Balzac, Literary Sociologist

Allan H. Pasco

Balzac, Literary Sociologist

palgrave
macmillan

Allan H. Pasco
University of Kansas
McLouth, Kansas, USA

ISBN 978-3-319-81868-9   ISBN 978-3-319-39333-9 (eBook)
DOI 10.1007/978-3-319-39333-9

© The Editor(s) (if applicable) and The Author(s) 2016
Softcover reprint of the hardcover 1st edition 2016
This work is subject to copyright. All rights are solely and exclusively licensed by the Publisher, whether the whole or part of the material is concerned, specifically the rights of translation, reprinting, reuse of illustrations, recitation, broadcasting, reproduction on microfilms or in any other physical way, and transmission or information storage and retrieval, electronic adaptation, computer software, or by similar or dissimilar methodology now known or hereafter developed.
The use of general descriptive names, registered names, trademarks, service marks, etc. in this publication does not imply, even in the absence of a specific statement, that such names are exempt from the relevant protective laws and regulations and therefore free for general use.
The publisher, the authors and the editors are safe to assume that the advice and information in this book are believed to be true and accurate at the date of publication. Neither the publisher nor the authors or the editors give a warranty, express or implied, with respect to the material contained herein or for any errors or omissions that may have been made.

Cover illustration: © Cover drawing courtesy of Dallas Designs, Lawrence, KS

Printed on acid-free paper

This Palgrave Macmillan imprint is published by Springer Nature
The registered company is Springer International Publishing AG Switzerland

To Dallas

Foreword

There are different approaches to the study of sociology, whether performative, developmental, constructionist, structural (functional), cultural, political, conflictive, or normative, or feminist. The theoretical impulsion orients and defines. But fundamental to any of the modes of study within the social science now called sociology is the consideration of relationships between more or less stable elements or constructs or, indeed, nuclei. Each of these nexuses and connections reveals and often explains some aspect of the social world created by human beings.

Because sociology is a "science," that is, subordinated to systematic investigation and reason, it is considered to be dealing with "reality." It does not take much time to understand that though we make distinctions between the real and the fictive, our distinctions are somewhat artificial and difficult to justify. As Georges May pointed out in *Le Dilemme du roman au XVIIIe siècle: Etude sur les rapports du roman et de la critique (1715–1761)*, the eighteenth century made few distinctions between fiction and history, since both had to be based on a recognizable reality. The word *histoire* with its meaning of both *history* and *story* continued on into the nineteenth century.

The following book suggests that although Balzac wrote "fiction," he believed he was writing the kind of cultural history (*histoire des mœurs*) that we would today call sociology. He was interested in the flux of connections between concepts that were forming a new society from enduring chaos created by the French Revolution of 1789, Napoleon's wars, and the Industrial Revolution. Convinced that the motivating force was money, whether coin, banknotes, bonds, debt, credit, land, or other forms of wealth, Balzac illustrated the results of the social pressures and activity inspired by the pursuit of such assets in various relationships between church, state, and family.

If Balzac had to justify his sociology, like many modern-day scholarly investigators involved with social phenomena, he might have pointed out that his "novels" were considerations of the most important relationships of his Restoration and July Monarchy world. The fact that he disguised the true names was merely an attempt to protect those involved, an idea that he exploited in *Cabinet des antiques* (see, Chap. 10, below). Certainly, the reports of many sociological studies hide the true names of real people whose behavior is studied in the authors' reports. I have hoped in the following pages to emphasize precisely these aspects of Balzac's work. *La Comédie humaine* has historical value because the author chose to examine and illustrate those systems or inter-relationships that made and explained his society.

I have three goals in mind for the following pages: (1) I have analyzed a number of under-studied novels of Balzac's masterpiece to demonstrate his aesthetic mastery once again. (2) These pages will also provide an example of the interlocking order that Balzac created from first to last in the *Scènes de la vie de province* and in the entire *Comédie humaine*. And (3), in a clear-cut fashion, I want to demonstrate that, like a few others in the late eighteenth and the first half of the nineteenth century, Balzac blazed a new trail as a proto-sociologist.

This book has been a major factor in my intellectual life since I began some years ago. I had long had a love for Balzac, for his perceptive, often-generous understanding of humankind and for his skeptical vision of the explosive world being created before his eyes. I found myself returning to the novels of the *Scènes de la vie de province* and was repeatedly amazed that their luxurious tapestry of inter-connected, rich imagery and themes had not attracted a lot more attention. Eventually, I began offering graduate seminars on this portion of *La Comédie humaine*. I am very grateful to the students whose very interest and insight helped me appreciate the complexities of nineteenth-century France all the more. At first it was the depth of Balzac's characters, then the sparkling but muscular style, then the images that established multivalent relationships between the characters and the society they were experiencing, but I eventually began to admire the accuracy of his multifaceted descriptions as France shifted from an agricultural to a capitalistic society. In the course of reflecting, parsing, reading, and rereading, I produced bits and pieces of manuscript that would eventually become this book. Everything has been extensively revised to emphasize the collective sociology of *La Comédie humaine* as I gained insight and understanding of Balzac and his world. I am grateful to have been able to try out gestating ideas in the welcoming pages of *French Review*, *French Forum*, *L'Esprit créateur*, *Nineteenth-Century French Studies*, *Symposium*, *Romance Notes*, and the volume *Currencies: Fiscal Fortunes and Cultural Capital in Nineteenth-Century France*. I also want to thank the Hall Family Foundation and the University of Kansas for their continued support.

Conventions

Unless otherwise mentioned, all references to Balzac's work are to Pierre-Georges Castex's edition of *La Comédie humaine*, 12 vols., Bibliothèque de la Pléiade (Paris: Gallimard 1976–1981). I shall refer to it without any attribution other than volume and page.When I call on other editions, usually to refer to the comments of editors, I either give the complete reference, or I precede the volume and page numbers with the following abbreviations:

HH   *Œuvres complètes de Balzac*. Ed. Maurice Bardèche. 24 vols. Paris: Club de l'Honnête Homme 1968–1971.
CI   *La Comédie humaine*. Ed. Pierre Citron. 7 vols. Collection l'Intégrale. Paris: Seuil 1965–6.
Hanska   *Lettres à Madame Hanska*, Ed. Roget Pierrot. 4 vols. Paris: Delta, 1967.

CONTENTS

1 Introduction   1

2 Through the Glass Darkly: *Ursule Mirouët*   35

3 A "Divine" Comedy: *Eugénie Grandet*   57

4 The Gerontocracy and Youth: *Pierrette*   81

5 The Tangible and the Intangible: *Le Curé de Tours*   101

6 The Dying Patriarchy: *La Rabouilleuse*   117

7 Nascent Capitalism: "L'Illustre Gaudissart"   135

8 A Provincial Muse: *La Muse du département*   151

9 Empty Wombs: *La Vieille Fille*   171

10 Restoration Boneyard: *Le Cabinet des Antiques*   191

11 Aeries and Muck: *Illusions perdues*	213
12 Conclusion	233
Works Cited	253
Index	271

CHAPTER 1

Introduction

> [Flaubert] then outlined a theory that I already knew about, since I'd heard it from Ernest Feydeau. "The novel is an outstanding historical document. In the future, no one will be able to write the history of Louis-Philippe's reign without consulting Balzac. The novel, a work of the imagination inspired by reality must contain indisputably true details that give it the value of a record book. It dismantles Paris, so as to describe the way it works. It is doing the work of a mechanic, taking Paris apart to transpose its mathematical movement into a novel. It is doing the work of a writer, hesitating is to do wrong, choosing badly is a crime." I confessed that I had decided to be both a criminal and a mechanic.
>
> [Flaubert] did not fail to make fun of me. Repeating one of his favorite comments, he said, "Look out! You have already quit using quill pens [...] which is the indication of a weak mind. In your preface to the *Chants modernes*, you reeled off a bunch of fairly dishonorable nonsense. You celebrated industry and sang of steam, which is idiotic and far too much like Saint-Simon."
>
> —Maxime Du Camp[1]

The late eighteenth and early nineteenth centuries in France were fraught with turmoil, and the populace was riven with insecurity, anguish, and fear. Diderot was reflecting the central agony of his society when he had one of his fictional characters remark "the instability of everything!"[2] The *philosophe*'s Tahitian responds to the cultural comment by wondering what would happen in the midst of a changing world if "there were neither true nor false, neither good nor evil, neither beautiful nor ugly"? Who would decide on one or the other? Priests? Judges? If one or the other or both, what would happen if "from one moment to the next, you were obliged to change your ideas and conduct"? Was anything stable? Was there no base in society that could stand strong without the support of either the Church, which had weakened, or the aristocracy, which had fallen into disrepute?

Looking for convincing answers to these widely voiced questions surely made people even more aware of the fractured social landscape. By the mid-eighteenth century, it was common to wonder whether there might be a basic idea that depended on neither church, nor the aristocracy and the monarchy, nor the law that differed depending upon jurisdiction, politics, and influence. The quest for a generative, foundational, and predictive idea that would explain the basis for rational order is one of the most significant characteristics of the late eighteenth and early nineteenth centuries. This desire is the source of such widely repeated catchwords as "science" and "progress." Both of these concepts were well rooted in eighteenth-century thought and writings, and were undeniably important to the attitudes of nineteenth-century French people as they looked to the future. They were, however, insufficient to satisfy such thinkers as Vicq-d'Azyr, Cabanis, Bichat, Condorcet, Henri de Saint-Simon, and Balzac, all of whom sought the seminal idea, what the novelist called the "seminal or generative idea [*l'idée mère*],"[3] that is, the concept or principle or, even, network that would explain both the causes of the contemporary topsy-turvy world and the future that was in progress.

Although I have found the term "idée mere" only twice in Balzac's writings, it is an extremely useful image for understanding a motivational force behind Balzac's theoretical thought. I translate it as either "seminal" or "generative idea." The sense of Balzac's term was very similar to *catallaxy*, a word invented by Ludwig von Mises and popularized by his student and colleague Friedrich Hayek. For these economists, it referred to a spontaneous order created within an economic system by exchange and specialization.[4] It occurs when people act for the simplest and perhaps most durable of motives: that is, enlightened or rational self-interest. While people might interact, and working together could be mutually beneficial, it need not be for the same reasons. As relationships formed and reformed within the shifting social landscape, whether because of regression or development and whether reciprocal or not, so too the catallaxy. Balzac found self-interest everywhere he looked, and his work makes it clear that the desire for money was, with a few exceptions in such marvelous, sacrificial people as Pauline Salomon de Villenoix, the guide and goal for human activity in the Restoration and July Monarchy. As Gobseck understood, whether gold or currency, money was easily transferrable into power, pleasure, fantasies, comfort, peace, luxury, or whatever (2.976).[5] The widespread, driving self-centered need for money could be summarized with the image of *gold*, and was a causative factor, the desired end point, and the basis for intervening relationships. Society was the result of the individual goals of a community, however diverse and different they might be, at least superficially. For Balzac, the egotistical desire for "gold" was the foundation of the entire society.

Investigations of the nature of human beings, their social constructs, and the consequent desire to predict where the world was going show up in many aspects of the events and writings of the late eighteenth and early nineteenth centuries. It is perhaps most obvious in the widespread, intense interest ignited by the discoveries of explorers of far-flung lands like Cook and Bougainville. Exotic places and people were in vogue. The numerous novels dealing with South Sea Islands and distant continents, while to some degree growing from missionary accounts, constructed imaginary worlds that reflected the hopes and needs of the French. By searching out isolated peoples who had not been "corrupted" by society, they hoped to discover the qualities that they believed resided at the core of human beings. Then, perhaps, they would be able to orient their own lives appropriately, in order to escape present problems and future uncertainties. Social philosophers like Thomas Hobbes, John Locke, and Jean-Jacques Rousseau constructed theoretical notions of a "state of nature." They felt that the whole of civilization required refashioning on the basis of this rediscovered Nature.

Many Frenchmen and women desperately dreamed of escaping the dismal reality of France. They wanted to try something different, something "other." Considering what that "other" meant to ordinary individuals of the late eighteenth and early nineteenth centuries often reveals through opposition to the novelist's constructs what it was like to live within both the overriding and the day-to-day conditions of society. The very fact that the French felt an impelling need to flee suggests fundamental weaknesses within the system. Whether the evasion was successful or not on the way to what Baudelaire would eventually call "Anywhere Out of the World" was left an open question. There were many possibilities for both goals and means—for example, Diderot's imaginative creation of exotic lands; popular utopian or sentimental literature; excessive use of alcohol, absinthe, opium, sex, or gambling—each of these escapes reveals social failures of daily life and, in addition, a significant fear, desire, or, more pointedly, a problem in French society.[6]

Our knowledge of how individuals felt about the tumultuous, societal changes that were taking place is quite limited. Historians tell us a lot about the major events, the roads, the coal production, the wars, and the leaders' speeches and activities, but very little about how the general population was actually living and what they thought and felt about the revolutions, riots, famines, and festivals. To some degree, the police and court records allow us to see into families with problems of inheritance, adultery, physical abuse, divorce, separation, abandonment, deaths, bankruptcy, and events that required official involvement.[7] Such insights gained from studying the legal records leave significant gaps about individual lives of the time, however. Indications of social turmoil are nonetheless many. I think, for example, of the particularly troublesome reality of suicide, which from the 1770s grew in frequency and appears to reflect the personal problems growing from severe weather, failed crops, hunger, disease, and general disruption.[8] Although reliable records of families' intimacy are not common, scholars have discovered several archives, including letters, a few diaries, and miscellaneous family accounts, in short documents that give us a peek at these lives, whether high- or low-born, whether rural or urban, in the streets, in houses, apartments, rooms, or miserable shacks originally made for animals.

Nonetheless, with all these, we remain virtually ignorant about the ordinary citizen who did not attract the attention of the police or people like the engraver Jean-George Willes who took no part in the Revolutionary uproar, but rather worked on the sidelines to improve his business and increase his wealth. On one occasion, he describes what must have been his customary behavior: "I did not see this march, not having wished to expose myself in any crowd, almost always dangerous."[9] For many, as for Benjamin Constant, the solution was even simpler: "As for me, I hide."[10] More thorough knowledge is, however, available. As I have argued before in *Revolutionary Love*, by looking to literature like Balzac's *Comédie humaine*, we may find useful commentary on a major period of France's history. Literature and art provide infrequently exploited historical archives and follow in the footsteps of the *Annales School*. Comparative study of such widely available texts can also result in significant new insights into France's political, economic, and social systems as the country morphed painfully from an agricultural to a capitalistic society. Many of these same systems can be seen in our current world.

The following pages pursue a more adequate vision of what has been called the "private life" of Balzac's culture by considering his *Scènes de la vie de province* [*Scenes from Provincial Life*], a major section of what Davin called a "gallery" of *La Comédie humaine*. Readers are invited into a series of the galleries' "rooms each of which has its purpose" (10.1204, 1207). Balzac investigates the relationship of Paris to the provinces as the capital city's values slowly infiltrated country life during the Industrial Revolution, and he provides important insights into the whole of society. The author's sophisticated literary devices used within the pages of his artfully composed masterpiece deserve close attention. Otherwise it is easy to go astray and miss the point or, even, to misinterpret his individual or corporate texts. It is also useful to note the careful arrangement of the novels within the cycle, demonstrating once again that he ordered his books so as to more fully develop his thesis and vision of the whole of society. The repeated claims that he made about the unity of his work were by no means idle. He meant exactly what he said.

His use of the reappearing character has been widely recognized. Reappearing themes followed, for they work together in a textual complex that includes character and plot "types." Such devices as the mock heroic have importance, as well. Certainly, he came to *La Comédie humaine* with an extensive knowledge of classical, literary, legendary, biblical, and historical material, which he exploited extensively in his allusions. Balzac was far more than a mere storyteller. He was rather determined to understand and portray his society. Indeed, *La Comédie humaine* gives the reader the opportunity to go to school with a great sociologist and join him in examining the interplay of competing individuals and groups within the French culture of his turbulent era. The portrayal he left us of Restoration and July Monarchy society is not only remarkably accurate; it predicts a future that continues to unroll in this aborning twenty-first century.

Discontent, even hostility toward established authority, was rife.[11] Public executions and torture were no longer successful at repressing or even diverting frustrations. Individual anger flowered in domestic and street violence and open revolt. The causes were many. Scholars have pointed to widespread crop failures, very cold weather, malnutrition, a weak economy exacerbated by an unbridled, profligate aristocracy, harsh taxation, institutionalized violence, an increasingly politicized clergy, the rise of the middle class, the costly wars against England and Prussia (1756–63, 1778), and the numerous failures and misjudgments of Kings Louis XIV, XV, and XVI.[12] All of these considerations made up a part of the nation's moral and physical bankruptcy. From the beginning to the end of the eighteenth century, there was an undercurrent of dissatisfaction that eventually brought France to its knees. Tocqueville, for example, describes a central administration staffed by a bureaucracy that was busily undermining the nobility,[13] and nobles themselves applauded the inflammatory remarks of Beaumarchais's wildly successful theatrical character, Figaro.[14] A man who lived through the period wrote, "People played, they danced, they made themselves dizzy, but this gnawing anxiety that resembles the quivering of the wind, the rustling of plants a few minutes before a big storm already reigned" (La Maisonfort 79). Later, in 1813, the social theorist Henri de Saint-Simon pointed out that Diderot's *Encyclopédie* (1751–72) was a critical work which highlighted numerous inconsistencies and failures, if not lies, within society, as well as major institutions that were revealing foundations of clay.[15] Saint-Simon felt that this encyclopedic undertaking effectively fanned the growing dissatisfaction by illuminating societal shortcomings.

The corrupt French church offers the first clear sign that changes affecting the very core of French culture were in process. Through the course of the eighteenth century, rural parishes were emptying as the faithful moved to more populous urban areas in search of employment. As Merrick and others have shown, the church itself had been losing respect for decades. Because church and state were so closely aligned, this growing disrespect for the ecclesiastical system undermined the monarchy and the aristocracy as well.[16] Within the church, the higher offices had long been reserved for powerful, aristocratic families, and the parish priests were often poorly trained, if not incompetent. When the Revolution confiscated the enormous, ecclesiastical land-holdings (over one-tenth of France), the secular base on which the Gallican church's spiritual power was established crumbled, and its spiritual foundations were ignored if not forgotten. With the further closing of numerous convents and monasteries and the permission, indeed encouragement, for clergy to wed there was no question about the split between Rome and Paris, between the church and the state, between the spiritual and the secular. The church's settled structure had long been fragile; now it seemed empty of substance.

"Although the revolutionary state envisioned far-reaching, state-run welfare and endeavored to put ambitious pension programs into effect, actual poor relief did not match the optimistic promises and predictions of the deputies."[17] The legislators apparently assumed that the clerics who had been involved in the church's far-flung ministry to the poor and needy would continue without funding. They were mistaken. As Richard

Cobb said, "It was not only that the Revolution had deprived charitable institutions of their financial support; it had done something even worse, killing the very spirit of charity itself" (Cobb, *Reactions* 166). Because the state was unable to fund social services, the misery grew. Corrupt to the core even before the revolutionary dismantling of the Gallican church, the institution had slowly lost not just members but influence and effectiveness. Increasing suicide rates were but one indication of the loss of ecclesiastical ascendancy, for the church had diminishing effect on French people's beliefs and behavior. As Balzac chronicles, people had lost respect for the church, a loss that had broad social repercussions. Why should an individual pay attention to St. Augustine's strictures against self-murder and resist the depression that is responsible for most of its victims?

In effect, the collapse of the eighteenth-century monarchy was not a matter of a few major events or of a single important cause. Revolutionary spillover of personal and public anger at the state of things continued and increased throughout society. Overall, the aristocracy had simply ceased to be important, though they long continued to impose heavy charges on society. Dissolute and ineffective, the nobles nonetheless demanded respect, and offices and honors continued to be awarded to them preferentially, rather than according to preparation and experience. In addition, as Robert Darnton put it, the king himself "had lost the last shreds of his legitimacy."[18] Worse, however, was that nobles as a class had come to seem negligible. The pretentious uselessness and foppery of too many aristocrats was exposed for all to see, whether in their dress or by their ostentatious carriages rushing hither and fro in the narrow, tortuous, sordid streets encumbered by shop displays, splashing muck onto pedestrians, occasionally crushing a child. They were justified by their notable ancestors, rather than by their own accomplishments. Their land, which had once been the foundation of their authority, was increasingly separated from their names, for it had been sold to pay the debts caused by their profligacy, leaving the names alone to remind people of the property that had once buttressed the families' importance. The contemporary descendants maintained their power, as Balzac illustrates, while having little real significance to society. Louis XV had successfully isolated himself, leaving the kingdom with feckless leadership. Though much delayed, it was no surprise that the monarchy was tossed aside, signaled by the decapitation of Louis XVI and his queen, Marie Antoinette, who had represented the apex of both the French church and state. In one of his vivid summaries, Tocqueville says the Revolution abruptly brought gradual change in society to a conclusion (20).

Fundamental transformation of society is neither rapid nor orderly. Although from the Revolution onward numerous officials were no longer appointed but rather voted into office, such "democratic" selection was by a very limited group and based on wealth. Furthermore, like deputies of the Revolutionary Assembly, those elected could be coerced by the threats of an unruly populace. The dwindling of the deputies' attendance at the Assembly in the early 1790s clearly demonstrates the influence of the menacing mobs that were wreaking havoc in the streets to the tune of vociferous demands. Mob rule is inconsistent, blown to and fro by every passing wind of doctrine, if not by the loudest clamoring voice. There was a period after Thermidor (27 July 1794) when Paris, if not France, had no government at all. If the political upheaval were not enough, the agriculturally based economy continued to be unpredictable. Not only was the weather unusually extreme, perfectly capable of destroying the livelihoods of families in one season, more and more land was bought up by untitled but wealthy bourgeois citizens, often as a means of cleverly transforming the increasingly worthless paper (fiat) money into land.

Social unhappiness, uncertainty, and disruption continued through the years of the Revolution. Because many of the nobles who had been competent and active in government were executed or frightened into exile, the revolutionary deputies effectively did away with experienced administrators. The idea, of course, was to confiscate the emigrants' property, combine it with the expropriated lands of the church and then sell it to pay for the wars that grew from the rebels' desire to export the Revolution to neighboring monarchies. The glut of property on the market resulted in government land sales for centimes on the franc, especially when payment was in depreciated *assignats*, the revolutionary fiat currency substituted for hard money. In addition to conserving the value of their assets, with the purchase of property, the new bourgeois owners assumed many of the rights previously reserved for nobles, as Balzac points out. Progressively the devalued *assignats* ushered in ruinous inflation. Illustrating the model of the fiat currency of John Law and the Weimar republic, the Revolution's *assignat* would lose all its value. In the conflagration that ensued, crops were neither planted nor harvested, people died from banditry, war, disease, and simple misery, and gold and silver disappeared from circulation, causing a severe lack of liquidity. In order to impose social control in the city, unjustifiable imprisonment, random searches of home and person, and capricious execution were common.[19] Social breakdown was not limited to urban centers. In the countryside, where abject poverty was the rule, drunken peasants periodically invaded chateaux, estates, and monasteries, smashing and grabbing, tracking mud on priceless rugs, senselessly destroying paintings and sculptures, indulging in uncontrolled hunting, and forcing their hereditary governors to flee to other countries (La Maisonfort 105–07).

The revolutionary decade sponsored major social concepts that would eventually lead to equality before the law, condemnation of torture and inhumane punishment, freedom of speech, a free press, liberty of association, and other freedoms that are enjoyed today, but they came too late to improve the lot of the general public, who were merely trying to survive. As Bourlin wrote of the revolutionaries, "They made brigandage systematic. Paris, this city that was once so brilliant, now offered to the saddened eye nothing but the hideous tableau of indigence, everyone showing off their rags, the comfortable citizen fearing to seem so, and seeking to slip away from the disquieting and jealous looks of an avid, cruel populace."[20] Alan Forrest put the general reality very simply: "[T]he enduring memory of the 1790s was one of hardship and poverty."[21]

The inept tyranny of the Revolutionary Assembly brought some progress, if only to highlight the need for important freedoms. Otherwise, as attendance at the legislative meetings declined (it was not safe to be noticeable or, indeed, noticed), mob rule grew with resulting confusion. Thermidor (27 July 1794) disposed of major bloodthirsty deputies like Robespierre and Saint-Just, slowed the guillotine, and signaled the middle class's defection, but it did not bring peace. The following Directory did no better than the various revolutionary Assemblies that preceded it. In effect, from 1790 until 1800, except for good theories, virtually nothing useful was accomplished. As Sainte-Beuve said later, "It is easy to imagine what the capital city, Paris, was like in 1800, after ten years of anarchy, sedition, and weakness, during which people had not undertaken a single useful work, not cleaned a street, not repaired a building, where nothing had been kept up, beautified or cleansed."[22] The Directory was dissolute, corrupt, and finally ruinous. The infrastructure of the big cities and elsewhere across France was in terrible disrepair. Danger and thievery were ubiquitous, and the French became increasingly cynical in the midst of seemingly endless war. Balzac's character Hulot calls those in authority under the Directory womanizing buffoons and asks, "What good would it have done to sweep away the abuses of the Old Regime if our patriots begin them anew."[23]

By 1799, although the lower classes never ceased believing in the promise of the Revolution, the idealistic fervor had faded. General conditions were so unacceptable that France enthusiastically welcomed Napoleon, who promised peace and justice. What in fact the jackbooted tyrant brought was constant war and bloodshed. While he and his wars provided upward mobility for courageous soldiers from the lower classes, it was no surprise when, fifteen years later, genteel ladies accompanied by their well-dressed husbands flooded the streets to welcome the allied conquerors by waving white handkerchiefs and wearing white rosettes, symbolizing a resurrected desire for the return of the Bourbon monarchy.[24] The bourgeoisie had once again withdrawn its support of the reigning government. Foreign though the allied troops were, they served France by forcing Napoleon's abdications. In effect, from 1799 until 1815, from the Directory to Waterloo, though Napoleon had indeed brought order, a generation of males died in the emperor's wars, fought to bring about, as Stendhal points out in *Lucien Leuwen*, an intolerable system of government rather like that preceding the Revolution.[25] At the end of the emperor's reign, as Balzac recognized, the surviving males of numerous towns across France were either invalids or aged. Tocqueville believed that, despite the political, economic, and social turmoil, the customs, conventions, and modes of thought that prevailed prior to 1789 persisted into the nineteenth century (vii). This consistency of social attitudes has led several recent scholars to wonder whether the Revolution was of negligible importance.[26] Indeed, if Persson is correct, "France stagnated" until the late nineteenth and early twentieth centuries, when the ideals and practice of universal education and democracy finally began to have positive results.[27]

Although the lower classes continued to support the emperor during the Empire (1804–1814), as they had supported the Revolution, the populace as a whole was too exhausted from one failed government after another to do anything but hope for peace. At first, the Revolution and the Directory promised much while delivering little. Napoleon likewise started strong. He spent money lavishly to beautify Paris and worked diligently to straighten out the legal snarl and social chaos left by the Revolution. Making peace with the church, establishing the Bank of France, and producing the Civil Code were major accomplishments that lasted long after his final departure for exile on Saint Helena. At the same time that he made these beneficial changes in the framework of society, the emperor moved toward totalitarian rule and multiplied police to keep the peace and enforce it.

Napoleon had clearly studied the defining characteristics of the long Bourbon reign. As Trotsky would later conclude, art was essential to forming public consensus that buttressed a lasting dynasty. The French Academy of 1635 was important in creating Classicism and establishing such brilliant writers as Racine, Corneille, and La Bruyière, to mention just a few of the seventeenth-century immortals. They had been supporting players in the panorama of the Sun King's glory, a continuing brilliance that illuminated France's reputation for more than a century. Napoleon seemingly thought that he could orient art and letters to bring back seventeenth-century Classicism for the benefit of his own heirs, and thus keep them in power for at least as long as the Bourbons. By supplying prizes and favors to writers that reflected his own often capricious understanding of classicism, coupled with rigorous censorship, he meant to build his own neo-classical dynasty. Of course, France's nineteenth-century, artistic neo-classicism was no more successful than the Soviet Union's socialist realism. Governments do not do well at establishing and maintaining aesthetic standards, schools, or traditions. Neo-classicism soon staggered off to the grave.[28] Napoleon also planned for Paris to become the artistic capital of the world. To this end he helped himself to the great paintings and sculptures that fell under his sway as he won battle after battle across Europe. Vivant Denon helped him choose the best examples to be shipped to Paris and the Louvre Museum. Later, Denon was also obliged to watch as all this magnificent art, stolen at least partially at his command, was returned after the emperor's defeat. The restitution is perhaps one more indication of how little Bonaparte achieved. In a memorable phrase, Fleming said, "Napoleon boasted of a new culture, yet he clothed it in a Roman toga."[29] And the emperor's clothing seemed increasingly ill-fitting, dated, even shabby.

The excitement that Napoleon's victories engendered soon turned to little more than tolerance. When the general began to lose his seemingly endless wars, his middle-class supporters started to count the cost of his rule, and their support was withdrawn. Rose-colored nostalgia made them forget the corruption and ineffectiveness of the Bourbon monarchy prior to the fall of Louis XVI's head. Unfortunately, to bring absolutism back, as indeed happened with Napoleon's Empire (1804–14) and the Bourbon Restoration (1814–30), was to revive an outdated system of governance, destined to pass away. Balzac excels at describing the street-level reality of these governments. Although as Waterloo approached, France's steadily rising bourgeoisie remembered selectively only the good aspects of the monarchy, they would soon learn that the cost to their own power and comfort during the Restoration of the Bourbon monarchy was too high. They then turned against the Bourbons, as they had turned against every previous government including the reign of Louis XVI. Whether Revolution, Directory, Napoleon, Restoration, or July Monarchy, none of these governments enjoyed a long life. The bourgeoisie was in fact the growing power that would not be denied, and it would eventually insist on a republic. By late in the nineteenth century autocratic rule was no longer possible in France.

Through the course of these different but similarly oppressive regimes, deputies and other administrators accomplished little. Part of it had to do with the lack of trust on the part of their colleagues and a very skeptical public. Functionaries changed parties and alliances with incredible ease.[30] During the "hundred days" of Napoleon's rule after he came back from Elba and before Waterloo, people changed from Bourbon to Napoleonic and back to Bourbon in such a brief span of time that they were termed *girouettes* (weathervanes). Divisions and a consequent lack of confidence within the society and government had had a long gestation period. The Bourbon rule of the Ancient Regime had weakened through the course of the eighteenth century, with increasingly ineffective government, agricultural mismanagement, and financial bungling that created rolling crises. One early result was the fear of starvation, which brought the bread riots in 1789. The inexperienced monarch, Louis XVI, confronting the bankruptcy of the French state and a tumultuous public, was incapable of assuaging the unrest. Despite his goodwill, Louis XV's negligent rule left an enormous burden on the new king. Unlike the latter's sexual problems, which only required minor surgery and a bit of instruction, the results of a century of misrule and distrust were not easily repaired.

Though governance and law changed under the Revolution's sway, social conditions were not better. Nor did they improve under Napoleon, whose need for order trumped the revolutionary demand for liberty. Police and spies that had multiplied under the Revolutionary government now increased again under Napoleon's minister of police, Joseph Fouché. Napoleon and Fouché also established an administrative system for state surveillance that was passed on to the Restoration. France felt the heel of a dictator's constant spying and created a "police state" that sowed discord and left what Sarah Horowitz calls a "legacy of distrust and division," which continued into the Restoration and beyond.[31] As Jacques Bainville puts it, "From fall to fall, from concession to concession, the people of 1789, tired perhaps by too great an effort, after having almost abdicated their rights and put themselves into Robespierre's hands, placed themselves in those of Bonaparte. [Soon] it will be freely accepted, almost hoped for tyranny."[32] Starting in 1799, the war-weary French surrendered their revolution-won freedoms to satisfy their yearning for peace and safety.

Of course, most of the citizenry was suffering from a lingering illness of some sort, and their widespread voluntary submission to the various governments could be explained by a lack of sufficient energy to object. Ubiquitous and potentially devastating epidemics of typhus, consumption, malaria, scarlet fever, cholera, tuberculosis, and venereal disease, complicated by barbaric medical treatment, poor sanitation, and malnutrition, were attenuated by the gradually improving diet. There seems little doubt, in addition, about the seemingly permanent reality of low-grade infections. Tight corsets were not the only reason for fainting women or, like Pierre Blanchard's Pauline or Rousseau's Julie, for the numberless romantic heroines who elegantly fade away from frustrated love (complicated almost certainly by unspecified diseases like tuberculosis). Malnutrition and one disease or another, moreover, put the lives of the vulnerable poor in continuing danger and claimed fully half of all children before their tenth birthdays.[33] In fact, without the constant immigration from the provinces to Paris, the city's population would have declined.

As the impotence of church, state, and the law became increasingly obvious, another institution, the family, was likewise weakened. Balzac gives numerous examples. The reasons were many. Farms were divided into smaller and smaller plots by inheritance and could no longer support the large families that had been necessary in previous centuries' agriculture. The weather was very harsh, and the price structure for grain seldom gave any advantage to peasants. The children then moved to the cities, in the hopes of finding employment. Away from the authority of father and church, morals broke down, suicide increased, venereal disease spread, and appalling numbers of infants were abandoned to die in foundling homes. The Revolution made waste of the institutions that had guaranteed some stability, while consciously attempting to destroy many of the nation's traditions. In the design to weaken the church, among other things, revolutionary deputies not only confiscated property, but also promulgated divorce, as mentioned above, which took a major sacrament out from under ecclesiastical authority and introduced more social malaise.

While Madame de Staël was in favor of divorce, as she was in favor of the Revolution, and, unquestionably, in favor of passion, *Delphine* of 1802 shows that she was conscious of the enormous changes, problems, and even dangers that each represented. Although marriage had been a sacrament since the eleventh century, suddenly in 1791, it was desacralized when the revolutionary deputies legalized divorce, thus turning marriage into a secular, legal contract that was, consequently, understood to be insecure. It could with little effort be abrogated. "The Supreme Being was no longer the third partner in a sacred union and could then no longer guarantee the permanence of marriage vows, just as a God ordained king no longer guaranteed the future" (Pasco, *Revolutionary Love* 123). Because of divorce, it became difficult, if not impossible, for either young people or their families to arrange their lives confidently for what was to come. Despite burgeoning opposition to the new law, divorce would not go away until 1816. Like the governments that only lasted a few years before another took over, divorce was a wild card of changing value that might efface tradition and destroy carefully laid plans. It put almost all middle-class citizens at risk. In the lower classes, where the poor often could not afford marriage, divorce was not a problem, since there were few assets to protect. Their interpersonal relational situation was already tenuous. There were likewise few divorces among couples at the highest levels of society, for the wealthy and well-connected worried about the stigma of shame and recognized the related financial dangers. Because it was paramount for ambitious upper-class bourgeois to preserve a large family asset base, it was likewise essential to prevent the expense or the capriciousness of the courts. Adultery was preferable to divorce. Balzac followed the results of poorly governed passion into the furthest corners of society. For virtually everyone during this era, nothing was certain. King, law, church, and family lacked permanence; indeed they changed with baffling frequency from 1789 until the July monarchy, which itself lasted less than twenty years. "Was nothing stable?"

Emigration was another indication of trouble throughout this period from the Old Regime through the July Monarchy. There was a profound reorientation occurring at every level of personal and public French life that drove people to consider other options. Unambiguously expressed in the letters of eighteenth-century French emigrants archived in Australia, people explained their departure because of social turmoil, financial problems, heavy, if not unfair, taxation, military conscription, and the Revolution itself. All these factors reveal the instability, rapid change, and fear for their own and their family's future as the French approached the end of the eighteenth century and suffered revolutionary changes in many aspects of their lives. Natalie Z. Davis has written that the "push toward planning" signals the change between early modern and modern France.[34] I would to the contrary suggest that for French people it was an *inability* to plan and prepare with any confidence for the potentially tumultuous future that constitutes a significant reflection of the social mood of late eighteenth-century France and may indicate why, in contrast to the later, nineteenth-century emigrants, those who left for Australasia or Canada generally did not go back home. The return of later California emigrants to France indicates that conditions improved in the last half of the nineteenth century and that there was increasing hope for the future. Confronted by the reality of seemingly unending flux, people from the Revolution through to the end of the July monarchy hoped to find some reasonable explanation for humankind and society that would allow them to make predictions of the future and, especially, that would permit arranging a safe and secure life.

Despite the appalling conditions and economic stagnation at the turn of the eighteenth and into the nineteenth centuries, the seeds of change had nonetheless been sown. The Industrial Revolution had begun in France, and although the changes were painfully slow, they were encouraging. Peasants and workers were increasingly moving around Europe and France in the effort to learn new skills, often finding work away from the family-owned plots of land that could no longer support them in such numbers. They found employment in workshops, small businesses, shipping, sales, and communication. Inventions became more numerous, and attracted Balzac's attention. By the time of the Revolution, newspapers were multiplying, and the burgeoning publication and sales of books, which had long been a major factor in the economy, testified to the startling increase in the numbers of those who could read. The critiques of the Enlightenment *philosophes* and others had an ever-widening audience as the Industrial Revolution matured and censorship diminished. The changes, both good and bad, were gradual and spread discontent irrespective of the actual government in control. Some enterprising people grew rich. Well-established bourgeois families like the Cochins consolidated and enlarged their wealth, founding a major hospital in the process.[35] Because Napoleon's Civil Code soon held sway throughout France, many aspects of business, property, family, and general behavior became more stable and predictable, though, of course, subject to the vagaries of the courts.

Both transportation and communication improved. As early as 1801, Commissioner Lépinard bragged about how quickly he could conduct passengers from Paris to Versailles, Orleans, and Marseilles.[36] In very few days, it was possible to cross France end to end, bringing manufactured goods, food, and, most important, information. By the 1840s France was well on the way to having viable mail and communication systems. With the deployment of the mid-century teletype, communication was virtually instantaneous. Although these innovations were positive, they came with bewildering rapidity.

Could no one make sense of all these changes? "Everyone realized that radical transformations were under way" (Piketty 3), but no one knew when they would occur and what exactly they would be. The yearning for insight into the meaning of human life was particularly acute. Henri de Saint-Simon enthusiastically believed he was providing increasingly satisfactory understanding of the social system. "It is a lot to know the reason for the things that successively preceded us," he writes, "since it provides the means of discovering what will come" (*Mémoire* 256). During the first half of the nineteenth century, extraordinary minds like Saint-Simon, Balzac, and, eventually, Auguste Comte carried on the work of Vicq-d'Azyr, Cabanis, Bichat, and Condorcet in the attempt to find the underlying, nuclear concept that would explain this incredibly tumultuous society. It was an item of faith that such an idea was generative and could be analyzed to reveal the future. As Saint-Simon explained, the general organization of our knowledge "will be based on the belief that the universe is ruled by a single immutable law. All systems of application, like systems of religion, of politics, of ethics will be arranged in accordance with the system of our knowledge" (*Mémoire* 368–69). Auguste Comte eventually termed this attempt to identify and codify group and individual interaction and motivational behavior as "sociology." While it was a simplification of the truth, the Revolution was cited as the cause of all these changes, though as suggested above, there were many currents in the social, spiritual, and physical world that were bringing what we may now understand as a new paradigm for the whole of society.

Certainly, France and, indeed, the Western world were transformed as the Enlightenment moved into the revolutionary age. It was not merely the addition of the *Droits de l'homme* (the *Rights of Man*) that enumerated many new rights and privileges for the common man in 1789, it was the church's loss of power, rotating governments, weakening family ties, the denial of hereditary rights, financial crises, and, perhaps most important, the modernizing exigencies of the Industrial Revolution itself. Everything was becoming new and different. People wanted to know what the future held. They were not even sure what their position would be in this post-revolutionary society. Thinkers tried with all their might to answer the persistent questions. Almost without exception their literature, whether fiction or drama, turned around the problems of the day, set in realistic venues. The *physiologie*, a new literary genre, exploded on the scene in the 1820s and 1830s, and readers purchased them in quantity. Many writers contributed to these descriptions of types of people and their professions, like the flower girl, the seamstress, the pianist, the miner, the soldier, the coachman, shop keeper, and bachelor, though it soon expanded to cover other kinds of topics, like "taste" or "wit." Subject matter was limited only by the imaginations of writers. In 1829, Balzac did a satirical *Physiologie du mariage*, Brillat-Savarin a *Physiologie du goût* [taste] in 1825. Seemingly, the reading public thought that if they could understand their present better, they would be able to grasp who they themselves were, what they were becoming, and where they were going. The questions of the age seemed to be "Why is this happening?" and "How does all this fit together?" Balzac, Saint-Simon, Comte, and others were actively attempting to provide convincing answers.

In the quest for a core reality, an understanding of which could perhaps protect them from the vicissitudes of constant change, the French public thoughtfully considered savages, whether "wolf child," "wild boy," or Tahitian, and they tried to divine what humankind would resemble if removed from the oppressive burden of civilization. Surely Nature would be more stable, thus more trustworthy. Henri de Saint-Simon was convinced that Cook's observations of various primitive societies, an attentive consideration of the recently "captured" *sauvage de l'Aveyron*, and the recollection of what was known of the early Egyptians, Greeks, Romans, and Saracens would help establish a "positive base for the science of man" and project a theory of how civilization might have been fashioned (*Mémoire* 333–40). Unfortunately, it was disconcerting when a "noble" savage brought back from the hinterlands needed no invitation to throw himself on any woman he found desirable.[37] Perhaps more bothersome for the *philosophes*, the Tahitian Aoutourou "could never learn to speak our language" (Diderot, *Supplément*, 968). The desire to see into the heart of what made men and women human was a widely held impulse. Although Balzac limited himself to the first half of the nineteenth century in his quest for understanding, Saint-Simon attacked the problem both chronologically (from primitive tribes to the modern day) and synchronically, implicitly comparing the "Wild Children" with adolescents, adults, and elderly freely chosen from current society, the implication being that his day offered an *a posteriori* example of the complete human being.

Saint-Simon pointed out repeatedly that a social system is in fact the implementation of a system of ideas: "the systems of religion, of political science, of ethics, of pedagogy are nothing but the applications of the system of ideas, or, if one prefers, the system of thought considered from different points of view " (*Mémoire* 249). The proto-sociologist wanted to forge both a method and a means for pulling together the knowledge necessary to perceive the basic, overriding idea.[38] This was within the realm of the possible, Saint-Simon thought, by using both analysis and synthesis. After all, he was quite sure that the universe was rational (Grange 16). Society was more than a mere agglomeration of individuals, as some claimed. It was rather a highly organized complex that could be seen as "a veritable *organized* machine, all of whose parts contribute in a different way to the progress of the whole" or, more commonly, as a living organism.[39] Delineation of such ideation was difficult, given that society was never static. It changed constantly, building, destroying, and developing. History was then neither a collection of facts, nor a sequence of events, but internally linked series within a growing, transforming complex of reality (Grange 24–25). Saint-Simon believed that once scientists had grasped this idea, they would better grasp the causal nature of the system and, thus, better organize the present and foresee the future.

Somewhere around the third and fourth centuries A.D., with the demise of the Roman Empire, Saint-Simon felt there had been other radical changes in man's social structures. A polytheist ideology and a societal order based on slavery came into place. Today, though Saint-Simon's historical dating is subject to challenge, we might call this a paradigm change. Perhaps as late as the eleventh and twelfth centuries another major break occurred and gave birth to a theological and a feudal military system. Then, in the late eighteenth and early nineteenth centuries, there grew a "scientific or positive" ideology, accompanied by an industrial system. While the third stage had not yet reached its full fruition, it was taking place before their eyes (Manuel 220). Hereditary, aristocratic power was being set aside, since the nobility had become unproductive, and society was transformed not so much by universal suffrage, but by profound reorganization of work, commerce, and property rights. It was in the process of generating a new social complex. For Saint-Simon, "the whole of society rests on industry [...]. Industry is the sole [force] guaranteeing its existence, the unique source of all wealth and of all prosperity" (quoted from Grange 34). Throughout this entire society, "Every man, every grouping of men, whatever their character, tend towards the increase of power" (Saint-Simon, quoted from Manuel 305). Power, for Saint-Simon, was the exercise of force on other human beings. Industry was not just the fabrication of manufactured items but agricultural production, banks, commerce, and "by extension all those who work or produce, including the domain of ideas, belonging to industrial society" (Saint-Simon, quoted from Grange 34). In sum, Saint-Simon felt he had opened a window onto a new society, which was industrial and "organized around production" (Grange 33–34). The only useful work was consequently scientific, artistic, technological, or industrial. "[E]verything else was parasitic" (Manuel 310).

Saint-Simon's "positive philosophy" was unsuccessful in discovering a "unified field theory" or "generative idea" capable of providing an explanation that elucidated the organization of modern society and of finding a way to see into the future. Indeed, although Durkheim considered Saint-Simon the founder of sociology, August Comte, dismissed him as a "depraved juggler."[40] Comte was one of the series of brilliant young men, including Augustin Thierry, Olinde Rodrigues, and Léon Halévy, who flocked around Saint-Simon and served to give order to his formative, but not always organized, musings. While one can appreciate the sweep of his thought, in the end it was the detail that defeated him. He was unable to show how the various parts of an art or science explained and sustained one another. For Manuel, "[T]he establishment of that interrelationship would facilitate the final acceptance of the idea that all were subject to a single law" (Manuel 131). Saint-Simon, who was not a scientist and consequently not, as Manuel says, "burdened by a scientific profession, was free to dream of the abstraction of general science" (Manuel 131). It was Comte who later elaborated a reasonably well-integrated, overriding system of religion, behavior, and ethics. Nonetheless, as Manuel argues, the germ of all the ideas in Comte's *Système de politique positive* (1851–54) was sown in Saint-Simon's *Mémoire sur la science de l'homme* of 1813 (Manuel 136).

As the epigraph of this chapter makes clear, Saint-Simon was in the air. He was a successful popularizer, ready to discuss his ideas with anyone at his beloved Café Procope or elsewhere. He crystalized a need to explain the organization of existence, a desire shared by Honoré de Balzac and other of his contemporaries. According to Augustin Pyramus de Candolle, one of Balzac's acquaintances, the novelist "claims that he is making a highly philosophical work that will hold the middle ground between Swedenborg and Saint-Simon."[41] Certainly, well before Comte coined the word "sociology," Balzac established himself as a particularly astute observer and illustrator of society. Indeed, one can read in Balzac's *Le Cousin Pons* of 1847 that "the great social force is character" (7.763). Like a number of other thinkers at the end of the eighteenth and beginning of the nineteenth centuries, Balzac sought the grail of an idea that would key the whole of civilization. As he put it in the 1842 "Avant-propos" to *La Comédie humaine*, "[S]hould I not study the reasons or the reason for social effects [and] surprise the hidden meaning in this immense gathering of figures, of passions and of events. Finally, having sought [...] this reason, this social motor, would it not be necessary to meditate on the natural principles and see how Societies move away or toward the eternal rule of truth, of beauty?" (1.11–12). Whether he had read Auguste Comte is open to question, but he did have some knowledge of Henri de Saint-Simon and his predecessors, all of whom could be termed cultural historians, each of whom analyzed texts, images, and practices in order to identify systems of thought and belief, and to each of whom the novelist refers on several occasions. It was for good reason that the author had his character Gaudissart call the proto-sociologist "the great Saint-Simon" (4.590), though I find no support for believing that Balzac held him in particularly high regard. In at least one case, he criticizes Saint-Simon's classifications (12.227).

Balzac's quest for the idea that would project the concept of a unified society is apparent throughout *La Comédie humaine*, but perhaps most clearly in the *Scènes de la vie de province*. The latter section of the novel was a major portion of his *Etudes des mœurs* and written during the period when the author was at the pinnacle of his literary form, from the early 1830s through the mid-1840s. This was when he wrote *Eugénie Grandet*, *Le Père Goriot* (*Father Goriot*), *La Recherche de l'absolu* (*The Quest of the Absolute*), and numerous other creations that perpetuate the majestic drumbeat of masterworks issuing from the author's pen to the printer and the public.

While never forgetting his commitment to art, Balzac was determined to uncover, examine, and represent the complex society surrounding him. He also knew well that he had to attract and keep an audience if he wished to have significant cultural and social impact. He needed to please readers who voted their approval with hard cash and demanded a "good story." Balzac did his best to satisfy his audience by offering well-crafted, realistic narrations embedded with social considerations rendered palatable, even tasty, by involving interesting characters working actively to better their situation. Almost always, however, we quickly perceive that the story is not central, but rather at best an illustration of a greater insight into society. Neither the story of Rastignac's move to the city and changing orientation on the road to his disreputable success, nor Goriot's fall from comfortable retirement into an impoverished death, tells the whole tale, which is basically a description of Parisians' avid quest for success at any price. All of Balzac's stories point to the larger underlying issues of social challenges and decay. In *Le Père Goriot*, he described a city and a society where success depended on the willingness to sell oneself and suborn others. It was a wholesale meat market where nothing was sacred and almost everything could be considered under the caption "Love for sale!"[42] Prostitution and trading in human beings were common and perhaps the only effective means of avoiding a descent into the stench of Parisian streets and ascending, rather, into the lights of perfumed success (3.1181).

The *Scènes de la vie de province* is particularly important, since it introduces a number of Balzac's most significant ideas. In *La Comédie humaine*, the author discussed and illustrated his thought on economics, fiat versus "hard" money, the opposition between Paris and the provinces, celibacy, art and journalism, creation and imitation, class structure, law, education, fatherhood, and the dissolution of families, to mention but those that are the most clearly emphasized. The sociologically oriented author incisively considers the condition of families, since the traditional family seemed to be atrophying if not disappearing, and he considered it one of the three major pillars of society (with church and state). Ineffective or substitute mothers in families lacking fathers could do nothing to soften the aggressively self-serving behavior of their sons, who had no respect for rules and laws, which is a common result in fatherless, male children, and who, deprived of prospects for upward mobility, thus easily slide into crime. Balzac rehearses many of the twentieth- and twenty-first-century conclusions of sociology, though in some cases the results that the novelist saw would not be apparent to other observers for well over a century.

The author's extraordinary, innovative nature is constantly at work throughout these novels and novellas. Understanding that he would not be satisfied with mere stories recounting the marvelous adventures of exemplar characters as they moved from glory to glory across this new world of the July Monarchy, much as one might find in popular literature, Balzac worked out a method to describe his society in ways that would include the most complex attitudes and realities. And as Hippolyte Taine put it, "With Shakespeare and Saint-Simon, Balzac is the largest storehouse that we have on human nature."[43] He was then able to communicate the depth, breadth, and inner-connectivity of this extraordinarily complex civilization as it was being industrialized, without neglecting the detail that defeated Saint-Simon.

The *Scènes de la vie de province* portrays the other side of French society, the provinces that served as the source of money and fresh human beings for the gluttonous maw of the insatiable Parisian monster. "[P]oets, nobles, and middle class people," the ambitious, the wealthy, the brilliant, the beautiful all went to Paris (Hanska, 21 December 1842, 2.139), where most were crushed by the brutal rapaciousness of the successful and the old. Starred and storied characters moved from social to political success, despite the tawdry secrets they dragged behind them, for they had long since sold their souls. The introduction to "La Fille aux yeux d' or" ('The Girl with the Golden Eyes') provides horrendous illustrations. The less successful settled for a sordid, gray existence serving the more adept, or they fell into the vile open sewers of Paris's streets that occasionally seeped into the basements and first floors of neighboring apartment buildings. Most either lived drearily hand to mouth, scurried home to the provinces, or, in despair, killed themselves. Balzac's poet and socialite, Lucien de Rubempré, did all three, one after the other, in the course of his career. Balzac boasted early on that he would "represent all social effects without forgetting either situations in life, or physiognomies, or men's and women's personalities, or ways of living, or professions, or social levels, or areas of France, or any effects of childhood, old age, maturity, politics, justice, war" (Hanska, Letter of 26 October 1834, 1.269).

With the exception of the fine work by Pierre-Georges Castex, Philippe Berthier, Andrew Watts, Nicole Mozet, and a very few others, little attention has been paid to Balzac's penetrating sociological analyses of the provinces.[44] Critics have seldom even attempted to demonstrate the startling unity of the author's magnum opus or, short of quoting what he or his spokesman Félix Davin said, how it fits into the rest of his literary creations. Indeed, as early as 1831, Philarète Chasles, another of Balzac's spokesmen, complained in respect to *La Peau de chagrin* (*The Magic* Skin) and the *Etudes philosophiques* (*Philosophical Studies*) that the "[t]he vast map, hidden beneath these imagined fantasies must have slipped past a number of people" (10.1189). Of the excellent novels in the *Scènes de la vie de province*, only *Eugénie Grandet* and *Illusions perdues* have stimulated much criticism or, indeed, much interest. In fact, all of them provide important, even essential, images that explain Balzac's insight into the causes and effects of his contemporary society, and they mark every aspect of the whole. The following study will focus on the *Scènes de la vie de province*. This section of Balzac's *Comédie humaine* includes ten of the author's best works, and gives an excellent idea of what he was attempting to do. The same literary and social concerns apply to it as to the rest of Balzac's cycle: Here and elsewhere he was attempting to illustrate his conception of Restoration and July Monarchy society. He also made use of a revolutionary means of organizing his work.

Balzacian Montage, my earlier attempt to deal with Balzac's cycle, considers the novelist's innovative system of composition. Confronted by the fact that the author of *La Comédie humaine* could not paint every single element of his society, he found a way of calling on the reader to fill in the gaps by bringing "fragments" into the whole of his masterwork.[45] Proust ungenerously claimed that in contrast to his rigorously organized *A la recherche du temps perdu*, *La Comédie humaine* is seriously faulty. Balzac, Proust pointed out, was obviously unable to see where he was going until very late. Readers are invited to compare Proust's own creation of both introduction and conclusion from the very beginning of his project, while Balzac's vision of the whole of *La Comédie humaine* arose when the opus was taking form. Proust emphasized his structural model by naming the Combray church after the French naturalist Saint Hilaire, who established the principle of "unity of composition" in the animal kingdom.[46] Balzac was very clear in his explicit recognition in the "Avant-propos" of what he owed to naturalists like Buffon, Geoffroy Saint Hilaire, and Cuvier (1.7–8nn4–5). All felt that similar, analogous "fragments" could stimulate the observant student both to join the individual pieces productively and fill in the empty spaces. In this way, the great naturalists were able to reconstruct prehistoric animals from a fossilized bone or two. *Disjecta membra poetae* (the scattered limbs of the poet), as Balzac proclaimed in what was likely a conscious emendation of the original Horacian epithet, could work like fossils.[47] He expected to join with his readers and reconstruct reality from the dispersed fragments he was able to envisage in the creative process that requires collection, analysis, synthesis, and invention. His examination of the cultural content, the connections, and the social ebb and flow of his era took on a distinctly sociological viewpoint as he detailed the interpersonal causes, effects, problems, and potential remedies.

A. Trillat makes the point that Balzac's scientists all adhere to his unitary theories. While it is easy to dismiss the novelist's Louis Lambert, his Balthazar Claës, and even his César Birotteau, or any of a dozen other examples, whose obsessive commitment to one goal or another encourages us to question their sanity, we should note, however, that for Balzac they were on the right path. They were successful adherents of truth, despite their inability to reach the perfection of a Séraphita, and their theories of unity are in fact connected to Balzac's method of composition: "For the execution of most of his novels, Balzac is inspired by the principles that he puts on display," as Trillat put it.[48] Without insight into the novelist's understanding and method of unification, misinterpretation becomes a real possibility. René Guise quotes a pertinent example of incomprehension from an anonymous critic attempting to come to terms with *Splendeurs et misères des courtisanes*: "In fact, M. de Balzac's books are different in that they almost all end without their characters having achieved what they were expected to do and disappeared from the stage. You are surprised to arrive at the end of the novel at the very moment that the action is the most active, the strings the most tangled, the interest at its highest."[49] It seems safe to say that the reader Guise quotes has completely missed the point of the novel, whose "generative idea [*l'idée mere*]" is the description of a capitalistic society that has laid all virtue to rest.

Balzac believed that there were two varieties of literature: that of ideas and that of images. A combination of the two may incorporate both action and lyricism, drama and the ode, in the hopes of offering what the novelist called "a complete view of things" (*La Revue Parisienne*, HH 24.214). He claims that a school which he termed "Literary Eclecticism" demands this kind of a vision in the creation of the world as it is. While ideas may exist in images, and images may occur in ideas, they are different, as different as "movement and reverie" (HH 24.214). It is a matter of whichever dominates. "Every image corresponds to an idea or, more exactly, to a sentiment which is a collection of ideas, and an idea does not always end up in an image" (HH 24.214). Balzac's definition of image parallels modern understandings; that is, *an image is a complex of (remembered) sensations*. In short, the various episodes highlighted in the *Scènes de la vie de province* provide a useful opportunity to consider both the ways Balzac formed his masterpiece and the ideas that he develops in this portion of his work. I am discomfited that I am largely limiting my examination of *La Comédie humain* here to the *Scènes de la vie de province*, since I agree with

George Sand that "[y]ou have to read all of Balzac. Nothing is indifferent in his general work."[50] Still, I hope that the limited number of avenues (or what he would call "galleries") that I have explored in this study will provide access to Balzac's exceptional creation more fully for today's readers and that it will facilitate sharing his vision in *La Comédie humaine*. Closer consideration shows how similar it is to the concerns of our day, for he discusses individuals, friendship, love, family, business, competition, class, war, and work that are common to Western civilization. He wrote at the budding of the Industrial Revolution and the naissance of capitalism. Now, we seem to be moving into another era, which is built solidly on the foundation that Balzac described. While I certainly celebrate the literary innovations of *La Comédie humaine*, I am perhaps equally drawn to the sociological insight that the novelist shows from beginning to end. He described the core of his transitional society, where class distinctions were being eroded, where peasants and laborers are rising in large numbers into the middle class, where the many little regions in France were being united into one nation through increased travel, commerce, and communication, where the French even in military defeat were a great people and nation. Kevin Ashton makes an important point in regard to Emile Durkheim's "macrosociology." For the latter, there was no practical way to observe the important "everyday interactions in detail." It would be necessary, he believes, to await "the invention of the magnetic tape recorder, the transistor, and mass-production electrical microphones."[51] In fact, of course, Balzac's analysis of everyday life provided introduction into both micro- and macrosociology.

The perceived distances that formerly separated the provincial countryside from Paris seemed to be shrinking rapidly. As roads and communication improved, effective means of transporting or exchanging people, goods, and information were established. Balzac considered the outlying provinces as the wellspring of the new economy and society. Some, like the Balzacian characters Savinien de Portenduère or Victurnien d'Esgrignon, having failed in Paris, return to the provinces and hew out a new life through advantageous marriages. Others like du Bousquier avoid the sludge of Paris streets by their subsequent success in the provinces. And others, having succeeded like Doctor Minoret, return to establish themselves more or less comfortably and on a smaller scale in Nemours. Still others, like Félix Gaudissart, serve to coordinate relationships between Paris and the provinces, living in two worlds that were rapidly becoming one. Or some, like the satanic colossus, Herrera, who comes to close out

Illusions perdues, signal the most common road to success through all the various kinds and levels of fraud, coercion, and self-abasement.

Balzac repeatedly painted the transferal of people from the provinces to Paris and back again. The novelist felt this continuing back and forth migration was essential to an adequate understanding of the heart of the July Monarchy.[52] What he saw better than many was that the shift of wealth, talent, and beauty to the capital to meet the crying needs of the Industrial Revolution was essential but almost always followed by failure and an ignominious return home to the provinces. Only individuals who understood the new commercial/industrial world and its basis in wealth and who could manipulate people and circumstances to get ahead could survive in the urban setting. By threatening suicide, Rastignac coerced his family into giving him support, which he was then able to exploit. Although others like Daniel d'Arthez sought a kind of comfort by joining groups of like-minded, each member was ultimately self-reliant. These artificial families were poor substitutes for the real thing, but in some cases they were effective.

Balzac's *Scènes de la vie de province* opens onto a France engaged in revolutionary reconstruction, new understandings, and the mental and physical reformulation of the social and economic systems. He comprehended that that old structures were no longer viable and that everything was changing to some degree: whether colonies, roads, finance, banking, education, manufacturing, building, communication, journalism, agriculture, or export. And all required capital. The *Scènes de la vie de province* was a major part of *La Comédie humaine* that took shape during the 1840s. These *scènes* focus on quintessential elements of the society, but more importantly, they dwell on the attitudes of people interacting in the midst of the transformation of one kind of society into another that was very different. They are particularly important, since they introduce and give life to a number of Balzac's most significant literary and sociological ideas that he further fleshed out in his encompassing masterpiece, *La Comédie humaine*.

In short, while considering ten novels in detail, in hopes of opening their significance further, I want both to insist on the careful order that the author chose for a major segment of his masterpiece and to show how his sociology, while predating the invention of the word, considered the connections linking the various aspects of his world and the specific, nuclear, generative concepts at the center of the systems or structures holding his society together.

Notes

1. Du Camp, *Souvenirs littéraires*, vol. 2. (1883; Paris: Hachette, 1892) 299–300. Considering Balzac and Saint-Simon together is not uncommon: see, e.g., Hippolyte Taine's statement quoted farther on in this chapter. Balzac even has one of his characters, Gaudissart, put Balzac and Saint-Simon together, as Frank Paul Bowman points out in, *Le Christ des barricades, 1789–1848* (London: Cerf, 1987) 250.
2. The interlocutor "B," in Denis Diderot, *Supplément au Voyage de Bougainville, ou dialogue entre A et B sur l'inconvénient d'attacher des idées morales à certaines actions physiques qui n'en comportent pas*, *Œuvres*, ed. André Billy, Bibliothèque de la Pléiade (Paris: Gallimard, 1962) 995. Diderot was not the only one to say such things. Pierre-Jean-Baptiste Nougaret's Rondin, for example, likewise pronounces, "There is nothing stable in the world"—*Paris, ou le rideau levé; Anecdotes singulières, bizarres et sentimentales. Pour servir à l'histoire de nos mœurs anciennes et nouvelles; avec des faits qui n'avaient point encore été publiés*, 3 t. (Paris: Chez l'auteur, 1799) 3.146. See, also, Restif de La Bretonne, *Le Palais royale*, 3 vols. (Paris: Guillot, Year VI 1798) 3.283.
3. Balzac, "Etudes sur M. Beyle (Frédéric Stendhalh [*sic*])," *La Revue Parisienne*, 25 septembre 1840, HH 24.253. As indicated in the frontispiece, references to these volumes will be preceded by HH. He also discussed principles in a letter to his mistress: Hanska 1.269–70. All further references to this work will be preceded by "Hanska." The novelist also mentions an "idée mère" or "generative idea" in a letter of 1832: *Correspondance*, 6 vols. (Paris: Garnier, 1960–69) 1.200.
4. Friedrick A. Hayek, *Law, Legislation and Liberty*, 3 vols. (Chicago: U of Chicago P, 1978) 2.107–09.
5. As indicated in the frontispiece, parenthetic references to Castex's Pléiade edition of *La Comédie humaine* will provide only volume and page.
6. Allan H. Pasco, "The 'Tahitian mirage'," *Revolutionary Love in Eighteenth- and Early Nineteenth-Century France* (Burlington, VT: Ashgate Publishing, 2009) 97–118.
7. Exploited repeatedly and fruitfully by Arlette Farge. See, e.g., *La Vie fragile: Violence, pouvoirs et solidarités à Paris au XVIIIe siècle* (Paris: Hachette, 1986).

8. See, e.g., Dominique Godineau, *S'abréger les jours: le suicide en France au XVIIIe siècle* (Paris: Armand Colin, 2012); Allan H. Pasco, "Death Wish," *Sick Heroes: French Society and Literature in the Romantic Age, 1750–1850* (Exeter: University of Exeter Press, 1997) 134–56.
9. Jean-Georges Wille's *Mémoires et journal*, ed. Georges Duplessis, 2 t. (Paris: Jules Renouard, 1857) 2.340–41.
10. Quoted by Colette Piau-Gillot, ed., "Préface," *Lettres trouvées dans les portefeuilles d'émigrés, 1793*, by Isabelle de Charrière (Paris: Femmes, 1993) 14. Richard Cobb discusses the issue of personal safety: *Reactions to the French Revolution* (London: Oxford UP, 1972) 14, 125–79, as does Georges Lefebvre, *The French Revolution*, vol. 2, tran. John Hall Stewart and James Friguglietti (New York: Columbia UP, 1964) 205, 271.
11. Roger Chartier, *The Cultural Origins of the French Revolution*, tran. Lydia G. Cochrane (Durham: Duke UP, 1991) 136.
12. Good summaries of the attempts to find the causes of the Revolution occur in Chartier's *Cultural Origins*, mentioned above, or in William Doyle, *Origins of the French Revolution* (Oxford: Oxford UP, 1988).
13. Alexis de Tocqueville, *The Old Régime and the French Revolution*, tran. Stuart Gilbert (Garden City, NY: Doubleday-Anchor, 1955) 19.
14. Antoine-François-Philippe du Bois des Cours, marquis de La Maisonfort [1763–1827], *Mémoires d'un agent royaliste sous la Révolution, l'Empire et la Restauration* (Paris: Mercure de France, 1998) 39.
15. Henri de Saint-Simon, *Mémoire de la science de l'homme* (1813), 2e partie, éd. Prosper Enfantin, *Science de l'homme* (Paris: Victor Masson, 1858) 384–85.
16. Jeffrey W. Merrick, *The Desacralization of the French Monarchy in the Eighteenth Century* (Baton Rouge: Louisiana State UP, 1990).
17. Suzanne Desan, *The Family on Trial in Revolutionary France* (Berkeley: U of California P, 2004) 247.
18. Darnton, *The Forbidden Best-Sellers of Pre-Revolutionary France* (New York: W. W. Norton, 1995) 166.
19. Suzanne Gireux Bertrand Morency-Quinquet, (pseud. Giroust de Morency, Illyrine de Morency), *Illyrine, ou l'écueil de l'inexpérience*, 3 vols. (Paris: Auteur, An VII—1798) 3.304, 341–42. Though there is some discussion about whether this work is a novel or an

autobiography, it unquestionably reflects the period. See, also, e.g., Jean-Pierre Béranger, *Les Amans Républicains, ou Lettres de Nicias et Cynire*, 2 t. (Paris, 1782) 1.186–88; C.-B. Le Bastier, *Dorbeuil et Céliane de Valran, leurs amours et leurs malheurs pendant la tyrannie de Robespierre*, 2 vols. (Paris: Lebastier, Brunet, An III—1795) 1.150–51, 2.77–78, 139.
20. Antoine-Jean Bourlin, *Les Amours et aventures d'un émigré*, vol. 2 (Paris: Marchands de Nouveautés, an VI—1797) 2.11.
21. Forest, *The French Revolution* (Oxford: Blackwell, 1995) 93.
22. Sainte-Beuve, "Frochot, Préfet de la Seine," *Nouveaux Lundis*, t. 11 (Paris: Lévi frères, 1869) 30.
23. Honoré de Balzac, *Les Chouans, ou la Bretagne en 1799* (1829), ed. Lucienne Frappier-Mazur, *La Comédie humaine*, 12 vols., Bibliothèque de la Pléiade (Paris: Gallimard, 1976–81) 8.964. Further references to *La Comédie humaine* will be to this edition and indicated parenthetically.
24. Charles Simond, "Deuxième époque: Le Premier Empire, 1804–1814," *Le Consulat—Le Premier Empire, La Restauration, La Vie parisienne au XIXe siècle: Paris de 1800 à 1900*, ed. Charles Simond, 2 vols. (Paris: Plon, 1900) 1.98, 272.
25. Stendhal, *Lucien Leuwen. Romans et nouvelles*, 2 vols., Bibliothèque de la Pléiade (Paris: Gallimard, 1952) 1.785.
26. J.M. Roberts, *The French Revolution* (Oxford: Oxford UP, 1978) 152; Alfred Cobban, *The Social Interpretation of the French Revolution* (Cambridge: Cambridge UP, 1964) 78–81. Cobban says pointedly, "[I]nstead of accelerating the growth of a modern capitalist economy in France, the revolution may have retarded it. [… T]he evidence in respect of trade and industry is that France was worse off in 1815 than she had been in 1789. After two decades of war this was perhaps only to be expected" (79). "Not until after 1825 did French external trade return to the level it had reached in 1788" (247).
27. Karl Gunnar Persson, *An Economic History of Europe: Knowledge, Institutions and Growth, 600 to the Present* (New York: Cambridge UP, 2010) 66, 211, and *passim*. Persson's estimates put economic growth in 1780–1830 at "only slightly higher than in the preindustrial period" (Persson 95). Thomas Piketty echoes this conclusion—*Capital in the Twenty-First Century* (Cambridge, MA: Harvard UP, 2014) e.g., 4, 7.

28. Allan H. Pasco, "The Incongruity of Resuscitated Classicism after the French Revolution," *XVIII: New Perspectives on the Eighteenth Century* 10 (2013): 38–50.
29. William Fleming, *Arts and Ideas*, 9th ed. (Fort Worth: Harcourt Brace, 1995) 507.
30. Horowitz, *Friendship and Politics in Post-Revolutionary France* (University Park: Pennsylvania State UP, 2013) 42–53.
31. Horowitz 22, 35–36; John M. Merriman, *Police Stories: Building the French State, 1815–1851* (New York: Oxford UP, 2006) 17. See, also, in this regard, Charles Pinot Dubois, *Mémoires secrets sur le règne de Louis XIV, la Régence et le règne de Louis XV* (Paris: Formin Didot, 1854) 112, 224, 230. Mémoires, diaries, and letters all have their dangers for those who seek the truth of history, for they were not really private and, therefore, possibly not candid. French rulers from the time of Louis XIV did not hesitate to violate the secrecy of the post, for example. Letters and diaries are particularly limited in number from the revolutionary period, when extreme discretion, codes, and prompt destruction were common—Colin Jones, *The Great Nation: France from Louis XV to Napoleon 1715–99* (New York: Columbia UP, 2002) 532.
32. Bainville, "1803," *Le Consulat—Le Premier Empire, la Restauration, la Vie parisienne au XIXe siècle: Paris de 1800 à 1900*, ed. Charles Simond, 2 vols. (Paris: Plon, 1900) 1.55. According to Stendhal, Napoleon exiled General Delmas for expressing a similar point of view—*Lucien Leuwen, Romans et nouvelles*, 2 vols., Bibliothèque de la Pléiade (Paris: Gallimard, 1952) 1.785.
33. Jacques Dupâquier, *Histoire de la population française*, Vol. 2 (Paris: P.U.F., 1988) 223–24.
34. Davis's argument is published in "Ghosts, Kin, and Progeny: Some Features of Family Life in Early Modern France," *Daedalus* 106.2 (1977): 87–114. For more detail, see Pasco, *Revolutionary Love* 27, 93, 99.
35. Laurence H. Winnie, *Family Dynasty, Revolutionary Society: The Cochins of Paris, 1750–1922* (Westport, CN: Greenwood P, 2002). For another example, see Christine Adams. *A Taste for Comfort and Status: A Bourgeois Family in Eighteenth-Century France* (University Park: Pennsylvania State UP, 2000).

36. Henri d'Alméras, "1801," *Le Consulat—Le Premier Empire*, ed. Simond 1.22.
37. Reported by Denis Diderot: *Supplément au Voyage de Bougainville* 968.
38. Julienne Grange, *Saint-Simon* (Paris: Ellipses, 2005) 14.
39. Saint-Simon is quoted from Grange 23. The reference to a more organic analogy is Frank E. Manuel's summary: "Society was a living organism, not a machine. The proper handmaidens for the new science of society would be physiology and psychology, not mathematics" (Manuel, *The New World of Henri Saint-Simon* (Cambridge: Harvard UP, 1956) 138).
40. I take Comte's quotation from Manuel 3. For a justification of viewing Saint-Simon as the founder of sociology, see Emile Durkheim, "Saint-Simon, fondateur du positivisme et de la sociologie," *Revue philosophique* 1 (1925): 99, 321–41.
41. Letter of 17 February 1830, *L'Europe de 1830, vue à travers la correspondance d'Augustin Pyramus de Condolle et Mme de Circourt*, ed. Roger Pyramus de Candolle (Genève: Jullien, 1966) 64.
42. This aspect of Balzac's vision was introduced in, Pasco, "Image Structure in *Le Père Goriot*," *French Forum* 7 (1982): 224–34, and expanded in, Pasco, *Balzacian Montage: Configuring* La Comédie humaine (Toronto: U of Toronto P, 1991) 22–47.
43. Hippolyte Taine, "Balzac," *Nouveaux Essais de critique et d'histoire*, 4th ed. (Paris: Hachette, 1886) 140.
44. Philippe Bertier, "Introduction," *La Vieille Fille* et *Le Cabinet des antiques*, by Balzac (Paris: Garnier-Flammarion, 1987) 7–43; P.-G. Castex, ed., "L'Univers de *La Comédie humaine*," *La Comédie humaine*, 1.ix–lxxvi; Nicole Mozet, *La Ville de province dans l'œuvre de Balzac* (Paris: C.D.U.-S.E.D.E.S., 1982); Andrew Watts, *Preserving the Provinces. Small Town and Countryside in the Work of Honoré de Balzac* (Oxford: Peter Lang, 2007). See, also, Bernard Guyon, "Balzac 'Invente' les *Scènes de la vie de province*," *Mercure de France* 333 (1958): 465–93; Michel Butor, "Les Parisiens en province," *Répertoire III* (Paris: Eds. de Minuit, 1968) 169–83; and Sharif Gemie, "Balzac and the Moral Crisis of the July Monarchy," *European History Quarterly* 19 (1989): 469–94.
45. Lucien Dällenbach makes a significant exception in that he submitted Balzac's claimed unity to intense consideration. In the end, his

attempt to recuperate *La Comédie humaine* into the conceptual realm of post-structuralist criticism suggests that intelligent readers must glory in its fragmentary nature: "Du fragment au cosmos: (*La Comédie humaine* et l'opération de lecture I)," *Poétique* 40 (1979): 420–31; "Le Tout en morceaux (*La Comédie humaine* et l'opération de lecture II)," *Poétique* 42 (1980): 156–69. See, also, Lucienne Frappier-Mazur, "Lecture d'un texte illisible: *Autre étude de femme* et le modèle de la conversation," *MLN* 98 (1983): 712–27. Recently, though she does not give credit to what is truly innovative in the novelist's organization, Dominique Massonnaud argues that Balzac was attempting to produce a unified work: *Faire vrai: Balzac et l'invention de l'œuvre monde* (Geneva: Droz, 2014). Jeannine Guichardet takes Balzac's usage of "mosaic" to indicate that the author meant his often fragmentary work to create a chronological/spatial tableau that invites and includes critical appreciation as well—*Balzac-mosaïque* (Clermont-Ferrand: UP Blaise Pascal, 2007). For work that complements my view of Balzac's composition, see, for example, Max Andrioli, *Le Système balzacien: Essai de description synchronique*, 2 vols. (Lille: Atelier National Reproduction des Thèses, Université de Lille III, 1984); Roland Le Huenen and Paul Perron, "Balzac et la représentation," *Poétique* 61 (1985): 75–90.

46. Proust was ungenerous in his failure to highlight his significant debt to Balzac. See, e.g., Proust, *A la recherché du temps perdu*, ed. Jean-Yves Tadié, 4 vols. Bibliothèque de la Pléiade (Paris: Galliard, 1987–9) 3.666. For Proust's more complete and somewhat more adequate critique of Balzac, see *Contre Sainte-Beuve*, Bibliothèque de la Pléiade (Paris: Gallimard, 1971) 263–78. Cf., Annick Bouillaguet, "La Dette de Proust envers Balzac," *Le Courrier Balzacien* 27 (janvier 2014): 40–53.
47. Pasco, *Balzacian Montage* 321. The quotation is from 5.831. I am grateful to my colleague Anthony Corbeill for help with the passage.
48. Trillat, "Les Savants et la théorie unitaire dans *La Comédie humaine*," *Revue d'Histoire de la Philosophie*, 3 (avril 1935): 140.
49. Guise, "Balzac et le Bulletin de Censure," *Année Balzacienne* 1983: 283 (269–301). This may well have been Davin's position, as he seems to have had some doubts about Balzac's genius—Citron, "Un Article sur la mort de Balzac," *L'Année Balzacienne* 1977, 192.
50. George Sand, "Honoré de Balzac," *Autour de la table* (Paris: Michel Lévy, 1876) 203.

51. Ashton, *How to Fly a Horse: The Secret History of Creation, Invention, and Discovery* (New York: Doubleday, 2015) 223.
52. Hanska, 21 Dec. 1842, 2.139. I am using Madeleine Fargeaud's archival work, 1.1109–10, 1143–72, that of Pierre-Georges Castex 1.xii–xiv, xxxvi–xlviii, and that of Bernard Guyon, "Balzac invente." While Castex puts that turning point at 1829–30, Guyon believes the Balzac's understanding and crystallization of what he was about came in 1832–33 (see, especially, Guyon 477–78).

CHAPTER 2

Through the Glass Darkly: *Ursule Mirouët*

The novels that Balzac placed at the beginning of each of his *Scènes* set the stage, introducing the kinds of characters, the patterns of plot, and the major themes of the entire section. In some instances, they may prepare a reversed, mirror image which recurs many hundreds of pages farther on in the section's last novel. In the *Scènes de la vie parisienne,* for example, the secretly destructive league of the introductory *Histoire des treize* (*History of the Thirteen*) establishes the equally covert but beneficent image of the *Frères de la consolation* (*Brothers of Consolation*) in the terminal *L'Envers de l'histoire contemporaine* (*The Seamy Side of History*).[1] Likewise, God's activities preparing for the marriage of a lovely young woman to a dashing young man in *Ursule Mirouët* (1842), that opens the *Scènes de la vie de province*, are reversed in those of the satanic abbé Herrera's homosexual union with Lucien in *Illusions perdues,* which brings the *Scènes de la vie de province* section to a close. Other of the initial novels serve as links with the works that concluded preceding *Scènes* or that introduced their own *Scènes*. It was for Balzac a standard strategy.

If *La Comédie humaine* is read in the order of Balzac's definitive arrangement, on turning from Balzac's *Autre étude de femme* (*Another Study of Woman*), the reader leaves the *Scènes de la vie privée* and Vendôme, on the banks of the Loir, and opens the *Scènes de la vie de province* and the initial *Ursule Mirouët* set in Nemours, on the banks of the Loing. Although the geographic displacement is of little importance, other than revealing Balzac's efforts to make the setting realistic and recognizable, the similar settings provide a common element to help connect the two contiguous works. Both *Autre étude de femme* and *Ursule Mirouët* are situated in the provinces, a general reference to regions which are, in Balzac's world, defined primarily by what they are not, a difference that can be explained briefly as the radical opposition between the provinces and Paris. When Désiré went to the capital city, for example, he acquired "ideas that he would never have had in Nemours."[2] Paris is different in form and substance from the provinces, and one needs to have particularly strong personal qualities to succeed in France's capital. Savinien is, for example, "a little too simple to live in Paris without a mentor" (3.872). While provincials usually stick together, Parisians are highly independent, often solitary creatures. The latter may be seen shifting from one group to another, but their primary allegiance is always to themselves and their goal to better their personal welfare. Those who are too weak to stand alone are destroyed. Nonetheless, despite the many common factors connecting *Autre étude de femme* to *Ursule Mirouët*, a major change distinguishes the prior work and section from the latter. With the last words of the former we close the *Scènes de la vie privée*, a series of private dramas which explode, destroy, and die within the confines of families. Though still in the provinces, we move to a larger stage, opening the pages of *Ursule Mirouët* and the *Scènes de la vie de province*, where we can watch as the osmotic influences of Paris spread throughout France and build the new capitalistic, industrialized society.

Like the proto-sociologist, Henri de Saint-Simon,[3] Balzac portrayed humanity by representing the singular ages of human beings from infancy to adulthood. According to Félix Davin, one of Balzac's spokesmen, the *Scènes de la vie privée* were the portrayal of infancy and adolescence: "There, then, principally emotions, unthinking sensations; there, mistakes made less because of the will than by inexperience with the customs and because of ignorance of the way of the world" (1.1146). The *Scènes de la vie de province* represent a new period in a process of development, "this phase of human life when passions, planning, and ideas take the place of sensation, unthinking movements, images taken for reality" (ibid.). As Balzac summarized in his "Foreword" to the *Comédie humaine*, it is "the age of passions, careful planning, self-interest, and ambition" (1.19) or, phrased somewhat differently, it is the age of those on the threshold of maturity, a time when young men and women set aside their unbridled passions and begin to think strategically, both to avoid obstacles and to gain the goal they have consciously or unconsciously formulated. In general, what they want is very simply a fortune and the power that accompanies it in the July Monarchy. They give free reign to their ambitions, plot the path necessary for success, or wait patiently either to seize their prize when the right moment comes or to receive it more or less passively through inheritance.

For those sensitive to names, the title suggests something of what readers will confront in the subsequent pages. Madeleine Ambrière-Fargeaud points out that *Ursule Mirouët* had been in Balzac's mind at least as far back as his drafting of the unfinished *Héritiers Boirouge*.[4] In the second chapter of the fragment, Balzac wrote, "Never has a name belonging to a person painted them better: does not Ursule Mirouët raise the image of a..." (3.753). Unfortunately, the novelist never completed the sentence, and only by implication did he reveal his thought. Ursule derives, of course, from the Latin for bear, *ursus*, which has long symbolized primitive and cruel forces that may, however, be tamed.[5] "Ursule is worthy of her name," Dr. Minoret tells Mme Crémière, "she is very wild [*sauvage*]" (3.848). Indeed, the good doctor says later, "She is ferocious" (3.941). Chevalier cites Jung in claiming that the bear represents the dangerous aspect of the unconscious, but it is perhaps more interesting to note that "the bear opposes the hare." Both are lunar creatures, both legendary antagonists. The bear usually kills the hare (Chevalier 573). It is certainly of interest that Ursule's most vicious antagonist is named Levrault-Minoret, since Levrault derives from *lièvre* or hare.[6] The fact that the hare is also a virtually universal symbol for timidity or cowardice (Dauzat 390) may also prepare the stationmaster's craven behavior. It is in respect to Levrault-Minoret that the narrator says, "[S]hould we not recognize with Sterne the occult power of names that sometimes mock and sometimes predict character?" (3.772). And Balzac takes a little extra, explicit trouble for those who have not understood the important connection provided by his characters' names. Balzac's highlights this aspect of his creation by explaining that "Goupil is a corruption of the Latin word *vulpes*, fox" (3.870).

In respect to Ursule's name, S. de Sacy remembers the martyrdom of St. Ursula and the 10,000 virgins (Sacy 341), though I suspect the saint's famous dream, magnificently portrayed by Carpaccio, has much more importance, for it opens the text to supernatural, prophetic dreams that Balzac employed to actuate the unwinding of the criminal activities of the stationmaster. References to Mesmer and Mesmerism highlight the novel's use of saints' names and the associations they bear. To test the somnambulist's prediction, Denis Minoret opens the almanac from Ursule's room and learns as predicted that someone has marked the names of St. Denis (martyred patron saint of Paris, where Denis Minoret gained his fortune and for whom he is named), St. Savinien (another martyr for whom Ursule's beloved is named), and St. John (author of the Gospel that is the primary interpreter of the Holy Spirit, God's powerful right arm commissioned to work His will in the world, and Father Chaperon's first name). The somnambulist learned this in a strange dream/vision. Ursule will likewise have visitations, which bring her namesake more vividly to mind. It was by means of a dream that St. Ursula learned the truth of her coming martyrdom, while Dr. Minoret came back from death in the form of a nocturnal apparition to reveal Levrault-Minoret's theft of the will and bearer bonds. The further fact that Saint Ursula is the patron saint of students opens the important theme of education that ties Ursule to Denis's carefully chosen cadre of friends, as they unite to raise her properly.

Ursule's family name is even more suggestive, for it is loosely reminiscent of Denis's family name of Minoret. Dauzat thinks that *Mirouet* may even be a misspelling of *miroi, -oy* or mirror (436). If one inverts the *u* of Mirouët, thus making an *n*, and then exchanges the positions of *r* and the resultant *n*, the common features make it seem likely that Balzac had mirrors and mirroring in mind. Like mirror images, where relationships are inverted, the strong resemblance emphasizes the mutual affection tying Ursule Mirouët and Dr. Minoret together. She is not his "natural" (illegitimate) daughter. Their relationship is perfectly legal; she is his goddaughter and ward. In addition, mirrors take us once again into the lunar realm of bears and hares, the magical world where a looking glass reveals the truth, whether future or past, and evokes the spirits of the dead (Chevalier 512). It also serves as a glass through which one may see or pass into another world. The Bible uses the symbolism in 1 Corinthians 13.12, as does Lewis Carroll in *Through a Looking-Glass and What Alice Found There* (1872). Ursule does not pass through the portal, as does Alice. Nonetheless her dreams give her access to a world of truth, where the perfidious theft by the brute Levrault-Minoret comes out of the shadows into the light.

All art is internally redundant, providing several indications of what is especially important to communicate. As Balzac multiplies his suggestive images, he also increases aspects of the reality they represent. So it is that when we move beyond the title and into the pages of the text, we approach Nemours from Paris by moving along a canal to a bridge—a symbol of transition and a link between worlds—joining the *Scènes de la vie privée* to the *Scènes de la vie de province*. Because bridges may also symbolize the danger of passage, readers will surely not be surprised to discover Minoret-Levrault himself "seated at the very end of this bridge" (3.770). Described as a "brute" (ibid.), a "giant" (3.771), "violent and incapable of reflection" (ibid.), and compared to Caliban (3.770), the animal nature of the "master of Nemours" is repeatedly emphasized: "This man's chest was a block; you would have said that he was a bull raised up on his two hind legs" (3.771). He serves as another link to the *Scènes de la vie privée*, for he is too primitive to be capable of reflective consideration. His theft is an unthinking reflex rather like an animal incapable of resisting the temptation of instantaneous wealth. In those opening pages usually termed the "overture," the image of a malevolent giant guarding Nemours from outsiders predominates, though the narrator reveals that this apparent Minotaur is involved in the innocent enough activity of awaiting the arrival of his son.

The rich symbolism surrounding bridges also suggests the passage to other realms, and some readers may grasp its preparatory connotations in the conversion of Dr. Minoret. There is of course reason for the Minoret family to be outraged by their relative's accompanying his goddaughter to mass. His fondness for the faithful girl and Father Chaperon's catechism instruction had previously signaled a danger to the watchful eyes of the family. They feared that Dr. Minoret's indulgent love might encourage him to acquiesce to the girl and leave part of what they considered their financial heritage to the church. While they had never really believed that the eighteenth-century philosophically oriented doctor would go so far as convert, their uneasiness remained and was a constant reminder of their fear. What they do not know is that the ward's adoptive father has not only passed into the spiritual world of the Church because of his conversion but has also pursued the revelations of Mesmer into the realm of the occult. In Balzac's terms, he has effectively come to fill his role as godfather.

A German physician, Anton Mesmer (1734–1815), claimed to have discovered a mysterious fluid he called "animal magnetism," which he believed he could control, so as to produce prophesies and cures. Official investigators in both Vienna and Paris were skeptical. Mesmer had nonetheless an enthusiastic following that attended his Parisian lectures and demonstrations in the 1780s and 1790s, though his controversial influence continued long afterward. Having witnessed the incredible, supernatural insights of Mesmer's somnambulant seer, Balzac's Dr. Minoret believes that he has glimpsed another realm and is thus encouraged to claim that he can return from the dead, as indeed he does later (3.839, 853, 959).

The expected arrival of a visitor from Paris recalls Nicole Mozet's insight into the *modèle* or "pattern" of the novels set in the provinces: "[I]n the close environment of small towns, the arrival of a stranger provokes a series of chain reactions " (3.1010). I would quibble that those novels set in the provinces but included in other parts of *La Comédie humaine* may also include structures similar to the one Mozet indicates, though they are significantly altered by differing contexts and other impulsions. Still, that in no way impugns her apt comment in relation to the *Scènes de la vie de province*, though it should, however, be expanded.[7] It is noteworthy, for example, that these quintessential arrivals are coupled with the story of an inheritance and of ambitious youth, a combination that is at the heart of the novels in this section of *La Comédie humaine*. As Mozet also recognizes, *Ursule Mirouët*, "this disconcerting novel," is also a novel of miracles: "the imbecile becomes a saint, the incredulous believes, the indebted young man becomes serious, and his old mother consents to his marriage with Ursule, through generosity rather than selfish desire," the latter being perhaps the greatest miracle of all ("Test" 218, 223). As Claudie Bernard moreover points out, both Ursule's and Mme de Portenduère's maiden names end in the same way: Mirouët and Kergarouët thus prepare them to share the same married name.[8] A single bridge has led to two faiths—the one Catholic and the other occult (though Balzac apparently felt them to be reflections of the same underlying belief system)—and it has brought together two lovers in marriage.

The image of an armature is useful here. In a sense, a character type illustrates the concept. Take, for instance, the miser, a type that Balzac used on several occasions, notably for Gobseck and Grandet. If one thinks of misers that have been incarnated in the course of European letters, from farce and the Pantalone of the *commedia dell'arte* to Molière's Harpagon of *L'Avare*, to *La Comédie humaine*'s further examples, there is a consistency within the type that can nonetheless include different traits and qualities, depending on whether the miser is a thief, or charitable, or unintelligent, or brilliant, or married, or in a small town, or in the country, or in a large city. The basic stereotype varies considerably. As just one example of contrasting characters within the same type, one could think of the extraordinarily generous Father Chaperon, who has a character joining avariciousness with charity, unlike the self-centered nature of most misers like Gobseck (3.792). The priest's apparent greed is only so that he may give more abundantly to the poor and needy.

As with a character type, so with the armatures of plot or situational types. According to Vladimir Propp, the apparent multiplicity of the Russian folk tale can be reduced to a very few plot structures. The *Scènes de la vie de province* are prototypical as well. The first half of these *scènes*, from *Ursule Mirouët* through *La Muse du département* (*The Muse of the Department*), are organized around the repulsion of foreigners, of strangers, usually from Paris, in order to maintain an indigenous monopoly. Without exception, the novels portray rival groups of provincials that band together at some point to repel the outsider, all for the purpose of retaining any inheritance or advantage within the community. Although the locals do not always succeed—Ursule Mirouët and the Parisian Joseph Bridau eventually inherit despite the efforts of the country people—the inheritance, which has constituted the basic subject of these creations, forms a thematic armature around which there is considerable room for variation.

Much as Dr. Minoret's heirs unite to reject Ursule, the Cruchotins and the Grassinistes forgo their rivalry in the next novel, *Eugénie Grandet*, in order to expel Charles. He eventually does leave, though not due to their efforts, and even with Cruchot's marriage to the heiress, whatever success this brings is only temporary. Cruchot, who now calls himself M. de Bonfons, arranges in the wedding contract for whomever lives the longest to inherit everything, whether himself or Eugénie. This, of course, is a clever ploy, which would enable the enormous Grandet fortune to flow into his family's assets, but only if he is the longest lived. Regrettably for him and his relatives, he misjudged Eugénie's and his own health. He dies first, thus depriving his family of his personal wealth and endowing Eugénie with an even larger fortune. The narrator considers his early demise the vengeance of Providence (3.1197).

The details of the inheritance paradigm change in *Pierrette*, as they do elsewhere in the *Scènes de la vie de province*. After making something of a fortune in Paris, Denis Minoret and the Rogrons return to the provinces where they were born. Also like Dr. Minoret, though for different reasons, they have problems with the local families, and they begin slowly to build their own group. Minoret brings his ward with him, and does everything he can to protect her from his preying relatives, while the Rogrons do not import their cousin, Pierrette, until long after their own arrival. Despite their promises to leave their fortune to the girl, the Rogrons abuse and eventually destroy her. In *Ursule Mirouët*, Minoret creates a support group of men of intelligence, substance, and authority within the community, including not just a justice of the peace, a clergyman, and a soldier, but God as well, in order to see that Ursule eventually inherits. The situations and the characters are different, as is the conclusion, though the inheritance remains important.

Since families through the late eighteenth and early nineteenth centuries were weakened due to the war-torn and economically challenged society, historians like Lynn Hunt and Michelet have argued that the Revolution dismantled *ancien régime* paternity.[9] Family might have been replaced by cohesive relationships of friends, almost a substitute or artificial family. Reflecting the world of the July Monarchy, Balzac repeatedly constructed such pseudo-families. The Rogrons, for example, form a group of liberals in *Pierrette* which becomes so powerful that, while rightfully charged with responsibility for Pierrette's death and brought to court, the brother and sister get off without penalty because of their political, rather than family, affiliations. Hunt goes on to argue that around 1750 the "bad" father of literature was replaced by a "weak," but "good" father without authority. As the novelist put it, "In cutting off Louis XVI's head, the Revolution cut off the heads of all fathers" (1.242). For Hunt, impotent fathers augur the end of fatherhood, which will be replaced by fraternity. My own research, like that of Marcel David, would suggest that no such chronology leading from loveless, tyrannical paternity, to feckless fatherhood, to brotherhood can be sustained beyond Balzac and a very few others. Across what I and David have been able to consider, the post-revolutionary fraternity indicates that neither the term nor the concept of brotherhood had much significance beyond the rhetorical realm of the workers' movements.[10] In point of fact, "Fraternity faded away during the Consulate and the Empire, until you would have been justified in believing that it had had its day" (David 276).

Sarah Horowitz turns in a different direction and points out that friendship made business and political life possible after the French Revolution and during the Restoration. As the Terror atomized society, she argues, the widespread perfidy and constant spying destroyed trust, dividing the nation according to ideology and, simultaneously, making it virtually impossible to either govern or do business. Friendship displaced other potential systems of relationship and rebuilt trust and cohesion on the basis of affection rather than political or financial position. Friends depended on each other for pleasure, contacts, and protection. Horowitz concludes that the power and efficacy of this amity was very important and very real, though she shows that it faded during the July Monarchy to become little more than a useful tool to motivate groups for political reasons.[11] Though she does not mention the actual breakdown of family during the first third of the century that Balzac describes regularly, it surely provides another reason for the emphasis placed on friendship. With the fragmentation of family and its loss of power and influence, an older form of tribalism revives. People banded together, not on the basis of blood, but for mutual advantage. Even when a group like the Minoret-Levrault-Crémière-Massin family grow closer because of their blood ties, they do so, not out of love or even affection for the family, but out of the desire to strip position and wealth from the "other," the outsider, the foreigner.

Legions of weak, selfish, and cruel fathers continue to appear in literature across the eighteenth and nineteenth centuries. They occur well after the Revolution, and they move aside not for reasons of fraternity but for extreme forms of individualism. As Balzac has Monsieur de Chaulieu explain, "Today there are no longer any families, there are only individuals" (1.242). Savinien echoes the perception in an already quoted passage (3.883). Along with many other examples outside of *La Comédie humaine* that come readily to mind, there are Benjamin Constant's sister Louise d'Estournelles, a novelist who had M. de Laval unreasonably oppose the love match between his son and Eugénie in *Pascaline* (1821), Stendhal's hated father figures in the 1820s and 1830s, and Flaubert's appalling father, Charles Bovary (1857). A radical change was unquestionably taking place in families. Increasingly unattractive examples of fatherhood appeared in literature as paternal mortality rose during the wars.

The growing disappearance of all fathers from Romantic literature is also telling. Not only do fathers disappear from the books written for children, either because they are away on a trip or because they are said to be too busy with various affairs to take a significant part in the family, they constitute a remarkable absence from the majority of all novels. Occasionally, fathers are explicitly dead, as in *Ursule Mirouët*, the anonymous *Confessions d'une courtisane devenue philosophe*, or legions of other novels, but most often the family patriarch is simply not there. Stephen's childhood took place far from his father, for example, in Alphonse Karr's *Sous les tilleuls* (1832). In 1836, Saint-Estève nonetheless draws a more encompassing conclusion: "There are no fathers in nature [...] there are only mothers. Fathers are a social fiction."[12] In 1793, the Convention even decreed that children could choose whatever last name they wished.[13] For

Balzac and for others, family ties were dissolving. There are many explanations for the lack of fathers. Seasonal migration, numerous wars, and business removed fathers of all classes from the homes. All took their toll. I earlier suggested that the unrealistic plethora of orphans in Romantic literature might have indicated widespread feeling of abandonment caused both by absent fathers and by the methods of childcare that frequently sent children off to the wet nurse away from parents as soon after birth as possible, until they were abruptly returned to the natural family or abandoned (*Sick Heroes* 61).

In *Ursule Mirouët*, the little group of friends around Minoret were people he enjoyed, and, crucially, they also helped him raise and educate his goddaughter. "[T]he priest thought about the soul, the judge was the guardian [concerned with legal matters], the soldier promised to become the preceptor, and, as for Minoret, he was simultaneously father, mother and doctor" (3.798). In addition, Minoret depended on secrecy. "These wise operations thought out by the doctor and the judge were accomplished in the deepest secret" (3.903), because they believed that happiness is impossible unless one guards one's privacy with the utmost care. This lesson will be repeated regularly throughout the *Comédie humaine*. "Children," Dr. Minoret tells Ursule and Savinien who are aglow with love for each other, "you put your happiness at risk in not keeping it secret except for yourselves" (3.899). Of course, his tactics for maintaining his privacy do not always succeed. He refuses, for example, to bring his housekeeper with him from Paris, but somehow she and the stationmaster's wife meet. "[F]urious to have not accompanied [Minoret] to Nemours, [she] said to Zélie Levrault [...] that she knew the doctor has fourteen thousand francs invested in treasury bonds" (3.789).

Minoret's friends do not object to being used to advance the doctor's plans. Still, as Sarah Horowitz argues, with an important observation, friendship and love did not exclude being used for political and personal ambition. That mutual affection served a practical purpose within society neither discredited nor reduced either the value or the importance of true friendship. Such amity between men and women might or might not include sexual relations, and it might for various reasons be kept secret, but from Thermidor through the Restoration it was an important part of the social complex. It was never viewed as separate. Participants in such sentimental relationships were aware that the responsibility of love and friendship went beyond mere feelings. Because Dr. Minoret chose his friends carefully, they are also important to his primary mission, the education and suitable marriage of Ursule. He knew that membership in an active group was essential to his success with his ward. Neither he nor they feel diminished by Minoret's goals and the fact that he depends on them to accomplish what is necessary for the girl.

Minoret understands that solitary people cannot succeed in the provinces. In Paris, it is quite a different story. Those who cannot find success by themselves will fail. The *Scènes de la vie de province* give a series of examples of young people whose incapacities leave them with no recourse but to scuttle back to the provinces, but who, in one way or another, later put together a life of comfort and pleasure in a context of provincial support. To combat the large family of his relatives, Dr. Minoret needs a family of his own with shared goals and ambitions. Given that his extended family has come together with the shared ambition to disinherit the doctor's ward, he needs to construct his own pseudo-family based not upon greed or lust but on friendship. Balzac clearly felt that the family did not necessarily function appropriately. He deals extensively with the opposition of family and support groups in a number of other novels. In *La Rabouilleuse*, for example, he follows Philippe, who successfully marshals a group, including several relatives, to defeat his brother, mother, and other interested parties. It is particularly important that this family-like group fails in the primary purpose of families. Philippe works not for his loved ones but for himself alone.

After Napoleon, French families were in significant difficulty. Some 1,700,000 Frenchmen, or more than five percent of the population, died in the revolutionary and Emperor's wars, leaving only approximately 30,000,000 French people alive in 1815, after the Emperor's defeat at Waterloo. France had become a nation of grandfathers and children. It is no wonder that, as demographers have pointed out, France grew so slowly during the nineteenth century, much more slowly than either Germany or England.[14] While there were certainly more real families than Balzac portrays, he points to a gaping absence of leadership that had become a retrograde force within the culture. In particular, he accuses the extremely conservative gerontocracy that has tightened its hold on the financial and political power of the nation and used it to exclude France's young, thus impeding progress.

The colossus Minoret-Levrault waiting at the Nemours bridge, fully capable of repelling any stranger, serves as a thematic image for *Ursule Mirouët*'s introductory scene, and for a significant portion of the *Scènes de la vie de province*. In this case, Levrault merely awaits the coach bringing his son, Désiré, who has just completed his legal study in Paris. Especially when Minoret-Levrault turns back toward town to consult about the inherent danger of Dr. Minoret's conversion with the gathering relatives, all of whom hope to disinherit Ursule and the Church in their own favor, the picture of the stationmaster at the bridge reinforces one of the major movements of this section of *La Comédie humaine*. Ursule is an outsider (the dieresis in her last name may even mark her as foreign or, in line with Bernard's previously mentioned suggestion, a throwback of some sort). One and all, Minoret's family oppose all aliens and would like to get rid of the doctor's ward. The mention of the coachman and coach also opens the door for Balzac to emphasize the sociological changes taking place in this society.

Advances in transportation and communication radically transformed peoples' lives. As Minoret-Levrault is in charge of the local way station, his wife is in charge of the post office, thus potentially with their fingers on the pulse of the town and nation. Whether by mail coach, stagecoach, or horseback, people and documents moved rapidly across France, simultaneously introducing a new understanding of the importance of information and speed. The coach Levrault waits for is late, so he is uneasy, given the mishaps that still happen in the modernized system, and, indeed, at the end of the novel Désiré will die in a perfectly horrendous coach accident. This time, however, it is only a wheel needing repair, and the son will soon be welcomed home. Still, everyone remembers what it used to be like, for it is only 1829 in *Ursule Mirouët* and not very far removed from the appalling roads at the turn of the century. Jean-Georges Wille, for example, describes an episode in a trip he took in 1791 to attend a wedding. "[S]ince the path from the inn to the barrier is known for being very bad, a domestic from the house lit our way [...]; despite that the carriage became so caked in mud that the barrier agent began to push on the wheel and freed us."[15]

Better roads and equipment allowed people, products, documents, and news to cross France "like lightning." As horses were exchanged, coachmen and passengers gossiped, and important news spread. Information that formerly took days and weeks to affect the market was suddenly available to the quick and the knowing. They not only made fortunes but also wielded power. Old Grandet accumulated a small fortune by exploiting the change in the price of gold before others knew. He surely took advantage of this remarkable network of information. Given good weather, daylight, and alert drivers and staff, news from the provinces could be transmitted to Paris in a few hours. The teletype would soon make it even faster. The roar of the passing stagecoach and, later, the bellowing of trains marked a new world. In the July Monarchy, the town of Nemours had suddenly "moved" much closer to Paris and seemed, given the speed of transportation, "right next door."[16] Even when one was in Paris, the amazing ubiquity of Mesmer's prophetess was hardly necessary for virtually simultaneous knowledge of occurrences in Nemours. As this novel and others like *Le Cabinet des antiques* unfurl, numerous characters move with apparent ease between the provinces and the capital city. As people move, so eventually will ideas.

There are three arrivals in *Ursule Mirouët*. The first occurred many years before the action of the novel, when Denis Minoret arrived with his ward, and it serves as the stimulus for the rest of the narration. Still, the spaced arrivals of Désiré, who is the pampered offspring of Minoret-Levrault, and Savinien, the equally spoiled child of local aristocrats, give the impression of activity while describing the strategies, the changing alliances, and the opposing forces of two families, the one a rather impressive number of Minoret-Levraults, Crémières, and Massins,[17] all related, and the other, a group of friends, an artificial family organized by Dr. Minoret.

Zélie briefly touches on the associated class structure, when she claims that the five hundred years of the Minoret family history "is worth nobility" (3.845). Not everyone would agree, though bourgeois roots lost in the distant past certainly justify the respect due a few worthy families. Grandet enters the middle class by means of money. Savinien's fatherless family has little to recommend it in this period, despite its impeccable heraldic credentials, for they were impoverished by the Revolution. The snobbery that Zélie reveals in her refusal to allow her son to marry a bastard's offspring seems as ridiculous as Mme de Portenduère's adamant refusal to permit her son's marriage to a commoner, however noble might be Ursule's innate character (3.884). Savinien is attempting to explain his lack of success during his time in Paris when he says, "Family no longer exists today, Mother, there are only individuals. Nobles no longer stand together. These days no one asks if you are a Portenduère, if you are brave, or if you are a statesman. They only want to know how much your taxes are" (3.884). In *Ursule Mirouët*, Balzac will follow the theme of family in its numerous ramifications to suggest that all nuclear families, at all levels of society, are slowly being destroyed, if not by war then by social breakdown. The theme will be explored repeatedly throughout this portion of *La Comédie humaine*.

The overture of this novel is long even for Balzac. It takes up almost exactly the entire first half of the novel, and it ends only because the narrator says it does: "If we must apply scenic rules to the tale, Savinien's arrival, in introducing to Nemours the only character who was still missing from those who must be present in this little drama, ends the exposition here" (3.883). In fact, we understand that the events of this story are continuing to take place in the background of the overture as the narrator sets the scene for the crisis. With all due apologies to the narrator, Savinien's return from Paris, the event which supposedly marks the beginning of the novel, has no real impact on the occurrences which actually bear on the inheritance. Ursule, who feels attracted to Savinien and is thus responsible for her uncle's rescuing the boy from debtors' prison, receives an invitation to visit the young man's mother, Mme de Portenduère. The love that blossoms despite the punctilious aristocratic mother's disapproval of Ursule, whom she views as the middle-class spawn of a bastard, then serves as the opening of a story which is closed by the marriage of the wealthy Ursule to the penniless Savinien de Portenduère. The more inclusive plot turning about the inheritance, however, begins with the novel's first few pages, when we are introduced to the local families who are determined to usurp Ursule's rightful inheritance, and it ends with their failure. From the opening vision of the doting father Levrault-Minoret at the bridge to the closing death of his son, likewise at the bridge (as Mozet points out—*Ville* 218), the novel prepares for Ursule, the rich heiress, to ride off and live happily ever after with her husband, Savinien.

Dr. Minoret asked about his heirs when he first came to Nemours. The doctor's concern is difficult to understand, since before the law there is no real reason why he cannot leave everything he wishes to his ward. Balzac makes it very clear that the nieces and nephews have few, if any, claims to his estate, though the doctor's questions make his awareness of potential problems clear.[18] The law did indeed protect legal children's inheritances from the claims of those born out of wedlock—as Bixiou points out in another context: "[W]e are only the fathers of our legitimate wife's children" (4.748)—though this has but the vaguest pertinence to the legal child of an illegitimately born father, who was moreover but distantly related by blood to Dr. Minoret's wife and not to the doctor. Madeleine Ambrière-Fargeaud also considers the rights of the doctor's relatives "a false problem" (3.1588n2), but Minoret's friend Bongrand assesses the potential complications of the case more adequately:

> [Ursule] was unrelated to Doctor Minoret, but [Bongrand] clearly felt that the spirit of the legislation rejected illegitimate additions. The authors of the code [law] had not foreseen anything but the weakness of mothers and fathers of bastard children, without imagining that uncles or aunts would espouse love for the bastard child in favor of legitimate offspring. Obviously, there is a lacuna in the law.
>
> "In any other country," he said to the doctor as he finished exposing the state of jurisprudence to the doctor, [...] "Ursule would have nothing to fear; she is a legitimate daughter, and the legal limits of her father [in regard to being illegitimate and unable to inherit] should have no effect in respect to the succession from Valentin Mirouët [...]. Nonetheless, in France, the magistracy is unfortunately very clever and consequential. It looks for the spirit of the law. Attorneys will speak of morals and will demonstrate that the code's lacuna comes from the legislator's failing from good will to foresee the possibility. They have nonetheless established a principal." (3.851)

Only excessive judicial ratiocination, if not capriciousness, would prevent Dr. Minoret from preferring his ward to such distant relatives as those in Nemours who scheme to inherit his fortune—which is precisely the point behind the doctor's concern.[19]

If one pays close attention to the notary Dionis's explanation to the relatives, a will in Ursule's favor "could perhaps be attacked" (3.843), though it would be "a rather bad lawsuit for you" (ibid.). Goupil pushes the explanation further, making the tenuousness of the nieces and nephews' position all the clearer, but Dionis understands that the law can be used as a club and thus work for illegitimate ends. "[T]he lawsuit would certainly frighten a defenseless girl and would open the possibility of transaction" (ibid.). As any trial lawyer knows, clients with "deep pockets," whether individual or corporate, can by intimidating, wearing down, or simply allowing time to pass bring about concessions and settlements which are in every way unjust. "Consequently, I would answer that in this lawsuit, there would be a settlement, especially if they knew that you were willing to take the suit to a court of appeals" (3.844). Dionis's strategy might have been different had their prey not been young and a girl. If the relatives act aggressively, she will have limited funds and be subject to considerable embarrassment in her provincial society when the lawyers capitalize on her father's illegitimacy. It should be a simple matter to intimidate her.

Denis Minoret's grasp of the situation is far more profound, though it only grows clear through his actions, as well as through what the reader learns of the provinces. While Minoret understands the mores of those French people situated away from Paris, he underestimates the depth of his relatives' greed. After inquiring about his potential heirs—"'In short, I don't lack heritors,' the doctor said merrily" (3.787)—he does not depend on the law, since the law is the undependable servant of the powerful. His plan is relatively simple. First of all, he endows his relatives. Mme Massin receives ten thousand francs, with which her husband becomes a successful usurer. The doctor calls on his influential friends to gain the position of tax collector for Mme Crémière's husband and then puts up the amount required for the security bond. And for his nephew, Désiré, he arranges a partial fellowship at school. Then he lets his heirs know that they will indeed inherit from him. To this end he dedicates the sum he had accumulated before his arrival in Nemours. The most obvious, hoped-for-benefit is that his relatives will leave him alone. "[T]o his great contentment, they stopped seeing him" (3.798). He apparently also hopes that they will be sufficiently satisfied at his death with the previous help and generous inheritance he reserves for them that they will not attempt to take the small fortune he plans to leave his ward. In this, he was mistaken. He has misunderstood the depth of their greed and only whetted their appetites for more.

The third and fourth strategies show exceptional cunning and insight into the ways of provincials. Dr. Minoret lives a quiet, withdrawn life, thus avoiding the curiosity of his neighbors and indeed attempting to keep them absolutely ignorant of what went on inside the walls of his home. "He wanted to concede nothing to the changing goddess of public opinion" (3.798). To this end, Minoret dismissed the cook for gossiping to Zélie Levrault, as soon as Ursule was weaned and could walk independently. Because Balzac was convinced that the bond formed by a nurse and child was far stronger than that of blood, Minoret's only servant then became Ursule's wet nurse, Bougival, who "attached herself to Ursule in a natural way as wet nurses nourish their charges when they continue to look after them" (3.799). Bougival's loyalty is absolute, and the doctor's privacy virtually assured. He only needs to guard against what is elsewhere called "the analytical genius the provincials have" (3.1068). Indeed, he is not free from the scrutiny of his neighbors. The town's legal authorities have thoroughly discussed the question of Ursule's inheritance, for instance (3.850–51). Nonetheless, although Minoret has some success in protecting his privacy, his care in hiding his actions raises the relatives' suspicions. The town terms him *secretive* (3.921), implying that his reserved nature must cover something reprehensible, which is in fact simply to keep a portion of his personal wealth out of the hands of his predatory relatives. In most modern societies, success stemming from the relatives' attempt would be impossible. Given the legal confusion that remained from, and because of, the inconsistent efforts by the revolutionaries and Napoleon to reform the legal hodge-podge of the *ancien régime*, Dionis correctly evaluates the girl's danger. Denis Minoret's carefully planned campaign to ensure that the inheritance goes to Ursule succeeds only because God, the fourth partner of the group, intervened.

Dr. Minoret's astute understanding of the issues surrounding his family and Nemours led him to find a way to guard Ursule from the untrustworthy vagaries of the judicial system. By hiding a fortune in bonds between the covers of Justinian's *Pandectes*, he expected her to have millions despite any potential decisions of the courts and the skullduggery of his relatives. Had he not waited until too late, this last resort might well have succeeded. Unfortunately, his explicit instructions to Ursule about the bonds' hiding place came when she was unable to leave his bedside, preventing her from retrieving them. His nephew, the stationmaster Minoret-Levrault, overheard enough to find and steal both the doctor's will and the bonds. Sensing that a record might be kept that would prove Ursule's legitimate ownership, the thief is afraid to make use of the money. Shortly after God allows Minoret's return in the girl's dreams, Ursule becomes immensely wealthy and "the finger of God" (3.981, 986) brings true justice. The thief is exposed and repents.

The doctor's most important ploy to take care of his goddaughter consists of his support group of friends. Each participant is important. Prior to Minoret's conversion, there was Jordy, who tutored the girl and eventually left her the small bequest necessary to meet expenses while her inheritance is being arranged, Father Chaperon, who is essential in helping her understand and take advantage of the visions, and Bongrand, the justice of the peace, who is responsible for the legal protection of the inheritance. God, the fourth member of the group, did not join until the doctor's conversion, and even then He was perhaps no more important than the others. Contrary to all too many other examples of last-minute interventions of a *deus ex machina* in order to resolve plot issues, like the police officer who suddenly pops up at the end of Molière's *Tartuffe*, Balzac's use of God's activity is completely integrated into the story of *Ursule Mirouët*. After the demonstration with the somnambulist, which is credited to the power of God, and Minoret's subsequent tests, readers are encouraged and conditioned to accept Ursule's dreams announcing Savinien's letters before they arrive. Though such experiences are not unusual, her foresight is probably not enough preparation to make the reader take the doctor seriously when he announces, "Ursule [...] if you are ever menaced by danger, call me, I will come" (3.839), and still less effective at encouraging close attention to his threat against the relatives: "If one of them were to interfere with anything that I believe I should do for this child (he points to his goddaughter), I would come back from the other world to torment them!" (3.853). Still, the development as a whole is doubtless sufficient for readers to suspend their disbelief on reading the account of the various dreams. Certainly, Balzac was a firm believer in the occult occurrences connected with Mesmer and Swedenborg. While the Church did not approve of all of Balzac's occult allegiances, the novelist viewed the supernatural as a normal part of Catholicism and an acceptable part of both life and a realistic novel.[20]

But it is Ursule who remains at the center of every complex of the novel's images and themes, like those of the occult and of justice, and of every plot, whether the love story, the inheritance, or the conversion of her atheistic guardian. She is the pivot for the well-delineated social groups that for Balzac defined provincial life. Minoret's relatives are outraged at the beginning of the novel because the doctor has started going to mass. They fear he might leave part or all of his fortune to the Church, though in fact the real danger is that with Minoret's conversion, God may decide to see divine justice done here on earth. The relatives are in significant jeopardy, but only because God rather than man may judge the issues. Although Désiré warns his father that "[i]f justice could not always punish everything, it will know everything in the end and keep a good record" (3.948), in fact, of course, without God's revelation Minoret-Levrault's crime would have been neither known nor punished. Ursule herself is the glass through which on one side we see the inadequacy of human law, and on the other the righteousness and thoroughness of God's justice. Though she never crosses over or passes through the glass, as did Alice, she is allowed to perceive the truth of her situation. "Ursule became the pious, mystical girl whose character was always above events, and whose heart dominated all adversity" (3.817). She is the candid person through whom God can shine the light of his truth when human justice fails. While it may be correct, as Bongrand claims, that "[h]uman justice is [...] the development of a divine thought that soars over the world!" (3.890), as the rest of the *Scènes de la vie de province* proves, justice in the world of *La Comédie humaine* is seldom so satisfying. *Ursule Mirouët* ends, unlike the other novels in this section, with the happy resolution of her circumstances, illuminating the possibility of fairness and honorable dealings. The heroes are triumphant and joyous, the villains roundly punished and agreeably repentant.

Ursule Mirouët is on its own terms a very fine literary work, powerfully arranging novelistic and sociological elements, title, names, images, themes, and story to project a vision of the July Monarchy's legal system and intense interest in the occult, to insist on the cohesive interface between our world and the other, and to serve as a transition into and overture for the *Scènes de la vie de province*. The title itself serves to suggest its function as gateway, both in respect to the major themes, the plot, and the heroine. A series of young women will, in subsequent novels, have to cope with the problems of inheritance and, more generally, of the society-wide effects of modernity that is pervasively spreading throughout the provinces. Variations on the paradigmatic plot, characters, and themes of the introduction are replayed in the entire section of novels and short stories. In this light, as readers are brought gently through the mirror to Balzac's provinces, they are reminded once again that Balzac is the creator of a series of rather disparate novels that coalesce into an enormous, pulsating, vital, unified *Comédie humaine*.

Notes

1. See Allan H. Pasco, *Balzacian Montage: Configuring* La Comédie humaine (Toronto: U of Toronto P, 1991; rept. Charlottesville: Rookwood P, 2002), ch. 4.
2. 3.773. As stated in Chap. 1, all references to *La Comédie humaine* are, unless otherwise indicated, to the Pléiade edition.
3. Henri de Saint-Simon, *Mémoire de la science de l'homme* (1813), 2e partie, éd. Prosper Enfantin, *Science de l'homme* (Paris: Victor Masson, 1858) 333–40.
4. Anthony R. Pugh convincingly dates the fragment: June 1836, in his *Balzac's Recurring Characters* (Toronto: U of Toronto P, 1974) 135.
5. Jean Chevalier and Alain Gheerbrant, *Dictionnaire des symbols* (Paris: R. Laffont, 1969) 574. I refer to Jung and such editors as Chevalier and Cirlot as well-documented elucidations of widely recognized associations, but only when Balzac's context is congruent.

6. Albert Dauzat, *Dictionnaire étymologique des noms de famille et prénoms de France* (Paris: Larousse, 1951) 389.
7. As Nicole Mozet has in fact done, though in a different way. See her *La Ville de province dans l'œuvre de Balzac: L'Espace romanesque: fantasmes et idéologie* (Paris: Société d'Edition d'Enseignement Supérieur, 1982; and "Ursule Mirouët ou le test du bâtard," *Balzac, Œuvres complètes: Le Moment de* La Comédie humaine, ed. Claude Duchet and Isabelle Tournier (Saint-Denis: PU de Vincennes, 1993) 217–28.
8. Bernard, "La Dynamique familiale dans *Ursule Mirouët* de Balzac," *French Forum* 24.2 (1999): 196.
9. Hunt, *The Family Romance of the French Revolution* (Berkeley: U of California P, 1992).
10. Susan Dunn's development on fatherhood is particularly important: *The Deaths of Louis XVI: Regicide and the French Political Imagination* (Princeton: Princeton UP, 1994) 67–92. For other pertinent work, see J.-C. Bonnet, "La Malédiction Paternelle," *Dix-Huitième Siècle* 12 (1980): 195–208; Joan B. Landes, "Representing the Body Politic: The Paradox of Gender in the Graphic Politics of the French Revolution," *Rebel Daughters: Women and the French Revolution*, ed. Sara E. Melzer and Leslie W. Rabine (New York: Oxford, 1992) 15; and, especially, Marcel David, *Fraternité et Révolution française* (Paris: Aubier, 1987), and Pasco, *Sick Heroes: French Society and Literature in the Romantic Age: 1750–1850* (Exeter: U of Exeter P, 1997) 61–65, though I shall argue farther along in these pages that Balzac is primarily concerned with family in crisis.
11. Horowitz, *Friendship and Politics in Post-Revolutionary France* (University Park: Pennsylvania State UP, 2013).
12. Anonymous, *Confessions d'une courtisane devenue philosophe* (London, B. Le Francq, 1784) 7. See, also, Karr, *Sous les tilleuls* (Paris: Calmann Lévy, 1881) 60; Sophie Pannier, *L'Athée*, 2 vols. 1835 (Paris: Fournier, 1836) 1.21. For analyses of the phenomenon, see M. Sonnet, "Les Leçons paternelles," *Histoire des pères*, ed. Jean Delumeau and Daniel Roche (Paris: Larousse, 1990) 264–65; A. Cabantous, "La Fin des patriarches," *Histoire des pères* 323–25; Hunt, *Family Romance* 22, 40.
13. Several months later the deputies had a change of heart, however, insisting that the family name on the birth certificate was obligatory— J.-C. Bonnet, "De la famille à la patrie," *Histoire des pères* 256.

14. Karl Gunnar Persson, *An Economic History of Europe: Knowledge, Institutions and Growth, 600 to the Present* (New York: Cambridge UP, 2010) 66. The French mortality during the Revolutionary and Napoleonic wars is based on estimates published in Matthew White, "Selected Death Tolls for Wars, Massacres and Atrocities Before the 20th Century," *Historical Atlas of the 20th Century*, http://necrometrics.com. See, also, Jacques Dupâquier, "La Population française de 1789 à 1806," *Histoire de la population française*, éd. J. Dupâquier, 4 vols. (Paris: PU de France, 1988) 3.64–83. F. Bluche, S. Rials, and J. Tulard say flatly that a minimum of 5 % of the population died at war—*La Révolution française, Que sais-je?* (Paris: PU de France, 1989) 120. These estimates are far from certain, though not unreasonable.
15. Wille, *Mémoires et journal*, ed. Georges Duplessis, 2 vols. (Paris: Jules Renouard, 1857) 291.
16. Because the new speed contrasted with the traditional and expected normal rhythms of life, David F. Bell suggests that time seemed compressed—*Real Time: Accelerating Narrative from Balzac to Zola* (Urbana: U of Illinois P, 2004) 9. For his remarks on *Ursule*, see pp. 9–32. For a more inclusive grasp of the concept of travel that suggests the vertiginous, breathless quality poets sensed while experiencing the changes occurring around 1830, see Claude Pichois, *Littérature et progrès: Vitesse et vision du monde, essai* (Neuchatel: La Baconnière, 1973) 11–19.
17. Armine Mortimer has unsnarled the complicated interrelationships of this family whose members served in the areas' most important professions—*For Love or for Money: Balzac's Rhetorical Realism* (Columbus: Ohio State UP, 2011) 151–66.
18. Madeleine Ambrière-Fargeaud presents the legal case clearly: 3.1588–91, 1595, in the notes to 3.843–44, 851.
19. The scandalous, long-term disregard of the courts and inheritance law, whether revolutionary or Napoleonic, has been described in detail by Suzanne Desan, *The Family on Trial in Revolutionary France* (Berkeley: U of California P, 2004) 141–318.
20. See Anne-Marie Baron's excellent book *Balzac occult: alchimie, magnétism, sociétés secrètes* (Lausanne: L'Age d'homme, 2012). Although she deals only briefly with *Ursule Mirouët* (51–55), her overview of the occult practices of Balzac's day is very helpful.

CHAPTER 3

A "Divine" Comedy: *Eugénie Grandet*

Balzac's *Eugénie Grandet* (1833) turns on concepts and precepts of Christianity, and specifically of the French Catholic Church, which had been substantially weakened by a century of flaccid theology and subsequent loss of its property during the Revolution. Anyone interested in the social interrelationships of the Restoration and the July Monarchy will unfailingly be brought to consider the French church, if only because it was the focus of considerable, continuing disagreement. In addition, society was failing in many of the areas of education and welfare, where the French religious institutions had previously demonstrated some effectiveness. Prior to the social conflagration and upheaval of the Revolution, the ultramontane church owned in the neighborhood of ten percent of the land, and if other property like cash, artworks, and movable property are included, the estimates rise much higher. In some parts of France, like Picardy and the Cambrésis, a third of the real estate belonged to the church.[1] Protected by its exemption from taxation, the ever-increasing material wealth of the eighteenth-century Gallican church made it a powerful force within society, strength that the Revolution revoked through confiscation and legal interference with normal church practice. With little more than the stroke of a pen, all of the church's material goods were now owned by the state. With another, priests could and in the opinion of many revolutionaries should marry. By 1819, when Balzac's *Eugénie Grandet* begins, many properties previously owned by the church had been sold, forcing French Catholicism into the background as a social

© The Editor(s) (if applicable) and The Author(s) 2016
A.H. Pasco, *Balzac, Literary Sociologist*,
DOI 10.1007/978-3-319-39333-9_3

force. Indeed, the church was compelled to have its authority limited to little more than its spiritual beliefs and doctrines. This development, while championed by many middle-class Frenchmen, was not viewed with universal favor. The revolutionary decisions to strip the church of all material property, if not all of its spiritual authority, had infuriated many of the faithful, as the particularly vicious Vendean uprisings of the mid-1790s against the Revolution prove.

Successful rule of France required peace with Catholic believers. When Napoleon approached Pope Pius VII about an official revision of the revolutionary efforts toward dechristianization, he had just won the major victory of Morango, and was then negotiating from a position of strength. He agreed that "Catholicism was the religion of the great majority of the French," but he insisted that it was not the official state religion. This was an important change from the Catholicism of the *ancien régime*, though Jeffrey W. Merrick argues that it had been the basic position of Louis XV. The new agreement permitted some freedom to both Protestants and Jews. Leaving intact the material poverty of the church imposed by the Revolution, and accepted as permanent, the Concordat of 1801 permitted basic Christian moral tenets and beliefs as they were defined and understood by Catholics. The Concordat agreed to open worship supported financially by the state and to permit doctrinal freedom, with a few reservations in particular about the authority of the Papacy, but the religious functionaries became employees of the state. The agreement had immediate impact. As Napoleon explained, mimicking Henri IV's conversion to Catholicism, "It was by making myself a Catholic that I finished the war of the Vendée."[2]

The Concordat was a political coup for Napoleon. It undercut monarchical support in a period when there were significant elements agitating for restoration of the Bourbons. It also left the French church in a shambles. As Merrick describes the situation of the Gallican church at the end of the eighteenth century, so were the conditions on into the nineteenth: "delayed baptisms, indifference concerning burial, omissions of religious invocations and intercessory clauses from wills, bequests to subsidize charity for the living rather than masses for the dead [...], fewer theological titles in print, more Sabbath-breaking, blasphemy, suicide, premarital sex, illegitimate births, abandoned children, contraception, adultery, prostitution, less regularity in attendance at Sunday mass and fulfillment of paschal obligations [...], more friction between clergy and laity over tithes [...], administration of the sacraments, observance of holy days, and standards of moral conduct."[3] Though one could argue that the church's impoverishment opened the opportunity to emphasize spirituality, the terrible reality was the converse, as the narrator pointed out in *La Cousine Bette*: "The Church is excessively fiscal in France. It has devolved in God's house to the ignoble trafficking in little benches and chairs [...], although it cannot have forgotten the Savior's anger in chasing the vendors from the temple" (7.436). The churches and convents that had not been sold were in disrepair, and sacred vessels and altar appointments needed in worship services were often either missing or damaged.

Many children had grown up outside the regular practice of their faith, and those that wished to re-establish organized worship were confronted with a shortage of priests (Desan 220-21). While in 1789 there were 60,000 priests, in 1814 there were only 36,000 (Aston 339). Furthermore, as Gérard Cholvy makes unequivocally clear, the church was detaching itself from the doctrine of divine revelation, a central tenet of Christianity.[4] Despite claims by writers like Chateaubriand, believers increasingly felt that reason and a simplified Gospel sufficed for a modern faith (Bowman 72, 118-27). They were convinced, with Mme de Staël, that "[y]ou demonstrated the love of God by doing good" (Bowman 42). In addition to insisting on a religion of works, France of the July Monarchy had institutionalized a division between the secular and the sacred. There was a secular and a religious press, secular and religious schools, and social services that were separated into the secular and the religious. Most important, as Daniel Stern said in 1849, was "the continuing and universal weakening of Christian faith."[5]

As Balzac's *Eugénie Grandet* makes clear, another religion had come to fill the gaps left by the Revolutionary depredations. Balzac marshaled a series of allusions to the Bible and to saints' lives to make his point. Grandet represents a new faith. "Was he not the only modern god in whom people had faith, Money in all its power [...] ?" (3.1052). Although the novelist refers to the Catholic Church in other of his works, in none does he so clearly set it in opposition to that of a false god, the worship of material wealth or Mammon. Of course, Balzac was neither alone nor even the first to suggest that French society had welcomed a new force accompanying the Industrial Revolution and the rapidly expanding middle class. To Stendhal it seemed very simple. As he wrote to his sister, "This century [...] has only one motivation: money."[6]

Eugénie Grandet (1833) has been the most persistently misunderstood of all Balzac's novels. Despite its popularity and the regularity with which it has been read and analyzed, from the beginning its secondary literature has been filled with equivocal or flatly negative judgments. Even so fine a Balzacian as Pierre Citron views the novel with a notable lack of enthusiasm. He sees it as "a lusterless novel."[7] There are several explanations for this unrelenting misprision, thrusting critics into a sad *Flatland* where this brilliant novel lacks vitality. On the one hand, the novel exploits an oppositional allusion that even the best readers have missed. The text elicits two completely different religions to stand in opposition to each other, the one representing the feckless church that lives on after being effectively disemboweled by the Revolution, the other portraying the new god of the middle-class market economy and the greed that inspires it. Sainte-Beuve's wrong-headed praise has led generations of readers astray. Bardèche echoes Balzac's own discomfort by terming the nineteenth-century critic's evaluation as "perfidious," since it congratulates Balzac for all the qualities that he does not have: delicacy, measure, sobriety, gracefulness.[8] To see only the simple story Sainte-Beuve and others like Percy Lubbock have enjoyed, it is necessary to remain oblivious to those qualities that raise the novel above the norm.[9] Similar to Edwin A. Abbott's *Flatland*, critical evaluations of Balzac's multi-leveled creations lack essential dimensions. Although the Balzacian secondary literature has insisted on those qualities that made him a successful popular writer, a deeper consideration of his work highlights the reasons why some consider him a truly outstanding creator and artist.

Though sometimes labeled a love story, the love of *Eugénie Grandet* is unrequited, and we leave the novel when the sweet young maid of the beginning has become the desiccated widow of an unloved husband in an unconsummated marriage. Not surprisingly, she has developed an old maid's stiffness and the pettiness encouraged by the narrowness of provincial life (3.1198). She has, nonetheless, a beautiful soul, is dedicated to her Lord, and has become His agent in helping those in need. Still, for the title figure of a novel, Eugénie does very little of apparent importance. In fact, for all the words that have been written about *Eugénie Grandet*, it is the girl's father, Félix Grandet, who has attracted the most attention. Nicole Mozet goes so far as to suggest that the novel's symbolic structure is constructed on the character of the father (*Ville* 151). One might wonder whether Balzac mistitled the work, though there is reason to believe that Father Grandet's primary function is to set off the powerful image of his daughter. But even M. Grandet does little during the course of the story. "The novel is new," comments Citron, "because nothing novelistic happens" ("Préface" 12).

In fact, by the time the novel actually sets things in motion, Grandet has already progressed up the social ladder of his society. Originally, that is, prior to the Revolution of 1789, he was a master cooper. Such an artisan could make a good living. The fact that he could read, write, and keep accounts additionally gave him the tools to begin to make his fortune and move into the middle class. Indeed, in this society committed to money, "Monsieur Grandet gained [...] the new aristocratic title that our little egalitarian ways will never efface: he paid more taxes than anyone else in the district" (3.1032). On marrying the daughter of a rich timber merchant, he received a substantial dowry to add to his savings and thus finance his dreams. Little of further importance happens to Grandet after the opening pages. Well on his way to an enormous fortune, he consolidates his financial position with a few astute, if not entirely honorable, financial successes during the actual time period of the novel's action. Except for the La Bertellière inheritances that Mme Grandet promptly turns over to her husband, she has been almost inconsequential since her husband first took her dowry and used it to continue his pursuit of riches.

The date of Grandet's purchase of the region's best vineyards, an old abbey, and several farms for 40,000 francs is not completely clear. Castex tells of a similar purchase of some 600,000 francs for property officially appraised at more than twice that sum, which he terms "a good deal."[10] Grandet's purchase price is so much more advantageous that one must wonder at the narrator's conclusion that the exchange was "legally, if not legitimately" acceptable (3.1030). The discrepancy in the figures may be explained by the possibility that Grandet paid partially in the much devalued, revolutionary fiat currency (*assignats*). Already in early 1792, inflation had seriously eroded the legal tender, perhaps by as much as half (White 13, 34). There was a market in the currency, permitting purchase for far less than the indicated value. The miraculous bargain may also have something to do with the 200 double-louis (8000 francs) that Grandet's father-in-law gave the "ferocious Republican" overseeing the sale of the confiscated property (*biens nationaux* 3.1030–31). Grandet's further wealth came from his wife's inheritances, by supplying wine to the republican armies, and through clever exploitation of political office. The progression in the ways his neighbors addressed him, from "*Old* Grandet" (*Père* Grandet) to *Monsieur* Grandet during the Empire, further signals his successful rise to the bourgeoisie, like many others in the post-revolutionary period. Furthermore, Grandet now owns one of the houses in the upper part of Saumur that formerly belonged to the local aristocracy (3.1030).

Eugénie adds little to the novel's action. She does fall in love with her cousin, Charles, and though they exchange vows, it all seems adolescent and unimportant except to Eugénie. Charles's love is not strong enough to last the seven years it takes for the young man to make his fortune, and he is seduced by greed and the promise of wealth. (On repaying the money Eugénie meant as a gift, he calls their early love "our childishness"—3.1187.) And when Grandet eventually dies, his household continues to operate as it always had: Eugénie who, unlike Ursule Mirouët, was thoroughly trained by Grandet to become an excellent steward of her enormous fortune, lives virtually as she did when her father was alive, though with different motivations. She lights the fire only on those days when it was permitted in her youth, she dresses as her mother did, and she remains in the dark, cold, melancholy house where she was raised. Balzac picked up the images of the beginning and repeats them in the end, thus insisting on a continuation of the cycle of provincial behavior. And, while on the surface, there has been a small turbulence in the placid pond of Saumur's society, it has passed, and equilibrium has returned. On a spiritual level, however, Eugénie displays progress of major importance.

Balzac's dazzling description of Saumur and Monsieur Grandet is merely the background for the true plot, the story that begins at the beginning and does not end until the conclusion of *Eugénie Grandet*. We watch while an innocent girl gains the strength to oppose her father and his absolute commitment to wealth, especially gold. Sainte-Beuve and his followers have not paid sufficient attention to the quiet, steady maturation of Eugénie's character. While the noise and the violence answering her growing self-assurance comes from Grandet, the change is emphasized by Eugénie's very natural development toward maturity and independence, at least as "natural" is understood by modern parents and children. The stimulus for Eugénie's blossoming into a functional personality (or deviation from her father's expectations) comes after falling in love. It stuns and outrages her father.

Although there had been a momentous change in society's prevailing attitudes toward the rights of offspring to choose their own mates, this freedom was not recognized universally. It required parental permission, and it caused enormous contention within many families.[11] Grandet's home is not alone in being immersed in trouble brought by young people. From the early 1700s and much of the first half of the eighteenth century, marriage was considered a social act within the harmonious context of family, state, and church. Although it was often a business arrangement, it was even more a matter of duty. While marriages were arranged in all classes, the more significant the family fortune involved, the more likely it was that the marriage was determined by the head of the family, that is, by the father.[12] Children were, however, increasingly listened to, considered, and often heeded as these crucial decisions were made, especially as the late eighteenth and early nineteenth centuries rolled on. The concept of a sacred union of husband, wife, and God that had long been an essential part of the sacrament joining two young people and their families moved to the background and diminished in importance. Marriage became a personal matter between two individuals. Some even claimed that it was wrong to marry when the partners were not bound by a shared, passionate love. The important emphasis on the attitudes (*mentalités*) surrounding the individual and individual rights was felt throughout society. To some degree this commitment to passion trumped marriage and led to an insistence on what Stendhal called *amour-passion*, and an explosive growth in illegitimate births and venereal disease (Pasco, *Revolutionary Love* 149–74).

Eugénie realizes that she has changed. While it is not at all certain that she was sufficiently far along in her development to sustain the kinds of lawsuits brought within families to enforce the patriarchy that Maurice Daumas describes in his *L'Affaire d'Esclans: Les Conflits familiaux au XVIIIe siècle*, and while it is true that in most cases Balzac stood for traditionally and legally sanctioned marriages (see, for example, *La Femme de trente ans*), Eugénie's independent choice of Charles would have been popular with readers. Literally hundreds of novels demonstrate the need for liberalization of old ways, claiming that children should be able to choose their mates. Eugénie chooses Charles, despite her father's opposition and in disregard of her mother's warning that "it would be wrong" (3.1085). Perhaps even more startling, "[S]he begins to judge her father" (3.1093). Although never before had she even disagreed with him, suddenly she feels constraint on being in his presence (3.1096). Indeed, she goes so far as to counsel Father Grandet to help Charles, something he had already firmly rejected (3.1099). Grandet's consternation at her brazen advice is compared to "Balthazar's astonishment, anger, stupefaction in seeing the *Mane-Tekel-Upharsin*," and the narrator recognizes clearly, "[h]er life of ignorance had ceased suddenly, she was reasoning" (3.1103).

Eugénie is so certain of the rightness of her position that she refuses to follow her mother's suggestion of enlisting M. des Grassins. Revealing her father's attitudes in the midst of her rebellion, she says she does not wish to be dependent on the banker (3.1149). On finally telling Grandet without apology that her gold is gone (3.1153) and on actually rejecting Grandet's New Year's gift of gold (3.1154), she reveals that she has developed many of her father's strong-willed traits, without bowing to his wishes or his set beliefs. Eugénie has indeed come of age (3.1155), for she will not ask for anyone else's help. During the remainder of the novel, she learns how to become a good manager and steward, all the while rejecting the "love of money." As with Father Chaperon, her "avarice" benefits the church and the poor, thus closing the novel's most important plot. By turning from gold to God, she quietly rejects her father's false god. Eugénie's maturation accords with her gentle nature, avoiding as much as possible any *Sturm und Drang*. The development in her character is nonetheless profoundly important.

While I do not wish to contradict the claim for *Eugénie Grandet*'s artistic economy, I would argue that it differs from much of Balzac's work in that the economy he always sought was achieved with less apparent prolixity. At base, the novelist's creations are usually quite simple and straightforward—Balzac tended to be a narrational minimalist. The descriptive complexity comes from his desire to fit his characters and their lives into the context of a physical and metaphysical world that would satisfactorily highlight the sociological or aesthetic point he wanted to make. His plots are most often subordinated to the overriding description. The apparent simplicity of *Eugénie Grandet* comes from Balzac's decision to allude to the Second Coming of Jesus, an extremely well-known story of the Christian New Testament, and thus incorporate a larger literary and religious dimension. Equally important, once the basic narration is understood, it illuminates the complex movements and attitudes of Restoration and July Monarchy French people.

Here, Balzac did not need to create his own myth and thus did not need a plethora of detail. Under the descriptions of seemingly trivial events and objects, there has been a development of considerable significance, though it only becomes clear on reading the account with an awareness of the fuller potential of the story's images. After preparing and presenting a supernatural reading in the preceding *Ursule Mirouët*, with the essential visions that lead to the discovery of a vile criminal and the salvation of the heroine, the reader should be ready to recognize a depiction of the Holy Spirit's activity in the physical life of a Balzacian saint, Eugénie Grandet. The occult of the preceding novel joins forces with the description of the normal world that one usually finds in *La Comédie humaine* and other contemporary novels. In *Eugénie Grandet*, the fiction recognizes the enfeebled reality of the Catholic church while insisting as well on its potential. In *Ursule Mirouët*, one bridge led to two visions, but the two visions finally united to reveal the efforts of God in His purposeful activity to save Ursule. The occult then becomes one of God's spiritual weapons. In *Eugénie Grandet*, the subsequent book, there are two churches, one the Catholic faith, which is set in opposition to that of the other atheistic commitment to money and greed. *Eugénie Grandet* recounts the story of the heroine who, in spite of being immersed in the environment of her father's gross materialism, has considerable success in establishing and pursuing spiritual values. Balzac calls God and the Church into battle against money.

As Victoria E. Thompson's *Virtuous Marketplace* argues, with the momentum of all the changes taking place in the culture, old values were moving aside for the new. Previously, advancing in society almost required being a member of the aristocracy. Many posts that carried with them a title had long been available for purchase, and the ambitious knew that with sufficient funds they could either arrange an aristocratic marriage for their child or negotiate an appointment as a judge or other official that was accompanied by a title. Money could buy almost anything. The guillotine had eventually raised doubts about the desirability of moving into the nobility, of course, but the other factor in the equation remained even after the social reordering. Control of capital was essential. As money and goods flowed into France from the colonies and from foreign trade, so various segments of the French economy were stimulated, and wealth became a possibility for those who were willing and able to learn, work, save, and invest. Napoleon's creation of the Bank of France was an important facilitator as the Industrial Revolution gained power, since financial liquidity was essential in the new economy. It is not by accident that *La Maison Nucingen* serves as a nucleus for a number of Balzac's stories involving power. It turns on a disreputable banker who exploits credit to make several fortunes for himself and his bank.

In *Eugénie Grandet*, readers can watch as Grandet's pragmatically governed, flexible conscience allows him to betray his neighbors in order to market his wine. He had agreed to join them withholding produce to drive the price higher, only to abandon solidarity with his fellow vintners and jump at an initial good offer in the artificially restricted market. Grandet constitutes an exception to the general Balzacian concept that provincials only succeed when they are an integral part of a faction, for he regularly acts independently against such cliques as he increases and consolidates his wealth. His astute deals allow him to best others whether in the provinces or in Paris, whether dealing in gold or manipulating creditors. Since Balzac detailed the greedy miser's tactics in encouraging the des Grassins and Cruchot families to serve *gratis* as his agents in order to avoid his brother's bankruptcy, in explaining his calculations for selling his trees, in the wine manipulation, in trading the gold, and in pocketing his wife's inheritance, it is no surprise that he was able to purchase some of the best land in the region for little money (3.1030–31). Capital has become the only virtue and greed the only motivation.

As the novel builds on the devotion to gold, it provides an excellent example of an oppositional allusion to the Biblical drama of Christ's departure and promised return, and, as well, it plays out the divine/human comedy more fully than any other of Balzac's works.[13] From the opening lines, which mention how much Saumur's houses resemble cloisters and monasteries, to the terminal announcement that Eugénie is moving toward heaven accompanied by quantities of good deeds (3.1198), frequent references establish an allusion to the divine drama of Christ and His Church subsequent to the passion. Jesus promised His people that He would return. In the meantime, He sent the Holy Spirit to help the congregation of His saints, the Church, in the tribulations and persecutions which would take place before His second coming. Balzac was to use the account again in *Mercadet, le faiseur* (1851), but only in *Eugénie Grandet* does it assume so much importance. At the conclusion of the novel, Eugénie has moved well beyond her father's faith in gold into a spiritual system of Christian belief—Father, Son, and Holy Spirit—which, though perverted by worldly influences, is nonetheless recognizable.

The French church of 1819 had been seriously eroded. Elsewhere, Balzac terms it "without strength" (4.505) and "impotent" (4.664). In many ways, including decimating the clerical ranks through exile and execution (4.392), the revolutionary state had attempted to subordinate the church to itself. Balzac's narrator goes to considerable lengths to illuminate the opposing religion that had been established and was flourishing in the provinces, as it had long reigned in Paris. As for Grandet himself, "Was he not the only modern god in whom people have faith, Money in all its power, expressed by a single physiognomy?" (3.1052). Appropriately, the name, Grandet, is an anagram of *d'argent* (money).[14] His life is "entirely material" (3.1053). A mirror or inverted image of the Father in Heaven, Père Grandet (e.g., 3.1030, 1033, 1034) lives at the top of what in Saumur was formerly named the Grand'Rue, and which as Fischler says surely suggests "a heavenly abode."[15] In addition, Grandet "sees everything" (3.1060, 1090) and distributes the daily bread (3.1041, 1077–78), though otherwise the novel stresses his negative, rather than divine, traits. While the Judeo-Christian God is the generous "I am" (Exod. 3: 14) of eternal life in whom "all the promises […] are yea" (2 Cor. 1: 20), Grandet's four standard responses are essentially negative: "I don't know, I can't, I don't want to, and we'll see about that" (3.1035).

Superficially, many of M. Grandet's positions seem modeled on Biblical principles. God proclaimed, for example, "all the earth is mine" (Exod. 19: 5). As the parable of the talents implies, however, all of His gifts are held in trust, and His people are responsible for them until He returns to ask for an accounting. It is clear that Grandet's gifts to Eugénie are not free gifts either. The strings he attaches are more like steel cables. Furthermore, while God "maketh His sun to rise on the evil and on the good, and sendeth rain on the just and on the unjust" (Matt. 5.45), Grandet's generosity is limited to his own household and, for anything significant, to himself only or, perhaps, to Eugénie. What he gives to his wife, he quickly takes back, and she is only too happy to give it, since she knows from experience that it produces peace in her household (3.1108). And the gold he "gives" to Eugénie is to be displayed regularly for his own enjoyment.

In a somewhat different vein, both Grandet's religion and Christianity are essentialistic (essence precedes existence, to use a distinction of the Existentialists). For Grandet, however, the value which gives essence comes only from the material possession of capital. A person lacking wealth has no value. "Charles is nothing to us," he points out, pertinently cutting through whatever family sympathy might be expected for his nephew, "he hasn't a cent; his father went bankrupt" (3.1094). Likewise, his cavalier treatment of his wife, after he takes her dowry and inheritances for his own purposes, sets up a significant pattern that is repeated when he learns that Eugénie no longer has her gold. At that point, Eugénie has lost her value and is sent to her room and locked up "in prison" on bread and water (3.1156). Later, after it is brought to his attention that much of the wealth he has been using as though it were his own continues legally to be his wife's, and that he may be forced to divide "his" property and allow Eugénie to receive her mother's inheritance, he suddenly alters his behavior and plays the toady. When the day arrives that Eugénie becomes the heir and owner of her mother's wealth, Grandet "hovers over her as though she were made of gold" (3.1171).

The major difference between Grandet and God has to do with eternal life. If Grandet is the "High Priest" of the gold cult (Hoffmann 212), his belief in eternal life is conversely very slight. After his mind weakens and he spends hours with his eyes fixed "stupidly" on the gold coins which the heroine spreads before him (3.1175), and he later attempts to seize the gilded cross extended for him to kiss, he tells Eugénie that she will give him an accounting "over there," thus proving, the narrator maintains, that Christianity must be the religion of misers (ibid.). Of course, it seems as likely that Grandet is using his daughter's religion as a means of threatening her. Previously, however, the narrator says flatly that misers do not believe in eternal life (3.1101). Elsewhere Balzac warns ominously:

> This reflection casts a horrible light on our era, when, more than in any other period, money dominates law, politics, and general behavior. Institutions, books, men, and doctrines, everything conspires to undermine the belief in a future life on which the social edifice has been founded for eighteen-hundred years. Now the casket is a little feared transition. The future which used to wait for us on the other side of the requiem, has been transposed into the present. To arrive *per fas et nefas* at an earthly paradise of luxury, vanity, and enjoyments is the general idea, rather than to petrify one's heart and mortify the flesh with a view toward ephemeral possessions, as people were once martyred with a view toward eternal treasures! [...] When this doctrine has passed from the bourgeoisie to the lower classes, what will become of our land? (3.1101–02)

The passage is important, for it places in explicit opposition the worship represented by the Church and the reverence for gold. If gold in the person of Grandet is the new god, he provides a clear opposition to the eternal God of the Judeo-Christian tradition, who does not change.[16] Grandet, after all, dies, without being resurrected.

Balzac indicates that Grandet is but one part of an unholy trinity. Just as the Christian Trinitarian God includes not only a Father but also a Holy Spirit, who is essentially God's action officer, through whom His power, knowledge, and wisdom are manifested in the world, so Grandet has

Nanon. She is Grandet's "prime minister" (3.1077). He trusts her more than the members of his own family. Though she does not manifest herself as fire itself, as does the Holy Spirit (Acts 2: 3), she lights the fire (3.1044) and carries candles (3.1053) or torches (3.1107) to illuminate the way. And while the Holy Spirit only speaks what He hears in accordance with God's will (John 16: 13), Grandet has to remonstrate with Nanon on several occasions for saying things which do not correspond to his desires: "I'm not speaking to you, Nanon! Hold your tongue" (3.1083). He expects her to speak *his* word or not at all. One of the most important of the Holy Spirit's functions is as the Comforter for God's people after Jesus rose and went to heaven (John 16: 7). Nanon serves a similar task during Charles's long absence, especially while Grandet persecutes his daughter, and after Eugénie is alone, both of her parents having died. Finally, given the fact that the Holy Spirit represents the earnest or down payment on all the promises of God (2 Cor. 1: 22), it is also worth mentioning in respect to Nanon that *nans, nant* in Old French meant "earnest," "surety," or "down payment," and *nanter* "to provide a surety."[17]

Nanon's refusal to obey Father Grandet in all cases has considerable importance in distinguishing the unholy trinity from that of the Christian God. As was extensively discussed and eventually established in the doctrine of the third- and fourth-century Christian Church, God is a Trinity. While each member of the Trinity can function individually, they always work in accordance with the whole. Consequently, Nanon's refusal to parrot her master's will, her readiness to provide food and a certain amount of freedom to Eugénie after her father had put her "in prison," and her delight in the love that blossoms between the girl and Charles marks the disunity of this false god. The three members of the unholy religion are not cohesive; they do not reveal one will, but to the contrary act in opposition to each other.

The other member of the Christian Trinity was Jesus, who referred to himself as the Son of Man (Matt. 8: 20) and as a shepherd (John 10: 11). The Son displayed nothing but love for humankind during His life and ministry, but Charles became a slaver. The explanation for such a disreputable decision are simple: "[T]he best means for becoming wealthy was, in tropical regions as well as in Europe, to buy and sell men" (3.1181). Although revolutionaries abolished slavery, Napoleon revoked the decree in 1802. Slavery continued to be legal in the French colonies until 1848. Nonetheless, slavery was in very bad odor on mainland France and marks Charles as unsavory. "Father" Grandet has long disdained Charles, though for different reasons. He loves gold more than he loves Charles, his nephew and symbolic son, who is penniless. Likewise, his love is limited within the nucleus of his own family.

While Charles's pseudonym in the early versions of the novel was Chippart (possibly constructed on *chiper* "to steal"), the etymon of his given name, Charles, means "man," and Balzac replaced the earlier assumed name in the Furne edition with Carl ("man") Sepherd (which may suggest the English word "shepherd") (3.1182). In the same vein, Jesus raises Lazarus from the dead, and Grandet condemns Charles because he cares more about his dead father than about money (3.1093). Jesus leaves for heaven; Charles for the Indies. Both promise to return for their "brides," but Charles's egotism hardens the young man (3.1126), and he becomes callous and skeptical (3.1181). He does not return and leaves Eugénie in the lurch, a victim of his breach of promise. Appropriately, the local grocer, M. Fessard, compares the excitement around Charles's first visit to the three wise men who came to worship the child, Jesus (3.1085).

Eugénie's identification with the Church, that is, the congregation of the saints, is emphasized by the traits which relate her to those particularly holy examples of the faithful who have been admitted to sainthood.[18] Her masculine attributes (e.g., 3.1075) have several functions. On the one hand, they prepare her impressive strength of purpose in opposing her father,[19] and on the other, they might remind us of Saint Eugenia of Alexandria, who dressed as a man and passed for many years as a monk. On joining the monastery, Helenus who was supernaturally informed of her true sex said, "Thou dost well to call thyself a man, for woman though thou art, thou doest manfully."[20] It is perhaps more important to note that the M. Cruchot de Bonfons's uncle terms the young man whom she eventually marries a *cruche*, that is, a "pitcher" or a "fool": "My nephew is a *cruche*," Father Cruchot says with disgust (3.1051). Saint Eugenia of Alsace is normally represented holding a pitcher.[21]

Eugénie's appropriateness as a symbol for the Christian Church, however, is most obvious in what she actually does. The significance of her actions also helps to explain why she, rather than her father, is the title character of the novel. The Bible refers to the Church as the bride of Christ and uses the betrothal customs in the intertestamentary and early Christian era to illuminate the image. As Joseph's decision to break with Mary on learning of her pregnancy indicates, although a betrothal did not absolutely have to lead to marriage, it was in fact a binding contract that was expected to move with well-regulated deliberateness to the actual marriage ceremony and consummation. Joseph accepted Mary's pregnancy as God's will and completed the contracted marriage. A similar pattern recurs when Jesus rose to heaven. He promised to return for His bride, that is, for His people or His Church, at which time the actual marriage would be performed (e.g., Matt. 26.64; Rev. 19.7). Charles, the unholy son of man in Grandet's trinity, does not honor his word. He does not come back for his promised bride. The Church, while awaiting the Messiah's return, is expected to love (2 Thess. 3.5), to remain obedient (1 Tim. 6.14), charitable (1 Cor. 1.7), faithful and ready (Matt. 24.44; 25: 1–13), while manifesting good stewardship (Luke 19.11–27). Eugénie corresponds to the model.

In this context, many puzzling aspects of Eugénie's behavior are resolved. There is no question that the heroine looks upon the kiss and promise she exchanged with Charles as betrothal: "I will wait," she says (3.1139). And so she does, though as it finally turns out she awaits a bridegroom who changes his mind. The solemnity of the occasion where the two commit themselves to each other is highlighted by Nanon's sudden appearance. "Amen! [*Ainsi soit-il!*]" (3.1140), she says. As a witness, the servant not only makes the agreement official, she also brings in the religious element. Nanon is elsewhere said to be "conserved as though in brine [*saumure*]" (3.1177), which may recall Jesus telling His people, "Ye are the salt of the earth" (Matt. 5.13). Of course, all members of Jesus's Church or bride are to give flavor to the world. It is surely no accident that Balzac sets his exploitation of the Biblical drama of Christ's departure and promised return in Saumur, homonym of *saumure*.

As she waits, Eugénie's life is dominated by love. "[S]he could only exist through love, through religion, through her faith in the future" (3.1178). She is so obedient and submissive to her father's will that, at her father's demand, she signs away her rights to her mother's inheritance. Although her charitable spirit bears notable fruit only after Grandet's death, she becomes an excellent steward of the family fortune. And, despite the lack of communication from Charles, she remains faithful during the long years after his departure. When she learns the truth of his inconstancy, she begins what was to be an important shift in her love. Earlier, in respect to the affection she bears Charles, the narrator tells that "[l]ove explained eternity to her. Her heart and the Gospel signaled two worlds to look for. Night and day, she meditated on these two infinite ideas, which for her were perhaps brought together in one" (3.1178). While there is no doubt that her love of Charles is the "inextinguishable sentiment" (3.1193) preventing her from considering other suitors, she later seems to have made an important change. Much as Dante shifted his focus from Beatrice and Petrarch from Laura, in both cases toward the divine, so Eugénie turns from Charles to God. She has all her mementos of Charles turned into a gold monstrance, which she then donates to her parish church.

As the narrator would clearly wish, given his opposition to society's commitment to money here on earth, rather than living as did early martyrs "with a view toward eternal treasures" (3.1101), Eugénie turns toward heaven. Although she has from the beginning lived in the midst of a "people whose life was purely material" (3.1053), Balzac's heroine is indifferent to gold and "aspired to heaven" (3.1198). She "lived, pious and good, filled with saintly thoughts, [and] constantly helped the unfortunate in secret" (3.1198). Eugénie "walks toward heaven accompanied by a long procession of good deeds" (3.1198). She is a *beati*, one of the blessed. She stands in opposition to her father, Félix. Both *beati* and *felix* occur in the Vulgate Bible, and both words can mean happy, but *felix* (e.g., Sirach 14.2) leans away from holiness toward material benefits and good fortune. It is surely no accident that M. Grandet's first name is Félix, given the pagan and materialistic Roman deity Felicitas, the goddess of happiness. Charlotte Yonge tells us that this name was frequently given to particularly fortunate individuals.[22]

Monsieur Grandet is so obvious a focus of attention from the very beginning that Guyon considers that the novel might have been called "Father Grandet" [*Père Grandet*].[23] We learn how he arranged one financial deal after another, whether in the case of the wine he sells (despite the agreement he made with his fellow Saumurian winemakers), the fast turnaround to market the gold, the poplars he clears, or the property that he bought at an advantageous price. Readers observe as he rules his home despotically, and can further watch him as he entertains and takes advantage of his guests. When Charles arrives, Grandet continues to be in command, and, in the early portion of the novel, there is no deviation in the focus. After that, Eugénie begins quietly to revolt. At first it is only in order to secure delicacies for Charles, but the rebellion grows. Contrary to her father's rules, she then offers the young man her gold, an action that is far more serious than her agreeing to become his promised, despite the lack of her father's permission. Little by little, as her father punishes her, she gains independence and maturity. The fact that he cannot bend her will is another indication that his dominance is slipping, even after he successfully protects his nephew in the negotiations with the Parisian moneylenders. Soon, as the allusion to Christ and His promised return is played out negatively, she has taken over the central role of the novel. She does not relinquish it, and, in the end, her "husband dies" and she inherits his fortune, thus able to add it to her own. To Eugénie go the spoils. She has vanquished her father and his faith.

Whatever the conflicting hints pertaining to the reality of Balzac's religion, the text shows that he recognized the literary advantages to be reaped from a stable, reasonably well-known reference to a text like the Bible. Most of the biblical passages referred to above were culturally embedded, since they were included in the Mass at some point in the liturgical year. Balzac's charming, innocent, defenseless heroine looks for guidance to a weak church represented by Father Cruchot, a priest who in order to benefit his own family's fortune will not only permit but also encourage an unsuitable relationship between Charles and Mme des Grassins and, later, an unconsummated marriage between Eugénie and his nephew, M. Cruchot de Bonfons (3.1192). Such positions are of course absolutely unacceptable to the Church. The reader then watches Eugénie live at the heart of a cult of committed materialists worshipping gold and earthly success as she plays out a perverted and failed drama of Charles's betrayal, before committing herself to heavenly goals. The allusion marvelously implies the stable French society that used to be and is no more. Balzac believed that at one time the pattern of Christian belief and action within a strong Church served the salutary end of protecting society. Now, however, the Church was being overwhelmed by an egocentric, greedy, destructive worship of gold. In one instance, at least, the heroic Eugénie resists Grandet/*d'argent* and suggests another possibility where a socially functional stewardship, charity, and faithfulness remain operative. Eugénie becomes God's handmaiden. She then represents the bride of Christ, that is, the Church, for whom Christ has promised to return.

Such extended allusions as in *Eugénie Grandet* gain power by their extension and consistency. They require a relatively fixed external text, usually as in this case indicated initially by the suggestion of a parallel. Antiphrastic allusions, however, require considerable knowledge on the reader's part, much more than in a text composed of an extended parallel allusion like Bernanos's *The Diary of a Country Priest* (1936), since the reader must keep in mind both the lessons of the pattern of meaning alluded to and the distortions occurring in the text in hand. This example in *Eugénie Grandet* is not satire or parody, for the passages neither mock nor ridicule the Bible or the Church. It directs the reader's attention to the work in hand, rather than to an offending person, object, or text outside the reading experience. In *Eugénie Grandet*, Balzac's emphasis is not on the Bible, rather on what his novel does with the theme of the Second Coming. One is expected to keep present both the Christian drama and an opposing materialistic antithesis in order to appreciate the full implications of the work. Similarly, to take another example, in Gide's *The Return of the Prodigal Son* (1907) those readers who are not aware that Gide's prodigal son is not following biblical precedent when he encourages a younger brother to imitate his profligacy will remain insensitive to the full, antibiblical ramifications of the Gidian creation.

Eugénie Grandet emphasizes the differences between genuine Christian faith and the monstrous perversion represented by Grandet, and readers should consciously or unconsciously seek a way of reconciling the two. As Genette said in *Figures II*, "In fact, the opposition between two terms gains its meaning only in relation to what establishes their reconciliation, and which is their common element: phonology taught us that difference is pertinent, in linguistics as elsewhere, only on the basis of ressemblance."[24] Readers are expected to go beyond the similarities to sense Grandet's perverted theology and the implicit warnings. Eugénie serves as the fulcrum. Her role throughout the novel remains essentially the same, though the others change radically. Grandet dies, Charles fades away, and Nanon marries, thus securing a life of her own. While still a servant and a comforter to Eugénie, her previously total allegiance to the godlike Grandet has been weakened. Eugénie's character remains essentially the same despite her reorientation. She turns from the perverted religion of gold, which has disappointed her, and, while storing up treasures in heaven by her good deeds, she waits for the return of her Lord. In the process, as Balzac's touching heroine plays out the divine comedy in a human context, *Eugénie Grandet* emphasizes the changes taking place in the Church in the first third of the nineteenth century and society's need for religion's stabilizing influence.

Revolutionaries had done everything they could to stamp out religion, and they failed. Though it was in fact to avoid taxes, Balzac percipiently has his unbelieving Grandet wall off his abbey's windows and doors. What those in power did not understand was the deep-seated belief of the faithful, who would continue to practice their religion despite any difficulties. However much the faithful were termed *oies* ("geese") or *ouailles* ("sheep"), the strength of their belief forced major concessions. As the representative sent by the National Assembly in 1794 on a mission to confront the Lutherans of Montbéliard concluded, "What is inconceivable is that they love their Good Lord [*Bon Dieu*], and are neither republicans, nor patriots, nor aristocrats."[25] As revolutionary history could have elucidated, whether summary execution with guns (*mitraillades*), or drownings, or more leisurely and individualized death by hanging or the guillotine, persecution increased fervor. Napoleon had indeed brought nominal peace to religion and the state, but neither he nor his ministers seem to have understood the depth and importance of this Christian belief that they termed "fanaticism" (Cholvy 16). The disruption took its toll, however. Around 1830, according to Cholvy, French religious knowledge and understanding had reached its nadir (25).

There began simultaneously a renewal of faith, called the *Renouveau* (Renewal) or, among Protestants, the *Reveil* (Awakening). To some degree Chateaubriand and another whole series of writers and thinkers—Lamennais, Bonald, Lacordaire, Montalembert, Maistre—had increasing impact on society and helped spread the movement. Balzac was surely sensitive to this societal impulsion. Lamennais left the Catholic church and kept the renewal in the headlines as he fulminated against the pope. From 1816, there was a significant and successful attempt to implement a nationwide system of instruction within the Catholic church. State education had little choice in the matter. While not welcoming the competition, it continued its efforts to broaden and deepen education. For church schools, religion was a part of the whole of life; for those institutions run by the state, education was based on reason. Increasingly, as the state developed its care of the needy and the young, so believers gathered together to help the destitute and the sick, to promote missions, and to support education. Perhaps because women were so important in maintaining the faith through the dark years of persecution and skepticism, there was a particular effort to provide a basis in the faith for the young ladies for whom convent education was no longer possible. This early nineteenth-century effort emphasized solid instruction in reading. As a result, it is generally agreed that by mid-century illiteracy was no longer a major problem. Accompanied by a new emphasis on religion, the French cities of Lyon and Toulouse became centers for edifying publications for juveniles. From novels, to biographies, to guides, religious tracts and testaments, hundreds of books and pamphlets designed to attract and hold the attention of children and young middle-class girls were put on sale. Balzac likely had this well-primed market in mind as he penned *Eugénie Grandet*.

The country girl's struggle to rise above "the world's corruptions" (3.1199), in a thoroughly secular society committed to reason and capital, draws its power from its relationship to bourgeois France. Eugénie has been prepared to take her place as a saint in a new world of faith in a Trinitarian God and, in the process, illustrates the condition of the nineteenth-century French church. As almost all major writers recognized, reason was insufficient. Especially the Romantics knew without question that love was not reasonable but spiritual and that people who were not open to spiritual realities were downright absurd. Nodier, Gautier, and Nerval, not to mention Baudelaire and Hugo, continued to poke pointed sticks at bourgeois businessmen enslaved to the marketplace in the attempt to awaken them to a larger spiritual reality that would include human beings and humanitarian values. Money was not enough. Grandet's faith is as ridiculous as the terminal vision of the pathetic old miser receiving last rites, mindlessly focused on a pile of gold coins, and attempting to add the priest's silver-gilt cross to his hoard.

Notes

1. Susanne Desan, *Reclaiming the Sacred: Lay Religion and Popular Politics in Revolutionary France* (Ithaca: Cornell UP, 1990) 5. Of course, the church's property was not limited to land. Overall, it constituted the accumulations of fifteen hundred years. There were princely estates in the country, bishops' palaces and conventual buildings in rural and urban areas. White estimates that "these formed between one-fourth and one-third of the entire real property of France, and amounted in value to at least two thousand million livres"—Andrew Dickson White, *Fiat Money Inflation in France* (New York: Appleton-Century, 1933) 4. John McManners says that the estimate is inflated and should be no higher than 6–10 % of France, though he states that the yearly income from the property was immense, somewhere in the neighborhood of 100 million livres, "nearly enough to have paid a living wage twice over to all the priests of the Gallican Church. And in addition there was the tithe, yielding a revenue of at least half as much again"—*The French Revolution and*

the Church (New York: Harper & Row, 1970) 6–7; see, also, his more detailed *Church and Society in Eighteenth-Century France*, Vol. 1 (Oxford: Clarenden P, 1998) 98. Although this wealth was enormous and there were many abuses, it must be added that the church expended vast resources to take care of the poor and the sick, and had a virtual monopoly on education in the late *ancient régime* (McManners, *French Revolution* 7–8).

2. Quoted from McManners, *French Revolution and the Church* 142.
3. Jeffrey W. Merrick, *The Desacralization of the French Monarchy in the Eighteenth Century* (Baton Rouge: Louisiana State UP 1990) 43; Nigel Aston, *Religion and Revolution in France, 1780–1804* (Washington, D.C.: Catholic UP, 2000) 49–52. Frank Paul Bowman returns repeatedly to the sad state of the early nineteenth-century church, see, e.g., *Le Christ des barricades 1789–1848* (Paris: Cerf, 1987) 35–37.
4. Cholvy, *La Religion en France de la fin du XVIIIe siècle à nos jours* (Paris: Hachette, 1998) 9.
5. Stern (pseud. Marie de Flavigny Agoult), *Esquisses morales et politiques* (Paris: Pagnerre, 1849) 185.
6. Letter of 19 April 1805 to Pauline Beyle, Stendhal, *Correspondance*, 3 vols., Bibliothèque de la Pléiade (Paris: Gallimard, 1962–68) 1.192.
7. Citron, "Préface," *Eugénie Grandet* (Paris: GF-Flammarion, 1964) 5.
8. "[I]t lacks very little for this charming story to be a masterpiece"—Sainte-Beuve, "Poètes et romanciers modernes de la France: Balzac," *Revue des Deux Mondes* 333.4 (1834): 450; Maurice Bardèche, "Notice," *Eugénie Grandet* HH 5.244. See also, in this regard, Balzac's letter to Mme Hanska of 10 Feb. 1838, his additional comment (5.115), and Nicole Mozet's remarks in her introduction to *Eugénie Grandet* in the Pléiade edition (3.991). As just one example of a suggestive objection to the novel's widely perceived simplicity, see John T. Booker, "Starting at the End in *Eugénie Grandet*," *L'Esprit Créateur* 31.3 (1991): 38–59.
9. Sainte-Beuve, "Poètes et romanciers," esp. 450–51; Percy Lubbock, *The Craft of Fiction* (1921; New York: Viking, 1966) 203–35.
10. Pierre-Georges Castex, "Aux sources d'*Eugénie Grandet*. Légende et réalité," *Revue d'Histoire Littéraire de la France* 64.1 (1964): 88. Precision about these sums is impossible, as Castex and Nicole Mozet, "Introduction" 3.1008–09 make clear. The constitution of Grandet's fortune is however realistically possible.

11. See my "Love at War," *Revolutionary Love in Eighteenth- and Early Nineteenth-Century France* (Farnham, UK: Ashgate, 2009) 32–62; and Patricia Mainardi, *Husbands, Wives, and Lovers: Marriage and Its Discontents in Nineteenth-Century France* (New Haven: Yale UP, 2003) 21–46.
12. Maurice Daumas, *L'Affaire d'Esclans: Les Conflits familiaux aux XVIIIe siècle* (Paris: Seuil, 1988).
13. See Léon François Hoffmann & the Princeton Balzac Seminar, 1974, "Thèmes religieux dans *Eugénie Grandet*," *L'Année Balzacienne* 1976: 201–29.
14. Harry Levin, *The Gates of Horn: A Study of Five French Realists* (New York: Oxford UP, 1963) 192.
15. Alexander Fischler, "Eugénie Grandet's Career as Heavenly Exile." *Essays in Literature* 16.2 (1989): 271.
16. Mal. 3.6. Joan Dargan's interesting insight about the comparison of Grandet to a basilisk adds further support for the belief that the miser becomes a perverted, monstrous god: "[T]he root *basileus* (Greek, king) is also that of *basilica*, incorporating in a single image Grandet's sovereignty in his household and religious devotion to his fortune [...] And finally, the legendary basilisk, with that calm, devouring and also fatal gaze, is a heraldic monster, an emblem of this tale of inheritance"—*Balzac and the Drama of Perspective: The Narrator in Selected Works of* La Comédie humaine (Lexington, KY: French Forum, 1985) 137.
17. Cf. today's French *nantir, nantissement*.
18. The fact that the late, definitive, 1843 version of *Eugénie* minimized the previously much more salient association of Eugénie to the Virgin Mary, which Fischler skillfully elicits, may be explained by the traditional emphasis of Mary as linked to Jesus rather than as linked to the Church, the bride of Christ awaiting His return. Balzac's earlier allusions to Mary were doubtless to emphasize Eugénie's saintliness, but at some point he must have realized that they raised dissonances with his central reference to the Second Coming.
19. Pierre-Georges Castex, "Introduction." *Eugénie Grandet*, by H. de Balzac (Paris: Garnier, 1965) lxv; Bardèche, *Balzac, romancier* (Paris: Plon, 1940) 466–67.
20. Jacobus de Voragine, *The Golden Legend*, tran. Granger Ryan and Helmut Ripperger, 2 vols. (London: Longmans, 1941) 1.537.

21. Louis Réau, *Iconographie des saints*, t. 3 of *Iconographie de l'art chrétien*, 3 vols. (Paris: P.U.F., 1958) 1.462.
22. Yonge, *History of Christian Names* (1884; rpt. Detroit: Gale, 1966) 163.
23. Guyon, "Balzac 'invente' les *Scènes de la vie de province*," *Mercure de France* 333 (1958): 478.
24. Gérard Genette, *Figures II* (Paris: Seuil, 1969) 103.
25. Quoted from Cholvy 16; see, also, Aston 207.

CHAPTER 4

The Gerontocracy and Youth: *Pierrette*

Despite its popularity—if one can consider successive paperback editions an indication of popularity—Balzac's *Pierrette* (1840) has had remarkably little attention from critics and scholars, no more than passing references and a handful of studies.[1] These professional readers have frequently mentioned Balzac's early plans for the short novel, indicated in a letter to Mme Hanska on 4 June 1839: "I will dedicate the first girlish work [*œuvre un peu jeune fille*] that I am doing to your dear Anna…" While Jean-Louis Tritter explains that Balzac later set aside the expectation of what he calls "a more or less sentimental, little work" (4.3) for something much darker, his explanation does not give hope for a powerful masterpiece, and it remains to consider the mechanisms and setting through which Balzac turned that same story into "one of the most desperate scenes of *La Comédie humaine*" (Tritter 4.3). Tritter's Pléiade edition makes it clear that the novel's creation was not easy, involving as it did many false starts (Tritter counts sixteen) and numerous corrections. Balzac's promised dedication to Anna de Hanska and the text itself leave no doubt that the work was not in the end "girlish." Balzac apologizes for its bleakness and explains that the story as finally told was imposed on him: "In the history of our society, it is so difficult to find a story worthy of passing before your eyes, Anna, that the author had no choice" (4.29). Conditions in France, particularly for the rising generation, had grown so desolate that it was impossible to candy-coat reality.

Works like "Ferragus" (1834), *La Vieille Fille* (1837), "Z. Marcas" (1840), and *Sur Catherine de Médicis* (1830–42) show conclusively that by 1839, when Balzac wrote *Pierrette*, his opposition to the July monarchy was firmly established, and he had moved far to the political right. As a budding sociologist he looked to the relationships within society for an explanation of what he sensed to be ominous developments in France, and he was especially unsettled by the demographic situation remaining from a quarter century of wars. He was convinced that the avariciousness of the middle-class gerontocracy, controlling society for the sake of its members' own self-centered desires, was shackling youth to such a degree that they were often confounded and in some cases destroyed, thus nullifying any hope of a better future for the whole of society. Perhaps this is why the Physiocrats argued that only an enlightened monarchy was "capable of forcing natural order upon recalcitrant humans."[2] In numerous passages, Balzac leaves no doubt that stultified egotism and greed were crushing the brilliant young people of the middle and working classes. Pierrette, herself, is but one more example of the poor and the innocent being ground to a tasteless bolus in the aging maw of bourgeois ambitions.[3] The young were everywhere frustrated. They were allowed no avenues to effective positions where they might work the changes desperately needed by French society.

While there remains little mystery about Balzac's politics, we continue to have difficulty elucidating reasons for the power of his work. If literature is viewed as prepackaged experience, why would readers continue to seek out Balzac's creations, especially such bitterly discouraging tales as *Pierrette*? The story of an abused child, while touching, was a commonplace in the novels that since the late eighteenth century had detailed the pathetic plight of legions of orphans. Some of these waifs, like Pigault-Lebrun's Happy in *L'Enfant du carnaval* of 1792 or Ducray-Duminil's Dominique in *Le Petit Carrillonneur* of 1809, manage to rise to wondrous heights of joy and wealth, while others like the title character of Edouard Ourliac's *Suzanne* (1840) move from one disaster to another until they die a miserable death. Of course, Balzac frequently took the clichéd character types and tired stories of popular novels and recast them into works of astonishing impact. *Pierrette*, a relatively short novel of 134 pages in the Pléiade edition, offers good ground to study aspects of Balzac's aesthetic practice in order to envision the social environment more adequately.

Pierrette's narration reveals Balzac deploying an arsenal of his most effective literary devices in order to expose the gerontocracy, one of the most troublesome social realities of his day. His use of allusion is particularly important. Once again, I employ the traditional term of "allusion" to mean "the metaphorical relationship created when an alluding text evokes and uses another, independent text"[4]—reserving that of "intertextuality" as a generic designation for "any textual exploitation of another text [, including] satire, parody, pastiche, *imitatio, refacimento,* reference, allusion, modeling, borrowing, even plagiarism" (Pasco, *Allusion* 5). The last chapter of *Eugénie Grandet,* the preceding novel in the *Scènes de la vie de province,* lays the groundwork for literary allusion by looking at allusive oppositions. Resourceful writers often weave a tapestry of allusions that could be termed an allusive complex and that gives their creations considerable resonance. Particularly interesting in Balzac's *Pierrette* is an allusive complex of intertextual references and images that evoke a comic, Molièresque structure, hagiography, the Passion of Christ, *Paul et Virginie,* and Béatrice Cenci, all in the service of eliciting an image of society.

Balzac's allusive referents are varied but effective as the novelist used them to draw his readers into the story and to infuse a fuller understanding into various aspects of his vision. Despite this variety, the allusions themselves work together to produce the final aesthetic experience. That the book opens onto a scene that would make *aficionados* of traditional comedy smile with anticipation is surely not an accident. Just a few years before, Balzac had similarly set up his readers to expect a comedy before twisting *La Vieille Fille* into the tragic suicide of Athanase Granson and the pathetic destiny of Rose Cormon.[5] Here in *Pierrette,* Brigaut, a young man, whose "physiognomy [...] became entirely happy" (4.31), serenades Pierrette, the ward of M. Rogron, a wealthy, former shopkeeper who was also one of her cousins. The latter's name itself, with the growling echoes of an angry ogre ["le ton rogne d'un ogre qui grogne"],[6] prepares us for the horrendous apparition of Sylvie at the window. After greeting Pierrette with a single yellow flower, Brigaut is forced to flee by the sudden specter of this "ugly old maid" (4.32), who is committed, we shortly learn, to protecting her brother's interests. As the narrator explains, "When there is an old maid in the house, there is no need for guard dogs" (4.34). The girl's pale skin reveals her severe anemia, and we later learn that she is "a little girl with deliciously white skin, with eyes so tender that they could warm a dead heart" (4.106), but we are told nothing that would prevent us from expecting the joyous but clichéd conclusion of Molière's *L'Ecole des femmes* (1662) and hundreds of other, similar works where youthful lovers are united. When a young man surreptitiously visits a girl held captive by a dreadful warden, legions of comic stories with similarly threatening early scenes and yet with joyously happy endings give us every right to settle back and anticipate the pleasurable victory of love over an inappropriate marriage. Surely the comedy will not only prevent a marriage between the lovely ward and her repugnant guardian, we can also expect him to be punished for his disgusting plans, since comedic tradition leaves no doubt that ugliness and old age should never be joined to beauty and youth.

Rogron is without question unattractive; he sports "the most foolish, inexperienced, and awkward physiognomy that any counter has ever presented to customers. His seemingly crushed brow, depressed by fatigue, was marked by three arid lines. His sparse gray hair, cut to the skin, expressed the indefinable stupidity of cold-blooded animals" (4.42). Who would not suspect a worthy descendant of Molière's Arnolphe? Even the fact that "Pierrette ought to have been gay; she was sad" (4.36) does nothing at first to discourage associations with the optimistic, comic structure. In fact, it emphasizes the anticipated comedy. Audiences are invited to hold the guardian's plot for his ward in contempt as they await the delight of his frustration when the handsome hero rides off in the distance with his bride. The strength, however, of what will shortly be understood as an oppositional allusion, where two or more literary patterns resist integration and emphasize disparateness, exacerbates the reader's disappointment, for the girl does not live happily ever after, but rather dies leaving a disconsolate, young suitor. Although compared to a "ewe" (4.88), she is in no sense a descendant of Molière's Agnès, suggestive of *agneau* or lamb, whose love will soon be crowned with success. Pierrette is instead a poor little lamb sacrificed to the vanity and avariciousness of the nouveau riche Rogrons and their ambitious acquaintances. Encouraged initially to expect comedy by Balzac's clever allusion to a well-known humorous pattern, readers are invited to react strongly to the tragedy of the girl's fate when their confident expectation of a happy ending is betrayed. Thwarted expectations are a very effective way of emphasizing the tragedy of an unrestrained gerontocracy set loose on the land. The oppositional allusion works in conjunction with several parallel allusions, where allusions merge (or more precisely concatenate) with one or more elements of the text.

Both Brigaut and Pierrette are orphans. It was not uncommon in the first third of the nineteenth century for children to lack fathers, given the high death toll of combatants in the unceasing wars. The minute the revolutionary assembly had excitedly "challenged the bases of absolute monarchy and social privilege, not just in France, but everywhere in Europe,"[7] European monarchies paid close attention to the French intentions to export revolution to the neighboring countries that French rebels viewed as shackled by monstrous tyrants. From 1792, with the declaration of war against Austria, France was internally and externally at war with but brief intermissions, encircled on land and sea with enemies, until Napoleon was definitively defeated at Waterloo in 1815. As mentioned before, for two and a half decades, the blood of young Frenchmen had been spilled across Europe in seemingly endless wars. The mortality came to at least 5 percent of the population, and perhaps a good deal more.[8] France had become a nation of women, grandparents, and children. The resulting absence of fathers was not just another sign of the terrible cost of war or of the dying patriarchy. It signaled a generation of children who had been deprived of a father's love, guidance, and protection.

Balzac's charming orphans are not simple accidents of fate. They represent the tribute being exacted from a new generation ready but prevented from taking on the challenges of French society. Lacking parental affection, defense, and tutelage, they are helpless. Their elders, who view them not with paternal affection, but as simple pawns in their own scramble for riches and power, do not hesitate to toss them aside when they are no longer useful. Balzac surely chose Pierrette's family name of Lorrain to suggest a person representing the glories of ancient France. He repeatedly presented the young as the future hope of a languishing country. Pierrette is, in effect, a nice young woman with the most attractive virtues: anxious to please, delighted to help, obedient, kind, intelligent, charming, in every way someone who would be advantageous to the future of France, particularly when coupled with her childhood friend Brigaut, a master artisan who would soon become a military hero. Too courageous to commit suicide after Pierrette's death, his noteworthy bravery occurs because he is recklessly inviting death. Vicious republican and royalist factions had destroyed the love of his life, leaving him with empty heart and arms. Silvie and Denis Rogron become the instruments of several factions that will immolate the charming couple. The rapacious brother and sister are the most obvious examples of the July Monarchy's gerontocracy that destroys those exceptional young French people who might have had both the energy and the intelligence to lift France above stagnation.

The Rogrons have a long history of mistreating their youthful apprentices. Balzac's narrator explains that such behavior is to be expected of old bachelors and spinsters, and he emphasizes it by bestowing names on the pair that mark them as uncivilized. One of Jérôme-Denis Rogron's given names, for example, derives from Dionysos, while Sylvie's comes from Silvanus, one of the wine-god's followers. In ancient Greece, Dionysian festivals frequently included flagellation and the immolation of children. The number of times that Balzac insists on the importance of names and draws attention to their meanings raises a question about the meaningful intent of naming Denis Rogron's puppet-master *Vin*-et (French *vin* means "wine"). It is one of Balzac's imaginative ways to prepare for the liberal group that will protect the Rogrons and bring both the liberals and Vinet to power.

In Balzac's preface, he claims to despise celibates, for they are "unproductive" (4.21), an opinion he will repeat in detail in the following *Curé de Tours*. He recognizes certain anomalies, people that are "noble and generous, like priests, soldiers, and a few, rare sacrificial types" (4.22). We remember Eugénie Grandet, who was an exception to the general run of Balzac's celibates, for she experiences a profound love that could never be understood by such unmarried people as Sylvie and Denis, who are "serious singles, stealing from civilization and returning nothing" (4.24). They, like most of their breed, replace natural affection by the artificial, loving dogs and cats or, in the Rogrons' case, by an immoderate love for their house and furnishings (4.78–79). Balzac gives the Rogrons even more reason to be abusive. As children, they were abandoned to a cheap, country wet nurse, who went off to work and left them locked up in the dark, humid dwellings typical of French peasants, crying "long and often for their nurse's breast" (4.40–41). In the days when the Rogrons were running their shop, their reputation was so bad that they would have had no employees at all without the help of their father, who sent them "all the unfortunates who had been committed to commerce by their parents [... H]e became the slave trader of apprentices" (4.45). The Rogrons, "repulsively cheap, soulless tormenters" (ibid.), enjoyed few things more than making their victims miserable. Once retired, their new house redecorated, and barred from local society because of their appalling personalities, they are reduced to their own company. "These two machines had nothing to grind in their rusty, inner parts, which screeched" (4.66). Before Pierrette's arrival, because they are bored, they grow "weak from the lack of victims" (4.82).

Needing something new to fill their empty hours, the Rogrons write for Pierrette and eagerly await her arrival. "You would have to be [...] a little like a wild animal closed up in cage in the Jardin des Plantes, with no other prey than meat from the butcher shop brought by the guardian, or a retired merchant with no clerk to torment, in order to know how impatiently the brother and sister awaited their cousin" (4.67). Pierrette is like "a trunk on wheels" (4.73) delivered "like a package" (4.74). She then becomes their property—"she belonged to them!" (4.97). Sadly, the girl's immediate success with the neighboring Tiphaines of Provins does not please the Rogrons, since they receive no benefit. Despite the many invitations that shower Pierrette, Provins society remains closed to Sylvie and Denis: "their feelings, far from being paternal, were marred by egotism and a kind of commercial exploitation" (4.81).

Still, the persecution of their ward cannot be explained as sadism or even the indication of cruel, vicious natures; it is simply "imbecilic tyranny" (4.82). The Rogrons are unable to help themselves. At first, before Sylvie's jealousy is aroused, they even thought they were helping her (4.82). But when people who are variously described as "petty" (4.30), "foolish" (4.42), self-satisfied (4.30, 44), egotistical (4.40), and incapable of anything but "stupidity" (4.44), the results are disastrous for an affectionate, childlike Pierrette, who was made only for love (4.77). At this point, one of the Rogron house's new appointments begins to make sense. In the past, only nobles could put weather vanes on their houses,[9] and hunting was only for land-holding aristocrats. After the Revolution, the sport was open to the wealthy, propertied class, whether noble or not, and, as newly rich people, the Rogrons can reasonably install a weather vane that "represents a hunter set to shoot a hare" (4.30). Although Pierrette is nowhere compared explicitly to a hare, no one could doubt who is in the hunter's sights. Like Virginie, Pierrette is a victim and marked from the beginning for death. After all, as Gouraud implies, "a girl does not amount to much" (4.72). Certainly, Pierrette provides the Rogrons with the scapegoat they had lacked, and once she arrives "they are no longer bored!"[10]

As additional support, Balzac alluded to the well-known example of another long-lived love detailed in *Paul et Virginie* (4.98).[11] Bernardin de St. Pierre's book was a best-seller from its publication in 1788 until well into the nineteenth century, its popularity continuing through the nineteenth and, even, the twentieth centuries. It has gone through more than 200 editions, at least forty-five of them before 1800. By referring explicitly and unmistakably to the earlier novel, Balzac could resurrect the earlier circumstances in the reader's mind, thus infusing them into the reading experience, and create a parallel allusion with *Paul et Virginie*. Balzac then focuses on that portion of the victim's life that Bernardin slights, which took place in France where Virginie was sent to live with an aunt. When told that Pierrette is promised an inheritance, any reader of the mid-nineteenth century would recall that Virginie's aunt had likewise agreed to make Virginie her heir and to prepare a suitable life in civilization for the half-savage girl. Both Virginie and Pierrette learn to read and write after leaving the paradise of childhood for the heartless urban camps controlled by their aunts, and the deaths of both directly result from leaving their childhood homes. While Bernardin tells the reader little of Virginie's time under her aunt's tutelage, Balzac chronicles Pierrette's life of deprivation and misery in detail. In addition, just as Virginie "was condemned to die," in the words of *Paul et Virginie*'s narrator,[12] so we are warned early on in the narration that Pierrette will pass away. But while Virginie's return to her island paradise can be explained by her refusal to marry her aunt's choice and her drowning by uncompromising modesty, despite the need to disrobe and swim to shore, Pierrette's death comes from exploitation and abuse that can be neither satisfactorily explained nor justified.

By alluding to *Paul et Virginie*, Balzac was also able to limit himself to a few brief indications of Pierrette's childhood years in Brittany. Since Bernardin was, however, more interested in the portrayal of virtue induced by nature than in showing the corruption of society, he could leave Virginie's time in Paris in shadow. With the detailed picture of Virginie's childhood, Bernardin de Saint-Pierre intended to emphasize the intimate relationship between Nature and Virtue. Balzac's goal is, however, quite different, though he mentions that until she arrived in Provins, Pierrette "had no other education than that of nature" (4.77). He uses his character primarily to emphasize and illustrate the destructive cruelty of French culture of the day. Pierrette is then brought into focus during the period of her abuse, while that of Virginie is left in the background. Though the two texts have different objectives, the allusion brings them together to direct attention and highlight the point of Balzac's subject: a society ruled by the elderly with no interest in sharing power with its cadets and, thus, destroying its own future.

Balzac is, as always, primarily interested in the root causes of social phenomena. His allusion to *Paul et Virginie* emphasizes that Pierrette's tragedy arises from the sordid stupidity and egotism of greed-ridden bourgeois in a corrupt society. The novel concentrates on self-serving celibates like

Sylvie and Denis who join with the liberals in what will shortly be a successful revolution against the Bourbons and, on a smaller scale, against the local group of royalists. Focusing a brilliant light on the self-serving, egotistical old men that control the liberal July Monarchy, Balzac shows us French youth being crushed. Both the brilliance and the energy of young people will as a result be denied France, a fading nation. One of the wonderful things about "fiction" is that social lessons can be emphasized and rendered more touching with devices that are foreign to essays. Through allusion, Pierrette carries the aura of Virginie, Jesus, Béatrice, and St. Pierre de Vérone. By playing several concurrent roles, she becomes the unforgettable objective correlative of Balzac's teaching.

With the disappointment that builds as Pierrette's tragedy seems increasingly inescapable, readers may become aware of two allusions to martyrdom, that to Jesus and, especially, to the lesser known St. Pierre de Vérone. While the references to St. Pierre de Vérone may seem obscure, longtime readers of Balzac will not be surprised by his use of a name to key an allusion. He—and other authors—did so frequently. Names were all the more salient in that people of the day were encouraged to follow long precedent and choose names for their children that referred to saints of the church and, thus, were accustomed to associate stories and legends with cognomens. Balzac's Eugénie like his Pierrette, Flaubert's Félicité, and Zola's Etienne would all have evoked analogical resonances. Pierrette's name is, of course, particularly suggestive. In a splendid study of *Pierrette*'s hagiography, Timothy J. Williams points to the similarities between Pierrette and St. Pierre de Vérone: both are virginal and unexceptionably virtuous, both are victims persecuted by satanic people, both are falsely accused of having a lover, and both die from head wounds during the Easter season. Like Christ, the girl is "wounded on the head and hand" (Williams, "Dessein" 89, 93). Williams further quotes a passage where the grandmother "kept vigil beside her granddaughter, kissing her forehead, her hair, and her hands, as the saintly women must have kissed Jesus while putting him in the tomb" (Williams, "Dessein" 94). Both Pierrette and St. Pierre de Vérone are then martyrs, and both consequently allude to the life, ministry, and passion of Christ. This extended allusion serves to insist on Pierrette's absolute innocence. It may encourage readers to remember how she continued in the face of unrelieved failure and torment to try to please her tormentors. "With angelic patience, she bore the two celibates' black moods" (4.97). Who but a saint, after all, could ignore her terrible pain as she died, all the while begging "the assembled family to pardon her cousins, as she was doing herself" (4.157)?

When readers actually begin to experience the story, the allusions draw them toward the end and, along the way, highlight the most important elements and events of Pierrette's life. Alluding to *Paul et Virginie* elicits memories of Brigaut and Pierrette's joyous youth and emphasizes the injustices of a civilization sold out to money. Just as we begin to lose faith in the comic structure of the story, we realize instinctively, perhaps even consciously, that Pierrette like Virginie, Jesus, and St. Pierre de Vérone must die. We suspect that Pierrette's torments differ little from those of her predecessors as she suffers her martyrdom on the altar of virtue. Unfortunately, while Virginie would long inspire other girls to a virtuous life, and St. Pierre de Vérone would be beatified and thus inspire and be ready to receive the prayers of the faithful, Pierrette's many virtues serve only to prepare her to be martyred. She is a sacrificial figure. Perfectly willing to die for her God, she exemplifies virtue and dies as an extraordinary illustration. She does not die for the sins of others. Nor does she work the miracles required of sainthood. She does, however, provide an example of forgiveness, honesty, obedience, prudence, and restraint; her courage and humility are exemplary, as are her faith, her hope, and her love. She stands for all the strengths of old Lorraine. Readers easily find illustrations of the seven virtues in her life, with one exception. She does not exemplify justice, for her story has an outcome that is nothing less than outrageously unjust. At the conclusion of *Pierrette*, only Brigaut and Martener still remember her. Her sacrifice and her exemplary life are to no purpose. Her virtue has lost its importance in this society of old men that kneel at the altar of success.

In the activity of reading, readers make images or intricate, mental complexes of themes, feelings, and traits. When skillful writers like Balzac introduce allusions, the references to other creations—at least to those known by the reader of good will—stimulate the recollection of a previous experience, and the memory comes back to join metaphorically with the current reading. Although the alluding text must have salient similarities, it need not be identical to the text referenced. The reader should have no difficulty making meaningful applications and ignoring those elements and relationships that are inappropriate and unsuggestive, rather as readers suppress secondary and tertiary meanings of words and connotations that have nothing to do with the current context. And, of course, readers without the necessary background—perhaps a reader who knows nothing of saints' lives—will have an image of *Pierrette* that lacks the illustrative emphasis of St. Pierre de Vérone. *Pierrette's* allusion to *Paul et Virginie*, however, fills in most of the needed elements. Though the experience of those who are insensitive to the allusions may be less intense, since the unreasonable persecution that lacks redundancy will not be as powerfully evocative, *Pierrette* should nonetheless be comprehensible to any reader, sophisticated or not. By becoming a part of *Pierrette* and her story, however, the allusions serve primarily to intensify the girl's pathetic misfortunes. Without the requisite allusive sensitivity, the tale loses some its pervasive power and intentional meaning and becomes just another story.

Balzac waited until eight or ten lines from the end of his story to make another allusion, this one to Béatrice Cenci, a girl who also suffered legendary abuse. Stendhal speaks of her, as well: "[P]ushed to the edge by the terrible things that she had to suffer," the sixteen-year-old Béatrice decides to kill her father, François Cenci.[13] The elder Cenci had raped her repeatedly while forcing his wife to watch. The girl wrote to the pope for help, only to receive no answer. Although people were well aware that her father, François, had been jailed three times for "his infamous loves" (689–90), no one seemed willing to move against him, probably because of the liberal donations he had made to the appropriate authorities. Finally, there seemed no other solution, and Béatrice and her mother discuss the matter with the older brothers before arranging to assassinate their father. Béatrice and others of her family are condemned for the patricide, though Béatrice confidently commits herself to God's divine mercy. A procession including fifty large candles and all the Franciscans in Rome accompany her remains to a final resting place in front of Raphaël d'Urbin's *Transfiguration*, and her unjust, tragic death was not only regretted by an enormous crowd of people, Stendhal tells us, but it has not been forgotten by history. Balzac concludes by introducing Béatrice into his own story: "Today, based on faith in Guido Reni's portrait, both history and living people condemn the pope, and make of Béatrice one of the most touching victims of infamous passion and factions" (4.162–63).

What makes this example particularly interesting is that the story of Béatrice forms a paradigmatic relationship with that of Pierrette and then falls backward onto the syntagm, thus reformulating the tale. In Jakobson's words, "The poetic function projects the principle of equivalence from the selection axis onto the axis of combination [La fonction poétique projette le principe d'équivalence de l'axe de la sélection sur l'axe de la combination]."[14] Unlike other allusions that move readers toward the conclusion, the reference to Béatrice creates a new metaphoric combination that invites rereading and a different configuration. The story's concluding reference to a parallel with the story of Béatrice is neither emphasized nor exact, though it joins with other elements to increase the horror of Pierrette's treatment (Bardèche, "Notice," HH 5.667). The parallels between Béatrice and Pierrette are obvious, once the Italian victim is mentioned, and the explicit reference to another martyr joins with those of Virginie, St. Pierre de Vérone, and Christ to increase the pathos of Pierrette's abuse.

In addition, the reader is invited to rethink the story and its allusive complex, paying less attention to the characters and more to the infamous factions they represent. The final references to Beatrice alone succeed in casting a retrospective light on the political parties that are destroying France. The Tiphaine group has made an important step toward increasing their power by excluding the Rogrons. As the lovely Madame Tiphaine explains to her husband, "Where there are no enemies, there are no triumphs. A liberal conspiracy, an illegal association, any kind of a struggle will bring attention to you" (4.57). Mme Tiphaine does not say, though *Pierrette* illustrates, that such political conflicts may become surprisingly acute, breeding hatred and fear of one group for another. Small town hatreds are extraordinarily powerful, fueled as they are by ambition and greed, as Balzac well knew. His negative opinion of little provincial towns had recently been reinforced by his trip to Belley in the vain attempt to save Peytel (Tritter 20). In the fictional case, the Tiphaine group's aggressiveness fails to attain the expected victory, and the Tiphaines are forced to change parties with the Revolution of 1830, thus aligning themselves with Vinet: "[M]onsieur Tiphaine did not hesitate to join the July Monarchy" (4.161). The social forces of her day executed Béatrice Cenci; those of Pierrette go further and also sully her reputation. Perhaps the Tiphaines represent the empty, faithless, equivocating values generated by the worship of social position and wealth, the new god we have already met in *Eugénie Grandet* and whom we will meet repeatedly in Balzac's novels. Perhaps this explains why the author chose the name of "Tiphaine," which derives from etymons signifying "manifestation of God," or, more menacing, the "god yet to appear."[15]

The allusive references to *Paul et Virginie* and the account of Béatrice prepare another oppositional allusion. As mentioned above, *Pierrette*'s narrator says that history has condemned the pope for Béatrice's death.

Likewise, society comes to despise Virginie's aunt who dies impoverished and alone, while her victimized niece goes with her loved ones to be with God. Bernardin's narrator says that Virginie's virtuous deeds are kept faithfully in the hearts of those who knew her, and her story is immortalized in various place names. By contrast, Pierrette is destroyed and forgotten. At the end of the book, Vinet, Gouraud, the Tiphaines, and the Rogrons are all doing well. Vinet becomes a deputy and the public prosecutor, Rogron is the Internal Revenue director for Provins (*Receveur-Général*), M. Tiphaine makes his peace with Vinet and accepts an appointment as chief magistrate of His Majesty's court, and Mme Tiphaine happily frequents the salon of "the beautiful Madame Rogron." The author concludes that "Legality would be a lovely thing for social roguery if God did not exist." The reference to God is by no means idle. Balzac knew his popular audience well, and, however untraditional the Romantic God might be, the idea of God was very much alive in nineteenth-century France.[16] (As corroboration, it is clear that the socially aware Napoleon did not make peace with the Church to satisfy his personal religious needs, but rather as a political move to placate practicing Catholics.)

The allusion to Béatrice in *Pierrette*'s conclusion, then, expands the tale exponentially. By referring to the Italian girl and the "infamous passion and factions" that brought her death, Balzac sheds a new light back onto the story he has just told. What previously seemed merely a tragic account of a pathetic girl's victimization can now be reinterpreted in broader social terms as the tale of a France ruled by greed and factions, willing to compromise ethics for the sake of advancement and wealth, a society where virtue no longer exists. As the narrator puts it, "This world of mysterious things, that should perhaps be named the filth of the human heart, lies at the base of the biggest political, social or domestic revolutions" (4.101).

Pierrette becomes nothing but a means to be exploited to amuse the Rogrons and to increase Vinet's power. Sent as little more than a package to the Rogrons, the venal Vinet is ready to use the child and her supposed inheritance from the Rogrons to reward Colonel Gouraud. When he understands that Pierrette may well not inherit, Vinet points Gouraud to Sylvie and arouses the woman's interest, if not love. Because Balzac portrayed the affection of such an old maid as being expressed by jealousy, Sylvie has all the more reason to demonstrate her love for Gouraud by intensifying Pierrette's persecution. Later, however, Vinet decides that he would do better by marrying Denis Rogron to an impoverished but beautiful Chargebœuf girl whom he can control. Vinet's tractable doctor is then used to terrify Sylvie with an account of the dangers of childbirth, so as to keep her unmarried and thus protect the Rogron inheritance for the future Mme Rogron, *née* Chargebœuf. Vinet's tool, the young Bathilde de Chargebœuf, fearing that Pierrette might gain Rogron's hand, becomes the girl's enemy, as well. (Later when what one assumes to be the rigors of the marriage bed make Denis Rogron ill, it only advances Vinet, for at Rogron's death the beautiful widow will be another pawn whom he can marry off advantageously to increase his power.) The cliques are allied either expressly or through unconscious neglect to persecute Pierrette and, like Béatrice, cast her aside, leaving her dead.

Pierrette has the misfortune to fall between the two viciously opposing camps of Provins' bourgeois inhabitants. The royalists surrounding Mme Tiphaine are determined to reject the obnoxious Rogrons, Vinet, the shady lawyer, and Gouraud, a Napoleonic colonel and baron. Vinet and Gouraud use Denis Rogron's money to establish an opposition newspaper, *La Ruche*, which Vinet writes and Gouraud manages. And Vinet cunningly organizes social gatherings at the Rogron house. Recognizing that the political winds are blowing against the legitimists, he moves into the liberal camp and brings Gouraud and the friendless though monied Rogrons with him. Shortly, he succeeds in establishing the Rogron gathering as a liberal salon and a power in the provincial town (4.96). From the first, the text emphases duality. Provins has two rivers and divides into two sections, an upper and a lower city. The primary opposition, and the one that remains basic to the resulting plot, is between the offsprings of M. Auffay's two marriages. Denis and Sylvie descended from the second generation of his first matrimony, and Pierrette from his second. More important, there are two significant salons, two groups, and two newspapers. Two is, of course, the number of opposition and conflict, rivalry and antagonism.[17] Pierrette will be "ground up between implacable interests" (4.96).

The peculiar phrase at the end of the book presents the perhaps chilling possibility that God might have abandoned France. Explicit mentions of God make his absence seem all too apparent: because Pierrette learns "to see the finger of God in everything" (4.92), she rejects thoughts of flight and obediently submits to the Rogron brutality. When her case becomes so bad that even the famous surgeon Desplein fears to attempt surgery, Martener, "chagrined and morose" (4.157), tells Pierrette's friends that the girl's "salvation was only in the hand of God" (ibid.), and the angelic Pierrette insists "that the judgment of these things belonged to God alone" (ibid.). The phrase makes us realize that though Balzac's text mentions God four times, Jesus twice, and Providence once, there is absolutely no evidence of divine activity. Pierrette has been taught to love Jesus as her heavenly fiancé (4.92), but neither God's finger (4.92), nor his hand (4.157), nor his judgment (4.157) effect any change whatsoever. Instead of condemnation being called down on the heads of those responsible for Pierrette's death, they all achieve temporal success. Williams points out that however virtuous and pathetic Pierrette may be, unlike Pierre de Vérone and all canonized saints, she produces no miracles and can therefore not be a true saint, for "a saint without thaumaturgy is inconceivable" (Williams, "Dessein" 95). The other possibility, of course, is that the lack of miracles has nothing to do with Pierrette, but rather results simply from God's absence.

While Christ had Pierre, the rock on which God "will build [His] Church" (Matt. 16:18), France has only the youth of the country who like Pierrette are being disdained and ignored. They are closed out and, as a result, frustrated and stifled. Exemplified by Pierrette, whose name means "little stone or pebble," they have no value. Neither God nor anyone else punishes the rapacious liberals who are, on the one hand, responsible for killing Pierrette and, on the other, guilty of covering up the crime. They live on, rather, in positions of power. Furthermore, unlike Virginie and Béatrice, whose memories are carefully preserved by history, Pierrette leaves no monument to virtue. Only Dr. Martener and Brigaut still remember her at all. Then those who love Pierrette die, and the text mentions the tragedy of Brigaut who unsuccessfully seeks death in war. "[I]f God did not exist..." (4.163), the narrator says, but all the allusions and the outcome of Pierrette's life suggest that God has very little impact on the world of this story.[18]

Balzac's allusive complex effectively emphasizes the novelist's major conclusion growing from his observation of society's demographics. The young are being crushed by the venal gerontocracy. The oppositional allusion to a theatrical structure common to plays like Molière's *L'Ecole des femmes* leads the reader into the story, with the expectations of light, pleasant fare. The fictional reality proves very disappointing, however, and instead of amusement at the way young love can successfully overcome the most difficult obstacles and bring the guardian into ridicule, the tragedy of Pierrette is foregrounded, thwarting the reader's expectations, and offering as compensation one of Balzac's darkest tales. Allusions provide context. On occasion, they radically reorient a text's meaning by adding a new theme of significance. Prior to the last few lines of Balzac's novel, we have a startlingly vivid picture of egocentric, elderly celibates torturing and destroying a helpless girl. The indications of factions and of politics are in the text, but they lack much of their evocative power until they are highlighted by the allusion to Béatrice Cenci. Although seemingly a minor reference, when the history of the Roman girl is consciously recognized and enters into the reading, it throws a jarring, retrospective light across the whole of Balzac's novel. Suddenly, although the reader's attention had previously been directed toward the individuals of the story, now it is to the social fabric, the groups, the factions, the cliques, and the political implications of the Revolution of 1830 that are illuminated and emphasized.

Although, as Andrew Watts has pointed out, each of the provincial towns that Balzac chose for his settings "conditions its inhabitants," he also realizes that the novelist "confers upon Touraine qualities that extend his more general theories of provincial behavior."[19] Certainly, the narrator recognizes the particular beauty of the little town, and he remembers its glorious history, "dominated by the château's imposing remains [...], with its historic memories [and] melancholy ruins" (4.48). "[L]ike Auvergnats, Savoyards, [indeed like] the French," when locals leave Provins to make their fortune they love to return home (4.48). Despite the specific details that distinguish Provins [pʁɔ-vɛ̃], it is suggestive that the name of the town echoes the name of all the Provinces [pʁɔ-vɛ̃s]. There must be no mistake. *Pierrette* is not the rare story of just one pair of misfits. It concerns a major reality in modern France. Balzac focuses here on the gerontocracy that is in no sense limited to this small town. As Pierrette "was herself to fall in the social torrent" (4.82), so France, as a nation, is treating its young with similar cruelty. Like Chronus, it seems bent on devouring its children.

At the end, little Pierrette is dead and already in the last stages of being forgotten. Her persecutors have gone on to considerable success. In *Le Curé de Tours*, the next of Balzac's creations, we learn that the voracious society of the day denigrated virtue, especially defenseless virtue, so that even a harmless small town priest will not be spared. In the case of Athanase's destruction in *La Vieille Fille*, he "was promptly forgotten by society, which wishes to and, indeed, must promptly forget its dead people" (4.921). Because of the allusions that work together in *Pierrette* to form a tight complex, Balzac the sociologist leaves us with the vision of France abandoned to the machinations of insatiable, bourgeois cupidity. Indeed, because Pierrette does not seem to have the divine help that was available to Ursule, much less to Virginie, Béatrice, and the martyred

Pierre de Vérone as the allusions highlight, nothing impedes the vicious, self-centered gerontocracy. Barring radical change in the power structure, there seems little hope for France. Nonetheless, Balzac continues his work as what he elsewhere calls a "simple doctor of social medicine" (7.53). He diagnoses the various avenues of power within the July Monarchy, and he prescribes a cure. Society is creaking with the pathetic sound of old joints. It must be opened to the energies and talents of the young.

NOTES

1. To the works listed at the end of Jean-Louis Tritter's edition—Honoré de Balzac, *Pierrette*, *Œuvres complètes* 4.21–163—should be added: Maurice Bardèche, "Notice," *Pierrette*, HH 5.661–69; Lucette Chambard, and Marguerite Rochette, Pierrette *de Honoré de Balzac*, Folio Guides 2 (Paris: Armand Colin/Gallimard, 1976); Armine Kotin Mortimer, *For Love or for Money: Balzac's Rhetorical Realism* (Columbus: Ohio State UP, 2011) 117–27; Nicole Mozet, *La Ville de province dans l'œuvre de Balzac* (Paris: SEDES, 1982) 212–17; André Vanoncini, "*Pierrette* et la rénovation du code mélodramatique," *Balzac: Œuvres complètes: Le Moment de* La Comédie humaine, ed. Claude Duchet et Isabelle Tournier (Saint-Denis: PU de Vincennes, 1993) 257–67; Timothy J. Williams, "Dessein hagiographique balzacien: A propos de *Pierrette*," *Dalhousie French Studies* 28 (1994): 87–97; and Dorothy Wirtz, "Animalism in Balzac's *Curé de Tours* and *Pierrette*," *Romance Notes* 11.1 (1969): 61–67.
2. Elizabeth Fox-Genovese, *The Origins of Physiocracy: Economic Revolution and Social Order in Eighteenth-Century France* (Ithaca: Cornell UP, 1976) 9–10.
3. Balzac's move to the far right has drawn the attentions of many biographers and critics: see, e.g., Graham Robb, *Balzac: A Biography* (London: Picador, 1994) 189–330; Pierre Barbéris, *Balzac et le mal du siècle, 1799–1833*, 2 vols. (Paris: Gallimard, 1970); Sharif Gemie's "Balzac and the Moral Crisis of the July Monarchy," *European History Quarterly* 19.4 (1989): 469–94; Bernard Guyon, *La Pensée politique et sociale de Balzac* (Paris: Colin, 1967); Fredric Jameson, *The Political Unconscious: Narrative as a Socially Symbolic Act* (Ithaca: Cornell UP, 1981).
4. Allan H. Pasco, *Allusion: A Literary Graft* (U of Toronto P, 1994; rpt. Charlottesville: Rookwood P, 2002) 12. This study also includes extended consideration of allusion and *intertexualité* in its various

permutations, as investigated in major studies by Michael Riffaterre, Julia Kristeva, and others.
5. For the comic elements, particularly in *La Vieille Fille*, see, e.g., below, chapter 9, and Armine Kotin Mortimer, *For Love or for Money* 128–38.
6. Pierre Citron, "Préface," *Pierrette* (Paris: Garnier-Flammarion, 1967) 36. Sylvie is later compared to an "ogresse" (4.117).
7. Jeremy D. Popkin, *A Short History of the French Revolution*, 3d ed. (Upper Saddle River, NJ: Prentice Hall, 2002) 62.
8. I estimated in chapter 2 that something like 1,700,000 Frenchmen died during Napoleon's wars. One would not be too far out of line to assume a comparable figure for the wars during the Revolution and the Directory. Although these figures seem reasonable, they are not certain: Matthew White, "Selected Death Tolls for Wars, Massacres and Atrocities Before the 20th Century," *Historical Atlas of the 20th Century*, http://necrometrics.com. F. Bluche, S. Rials, and J. Tulard estimate that the bloodletting cost the lives of 600,000 Frenchmen from 1789 to 1799 and 900,000 in the Napoleonic wars, that is, "a minimum of 5 % of the population"—*La Révolution française, Que sais-je?* (Paris: PU de France, 1989) 120. See, also, Jacques Dupâquier, "La Population française de 1789 à 1806," *Histoire de la population française*, ed. J. Dupâquier, 4 vols. (Paris: PU de France, 1988) 3.64–83.
9. As Balzac well knew—4.848. Jeremy D. Popkin mentions it in his *Short History of the French Revolution* 9.
10. 4.82. From the beginning, as Timothy Williams suggests, she is the scapegoat of oppressive, abusive elders clawing their way to political and social success—"Martyrdom in *Pierrette*: Balzac's Unmasking of Scapegoat Violence." *Renascence: Essays on Values in Literature* 61.2 (Winter 2009): 91–102.
11. Balzac's subsequent, similar allusion to *Paul et Virginie* to suggest the joyous, youthful but long-lived love affair between Emile Blondet and the eldest Troisville girl is even more abbreviated in the *Cabinet des antiques*: "This affair was similar to that of Paul and Virginie. Madame Blondet tried to make it last, though ordinarily, such love should pass away like other childish things" (4.1067).
12. Jacques-Henri Bernardin de Saint-Pierre, *Paul et Virginie* (1788), ed. Pierre Trahard. (Paris: Garnier, 1964) 218. See, as well, Pasco, *Sick Heroes: French Society and Literature in the Romantic Age, 1750–1850* (Exeter: U of Exeter P, 1997) 109–15. A number of critics have

mentioned the allusion to *Paul et Virginie* (e.g., Tritter, in his edition of *Pierrette* 4.1140n1), but only Armine Kotin Mortimer has considered the parallels at any length ("Myth and Mendacity"). I expand on this excellent study to argue that Balzac uses Bernardin's work in conjunction with others to intensify the pathetic story of Pierrette through a series of supporting allusions.

13. Stendhal, "Les Cenci" (1837), *Chroniques italiennes, Romans et nouvelles*, vol. 2, Bibliothèque de la Pléiade (Paris: Gallimard, 1952) 678–709. The passage quoted is on 594. Tritter reminds us that Stendhal is not the only possible source for the Cenci story, though as Mortimer shows it is the most likely. Balzac's friend, the Marquis de Custine, had also produced a play on the subject in 1833. For Mortimer, the allusion to the Cenci story has the effect of raising *Pierrette* to the status of saint and of insisting on Balzac as a scribe who immortalizes her.
14. Roman Jakobson, "Linguistique et poétique," *Essais de linguistique générale*, tr. Nicolas Ruwet (Paris: Minuit, 1963) 220.
15. Edouard-Léon Scott, *Les Noms de baptême et les prénoms: Nomenclature, signification, tradition, légend, histoire: Art de nommer* (Paris: Alexandre Houssiaux, 1858) 28; Patrick Hanks and Flavia Hodges, *A Dictionary of Surnames* (Oxford: Oxford UP, 1988) 533.
16. For the Romantic God, see Frank Paul Bowman's classic *Le Christ romantique* (Geneva: Droz, 1973), and some of his more recent work in, *French Romanticism: Intertextual and Interdisciplinary Readings* (Baltimore: Johns Hopkins UP, 1990).
17. Jean Chevalier and Alain Gheerbrant, *Dictionnaire des symboles: Mythes, rêves, coutumes, gestes, formes, figures, couleurs, nombres* (Paris: Robert Laffont 1969) 286.
18. Mortimer ("Myth and Mendacity") argues that God's future punishment is implied by the phrase, "if God did not exist…" If so, the implicit, divine presence has no supporting framework. Since Grandmother Lorrain did not pray to God, but to Ste. Anne d'Auray, perhaps Balzac wished to suggest that she lacks faith in God.
19. Watt, *Preserving the Provinces: Small Town and Countryside in the Work of Honoré de Balzac* (Oxford: Peter Lang, 2007) 152; see, also, 96–99.

CHAPTER 5

The Tangible and the Intangible: *Le Curé de Tours*

Reading *Le Curé de Tours* (1832), in the light of Balzac's period, leaves little doubt about why it has been a particular favorite among Balzacians.[1] In but a few pages, it provides delicious melodrama and an exemplar instance of mock heroic. In brief, it makes use of narratological repetitions that have long fascinated readers. Headlined under the erudite Latin banner of *hoc erat in votis* (here is what I wanted),[2] an array of petty desires are eulogized, and like dominos one by one they either topple or quake dangerously: Birotteau's earnest wish to remain tucked comfortably away in his wonderful apartment is dashed; Sophie Gamard's cherished dream of mobilizing a scintillating group that would gather regularly in her house comes to naught; the Baron de Listomère's strategy for promotion is delayed, put into question, and fulfilled only after he has betrayed the little priest, who is a family friend; and the Marquis de Listomère's plan to gain admission to the peerage is thwarted. In fact, however, despite the Latin reference to "the battle between the people and the Roman senate in a molehill, or a tempest in a glass of water" (4.227), the narrator never forgets that his story takes place in nineteenth-century Tours. Whether the novel's mock heroic focuses on religion or the nobility, it describes the pathetic inadequacies and socially useless condition to which church and state have fallen. The French church in particular has lost its high calling.

Father Troubert, the evil genius behind the catastrophes that destroy Abbé Birotteau and fill the Listomère family with terror, uses the events to establish himself solidly as a power in the church and community.

He leaves Tours and his name Troubert (redolent of *trouble*) with his revenge on the dead Chapeloud accomplished and his future secure as the new bishop of Troyes. Only M. de Bourbonne and Father Chapeloud were insightful enough to recognize the danger he represented. Was it his red hair that warned them? Pierre Abraham notes that such hair is shared by Vautrin and constitutes a clear sign of the bestiality that furnishes a global impression of a menacing, wild beast.[3] Troubert's fiery orange eyes are even more significant, for they represent pride and ambition, ferocity, cruelty, and egoism (Abraham 160–65). It is not surprising that Father Chapeloud could warn, "Be careful of that big, gaunt man! He is a Sixtus V on the level of a cathedral town" (4.202). Historically, Pope Sixtus was an effective administrator, who brought many beneficent changes to the Papal States and ecclesiastical finances, though with such severity that by the end of his reign he was widely hated. We know Troubert's expert abilities only by his long-range planning and eventual success at gaining revenge on Chapeloud's friend, Father Birotteau. He will eventually be reborn in a new position as Monseigneur Hyacinthe, a name derived from Greek and Latin roots meaning "resurrection." By that point, poor Birotteau has been deprived of everything: exiled to the far side of the river and thus separated from his elderly companions by crippling gout and a 1900-foot bridge, denied his inheritance, banned from his priestly functions, and sick, a mere skeleton of his former pudgy self. In an example of Balzac's black humor, the little vicar's gout is exacerbated by his virtual entombment in the cold and damp of Saint Syphorien, a church named for the saint said to have particular powers against drought and dryness. He describes himself as a pitiable piece of dirty straw (*bourrier*) (4.235). He has in short been consumed by the fires of the *città dolente* of old maids' spiteful gossip.[4]

Several critics have refused to join the otherwise nearly universal admiration for Balzac's clean progression of ineluctable vengeance that destroys the poor abbé and brings Troubert/Hyacinthe to a bishopric in Troyes. The few negative views base their criticism on the author's long conclusion added to the second edition of 1834 (put on sale in 1833).[5] While Philippe Bertault terms it a flaw that overburdens the novel with theories, Naomi Schor argues that what she calls Troubert's apotheosis succeeds in the space of a page and a half in reversing the very thesis Balzac has argued throughout this veritable "thesis novel," namely, that celibacy and egotism are inextricably linked. In fact, on a first reading, the final pages seemingly shift the emphasis from Birotteau to Troubert. Though Balzac considered entitling the work "Father Troubert," after using the original *Les Célibataires* to serve as the title for the trilogy of *Pierrette, Le Curé de Tours*, and *La Rabouilleuse*, he settled finally on the title it now bears. The terminal emphasis on Troubert's success is, however, troubling. On reflection, he almost seems the subject of the novella. Still, as I have argued a number of times, Balzac's titles should not be dismissed lightly. They reward attention.

In this case, the title encourages readers to see the novel as Balzac did: as a window on the provinces as a whole. It is a mistake to get lost in the personalities of the main characters or the intricacies of the unequal war between the dead Chapeloud and the monstrous but living Troubert. Balzac always had the larger subject of French society in mind. Here, he returns to the corruption undermining the foundations of the Gallican Church, suggested earlier in *Eugénie Grandet* by Father Cruchot's ungodly counsel, in order to benefit his own family's fortunes. He insists on the way the French religion no longer fulfills its true role as the servant of God. Now the cathedrals are void of their sacrificial vocation. They serve only those they employ. In *Le Curé de Tours*, the novelist further insists on the pettiness of celibates, whether religious or secular, ready to move mountains to gain vengeance on a minor ecclesiastic functionary, who was guilty of nothing but being self-centered, thoughtless, and not terribly intelligent. His punishment for being the friend of the unambiguous object of Troubert's hatred is terrible. In order to effect a gargantuan revenge for a miniscule offense, Troubert was willing not only to destroy an inoffensive priest, but to bring an illustrious family to its knees. His activity is entirely extralegal, but it brings light to the decay growing throughout the church and the state. Neither nobles nor religious functionaries can operate effectively in this new post-revolutionary age. Major institutions are subjected to inconsequential personal needs and desires that undermine real values. As with Ursule Mirouët, the text leaves no doubt that Birotteau's case would surely prevail in court, though the little vicar cannot without the Listomère family's material support continue with his lawsuit. He loses not in court but before a society that serves as an unjust judge, and he will not be able to contest his treatment. Troubert has prepared too well.

The work also insists on a distinction at the center of *Les Scènes de la vie de province*, that is, as Balzac described it, the contrasting parallels that exist between provincial and Parisian life.[6] Indeed, one would not be too far wrong to say simply that the provinces are defined primarily by everything they lack in comparison to Paris. The brightest and the best leave the provinces to seek their fortune in the capital city. Failures either return to the countryside like Savinien or du Bousquier, or they sink like Lousteau to journalism and sloth, or they die like Lucien de Rubempré. The calm, monotonous provinces, enveloped in a pervasive sense of isolation, have a slower, more deliberate pace than Paris. Events and people tend to be vague and faded, as contrasted with the scandalously bright colors of the vivid Parisians in the City of Lights. The narrator insists on such traits, and Balzacians have noted them.[7]

Little critical attention has, however, been paid to provincials' limited ability to deal with imperceptible realities that can neither be grasped nor even touched. Provincials tend to be helpless when confronted by such intangibles. Whether facts are obvious, like Troubert's manipulations of Gamard and her friends, or in the shadows, like the mysterious *Congrégation*, provincials tend to be blind to all such invisible realities until their ramifications become overwhelmingly apparent. The perhaps mythical *Congrégation* that Balzac resurrects was rumored to be organized by ambitious priests for imposing their power on the church, government, and society. Certainly, in *Le Curé de Tours* no one recognizes the existence of this organization until Troubert makes his power felt. Balzac insists that the forces that are still hidden in the provinces need to be exposed and equated with the tangible degeneracy and depravity of Paris (3.1521).

The novella's overture points the way. There we meet Birotteau, a short, rotund priest hurrying through the rain toward his lodging. The narrator draws our attention to the little abbé's feet, carefully wrapped in flannel to protect them from the damp and thus shield himself from an attack of gout. We shortly learn that he has won several pounds playing whist, and he is cheered by that thought and by the knowledge of his wonderfully warm and comfortable haven awaiting him in the residence ahead. The vicar had long coveted the apartment in Mademoiselle Sophie Gamard's house because it would provide him with a good home, a good table, clean vestments, and, the text repeats, shoes with silver fasteners (4.183). With the death of his friend, Father Chapeloud, the legacy of the apartment and furnishings passed to him. His heartfelt desire has been gratified, leaving him with sense of well-being (4.188).

After the confiscation of the church's wealth, a passageway that had formerly separated these houses from the cathedral was turned into a street (4.182), but to no avail. Because the walls of the Gamard house are traversed by the church's flying buttresses, in every way it still seems a part of the magnificent monument to which it has been married (4.182). The house and cathedral form a unit into which Birotteau has withdrawn. Silence interrupted only by the expected noises of ecclesiastical activities and nesting jackdaws envelopes the house. Tim Farrant is correct to call Birotteau's satisfactions womb-like.[8] There is nothing really sinful in Birotteau's wish to escape to a place of sweet, creature comfort, but neither is it particularly uplifting. The little priest himself represents the principal thrust of the book. His unique focus on his physical comforts, in contrast to what was at one time the church's sacred calling, emphasizes the difference between intangible spiritual and tangible secular values. It is surely no accident that Balzac's Birotteau has found his womb in the Saint Gatien Cathedral, since iconographers most frequently portray Saint Gatien and his militant faith in a womb-like cave surrounded by his flock. He is said to have spent much of his life hiding from persecution in such grottos and caves.[9] What Birotteau wants from his comfortable womb differs markedly from Saint Gatien's expectations, however, but then the church has changed. Father Birotteau, resembling the big child he is (4.192), wants to belong to Mademoiselle Sophie Gamard as though she were a mother (4.224). And like the old maid's aborted desire for a salon (4.196), Birotteau will cast the premature enjoyment of his uterine dreams in a disastrous miscarriage.

With the exception of the hoped-for canonicate, Birotteau's desires are all physical and afford immediate pleasure. They are, in short, sufficient for "animal needs" (4.183). Though the vicar has long entertained his "furniture concupiscence," hungering to possess the apartment and its furnishings, his yearning was stimulated by a need for physical, appetitive satisfaction. Appropriately, the apartment resembled a beautiful woman.[10] He dreamed of living there, lying down in the bed with big, silk curtains where his late friend, the canon, used to go to bed, and making himself comfortable with everything around him as Chapeloud had (4.186). On moving in, he had begun to enjoy all the pleasures of material life that the deceased canon had bragged about (4.187): "Just think, Father Chapeloud used to say to Birotteau [...], I lack nothing. I always find enough of everything in its place, smelling like irises [...] The wood for heating is well chosen and the least little thing is excellent [...] That's what living really is! Not needing to look for anything, not even one's slippers. Always finding a good fire, and a good table" (4.187–88). Although Birotteau's life turns around tangible, present comfort, he lacks one thing to be content. It is a priest's desire that is already twelve years old (4.182).

He dreams of being named canon. His friends have told him that he will gain the appointment; it is "almost" guaranteed (4.182). He hears about the desired canonicate, he can almost see it, and its ramifications are nearly palpable. He is so certain of being promoted from his current position as vicar to replace Chapeloud as canon that, though the actual appointment is in the future, it seems a part of his present and within his grasp. Unfortunately, while the position is real and thus tangible, as a dream it is still intangible, and his ability to grapple with such unrealized essences is non-existent.

The opening pages offer another detail, which, if only because it does not seem at first significant, reminds us that the author's introductions generally make extensive use of minor elements. The abbé's shoes have large, silver fasteners. Because they are twice mentioned, they demand further attention. Given the orientation of the vicar to the here and now, one might remember that silver, like gold, has inherent value. If one were to melt the buckles down, the monetary value would be obvious and separated from their ornamental worth. As buckles, their preciousness has been set apart from their exchange value that exists but cannot be perceived. They are lovely to look at and have been configured into tangibly pleasant ornaments and trappings. M. de Bourbonne would call the buckles' monetary worth the "liquid part" (4.243), though Birotteau is not concerned with the clasps' pecuniary value. They are simply an appropriate part of his apparel, and, as such, they give him pleasure.

Modern man that he was, Balzac, of course, was a master of intangibles (to the despair of his debtors), and he disdained those provincials that were incapable of similar insight. However much Birotteau appreciated the physical things surrounding him, for example, neither he nor most provincials here and elsewhere in *La Comédie humain* give evidence of appreciating intangible wealth that both measures and stores value for the future, while serving in the meantime as a medium of exchange or as a reminder of loved ones or as simple decoration. Each of these values has importance and can exist simultaneously with others, or it may be separated and kept distinct and independent. We remember Monsieur Grandet. As he aged, his appreciation of intangibles diminished, and his life ends as he tries to grab the priest's vermeil cross during the last rites.[11] Grandet mistakes the gilded appearance for real gold rather than gilt. And, moreover, he is blind to the religious symbolism arising from the crucifixion and resurrection. The significance of the crucifix has no more value for the old man than the canonicate apparently has for Father Birotteau. For the vicar it is simply a promotion.

Appropriately, Balzac dedicated *Le Curé de Tours* to David d'Angers, a sculptor whose bronze medallions will, he says, last long after Paris is nothing but ashes (4.180). Throughout much of history valuable coinage served as monuments to important men or events. Gradually, however, they lost the former, fiduciary function, and the portraits inscribed on the medallions consequently have value only as a monument. Because d'Angers's creations neither represent people of importance to Birotteau, nor can be worn, nor are particularly attractive, and, to him at least, would have no monetary value, they would doubtless seem insignificant to the vicar. Likewise, while Birotteau attaches sentimental importance to Chapeloud's paintings, he does not grasp their monetary value for collectors. So it is that, while Birotteau can appreciate the tangible silver buckles as attractive parts of his apparel, their exchange value as a potential promise is beyond him. Like an inhabitant of Edwin Abbott Abbott's *Flatland*, mentioned before, Birotteau lives in a world of limited dimensions.

Birotteau's inability to see potential meanings beyond contemporary relationships and usages is shared by most of his provincial friends. M. de Bourbonne constitutes the major exception. Known as "*a crafty old fellow!*" (emphasis in original, 4.216), he "knows the provinces, men, things, and even better, local interests!" (4.225). We do not learn whether he would be clever enough to rise to power in the faster moving, more complex society of Paris (there are gradations in the understanding of the potential power of intangible forces), but he has long been able to understand provincial hungers and schemes, however occult. His insight has enabled him to manoeuver to increase his holdings. Although he does not immediately understand the ramifications of the threat to the little priest, he does recognize that there are shoals in the threatening waters. Despite M. de Bourbonne's quiet warning of the dangers, the others urge the vicar to fight for his rights. He could perhaps forsake his apartment, they suggest with seeming judiciousness, but he should definitely not give up his very reasonable expectation of being named canon. Again, M. de Bourbonne, who is beginning to sort out the tides arrayed against their friend, interjects another word of caution: Troubert will doubtless be named vicar-general and will thus have much to say about the appointment of the next canon. Bourbonne's warning does nothing to mitigate the growing outrage. Birotteau's friends urge the priest to go to court and fight for his rights. They reason that the nautical Baron de Listomère would enjoy an engagement between the *Gamard* and the *Birotteau* (4.217), especially since Birotteau is being treated unjustly. The vicar had not understood that he was signing over his material possessions, or that several of the paintings have great value. Unfortunately for Birotteau, however, he will not be able to seek justice, much less equitable treatment. The group, buoyed by the remembered power aristocratic families had under the *ancien régime* and unaware of contemporary weaknesses, had not considered that family relationships and ambitions are more important than the Listomère friendship for Birotteau. As the Baroness de Listomère explains to the priest, "Family duties are more important than those of friendship" (4.235).

The dozen old maids around Sophie Gamard, whom Troubert has spent years cultivating, turn their gossip to vicious character assassination of Birotteau. The new vicar-general is further able to exploit his membership in the powerful, underground *Congrégation* to put pressure on the Listomère family. Everything bows to the will of Father Troubert, soon to be Bishop Hyacinthe. As M. de Bourbonne says with close to absolute comprehension of the unfolding vendetta, if Birotteau wishes to live in peace, he should resign his vicariate and leave Tours (4.225). Birotteau is of course unable to muster the strength of purpose to do this of his own free will. Like other of Balzac's celibates, familiar things exercise astonishing influence over them. Consequently, the little vicar has become like vegetation with roots solidly implanted in Tours (4.226). He is unable to remove them and move. Nonetheless, the diminutive priest will be transplanted, thanks to the malevolent Troubert, who is determined to get revenge on the now dead Chapeloud by destroying his friend, Birotteau.

Balzac's position on old maids and priestly celibates was both more nuanced than is normally granted and an integral part of his philosophical understanding of society. While there can be no doubt of his conservatism, he saw his country as potentially on the move toward a more prosperous and glorious future. For this to happen, however, everyone had to be actively engaged and productive. Sterility was condemnable. "If everything in society as in the world must have a purpose, there certainly are some existences whose goal and utility are inexplicable. Custom (*la morale*) and politics reject individuals that consume without producing, who occupy a place on earth without spreading either good or evil around them" (4.206). Without directly attacking the church, the narrator wonders about the social usefulness of sterile old maids like Sophie Gamard and celibate priests of the post-Concordat Restoration period like the monstrous Troubert. "Today, the Church is no longer a political force, and no longer absorbs the force of solitary people. Consequently, celibacy creates the capital vice that, concentrating the abilities of a person on a single passion, namely egotism, it makes unmarried people either harmful or useless" (4.244). The reigning gerontocracy, including many celibates and beneath which everything is withering in France (7.808), should be opened up to youth.

Balzac returns to the theme of a destructive gerontocracy repeatedly. The provisions of the *Charte* (Constitution) of 1814 laid down that no one under 30 could vote in national elections, and no one under 40 could stand for parliament. It was moreover necessary to satisfy stringent property requirements before being permitted to vote. Although the required property tax of 300 francs per annum does not seem exorbitant to modern readers, it nonetheless raised a high bar and limited the electorate to between 88,000 and 110,000 people out of approximately 30,000,000 French people. As a result, the young saw the country being run by and for the rich, middle-aged and elderly people. Resentment of the disenfranchised was to a significant degree responsible for the underlying instability of the restoration régime. It is worth noting that the word *gérontocratie* appears for the first time in the French language in the 1820s. *De la gérontocratie* was the title of a pamphlet the political economist James Fazy published in 1828. His conclusions were harsh: "France had shrunk to a rump of seven or eight thousand individuals qualifying for election[. They were] asthmatic, gouty, infirm in body and mind [...], and it is to these wrecks from a stormy past that we look to give us resolute counsel relevant to present requirements!"[12]

As Balzac wrote in "Ferragus," the "youth, uncertain in everything, blind yet clairvoyant, was counted for nothing by the old men who jealously kept the reins of the State in their frail hands, while the monarchy could be saved only by their retirement and the admission of this youthful France [to positions of power]" (5.801). Not only are the elderly futile, they share with celibates the sin of infertility and selfishness. Their egotism is exacerbated by the narrow vision encouraged by provincial life. It is unproductive, and can be viewed in the sour unhappiness evident in their faces. As though it were of their own choosing, Balzac's old maids have denied their womanhood, "having refused the passions that make their sex so touching" (4.206). Moreover, they have refused motherhood. By "remaining a virgin, a female creature is no more than nonsense; egotistical, cold, she horrifies [the narrator]" (4.207). Such women, like Sophie Gamard, desperately need to dispense, to give, and thus fill their calm, monotonous, empty lives. Instead, these sad and socially unproductive creatures tend to become involved in petty schemes and gossip. As counterexamples, Balzac holds up other celibates whose committed lives constitute a daily sacrifice offered to noble sentiments. Some remain proudly faithful like Mlle Solomon de Villenoix, who sacrificed herself in order to care for Louis Lambert, or Mademoiselle de Sombreuil, who became a mother to her nephew Victurnien (4.220), or, finally, the elegant, well-doing widow, Madame de Listomère, whose name according to the narrator emanates everything that needs to be said of her (4.215). Certainly, her name suggests a "mother" surrounded by a "border." She also did what she could for Birotteau. In such noble commitment and sacrifice for the sake of others, a minority of celibates find their glory. Even when their wards no longer need them they continue a life consumed with magnanimity.

For the most part, in Balzac's mind, clergy shares the uselessness and social sterility of other celibates. Limited by jealousy, by their vocation, and by the strict confines of provincial appointments in an eviscerated post-revolutionary church, they tend to focus on their current needs and on the tangible benefits that go with their positions. Who knows what they could have accomplished, had they had broader horizons. The scheming yet seemingly faithful and patient abbé Troubert (4.198), who was able to defer his pleasures for years without appearing to suffer (4.198), feigns the canine-like loyalty demanded by Mlle Gamard, insinuates himself in her little group, cultivates the gossipy acquaintances, gains control, and thus exploits them. The position of Father Troubert in the midst of the female senate of Sophie Gamard, his consequent power in the community, and his personal abilities had caused him to be chosen from all the city's clergy by the *Congrégation* to be the secret proconsul of Touraine (4.232).

Although Gobseck's dozen friends who control Balzac's Paris come to mind as a comparison, the old maids of Tours have fewer abilities and less power. In Tours, nonetheless, these persons were lodged throughout the city in a way that configures a plant's capillary vessels, thirstily sucking up the secrets of every household, like dew from the leaf of a rose, mechanically pumping and transmitting them to Father Troubert, much as leaves communicate the freshness that they have absorbed to the stem (4.227). The women have negligible value until Troubert gains control and focuses their intangible rancor. At first people divined the ruthless ambition hidden beneath Troubert's sickly demeanor, and he inspired a feeling of involuntary terror (4.201). Later, having arrived at his fiftieth year, the canon "has dissipated this fear, by his appearance of an absolute lack of ambition and by his saintly life [...] His health itself having been gravely altered for the worse in the last year, his promotion to vicar-general seemed probable" (4.202). He describes the simplicity of his way of life for Birotteau (4.222), pointing out, as he surely had to others, "[f] or fifteen years I went to bed in a bare room without paying attention to the humidity which will finally be the death of me" (4.222). Given that his chronic sickness promises his early death, his competitors look upon his appointment as the opportunity to position themselves for his early replacement. Of course, it is all calculated pretense, as Balzac's narrator makes clear. During his years of apparently patient submission, he had cultivated his group of old maids and secured the position as the secret Proconsul of Touraine with the powerful *Congrégation*.

Although like Pope Sixtus V some of Troubert's acts were notable for their cruelty and violence, in a different age the focus encouraged by a celibate life might have resulted in beneficent kinds of activity needed by society. The fact that the bishop's disdain as he glances at the wasted Birotteau of the conclusion is colored by pity gives hope that the latter will be left in peace. As the narrator explains,

> Is not the apparent egotism of men who carry a science, a nation or laws in their breasts the noblest of passions, and in some way the motherhood of the masses? In order to give birth to new peoples and to produce new ideas are they not required to unite the breasts of a woman with the force of God in their powerful minds? The history of an Innocent III, a Peter the Great, and all those who have led in a century or in a country would if necessary provide convincing, very high level proof of the kind of thought that Troubert displayed deep in the cloister of Saint-Gatien. (4.244–45)

Troubert has precisely the same kind of vision that permitted his famous predecessors to perceive, grasp, and exploit those intangibles that bring them to positions of great influence. Remembering the power and importance of the self-seeking Henri de Marsay, whom Balzac unleashes in *Splendeurs et misères* and elsewhere, we are not surprised that the narrator of *Le Curé de Tours* suggests that in another age, Troubert might have been a Hildebrand or an Alexander VI. Unfortunately, the Church no longer has significant political force and no longer can absorb the activities of solitary, single-minded people (4.244). Consequently, Troubert is doubtless condemned like most other promising celibates to useless, if not harmful, lives. While Tours did not give Troubert the range to allow him to develop into an Innocent III or a Peter the Great, neither would his bishopric in Troyes, for the Gallican church no longer has either sufficient sway or influence. And the novella ends sadly. The impressive personal power of Troubert/Hyacinthe promises to fritter off into nothing in the future, and his helpless victim Birotteau is left but one pathetic step from the grave.

Though Mme de Listomère erroneously believes she successfully threatens him, Troubert wins on all fronts. The Listomère family agrees to talk Birotteau into dropping his lawsuit, before expelling their friend from their midst. With stunning servility they actually invite the vicar-general to their own social events, from which he has previously been excluded. When the dead Mme de Listomère defies the bishop by leaving Birotteau a small inheritance, at the behest of the powerful churchman, the baron de Listomère obediently breaks the will. Troubert even keeps the one thing that sentimental Birotteau had requested: Father Chapeloud's portrait. No doubt it allows the victor to gloat in private.

The work's title may explain the lesson. Undoubtedly, Birotteau might familiarly be called a *curé*, but it is worth remembering that he never has authority over a parish as the formal title of *curé* would suggest. We might further remember one of the etymological meanings of Tours is suggested by the homophonous, *tour* or tower. A *curé*, as his title suggests, is expected to watch for danger as he cares for his flock. Birotteau by gaining entrance to his apartment was moreover put in a sort of high retreat where he hoped for peace and safety. Traditional symbolism of towers, however, links them to vigilance and ascent.[13] Nonetheless, Birotteau is so wrapped up in his personal well-being and tangible comforts that he even neglects the necessity of self-protective watchfulness. His potential for rising into another position depends on his awareness of the intangible lines of power gathered in Troubert's ruthless hands. The vicar's tower is invaded, and he is cast out to sit broken, lonely, and sick on the other side of the river. The office of Tours' *cure* (parish), though the object of Birotteau's desires, passes from Chapeloud to Poirel.

As is often the case with Balzac's masterworks, critical controversies grow from the belief that, however masterful, the novelist was little more than a storyteller. These disagreements are frequently resolved on recognizing that plot and character are merely devices serving greater conceptual and social ends. The concepts of hero and narration have their importance for explaining book sales, but they should not be allowed to confuse the issues. They are the tangible story-line, easily accessible even to readers, who like Birotteau, may suffer from an incapacity to grasp intangibles. This level of reading suffices to provide a coherent narrative, but to glean the true authorial intent, it is just the beginning. An inquiring reader must extrapolate and see the greater sense. Balzac was especially a sociologist *avant l'heure*. He subordinated all aspects of his creations to his attempt to reveal the intangible, intricate workings of Restoration and July Monarchy society.

There is a lesson at another level of abstraction. As Balzac had one of his characters explain in "Aventures administratives d'une idée heureuse [The Administrative Adventures of a Happy Idea]" ideas are beings (12.775). Once this concept is grasped, his creations open the door to fuller and more significant meaning. In addition, the patterns of actions, or plot armatures, could be shifted to depictions of completely different social, political, or economic contexts without changing their essential relationships. The difference resides in the implications of the other sites or contexts for the plots. Should the Tourangeau setting be transformed into that of Innocent III, Peter the Great, Hildebrand or Alexandre VI, it might perhaps be easier to understand the patient rage and jealousy driving Troubert, the pathetic incapacity of Birotteau, or the cowardly betrayals of the Listomères, if for no reason but that they would seem more significant and worthy of attention. The human emotions and motivations are nonetheless the same, whether in the burlesque efforts of naming the next *curé* in little Tours or on a much grander scale. And that is the primary point. While Balzac's genius permitted him to make Birotteau, Troubert, and Mme Gamard come tangibly alive as they spill their sterile seed on the barren ground of France in 1826, for the novelist they were nothing but intangible images designed to reveal the limited triviality and sterility of Restoration mediocrity. In the process, the apparently simple burlesque of *Le Curé de Tours* is revealed as an example of much more powerful mock-heroic drama that casts intense light on the ineffective ridiculousness of Charles X's France.

Notes

1. Maurice Bardèche, for example, calls it "one of the most perfect and most illustrious works by Balzac"—"Notice," *Le Curé de Tours*, HH 13.
2. 4.201. As indicated in the frontispice, the reference to *Le Curé de Tours* is to Nicole Mozet's Pléiade edition. All further references to Balzac's text will be to this Pléiade edition and cited parenthetically.

3. Pierre Abraham. *Créatures chez Balzac* (Paris: Gallimard, 1931) 195.
4. 4.220. As the editor Nicole Mozet notes (1198n1), "*città dolente*" (doleful city) is inscribed over the door to Hell in Canto III of Dante's *Divine Comedy*.
5. Berthier, "Préface," *L'Œuvre de Balzac*, vol. 6 (Paris: Formes et Reflets, 1950) 529; Schor, *Reading in Detail: Aesthetics and the Feminine* (New York and London: Methuen, 1987) 145–46. For Nicole Mozet this disturbing conclusion was meant by the author to refer to his own creative "maternity"—"*Le Curé de Tours*, un espace œdipien?" *L'Œuvre d'identité: Essais sur le romantisme de Nodier à Baudelaire*, ed. Didier Maleuvre and Catherine Nesci (Montreal: Département d'Etudes Françaises, U de Montréal, 1966) 26–27.
6. Balzac, "Introduction," *Scènes de la vie de province* 3.1521.
7. See, for example, my *Balzacian Montage: Configuring* La Comédie humaine (Toronto: U of Toronto P, 1991) 134–37, 140–41; Pierre Barbéris, "La Province comme langage romanesque: La Dramatisation provinciale dans la constitution du héros balzacien," *Stendhal et Balzac II: La province dans le roman. Actes du VIIIe Congrès International Stendhalien, Nantes 27–29 mai 1971*, ed. Alain Chantreau (Nantes: Société Nantaise d'Etudes Littéraires, 1978) 130–41; Philippe Berthier, "Structure et signification d'un espace provincial chez Stendhal et Balzac: la ville," *Stendhal et Balzac II*, 187–201; Bernard Guyon, "La Province dans l'œuvre romanesque de Balzac," *Stendhal et Balzac II*, 117–27; and Nicole Mozet, *La Ville de province dans l'œuvre de Balzac: L'Espace romanesque: Fantasmes et idéologie* (Paris: CDU-SEDES, 1982).
8. Farrant, *Balzac's Shorter Fictions: Genesis and Genre* (Oxford: Oxford UP, 2002) 147.
9. James J. Baran, "Statues, Statutes and Status in Balzac's *Le Curé de Tours*," *Journal of Evolutionary Psychology* 14.3-4 (1993): 254.
10. 4.185. Léon-François Hoffmann highlights Balzac's comparison of Birotteau's "furniture concupiscence" [*concupiscence mobilière*] to a woman—"Eros en filigrane: *Le Curé de Tours*," *L'Année balzacienne* 1967, 95.
11. 3.1175. See the chapter above on *Eugénie Grandet*. Gobseck was much more aware of the power of intangibles. As he puts it, "Gold is the spirituality of your current societies" (2.976). Nonetheless, he also loses his ability to distinguish between tangible and intangible wealth. See my "Balzac's *Gobseck* and Image Structure," *Novel*

Configurations: A Study of French Fiction, 2nd ed. (Birmingham: Summa, 1994) 51–71.
12. F. W. J. Hemmings, *Culture and Society in France 1789–1848* (Leicester: Leicester UP, 1987) 128.
13. Jean Chevalier and Alain Gheerbrant, ed., *Dictionnaire des symboles: Mythes, rêves, coutumes, gestes, formes, figures, couleurs, nombres* (Paris: Robert Laffont, 1969) 762.

CHAPTER 6

The Dying Patriarchy: *La Rabouilleuse*

Balzac's *La Rabouilleuse* (*The Black Sheep* or, elsewhere, *A Bachelor's Establishment* 1842) has elicited no champions, a paucity of fans, and little scholarly interest. Notwithstanding Balzac's letter to Mme Hanska proclaiming its surprising success, critics, with the notable exceptions of Dorothy Magette and Lucienne Frappier-Mazur, have found the work difficult to appreciate. Even the sympathetic Fredric Jameson regrets that he has no choice but to recognize "the book's [...] structural dissymmetry," and André Le Breton went so far as to call it "a profoundly repugnant work," though few others would follow him to such an extreme.[1] Certainly, it cannot be said to resemble those highly regarded creations that pick up and exploit once again the structure Balzac employed to unify the *Comédie humaine* itself. In such cases, a sophisticated, finely tuned understanding of "image" dispels much of the confusion. What has been called an "image" or "spatial" or "descriptive" structure subordinates all the constituent parts, including plots, to most of Balzac's visions. As I argued in *Balzacian Montage*, such patterns or images are particularly significant in explaining how the novelist could emphasize his view of the entire society, rather than the coincidental actions of a particular character. Instead of having importance in and for themselves as isolated elements, such as in popular fictions, his characters and episodes serve as vehicles of significant meaning on the larger stage of the entire novel, of the entire *La Comédie humaine*, and indeed of the whole French society. When successful, the novelist was able to subsume the narrations of creations like "Gobseck," or *Eugénie Grandet*, or *Le Père Goriot* to a pattern that encourages an instantaneous comprehension of the whole[2] and a deeper understanding of the shape that the modern world was taking. Balzac was not, however, limited to image structure. The novelist was a master of many devices and patterns, and his work is no more tied to a particular technique than to an isolated subject. *La Rabouilleuse* illustrates a separate category from many of the novelist's other creations, for its structural coherence and unity depend upon different, though nonetheless effective, devices that reward close reading.

A more adequate understanding of *La Rabouilleuse* should attract knowledgeable Balzacians as well as a popular audience, for it both continues the author's socially perceptive description of the July Monarchy and reveals the novelist's mastery of sequential or process structure. On first reading, it would seem to justify the denigration that Robbe-Grillet, Nathalie Sarraute, and other Nouveaux Romanciers regularly heaped on the nineteenth-century novelist.[3] Bardèche more generously says that it is "a novel whose structure is rather strange, though its equilibrium is powerfully and extraordinarily naïve" (6.93). Still, while such masterpieces as *La Cousine Bette* might justifiably be preferred to *La Rabouilleuse*, the latter is a work of Balzac's maturity and well worth attention. In addition, I would differ with Bardèche and suggest that the novel's sophisticated structure is anything but naïve.

Like most novels that depend on narration, *La Rabouilleuse* may seem to follow the actions of a central character or group. The narrator mentions, for example, that the people in the area maliciously retained Flore Brazier's nickname of the Rabouilleuse, which encourages the reader to understand that Flore's importance is not in herself but in her activity with the fabulous *rabouilloir* (muddying stick). It seems reasonable to wonder whether there exist other *rabouilleurs* creating troubled water in society. Indeed, there are. She is merely the first to frighten the poor crustaceans into traps that render them helpless. Max Gilet portrays a similar figure. Not only does he keep extortionate pressure on the several men who erroneously thought they might be his father, he disrupts the Hochon home by corrupting their wards, keeps Issoudun in an uproar with successive pranks, and successfully lures Flore into partially abandoning her role as Jean-Jacque's kept woman by accepting Max as a new, in-house lover, though without resigning as the mistress of the doctor's scion and current heir of the Rouget fortune. Despite his mental limitations, Jean-Jacques long remains sufficiently prudent to avoid marrying Flore, since she then would have had limited but legal rights to the Rougon fortune. Max and Flore are consequently unable to break his hold on the inheritance.

Nonetheless, Flore is not the focus of interest, though her role is extremely important.[4] Rather than a picaro of eighteenth-century literature, the advancing focus or nucleus is not a picaresque heroine, since she does nothing of any significance. As a child, by agitating the muddy bed of a creek with her stick, she catches the attention of the crayfish that then feel threatened and scramble upstream. "[I]n their confusion [they] throw themselves in the fisherman's traps placed at a suitable distance. Flore Brazier held her *rabouilloir*, her stick for muddying the water, with the natural grace of innocence."[5] Her primary function is to trouble the water. By creating turbulence that directs the "fish" into the traps, the stick serves like the Rouget fortune to encourage covetous suitors into lethal nets.

The salient feature at the heart of the narration quickly appears to be less a character or even a role than the inheritance proper that passes from Dr. Rouget, to Jean-Jacques, partially and temporarily to Joseph, then, to Flore and to Philippe, and finally to du Tillet and Nucingen, before reverting to Joseph. Unlike fictional creations exemplified by Chateaubriand's René or Constant's Adolphe, Flore's character decreases in importance. She functions simply to represent or symbolize the Rouget family's assets. However much Jean-Jacques is the titular owner, she is the pretense for all the other main characters who in fact follow the money. Because effective control of the inheritance has passed out of the hands of the legitimate family, her role as representative of the wealth seems a wild card, her value depending on her connection to the various, passing men. How one gains and maintains control of the inheritance is the problem confronting all those attracted to the fortune. Each of Flore's suitors tries different means. After the doctor's son, Jean-Jacques, attempts to use the inheritance to maintain her in the role of *servante-maîtresse*, Max feigns love to gain control of the financial resources, Joseph tries charm and is offered paintings to deflect his interest, and Philippe keeps her subjected through fear until, when Jean-Jacques dies, he marries her himself. At this point, near the end of the novel, Flore passes from the scene, for she no longer holds sway over the inheritance. Philippe, as her legal husband, is now temporarily in control until the fortune eventually falls to the larcenous du Tillet and Nucingen, who focus not on the woman but, with concentrated directness, on the money. Joseph functions as a sort of pilot fish to whom the paintings, like the leftovers of a feast, fall. Although Flore muddies the water, the money is central and awaiting someone clever enough to gather it in.

La Rabouilleuse, then, deploys a highly complex plot armature that leads readers efficiently from first to last page. The term "plot armature" is intended to separate narration into its component parts and emphasize the abstract plot, free of the constituent characters. Aristotle defined narration as a work's sequence of episodes or plot when animated by a character. *La Rabouilleuse* emphasizes the sequence, including both direction and quantity, rather than the characters. The "plot armature" of a novel could be compared to a cable that includes any number of strands, that merge, twist, and turn around a central core throughout the story, but most of which do not continue from beginning to end. Names, symbols, mythical, biblical, and historical referents, descriptions, characters, and various themes feed into and around the central vector or core growing in importance as the novel's significance is constructed and illuminated within the encompassing, ongoing web. The themes are particularly salient, for they have cultural import, and Balzac both emphasizes them and depends upon them to carry the novel's sense of the surrounding society. But the core fortune retains the focus.

In most narrations, a character or a group of characters make up the sequence of what I just compared to the central vector of a "cable" that merges plot and character, providing an example of Aristotelian narration. For *La Rabouilleuse*, however, the armature is not a character, but rather a collection of elements that the novel weaves around the inheritance into a developing, encompassing textual cable as it moves from beginning to end and closure. Balzac does not neglect the well-worn means of closuring death to break the progression and end the book. Soon after we have attended the title character's pathetic illness, the novel follows with her own and Philippe's deaths. The novelist depends on more interesting devices to fill out the accumulation of signifying elements that are brought in at various points to unify the complex novel as it progresses. As an unusually strong texture is woven around the central sequence of the mobile Rouget fortune, the author highlights what is taking place in families like the Bridaus. The very innovative, literary progression also insists on the society-wide changes occurring in the nation, changes that warn of a dangerous future for France.

The narrator follows the nucleus of the inheritance gained and lost by successive "heirs" as it moves serially through the various characters' attempts to seize the money for themselves. They act, in short, like free radicals, able to join with differing couples and groups one after the other to advance their own careers and take charge of the nuclear inheritance. These characters generally become a part of a group, though they are essentially alone. To the unifying plot following the inheritance is tied the opposition between Paris and the provinces and a succession of irregular, though not always immoral, couples whose successive coupling and uncoupling emphases the dearth of legal fathers.

At the outset of the novel, the plot-vector opens with Dr. Rouget, a widower who intends to break the fraternal bond between his son Jean-Jacques and daughter Agathe. Mistakenly believing (or pretending to believe) that the girl is the result of his wife's adultery, he sends Agathe off to Paris and manages her marriage contract so that she will receive nothing at his death. As a result, when Agathe's overworked husband passes away, she is left in Paris with two sons to raise and insufficient funds. She then establishes a household with her friend Mme Descoings, the widowed wife of the grocer in whose home she had met her husband Bridau. "These two honest but weak creatures" (4.286) set about raising Joseph and Philippe without any help but that of three singularly unimpressive "wise men of Greece" (4.286) who visit them regularly. Clearly, mothering is not enough to protect and guide the children. Nor is the small group of male counselors. Balzac believed that the father was essential in resisting the crumbling society that he sensed surrounding him in the 1830s and 1840s. Philippe becomes a scoundrel (4.304), while Joseph commits himself to art.

Balzac's narrator repeatedly mentions the way he uses names and the importance of Sterne's influence on his practice all across *La Comédie humaine*. The importance he places on these names and their connotations is of even more profound significance in *La Rabouilleuse*. Several of Balzac's onomastic choices play more than usual on comparisons to animals. As the "Avant-propos" to the *Comédie humaine* claims, "Social Species" resemble "Zoological Species" (1.8). Of course, he expands the onomastic possibilities, comparing characters not just to various animals but also to natural objects, like Agathe's name, a homonym of "agate." Descoings clearly indicates quinces and Flore, flora. Flore Brazier's given and family names together further broaden her role beyond that of frightening crayfish into traps with her *rabouilleur* to that of allurement, for this "flower" attracts a number of creatures into the destructive "brazier" of her passion. The perverted Dr. Rouget and his retarded son bear the name of the red fish known in English as mullet, while the pathological

Philippe bears a given name deriving from an etymon for "horse" (which symbolically stresses his physical and soldierly aptitudes). The names may also depend on cultural associations. Balzac twice refers to the very unimpressive elderly counselors that Agathe engages to help her raise her fatherless children as *the three wise men of Greece*. Certainly, their careers had hardly been successful and their advice seems either inappropriate or decidedly wrong (4.286). Had they numbered seven, in accordance with the *Seven Wise Men of Greece*, as prescribed by the oracle at Delphos, they might have been more effective.[6] And every time the young Jean-Jacques Rouget's name occurs, one could well remember that Voltaire famously thought Jean-Jacques Rousssseau's work made him feel like "walking on all fours," thus facetiously accepting Rousseau's call to a "state of nature." Balzac was not enthusiastic about Rousseau either.[7]

At the apex of the pyramid within the natural kingdom that can be discovered in the text, from plants to fish to mammals to humanity, there stands Joseph Bridau, whose life has much in common with the biblical Joseph. Theologians consider Joseph a prefiguration of Christ, though Balzac's Chaudet only mentions the boy's "election by God" (4.293). Otherwise, French readers of the novelist's day might have remembered the scriptural son of Rachel and Jacob, who saved his father and brothers from a famine in Canaan (Genesis 37, 39–50). Not only is Balzac's Joseph falsely accused of a crime, he spends time in prison as did his epigone. His paintings may as well suggest visions resembling Joseph's Biblical dreams, and, as the latter supported his family in Canaan, so Balzac's character faithfully provides support for his mother and her friend, Madame Descoings. In addition, because he has "rare gifts" (4.293), he becomes a highly regarded July Monarchy painter.

Aside from being an outstanding painter, able to create beauty, Joseph has the knowledge to recognize and appreciate the true value of the paintings held by the uncultured Rouget clan. Despite considerable opposition, especially from his mother, Agathe, the young man's steely determination and concentrated focus make him capable of contributing great art to modern society, where few others have such success. His mother believes the career he has chosen to be disreputable, for she shares the disdain that the bourgeoisie had for art, artists, and the artistic. Nonetheless, for Balzac, only an extremely intelligent leader like the biblical Joseph was capable of saving a people and redeeming his terminally ill society. One of the book's lessons is clearly that youth can save the world, but only if young people are allowed to take their rightful place, a lesson that is more fully developed in a subsequent novel, *La Vieille Fille*. Balzac's Joseph

Bridau is a genius who like his biblical namesake makes a better future possible. By contrast, *Pierrette*'s Jacques Brigaut, though not a genius, had tremendous ability as a soldier. Nonetheless, he found no reason to live, and instead sought death on the battlefield. Athanase Granson, an intelligent young man with great potential, actually does commit suicide in *La Vieille Fille*. Such heartbreaking failures are sprinkled liberally across *La Comédie humaine*. Rare successes, like Daniel d'Arthez, are also recorded, but they occur so seldom that readers can scarcely doubt Balzac's anguish for the young people being wasted and, as well, for the future of France.

Occasionally Balzac's use of onomastics seems idiosyncratic, even playful if not bizarre. Though scholars have regularly sought the explanation for his names in the author's biography, the choices he makes for his characters usually have more to do with homophony (as with the pair Bette/Bête), with sixteenth-century words and names (like Goriot and *la grande Gorre*[8]), or puns (like *les cinq Hochon* [the five hogs]). In *La Rabouilleuse*, given Balzac's love of puns, which he shared with several of his creations like Mistigris, readers should note that finding himself eventually as the Count de Brambourg "often made [Joseph] burst out laughing with his gathered friends" (4:540). He then ends the book with several phonically twisted proverbs, implying that he might be laughing at the homophonous Branbourg or "city of garbage or excrement." This possibility is rendered more convincing on recalling that the young *Chevaliers de la Désœuvrance* (Knights of Idleness) had cried out on learning of Agathe's and Joseph's imminent arrival, "'Bran for the Bridaus!" (4.383).

Balzac was convinced that only families governed consistently by fathers could control self-centered young men like Philippe and Max. This opinion is widely accepted today, when similar effects are seen on the streets of major cities around the world in the children of one- or no-parent families. David Blankenhorn points out pertinently:

> The end of this process, the final residue from what David Gutmann calls the 'deculturation' of paternity, is narcissism: a me-first egotism that is hostile not only to any societal goal or larger moral purpose but also to any save the most puerile understanding of personal happiness. In social terms, the primary results of decultured paternity are a decline in children's well-being and a rise in male violence, especially against women. In a larger sense, the most significant result is our society's steady fragmentation into atomized individuals, isolated from one another and estranged from the aspirations and realities of common membership in a family, a community, a nation, bound by mutual commitment and shared memory.[9]

Balzac recognized that fathers had to a large degree disappeared from French society during the Napoleonic wars. As the novelist put it in *La Vieille Fille*, "Napoleon's system of politics [...] made many widows" (4.854). That *La Rabouilleuse* does not mention any fathers might even make one believe that Balzac's Issoudun completely lacks them. He shows that it is the untutored, the undisciplined, in short the fatherless who illegitimately usurp power and who become the unbridled, self-obsessed Philippe Bridaus and the Maxence Gilets. Ultimately, they destroy society. The novelist repeatedly showed that ungoverned young people lacking in long-term social vision disrupt society and commit their lives to frivolous goals and ideals. For their own and society's sakes, they need desperately to be put to good use.

The result of a weakened paternity is monstrous, Balzac claims, since it encourages "selfishness [...] without limits" (4.271). While it may take a moment to recognize that there is something monstrous in the single-minded commitment of great artists, there is no question that Joseph's brother Philippe's selfish plans to make money produce damaging, indeed horrendous, effects in the society at large. The point, as Balzac explains, is that the father is the only social force capable of forming character in his children and of opposing money in its capacity as the most powerful force in society. Money in whatever form has no morality, and is then very dangerous. "May a society based uniquely on the power of money shiver on noting the impotence of justice when confronting the complications of a system that deifies success and condones every means to achieve it!" (4.271). A society without fathers is sterile and results, in short, in Philippe. The implicit lesson is clear. Without the beneficent effects of the sharks Nucingen and du Tillet plundering Philippe's fortune, the entire family would have ended in disaster. Joseph salvaged the Rouget paintings, at least.

The situation in provincial Issoudun, where a major part of the action is set, warns of what the future holds for all of France. Although, as Armine Mortimer suggests, Napoleon constitutes a symbolic father for Max and Philippe, such abstract paternalism fails to shape sons into useful citizens.[10] Instead of acting regularly according to the Civil Code, society has been reduced to vicious rivalries, perverted strategies, and the stubborn retention of power in the hands of old men. In a better society, ruled by fathers concerned about guiding their sons honorably into useful positions of significance, Max would have been one of those men who can effectively perform momentous tasks (4.492). Like other outstanding young people, Max can simply not "remain in a hole like Issoudun without busying himself at something!" (4.502). Lacking the moral sense that should be instilled by fathers, his activity generated enormous harm and set him up to be killed by the psychopath Philippe, causing the narrator to mourn: "So it was that one of those men destined to do great things perished [...], a man [...] endowed by nature with courage, calm, and the political insight of a Caesar Borgia" (4.510). Unfortunately, lacking a father, and raised by an unmarried mother, "he did not learn that nobility of mind and conduct, without which nothing is possible in any kind of life" (4.510).

Curiously, none of the novel's young men behave normally. None wants to marry, for example; they do so only to serve other ends.[11] Jean-Jacques understands that marriage to the Rabouilleuse would cost him control, and Max wants a woman only if she has money (4.501). Prepared by the irregular upbringing of their childhood, the brothers forsake the normal path to marriage, for despite the fact that both eventually have brides, both are in essence bachelors. The fact that Philippe actually marries Flore does not abrogate the pattern, for he uses marriage not for love or for establishing a family and children, but to seize the Rouget fortune and destroy his wife. As further support, Balzac has the traitorous Hochon boys, both of whom are wards of M. Hochon, betray their guardian grandfather to Max and the illegitimate *Chevaliers de la Désœuvrance* (Knights of Idleness). For many reasons, Balzac believed that the father was essential in resisting and restoring the crumbling society of the 1830s and 1840s.

The novel is set in both Paris and Issoudun, giving the reader reason to expect that it resembles other of the paradigmatic *Scènes de la vie de province*, in which Balzac will illuminate further differences between Paris and the provinces. Issoudun has characteristics that the author invents, for its onomastic homonym implies another lesson: a society lacking the virile father will eventually self-destruct. The narrator explains: "The word 'Dun' is the province of any eminence sanctified by a Druidic cult and seems to specify one that the Celts' military and religious cult established. The Romans may have subsequently built a temple to Isis on the Dun."[12] We remember that the Egyptian goddess Isis was married to her elder brother Osiris, who was killed and cut into fourteen pieces by their brother Set. With the help of her sister Nephthys, Isis managed to bring Osiris back to life, having located thirteen of his fourteen parts. The emasculated brother/husband's genitals were not to be found, however, leaving him impotent. In the *New Larousse Encyclopedia of Mythology*, J. Viaud summarizes the myth: all that is creation and blessing comes from Osiris; all that is destruction and perversity arises from Set (16–20). Osiris has, however, been crucially mutilated. For Balzac, and for those who remember their mythology, the allusion to Isis serves to highlight an important pattern in the *La Rabouilleuse*: the lack of fathers and the opposition between the rascally Max and Philippe and the good son Joseph.

Balzac was also insisting on the incapacities of mothers, as his preface states clearly. He explained in his dedication to Charles Nodier that he wanted to plumb important lessons "both for Family and for Maternity" (4.271). It seemed to him that the weakening power of paternity had deleterious effects. "However tender and good the mother may be, she no more replaces this patriarchal royalty than a Woman replaces a King on his throne" (in France, of course, Salic law would not permit a woman to ascend to the throne) (4.271). Balzac will return to the theme of poor parenting and substitute mothers even more explicitly in *Le Cabinet des antiques*.

As in traditional melodrama, which notably fails to make fine distinctions, and perhaps influenced by the success of such popular writers as Dumas *père* and Eugène Sue, Balzac provided Agathe's sons with little nuance. Philippe is crude, even brutish, and profoundly depraved, a selfish womanizer, a gambler, a thief, a liar, and, ultimately, a murderer. In short, he is like the evil Richard III who, according to Pierre Citron, was one of Balzac's models,[13] with no virtue other than "that of the vulgar bravery of a swordsman" (4.297). Joseph, however, loves and cares for his mother; he is kind and quiet, an outstanding painter, though physically ugly. Still, the indulgent Agathe's continuing, overwhelming love for Philippe led her to undeviating attempts to come to his rescue in a succession of scandals, where she does her best to cover up his crimes and help him put himself back together. Her efforts might remind us of Isis. As the Egyptian goddess worked with Nephthys, so Agathe struggled with Descoings to reform Philippe. Joseph, who understands that Agathe prefers the handsome brother Philippe and cannot really help herself, lovingly refuses to condemn her, while nonetheless recognizing that she is "an imbecile of a mother" (4.357).

In the meantime, the author has extricated Philippe from a murky conspiracy, worthy of a good *rabouilleuse*'s skills, and sent him to Issoudun. Availing himself of Hochon's advice, he replaces Max and takes Flore, establishing a new, irregular couple, and reserving the Rouget inheritance for himself. While Flore continues to service Jean-Jacques in a new *ménage à trois*, there is no question about Philippe's dominance. He takes them both to Paris where he infects Jean-Jacques and Flore with the pleasures of the demi-monde. It does not take Jean-Jacques long to die of over-indulgence. Flore dies, as well, almost certainly of syphilis, the result of Philippe leaving her in penury and, thus, forcing her into prostitution. Fortified with unimpeded access to the inheritance, Philippe is then free to pursue a marriage of even greater wealth, an attempt that is foiled by Bixiou, before going on to die a lonely, brutal death on a battlefield in Algeria. His brother Joseph, however, like his biblical counterpart, is "the master dreamer" (Genèse 37.19), and like Jacob's son, he is able to rise from jail and follow his visions to a life of acclaim and fortune.

When the Parisian ladies Agathe and Descoings sink into the depths of poverty, Descoings dies, and Philippe, having been caught stealing from his aunt and brother, is shown the door. The family's misery is, of course, thanks largely to the latter's nefarious activity. To conserve their limited funds, Agathe moves in with her son Joseph, and thus establishes another of the novel's couples, this time a mother–son twosome. Agathe soon takes Joseph with her to Issoudun in an attempt to rectify the earlier paternal rejection and recuperate the Rouget inheritance. There, they join forces with the Hochons, who have a profound understanding of the mores of the people surrounding them in the provincial town.

As the unusual plot sequence, based on corralling the assets of the late doctor's fortune, follows a winding but nonetheless clear path from Dr. Rouget to Flore to Philippe, to the bankers and, finally, to Joseph, the trail reflects the changes Balzac saw in society. We have learned in other of his novels that the limited, indeed mediocre, rigid, fearful, arrogant, spiteful middle-class people that control society often succeed in crushing outstanding young people like Joseph whom France so desperately needs. In telling the story of the Rouget inheritance pursued serially by a number of characters, one after another, Balzac's innovative technique exploits a narration composed of a moving target where the wealth serves as the point of focus. The technique of organizing a narration around an object, in this case the inheritance, reflects and, thus, highlights the novel's significance. The novel is set in a society where neither people nor their moral characters are important. Only money matters.

Among the more significant failures of this society, religion and, more particularly, the church have lost its power. "Not only was the influence of religion nonexistent, the priest enjoyed no respect" (4.362). The narrator assures the reader that the local people enjoyed denigrating the priest by repeating the more or less ridiculous rumors about him and his housekeeper, and he notes the few things remaining from the religion of the *ancien régime*. There is a school, where children continue to attend catechism classes in preparation for their first communion, and people go to mass. They even celebrate the feast days. But it is all routine, lacking the impact of genuine belief. Given that it indicates lackluster religion and aesthetic blindness, it is not surprising that only one person tries to stop the demolition of the Saint-Paterne Church, one of the nation's loveliest examples of Romanesque architecture (4.365). Equally serious is the dearth of aristocrats, leaving the town without noble links to the rest of France and the vitality that two opposing classes would provide. Issoudun's bourgeoisie is proud of its triumph in expelling nobles, though in truth, combined with rural people's hatred of change, it is but one more reason for its "complete stagnation" (4.362).

"The decadence of Issoudun is explained then by a spirit of immobility pushed to the point of ineptitude" (4.362). Neighboring Bourges, the former capital of Berry, is much the same (4.362). Local government is so inbred that it is impotent (4.363), and change is impeded. The narrator warns, "Many French towns, particularly in the south, resemble Issoudun." His tone becomes even more ominous: "The condition caused by the triumph of the Bourgeoisie [...] is what awaits the whole of France, even Paris, if the Bourgeoisie continues to be our country's master of domestic and foreign policy" (4.364). Government is inept, the church is ineffectual, and, as the readers will see in heart-rending detail, the family is broken. Traditional, effective, patriarchal families have been replaced by such irregular couples as two weak women, a perverted old man and a little girl, a retarded son and a servant-mistress, and a mischief-making group under the leadership of a pseudo-father. In such a world, bourgeois mediocrity reigns, leaving an idle group of young people with no social goals and nothing productive to do. Nor does Balzac indicate that there is much hope for future amelioration.

Since the death of Dr. Rouget, who brought the pretty Flore home with the obvious plan of raising her for his private pleasures, Rouget's retarded son Jean-Jacques continues where his father leaves off and begins an affair with the Rabouilleuse, now the corseted Madame Flore Brazier (4.407). This new, unsavory couple does not stay the same for long. However much the aging Jean-Jacques is willing to lavish her heart's desire on Flore, he cannot satisfy the young woman, and she adds the former military man and bachelor Maxence Gilet to her bed. Like Philippe, Max's names suggest both leadership (Maxence) and military prowess (Gilet probably derives from etymons referring to the goatskin that covered shields[14]). The historical fact that the Roman Emperor Maxence died violently serves to prepare readers for Max's defeat. Soon Flore moves her new lover, Max, into the Rouget house. She does not dare to reject Jean-Jacques, since the fortune to be enjoyed is legally his, but she very quickly puts Rouget into second place and begins the process of stealing the inheritance. Max, of course, dominates his mistress and, thus, the *ménage à trois*, leaving him and Flore to face off against the other potential heirs, Agathe and her son, Joseph. Despite the support of Agathe's godmother, Mme Hochon, and the advice of her wily husband, the Bridaus are not up to the battle. Joseph finds himself incarcerated like his biblical namesake. When freed, he and his mother beat a retreat to Paris, where Joseph pursues his lonely struggle to rise to the heights of the Parisian art world, all the while caring for his mother.

Nicole Mozet points out that Flore serves to focus on the numbers of men that surround her and that are involved in irregular families. A list involves virtually every character in the novel.[15] Dr. Rouget, the father of Jean-Jacques and sister of Agathe, does not live long enough to consummate the relationship he intended with the pretty child he bought from the peasant. Jean-Jacques fills in after the father dies. Then, later, Flore establishes an illegitimate concubinage with Max, which lasts until Philippe kills her lover. Philippe offers another example of misdirection. He successfully integrates himself into the Issoudun society before luring Max to his death and taking Flore firmly under his control. Afterward, it is a simple matter to infect Jean-Jacques with the pleasures of the Parisian fleshpots, rapidly weakening his character and bringing him to his death. Flore finally inherits, though Philippe is waiting, ready to frighten her into marriage, so that he may legally take charge. While he continues after his marriage to hide his intentions, he abandons his new wife to poverty and prostitution. The fact that he is soon back in the military, where he suffers a horrible death, merely means that du Tillet and Nucingen, two other *rabouilleurs*, have succeeded in slipping behind his defenses and defrauding him of the inheritance. Since Flore is by this time already dead and the nefarious financiers have done their work, the inheritance is reduced to paintings and are free to pass to Joseph, the good brother. The latter's success and genius are finally crowned by the recognition of his artistic talent, the protection of the Count de Sérizy, a rich marriage, and what is left of the Rouget, now Bridau, inheritance.

The portrait that Balzac paints of the provinces in the preceding *Scènes de la vie de province* continues and deepens in *La Rabouilleuse*. Although success in Paris depends primarily on individual initiative, most often of a solitary nature, success in the provinces requires concerted group effort. Those individuals, like du Bousquier of *La Vieille Fille* and Philippe in *La Rabouilleuse*, who lack the power to rise to power and wealth in Paris may succeed in the hinterlands. They need to learn to fit in, to present the appearance of having become a part of the provincial scene, an endeavor that usually requires the active help of more knowing provincials like the Hochons. Few things please Balzac's provincials more than repulsing Parisians. Agathe and Joseph's flight, for example, "was celebrated by the entire town like a victory of the provinces over Paris" (4.466). They do not understand that they have merely opened themselves up to another Parisian predator, the sociopathic Philippe.

Balzac repeatedly returned to the dangers of a society ruled by money. His infernal vision of Paris at the beginning of "La Fille aux yeux d'or [The Girl with the Golden Eyes]" is merely the best known. He apparently felt that his message gained power when examined in a provincial setting. Although the essentially bachelor nature of the Parisians Henri de Marsay, Nucingen, du Tillet, and Rastignac, among others, is obvious, we expect family to continue to be important in the provinces, where, in fact, in the midst of stultifying inactivity, many of the same social forces are in place and result in the same social maladies as in Paris. Issoudun continues to be repressed by long lived, medieval, bourgeois attitudes. On the one hand, the provincials are committed to wealth and, on the other, afraid of change: "Issoudun's decadence is explained by a spirit of immobility pushed all the way to ineptitude" (4.361). And, as said before, the story takes place in a patriarchal vacuum. "The town of Issoudun has arrived at complete social stagnation [... It] would have bored Napoleon to numbness" (4.362–63). Religion has no influence at all (4.361), and the administration is so in-grown that one cannot expect any change. "Consequently, the administration's sluggishness admirably corresponded to the moral and intellectual situation of the country" (4.363).

Naturally, in such a town, "without even commercial activity, without artistic taste, without learned occupations, where everyone stayed in his place" (4.365), bored, idle young people become destructive, forming quasi-families devoted to their own self-centered, often malicious entertainment. By any objective judgment, they have nothing else to do in this society. Issoudun's community is controlled by undisciplined orphans like François Hochon and his cousin Baruch Borniche, who idealize Max Gilet. The latter becomes Grand Master of the occult *Chevaliers de la Désœuvrance*, which establishes a kind of corrupt family with Max as a spurious, counterfeit father. Max's illegitimacy is stressed in that he extorts money from several men his mother was seeing, which goes to pay for orgies at the Cognette's, and he leads his band in malicious, destructive, illegal pranks. François and Baruch themselves have no real tie to Max other than the thousand *écus* they owe him, yet are committed members of the group and betray their grandfather because of it. Money, not love, is the key to behavior in this society.

Not surprisingly, Mme Hochon obliges her husband to welcome her sister by threatening to direct her personal fortune away from him (4.421). M. Hochon gains absolute control of his grandsons by threatening to leave them with no inheritance (4.482–85). He wields a weapon of considerable power when he finally exercises the authority of a father over his wards, since, as Piketty notes, this was a period of extremely slow economic growth. Rising to a comfortable lifestyle required a personal fortune beyond the reach of those lacking a substantial sum, like an inheritance.[16] The boys have allowed money to turn them into spies on their own families, so that the pun on the Hochon name (*les cinq Hochon* or "the five hogs") becomes all too appropriate. M. Hochon brings them under control by wielding the only weapon they recognize. Another inheritance threatens to go astray, and they quickly come to order.

As usual, Balzac does not force us to guess the sense of his lesson: "The position into which the bourgeois triumph has placed this leading district town is the one that awaits all of France and even Paris, if the bourgeoisie continues to remain the mistress of the internal and external politics of our land" (4.364). Balzac recognizes that young people have been radically mistreated by their elders. Not only have women been virtually deprived of reasonable inheritances, allotting them at best a "minimum" portion, fathers often chose illegal primogeniture for the major portion of the family inheritance, thus disinheriting younger sons and daughters. The significant, widespread riotous behavior of youth during the Revolution was to some degree the result of this unjustifiably partial treatment of the young. Napoleon's Civil Code consequently became a means of keeping young people in subjection. There was much conflict internally as women and youngest sons tried to gain their rights. They felt they should be treated equally. The older generations, who remembered the troubles of the revolutionary decade acutely, were determined to avoid revolutionary turmoil, and they not only refused to give up their legal power embroidered on the Code; they expanded it to solidify their domination.[17]

Balzac's *La Rabouilleuse* illustrates that only with geniuses like Joseph Bridau can there be hope for rebuilding a functional society. As the biblical Joseph explains to his brothers: "[I]t was to keep you alive that God sent me before you [...], in order to assure you a portion within the country and to allow you to live through a great deliverance" (Genesis 45.5–7). Balzac prophetically exposes France's sterile mediocrity and stagnation, the consequences of a misguided genontocracy. Without the traditional power of the patriarchy and families both to guide young people and to guard morals, without the force of a strong church, Balzac believed France's only hope was in outstanding young people, in the Josephs. Of course, even in the case of such paragons, the author's hope is limited, as he reveals in works like *Z. Marcas*, *Pierrette*, and, perhaps most powerfully, in *La Vieille Fille*. These fictions reveal that in Balzac's literary critique of contemporary France, the middle-class arranges things so that vital young people have no future short of crime, exile, or death. France then forms an analogy paralleling the Isis myth Balzac perceived in Issoudun. As the reconstituted Osiris lacked his reproductive member, so Restoration and July Monarchy France lacks the virile power of youth raised in a disciplined fashion by fathers within the patriarchy.

Notes

1. Magette, "Trapping Crayfish: The Artist, Nature, and *Le Calcul* in Balzac's *La Rabouilleuse*," *Nineteenth-Century French Studies* 12.1–2 (Fall-Winter 1983–84) 54–67; Frappier-Mazur, "Max et les chevaliers, famille, filiation et confrérie dans *La Rabouilleuse*," *Balzac, pater familias*, ed. Claudie Bernard and Franc Schuerewegen, Cahiers de Recherche des Instituts Néerlandais de Langue et de Literature Française 38 (Amsterdam: Département de Langues romanes, U de Groningue, 2001) 51–61; Jameson, "Imaginary and Symbolic in *La Rabouilleuse*," *Social Science Information* 16.1 (1977): 64; Le Breton, *Balzac: l'homme et l'œuvre* (Paris: Armand Colin, 1905) 289.
2. Cocteau has succinctly described what happens when an author succeeds in offering such a structure to readers: "[Y]ou can dream in the space of a second the equivalence of Proust's work"—*Journal d'un inconnu* (Paris: Grasset, 1953) 153n1. For more detailed illustrations,

see, e.g., Pasco, "Balzac's 'Gobseck' and Image Structure," *Novel Configurations: A Study of the French Novel*, 2nd ed. (Birmingham, AL: Summa Publications, 1994) 51–71; *Allusion* (U of Toronto P, 1994; rpt. Charlottesville: Rookwood P, 2002) 211–20; *Balzacian Montage* (Toronto: U of Toronto P, 1991) 22–35, and, of course, the current volume.
3. I think particularly of, e.g., Nathalie Sarraute, *L'Ère du soupçon: Essais sur le roman* (Paris: Gallimard, 1956) 55–56, 60–64, 108–09; Alain Robbe-Grillet, "Une Voie pour le roman future" (1956), *Pour un nouveau roman*, Coll. Idées (Paris: NRF, 1963) 17–18; Jean Ricardou, "Le Nouveau Roman existe-t-il?" *Nouveau Roman: hier, aujourd'hui*, Communications et interventions du colloque tenu du 20 au 30 juillet 1971 au Centre Culturel de Cerisy-la-Salle, 2 vols. (Paris: 10/18, 1972) 1.20. Michel Butor, a major exception, maintained that those who wished to write anti-Balzacian novels had an insufficient understanding of Balzac—"Balzac et la réalité," *Répertoire* [*1*] (Paris: Eds. de Minuit, 1960) 79–80.
4. Lucienne Frappier-Mazur argues, conversely, "The Rabouilleuse's two marriages confer a pivotal position on her, which would alone justify the novel's title"—"Max et les chevaliers" 59.
5. This particular reference is on (4.387). Balzac's definition of a *rabouilleuse* has been contested. Rabelais used the term to refer to "un trou, un recoin" (4.1271n1 to p. 386). Consequently, "R. Guignard believes that crawfish don't throw themselves in the nets, but rather take refuge in holes. This perhaps allows the fisherman to catch them with his hand" (4.1271n1 to p. 387).
6. The Delphic oracle instructed that there should be seven wise men. Balzac's decision to limit his counsel to three may simply be a way of insisting on their inadequacies.
7. See Dorothy Magette's excellent discussion of Jean-Jacques Rougon's figural relationship to Jean-Jacques Rousseau 55–56.
8. Bette is a common nickname for Elisabeth, the title character of *La Cousine Bette*; *bête* is the French word for animal. J. Wayne Conner points out that *gorre* is a word that Rabelais used for syphilis: "On Balzac's Goriot," *Symposium* 8 (1954): 70–71.
9. David Blankenhorn, *Fatherless America: Confronting Our Most Urgent Social Problem* (New York: Basic Books, 1995) 4. For a discussion of fatherless works of art in the nineteenth century, see Pasco, *Sick Heroes* 168–71.

10. Mortimer, *For Love or for Money: Balzac's Rhetorical Realism* (Columbus, OH: Ohio State UP, 2011) 139–51.
11. George Saintsbury showed considerable insight when he titled his translation of *La Rabouilleuse*, *A Bachelor's Establishment*.
12. 4.359. I have found no recent etymologists who would accept Balzac's etymological embroidery. Albert Dauzat, *Les Noms de lieux: Origine et evolution: villes et villages, pays, cours d'eau, montagnes, lieux-dits* (Paris: Delagrave, 1963) 73, 102, and André Cherpillod, *Dictionnaire étymologique des noms géographiques* (Paris: Masson, 1986) 229 agree, simply, that Issoudun derives from the Gallic *Uxelodunum* or "fort on a height." The addition of Isis, however, provides the author with a powerful allusion that highlights the damage being done to families.
13. Pierre Citron, "Introduction," *La Rabouilleuse* (Paris: Garnier, 1966) lxxxvi.
14. 4.383. Charlotte M. Yonge, *History of Christian Names* (London: Macmillan, 1884) 79–80.
15. Mozet, *La Ville de province dans l'œuvre de Balzac: L'Espace romanesque: fantasmes et idéologie* (Paris: Société d'Edition d'Enseignement Supérieur, 1982) 234–52.
16. Piketty, *Capital in the Twenty-First Century* (Cambridge MA: Harvard UP, 2014) 238–43.
17. I take this summary from Suzanne Desan, *The Family on Trial in Revolutionary France* (Berkeley: U of California P, 2004). See, also, one of her very interesting sources, Alain Collomp, "L'Impossible mariage: Violence et parenté en Gelvaudan, XVIIe, XVIIIe et XIXe siècles," ed. Elisabeth Claverie and Pierre Lamaison (Paris: Hachette, 1982) 157–77.

CHAPTER 7

Nascent Capitalism: "L'Illustre Gaudissart"

Balzac's "L'Illustre Gaudissart" of 1833 poses a number of anomalies. It is, for example, the only creation included in *Les Scènes de la vie de province* that makes no more than a passing reference to an inheritance. Given the crucial significance of the theme, both in this portion of *La Comédie humaine* and in the society of the day, it is difficult to understand why the author was willing to deviate from the well-established pattern of these *scènes*. Still, the author may have felt that it was unnecessary to return to the subject, since the other stories emphasize the unquestionable importance of an inheritance to achieve even modest success in the life of late eighteenth- and early nineteenth-century France. Recent works by Alexandre Péraud, Thomas Piketty, and Karl Gunnar Persson make well-documented arguments that the general economy of the July Monarchy had reached a period of very low growth in which individuals had little or no chance of making a personal fortune without stumbling across or inheriting a substantial sum of funds.[1] As Piketty explains, "To live well" in Balzac's world, a person "needs 20–30 times the average income" (411), an extraordinarily unlikely possibility for any but the top 1 percent (411). "[I]t was totally out of reach for anyone content to practice a profession, no matter how well it paid" (411). Indeed, in Persson's words, "France stagnated" (66, 211).

"L'Illustre Gaudissart" may have justified its inclusion in the *Scènes de la vie de province* for Balzac in that, despite the peddler's significant failure when he was turned into the laughable object of a tasteless joke, he is on the road to gaining a substantial fortune, even without an inheritance. The novelist highlights the importance of money and wealth once again, even though he has expanded the focus on the means of accumulation. Gaudissart and his Parisian employers have found a way to use him as an "advertising genius" (e.g., 6.205–06) to shake loose essential capital from the recalcitrant provincials. Fueled only by increasing funds, the new capitalistic society desperately needs more liquidity. Gaudissart's task is to bring the ultra-conservative provincials into the modern world. Opposition is an important, rhetorical means of emphasis, and the author uses his comic story to insist on the important changes reforming France's economy. The story demonstrates that the provinces are creating a financial relationship with Paris.

Perhaps equally important for thematic consistency in the *Scènes de la vie de province*, "L'Illustre Gaudissart" provides a summative and explicit critique of provincials. The reader is entertained with Margaritis, a madman who exhibits the identifying marks of the stultifying masses of people outside of Paris who are holding up progress. He does not understand the essential details of possession and ownership, he hoards his money in ways that deny it the power of growth, and he greedily gobbles the delicacies that his family would have enjoyed. Chained to the present and immediate circumstances and pleasures, he is unable to see beyond the daily weather, and he has no grasp of the importance of events taking place outside his neighborhood. The French word *fou* is particularly appropriate in describing the madman, for he is both a "fool" and "insane." Nowhere else does Balzac describe so acutely or in such detail the reasons for his affectionate disdain of the provinces, provincial attitudes, and provincial life. Provincials resemble Margaritis all too much. They act like fools, if not like madmen.

As is often the case with Balzac's more interesting works, "L'Illustre Gaudissart" (1833) has elicited widely varying reactions. It started early, even with close friends. Zulma Carraud, for example, loathed the character Gaudissart, and remonstrated gently with Balzac, since she thought he had descended to "pure wit" and betrayed the wonderful gift that permitted him insight into the female sex. How could the novelist possibly imagine that any woman would ever behave like the fictional Mme Margaritis and allow her ill husband to be the unknowing participant in a practical joke?[2] Their mutual friend August Bourget agreed regretfully.[3] These two friends, at least, felt that Balzac had missed the mark of his high calling. More recently, Suzanne Bérard also considers the story "vulgar and poorly assembled,"⁴ and, in his earliest evaluation, Bernard Guyon agreed. There, he concludes that the tale was "rather coarse, to tell the truth, not very realistic." In addition, to make a farce of a madman is "in poor taste."⁵

Guyon nonetheless recognizes that the story has considerable importance, since it turns primarily on "aborning capitalism, speculation, the power of thought, and, less commonly, on the most modern form of published thought, the Press." Furthermore, he warns against the "mistake of turning one's nose up and not enjoying [the tale] wholeheartedly." Guyon becomes increasingly sympathetic and positive in several later studies and revisions. In the end, he says without equivocation that "L'Illustre Gaudissart" is "one of the successes of recent literature."⁶ Here, I want to expand on Guyon's perceptive insight that "L'Illustre Gaudissart" constitutes "a meditation [...] on the rapid expansion of capitalism at the beginning of the nineteenth century and on the role of [...] *Intelligence* in the form of *Speculation*" (ibid.). I suggest that the tale brilliantly illustrates one of the most important aspects of the period's nascent capitalism: to ensure success in the new economy, the financial system could not be confined to urban centers. It required the participation of the whole of society, and, to that end, the provinces had to be stimulated to take part in the Industrial Revolution and its sophisticated financial underpinnings. In the midst of this short but comic masterpiece, Balzac raises issues that will be central to the extraordinary changes that were taking place in the French economy. The old ways were no longer adequate for the enormous needs being generated as France turned away from an agricultural to a capitalistic economy. Paris desperately needed the provinces to unearth their gold and put it to work. To take part, retarded, foolish provincials could no longer ignore the implications of credit and debt, fiat money, or intangible values; for fear of becoming fools, even madmen, they could not afford to eschew speculation, and thus miss the tremendous opportunities of the new France.

Most scholars have ignored the cultural implications of Balzac's story to focus on the undoubtedly important literary thrust. Shoshana Felman reached the conclusion that Margaritis, the *fou* (whether *madman* or *fool*), and the attendant, linguistic comedy must be understood to highlight the relationship between the novel genre and madness.⁷ What has been taken as a simple device of comedy, a *dialogue des sourds* (a dialogue by deaf people), is in fact a highly sophisticated linguistic construction where Gaudissart's metaphoric language is uprooted and replaced by Margaritis's metonoymy. The speech of both traveling salesman and madman are, according to Felman, "deprived of referent." Furthermore, "the two discourses resemble each other [...], seducing, fascinating, dominating the other so as to sell him things that do not exist" (Felman 42). Balzac's comedy, of course, is to have a conversation without communication. Although the verbal exchange has seemed out of place to some, it is in fact ironic and has the value of being functional. For Felman, it serves to insist on the "insanity" of the story and of the novel genre, while it more directly continues Balzac's efforts to contribute to the nascent field of sociology by recognizing major, interacting, often competing forces within the society. The salesman representing the Parisian financial world is dealing in abstractions and potentialities, while the village *fou* can only grapple with his immediate concerns and experience.

Balzac acknowledged his friends' criticism—"We'll talk about it,"[8] he responded—but to the best of our current knowledge he never really answered their objections. Subsequently, by including the story in *La Comédie humaine*, he made it clear that he did not agree with their negative assessment and that "L'Illustre Gaudissart" merited inclusion among those works elected to comprise his epic creation, a selection that was by no means granted to everything he wrote. Perhaps with what we have learned through the years, we can explain why he included the episode on Gaudissart in his epic masterpiece, an answer he only gave by implication.

The story resembles one of the *physiologies*, sketches of types and vocations—soldier, seamstress, flower girl, mason—that were popular in the late 1820s, 1830s, and 1840s and had already drawn Balzac's attention. But "L'Illustre Gaudissart" goes further to create an exemplary literary facsimile, where he transformed the "type" of the commercial traveler into a powerful character that uses the devices of comedy to highlight significant points. The work rises above mere comedy, for the highly metaphoric speech of Gaudissart is, like Margaritis's metonymic understanding, the harbinger of the new world of capitalism. The comic effects have the very serious goal of stressing new economic ideas that were sweeping Europe. In addition, like other *Scènes de la vie de province*, the story raises important issues like speculation and the relationship between Paris and the provinces.

Throughout this portion of *La Comédie humaine*, we meet characters who migrate from the provinces to Paris. As Balzac explains in his "Préface de la première édition (1839)" of *Le Cabinet des antiques*, "In the provinces, there are three varieties of superior people who are constantly impelled to leave for Paris [...]. The Aristocracy, Industry, and

Talent are eternally drawn to Paris" (4.959). In fact, there is considerable traffic back and forth between the capital city and the provinces. In other stories, Rastignac, the Cointet brothers, and Troubert/Hyacinthe, for example, have sufficient vigor to leave the provinces and lay claim to a place on a larger stage. Some, like Denis Minoret or Denis Rogron who, having succeeded in Paris, then leave the city to retire to a small town in the country. Others, like Savinien de Portenduère, du Bousquier, and Victurnien d'Esgrignon, fail in the capital city and return more or less ignominiously to the provinces, where they can create a less demanding life in line with their abilities. Joseph Bridau and Lucien de Rubempré provide variant examples: having found no success when they go to the provinces, for good or ill they return for another attempt in Paris.

Félix Gaudissart, a *commis voyageur* or traveling salesman, differs from them all, even from other commercial travelers. He rises so far above the ordinary run of "these low end diplomats" (4.562), he is to such a degree "an incomparable traveler, le paragon of his species, a man whose nature possesses to the highest degree the qualities required for his successes" that he has earned the nickname of "illustrious" (4.564). A commercial Bonaparte, he plans extraordinarily well-prepared forays into the provinces, firmly intending to return to Paris from his campaigns a good deal wealthier than when he left. Unlike the peddlers who for centuries had followed similar paths, Gaudissart no longer welcomes commissions "for cotton cloth, jewelry, linens, wines" (4.565). It is only after special pleas that he deigns once again to act as a middleman for the fancy goods that appeal to women (*l'Article-Paris*). Not content to describe the "type" of traveling salesman, as one would find in the ordinary *physiologie*, Balzac turned instead to an "illustrious" individual who marks and depicts "the big transition that [...] joins material exploitation to that of intellectual exploitation" (4.561). As such, after 1830, Gaudissart pretty much leaves fancy goods and the hat trade behind "to leap into the highest spheres of Parisian speculation" (4.566).

"Speculation" had a particular sense for Balzac. Traditionally the word had the meaning of mental forays into abstract, theoretical research, but the Robert dictionary explains that in the 1770s it began to be used to refer to financial or commercial operations destined to profit from market fluctuations. Soon, it was regularly used to refer to the action of foreseeing "an exceptional value from which it will be possible to profit" or "to count, calculate in order to realize a gain" (Larousse, *Grand Dictionnaire*). As Littré makes clear, the word might be used to offer a pejorative description of an "action of betting on something for the sake of profit." For Balzac, as well, the word could have a definitely negative tint. We remember the Baron Hulot of *La Cousine Bette* whose selfish speculations brought an entire family to its knees. The Robert dictionary cites, for a specific example, a sentence from "Ferragus": "Lying becomes for [a particular kind of woman] the foundation of language, and truth is nothing but an exception; they speak truth as they are capriciously or speculatively virtuous" (5.834). In "L'Illustre Gaudissart" the word touches on all of these meanings, though the author uses the term especially to refer to the action of gambling a real, tangible asset on a potential, future gain, whether material, intangible, imaginary, or abstract.

While today one would scarcely apply the word "speculation" to taking out a subscription to a newspaper or magazine, any subscriber who had paid their subscription for forthcoming issues of *Lingua Franca* before it closed its doors, or those who have bought a subscription from door-to-door salespeople, may be more willing to accept Balzac's usage. Likewise, today we hope and expect that life insurance would be anything but speculative. One might become more sympathetic to the way the author used the word on noting that Gaudissart does not seem overly concerned about the possibility of the insurance company going bankrupt. Nor does he worry about the value a customer might put on his own life. As long as the client can pay the initial charges, there is no problem. If the payments are too high, and if the newly insured cannot maintain the payments, he may forfeit everything paid in. The policy will then be void, though Gaudissart will retain his commission. Today, while there are far more ingenious ways for insurance companies to avoid payment of claims than one might imagine, regulation has increased contract compliance and enforcement considerably. In Balzac's day, however, the word "speculation" for the purchase of insurance or a subscription to a publication was all too appropriate.[9]

Gaudissart himself is a "collection of prepared phrases that flow without stopping" (4.562). Having left behind the "business of mechanical and visible things" that occupy most commercial travelers (4.466), he has embraced abstract products, which he terms "thought." "He abandoned," he says, "matter for thought, manufactured products for the infinitely purer elaboration of intelligence" (4.566). In the new France after 1830, "ideas became values" (4.566). Whether or not the salesman understood his importance in the essential task of reshaping business, finance, and culture, he accepted the task of taking the exciting, Parisian ideas to the provinces and by one means or another turning his provincial prey into stockholders, corresponding members, "sometimes subscribers or patrons, but everywhere patsies" (4.567). Unquestionably, the ideas bubbling to the surface in the economic cauldron of Paris needed financing to survive and prosper. In a very real sense, as Sharif Gemie put it, Paris treats "the provinces solely as a source of revenue."[10] Where else but in the provinces could such funds be unearthed? And who else but a Gaudissart could find and lure the money back to be put to work in the modern economy.

Because insurance is so new, even Gaudissart needs to be stuffed with a completely fresh set of enticements and phrases, arguments and responses, all designed to bring the provincial dupes' wealth into the trap. The financial directors of several newspapers recognized his ability at promotion and filled this "living prospectus" (4.568) with the information necessary to sell subscriptions to Saint-Simonian and republican periodicals. Given his predisposition to sales, neither the additional *Journal des Enfants* (*Childrens' Newspaper*), nor the republican periodical posed any difficulties for him, though he needed considerable preparation to represent the Saint-Simonian publication properly. Because of his prodigious memory and intelligence he expeditiously learned the fine points of the financial and philosophical language and quickly mastered the new sales spiels, so that he could set out on his provincial foray with no delay. He has, in short, been enabled to "reason appropriately, so as [...] 'not to put his foot in it'" (4.568). "The king of travelers" (4.568) even condescended to accept a few other commercial and periodical commissions to round out his product mix, since he was going anyway.

At every step, Balzac's story "L'Illustre Gaudissart" emphasizes the use of language at a very limited linguistic level, rather than on a fundamental understanding of what the words, phrases, and arguments mean. The text insists on the process of speech, the speaker and the utterance, on the *signifying*, denuded of the *signified*, the actual meaning of his words. Consequently, the salesman believes that he has what is needed to rise to the heights of power: "If I were to take on the ways politicians talk, I would become a minister [in the government]" (4.571). For Gaudissart, only style and form have importance. There exists no real connection between words and objective reality. Even though he promotes sales that raise money for the tumultuous new society, nothing indicates that he believes the Saint-Simonian cant or would join the movement in attacking private property or the patriarchy, that he is in any sense a social utopian, that he opposes collateral inheritance, or that he believes in the emancipation of women, much less that he would accompany the sect's leader into celibate retreat in 1832. The fact that he has a mistress does not mean that he opposes bourgeois marriage. Indeed, although Gaudissart has firm mastery of the vocabulary and style of the material he sells, there is nothing to make one assert that he is any more involved in either insurance or Saint-Simonianism than necessary to sell subscriptions and gather in his commissions.

Gaudissart himself serves only as a connecting link, joining the high-flying financial future of Paris with the developmentally arrested, thus retarded and backward provinces. "Is not the traveling salesman to ideas what stagecoaches are to people and things? He transports them, puts them in motion, makes them bang up against each other. In the luminous Parisian center, he gets energized with light rays and beams them across sleeping populations" (4.561). His heart is in sales. Though his products, whether fancy goods, newspapers, children's magazines, or life insurance, have obvious potential benefits, he cares little about that. He wants only to sell, and thus bring back thousands of francs of commissions. The apparent conviction in his packaged patter has no necessary relationship with his true beliefs, all the less so in that the payments and products he sells are projected into the future. They are, so to speak, fiat products. They have value like government-issued currency only because he says so, only because his customers believe it. Nonetheless, his words have power. He demands that the customer give him tangible assets today in exchange for the promise of a more or less distant, thus, for the moment, materially inexistent or, at least, intangible result. The assets he collects in the provinces will flow into Paris. He was born lucky, he predicts; he will be a baron, a peer of the realm; he will be rich, and he insists, "[N]o one has ever put one over on me, and no one will ever put one over on me" (4.571).

Gaudissart's lady-friend, Jenny, recognizes that he cares not a whit for whether his customers will benefit, only that he make a commission, and she accuses him of fraud. He will get arrested, she opines (4.571), and will end up imprisoned in Sainte-Pélagie (4.569–70). He confirms her assessment when he tells her he has sold 162 shawls and comments, "On my word, I don't know what they will do with them, unless they return them to the backs of their sheep" (4.573). The newspapers are more difficult to sell, but he carries on. "There is a farmer who thought that the [Saint-Simonian] *Globe* concerned his land, because of the name, and I pushed him into it" (4.574). And, as a demonstration of his peerless ability to take cash in exchange for future development, he "produced two thousand *Enfants* [*Children*]," referring obliquely to the *Journal des Enfants*, another periodical he is marketing (4.547). He uses the vocabulary of a confidence man, as well: "[O]n my oath! We will take them in! They will be taken in! Taken in!" (4.575). Part of the humor grows from the fact that he is perfectly correct to aggrandize his role and differentiate his current work from that of previous commercial travelers: "I have a mission of the highest importance and which should make superior minds consider me a man devoted to bringing light to his country" (4.578).

Balzac's testy but affectionate opinion of the provinces has been clear throughout *Les Scènes de la vie de province* and, indeed, throughout *La Comédie humaine*. French society at a distance from Paris has become stultified, controlled by aging, complacent, ignorant middle-class people who care only for themselves and their self-centered interests. Elsewhere, the novelist gives a delightful list of ridiculous notions bourgeois people accept unquestioningly: for example, Potier, Talma, and Mademoiselle Mars were millionaires ten times over and did not live like other human beings; the great tragedian Talma ate raw meat; the emperor had huge pockets of leather in his vests so that he could dip tobacco by the handfuls, he rode his horse at a gallop up the staircase of the Versailles orangery; and so on (6.69). Such conceits simply enter the provincials' belief systems as random facts without significant connection to reality, but their intellectual energies are fully engaged in divining the activities of their neighbors and in avaricious hoarding. It is for Gaudissart to "go and fish five or six hundred thousand francs from frozen seas, from the lands of the Iroquois, from France!" (4.564). While Parisians tend to be solitary creatures, driving with manic concentration toward their goals of wealth, power, and glory, provincials generally work together to dampen the excessively effervescent peaks of Parisian inventiveness and turn the excitement into something more practically efficacious (4.561). Balzac was convinced that his century would take the force abounding in Parisian innovations and communicate it to the stubbornly indolent and backward provincial masses. The result would be far less extreme than the original impulsion, but the new ideas in particular would become more practical, beneficial, and more general in practice (4.561). Gaudissart functions to spread the word, the word of modernity. It is not an easy task, for few things please Balzac's provincials more than repulsing urban invaders and sending them packing. When, for example, Agathe and Joseph are forced to flee Issoudun in *La Rabouilleuse*, their flight "was celebrated by the entire town as a victory of the provinces over Paris" (4.466). Those of Vouvray are equally delighted to tar Gaudissart with ridicule.

The provincial innkeeper, Vernier, his wife, Margaritis's wife, and eventually the local drycleaner Mitouflet band together to protect their own and overcome the outsider, Gaudissart. Mitouflet enjoys the salesman's discomfiture when it becomes clear that he has been taken in by a madman and arranges things to protect Vernier, who set up the practical joke. Mitouflet convinces the furious Gaudissart, bent on a duel to avenge his honor, not to use swords that might hurt one or the other of the duelists and provides pistols that do not shoot straight. In general, for an erstwhile Parisian to succeed in the provinces, he must embed himself in the local community and gain allies, as Philippe does in *La Rabouilleuse*. Gaudissart attempts to ingratiate himself by learning the correct patter so that the provincial barbarians or "Indians" (4.576) will accept him as one of their own and agree to do as he urges. On the most obvious level, it is Gaudissart's mission, "by purely intellectual operations, to extract the gold from provincial hiding places, to extract it without pain!" (4.564). More importantly, however, this "human machine" (4.562) spreads the new ideas that make capitalism and the Industrial Revolution succeed. The "steam engine called Speculation" is essential to unrolling the future. "How can we forget the admirable maneuvers that mold the intelligence [...] of the most refractory masses and which resemble the untiring polishers whose files smooth the hardest porphyry!" (4.563). As he explains proudly, he is "a man who is committed to enlightening his country" (4.578).

The story in fact implies that the *fou*, Margaritis, personifies provincials to a large degree. One might even say that he represents his neighbors in claiming to be a "banker" (4.585). Unfortunately, when he deposits money in his "territorial Bank," the money is sterile, that is, unproductive. In a similar vein, Margaritis accepts the exact, same newspaper every day without learning anything new, since nothing ever changes in it. He is also something of a living barometer as the seasons pass. In addition, he enjoys walking bareheaded in his vineyard when it rains, instead of taking shelter, like a sensible person. "The *fou*'s most constant occupation is verifying the state of the sky, in relation to its effects on the vines" (4.579). While he *exists*, as he says, when they have guests he does little but mark time, so as to send the visitors home at ten o'clock (4.579–80). He is, nonetheless, capable of giving his wife excellent advice concerning the sale of their wine when his solipsistic madness lessens. Everything turns around himself and his needs. He takes the family's treats and eats them himself. Indeed, "he drank, ate, walked as would a man in perfect health" (4.580). In short, although the exciting urban innovations of the Industrial Revolution penetrate the provinces only with great difficulty, nonetheless, only a *fou*, whether fool or madman, would ignore the extraordinary new world— which, exemplified by Margaritis, is precisely what Balzac's provinces and provincials do. They eat their product and leave nothing for the market.

Away from Paris, the young who have energy and ideas are repressed. It is by no means an accident that Margaritis has no offspring, or that he hoards flour and hides his money, so that even his wife is unable to discover the secret trove (4.580). Elsewhere in Balzac's writings, discouraged young people may, like Athanase Granson, give up on their dreams and commit suicide, while still others, like the *Chevaliers de la Désœuvrance* (Knights of Idleness), fight boredom by wasting themselves in foolish, often destructive, practical jokes. Those who have sufficient courage emigrate, leaving the provinces for Paris or even for foreign climes. Legions simply give up and, like Jacques Brigaut, submit. Death, submission, or foolishness: the choices are few. But, despite the pervasive, entrenched obstacles behind which provincials hide, the new world of changes is unquestionably and unavoidably coming.

Such weighty themes as social progress and sophisticated finance are, of course, hardly common in the lower forms of comedy. Balzac, however, had ambitious goals for expressing and paradoxically illustrating the society he saw and that he predicted. There are several additional indications that Gaudissart is more than a single dimensional character typical of farce, "a hot water faucet that you turn on at will" (4.562). Though one might not admire the salesman, he is humanized by his relationship with Jenny, his ambition, his vanity, and even his anger at being the butt of the provincial tricksters. For all Gaudissart's repeated, emphatic pronouncements that nothing will ever succeed in besting him, most scholars who have published on the story agree that he was not only outwitted, but was also undone by a madman. "[I]n the joyous Vouvray valleys, his commercial infallibility perished" (4.575). In short, Gaudissart, who will eventually be a millionaire and able to start his own bank, has a startling failure in Vouvray, though it turns out to be but a temporary, partial setback. Similarly, despite his boasting about his future successes, readers of *La Comédie humaine* know he will never be a baron, much less a peer. His vainglorious boasting concerning his splendid, aristocratic future comes to naught and leaves him, if not entirely, at least somewhat like a blustering buffoon. If "L'Illustre Gaudissart" were mere farce, we would witness provincial mockery batter the one-dimensional puppet Gaudissart to the floor, with his nose rubbed in his failure, and pass on with little further thought.

He is more than a shallow, farcical creation, however. On reflection, his defeat in Vouvray was declared too soon, for though the object of a crude joke, his failure is by no means complete. After the duel, Gaudissart and the terrified Vernier make peace. The latter even agrees to purchase twenty subscriptions to the *Journal des Enfants*, Margaritis has already taken out a subscription to the same magazine, and, under threat of legal action, Madame Margaritis indemnifies Gaudissart with twenty francs for his loss of the wine that her mad husband sold but did not own and was, thus, unable to deliver. In truth, despite the contrary understanding of those who have written on the work, Gaudissart seems justified in claiming no one has the right to say that the "market town skinned the Illustrious Gaudissart" (4.598). Gaudissart may have been the butt of an unsympathetic practical joke, he may even have been "the greater fool," but he succeeded finally in pocketing a number of commissions and in gaining a profit from his visit to Vouvray.[11]

Gaudissart's imagination disgorges verbal creations that are analogous to the wine that Margaritis sells but does not own. Felman rightly insists that the *fou* Margaritis regularly interprets Gaudissart's metaphors metonymically. I am less convinced, however, by her conclusion that in the end, "Gaudissart's discourse is [...] dislocated by its own echo and itself dissolves in the pure emptiness of language" (40). While Gaudissart is lost in abstract, verbal speculation about the future that has not yet arrived, Margaritis, like all provincials, interprets all words in relation to his own present reality, at least, as he sees it. It is not that the wine he sells does not exist, for it does. It is simply that he does not own it. Margaritis is ignorant of the traditional and very important legal system that allows him to possess and to sell what does not belong to him, and he has no understanding whatsoever of the more modern, perfectly legitimate possibility of selling future produce on contract—an idea that the financial centers of the day appreciated. Although Margaritis is ignorant of abstractions like the Civil Code, Balzac was fully cognizant of the possibilities in such legalities.

During the conversations between the madman and the salesman, Gaudissart's fanciful ideas, abstract financial conceptions, and overarching societal constructs provide amusement as they are juxtaposed with Margaritis's literal understanding governed by in-hand physicality and present world application. The synecdoches of the dialogue, the misunderstandings, the same words repeated with different, unrelated meanings move from Gaudissart's grandiose visions to the madman's conception of the real: the salesman says, for example, "But I go further [...]." Margaritis concludes from this that his companion is leaving (4.584). Gaudissart projects a future death. "'But I am alive,' said the *fou*" (4.485). When Gaudissart persists, asking him "to follow him (*le suivre*)" as he talks of the ramifications of death, Margaritis responds by insisting that he exists: "I am (*Je suis*)" (4.585). Gaudissart discourses on "your intellectual capital"; the vigneron raises the issue of the two large casks of "heady" Vouvray wine that he wishes to sell (4.587). The commercial traveler talks of the superb feast offered by modernity; the *fou* realizes that they then need celebratory wine (4.588). Gaudissart mentions Ballanche, a writer given to mystical interpretations of history; Margaritis thinks of "la planche (the plank)" (4.591). And so on. There is no communication. From Gaudissart's images that are "abstract" in that they do not yet exist, however much they may perhaps play out in some projected future, the madman, like most of his fellow provincials, thinks only of the reality of the here and now outside of Paris. As the typical representative of a provincial, he remains incapable of grasping the application of abstractions that make the modern economy work.

The comedy functions to illustrate one of the Balzacian lessons. Gaudissart is actively involved in this "period of transition, of both transition and progress at the same time!" (4.589), which to Balzac's mind was a very good thing. Only someone who is extremely ignorant or foolish indeed would turn away from such opportunities as exist in the new, capitalistic world. In denigrating the Saint-Simonian *Globe*, Vernier unknowingly insists on the parallels between the provincials and the madman: "By my most sacred word of honor, old Margaretis says things that make more sense [than the *Globe*]" (4.595). The fact that this mention of honor has been highlighted through five previous occurrences emphasizes the word and insists on the substance of the claims in question. If a madman makes more sense than the anti-capitalist, socialist Saint-Simonian newspaper, few would have great faith in the Saint-Simonians.[12]

Vernier's explanation for his antipathy toward the *Globe* is also significant. He says scornfully that the *Globe* "preaches a religion whose first commandment of God commands, if you please, not to inherit from father and mother!" (4.595). The French verb *succéder* is a significant choice of words. While it can mean "inherit," the primary definition is to "come after someone, so as to take over his responsabilities, his dignity, his position [...]. By extension, *to inherit from one's father the management of a factory*, to assume his affairs" (Robert). The liberal Saint-Simonians did indeed oppose many inheritances, in the hope of weakening capitalism, just as they discouraged slavishly following in the footsteps of a father, whether apprenticing or taking over the family business. Balzac is apparently using the newspaper and the sect's beliefs to insist on the stagnation of the patriarchal provinces, where children are expected to remain in the rigid roles laid out by their families. Elsewhere, for example in *Le Curé de Tours*, the novelist focuses on the importance of intangible assets that, while beyond the ken of most provincials, are essential in the new economy.

Provincials may be shrewd in selling their crops, they may work with or against their fellows to get the best price (as in *Eugénie Grandet*), but their deepest desire is to exchange their tangible harvest for tangible gold. Nonetheless, though gold has both inherent and exchange value that fiat money does not have (we remember that Old Grandet bought his gold so that he could sell it later at a better price and that he sold his brother's debt at increasing profit), the metal has disadvantages, particularly in relation to transport. In the industrial economy, money must be freely and easily exchanged. For all the dangers inherent in fiat money, subscriptions, and insurance, people need to be able to conceptualize the future actualization of a present goal and work to bring it about, abilities that are baffling to most of Balzac's provincials. They need in short to be able to speculate, exchanging intangible, current wealth for the expectation of future fulfillment.[13]

The story of Gaudissart losing a minor skirmish and experiencing a small setback in Vouvray effectively emphasizes the character and the social role of provincials in this changing world of the Industrial revolution. While the provincials are sadly and stubbornly retrograde, Balzac's "L'Illustre Gaudissart" demonstrates the absolute necessity of their involvement in this world of invention, colonizing, communication, transportation, trade, and merchandizing that was inflicting major changes in everyone's life. Society-wide participation was essential to facilitate industrial and financial activity. Abstract ideas that represented opportunities had to be transported to the provinces, and provincials needed to be encouraged to unearth their treasure from its miry "bank." Money should be put to work—a major lesson from "L'Illustre Gaudissart"—so that the capitalistic society growing from the Industrial Revolution would result in spreading opportunity and prosperity throughout the country, from the urban centers to the provincial peripheries.

Notes

1. Péraud, *Le Crédit dans la poétique balzacienne* (Paris: Garnier, 2012); Persson, *An Economic History of Europe: Knowledge, Institutions and Growth, 600 to the Present* (Cambridge: Cambridge UP, 2010); Piketty, *Capital in the Twenty-First Century*, trans. Arthur Goldhammer (Cambridge, MA: Harvard UP, 2014).
2. Balzac, Letter of 8 February 1834, *Correspondance: 1832–1835*, t. 2 (Paris: Garnier, 1962) 463–64.
3. Bourget, Letter of 19 January 1834, *Correspondance* 2.451.
4. Bérard, ed., "Préface," *Le Curé de Tours; La Grenadière; L'Illustre Gaudissart* (Paris: Garnier-Flammarion, 1971) 34.
5. Guyon, respectively: "Balzac héraut du capitalisme naissant," *Europe* 429 (1965): 26, 140; "Introduction," *L'Illustre Gaudissart; La Muse du department* (Paris: Garnier, 1970) xiii–xlix, esp. xxii, xxvii.
6. "Introduction," *L'Illustre Gaudissart* (Pléiade) 4.546.
7. Soshana Felman, "Folie et discours chez Balzac: 'L'Illustre Gaudissart,'" *Littérature* 5 (1972): 34–44. Andrew Watts reasonably suggests that it can also be seen as a very realistic opposition between the capital and the provinces, between international markets and "France's Turkey"—"An Exercise in International Relations, or the Travelling Salesman in Touraine: Balzac's 'L'Illustre Gaudissart'," *Currencies: Fiscal Fortunes and Cultural Capital in Nineteenth-Century France*, ed. Sarah Capitanio, et al. (Oxford: Peter Lang, 2005) 164, 167, 170.
8. Balzac, Letter of 30 January 1834, *Correspondance*, 457.
9. Michael Tilby gives a useful introduction to nineteenth-century insurance and the reasons for Balzac's mistrust of the business: "Playing with Risk: Balzac, the Insurance Industry and the Creation of Fiction," *Journal of European Studies* 4.2 (2011): 107–22.
10. Gemie, "Balzac and the Moral Crisis of the July Monarchy," *European History Quarterly* 19 (1989): 4.652.
11. Andrew Watts arrives at a similar conclusion—*Preserving the Provinces: Small Town and Countryside in the Work of Honoré de Balzac* (Oxford: Peter Lang, 2007) 235.
12. Franc Schuerewegen, *Balzac contre Balzac: Les Cartes du lecteur* (Paris and Toronto: Paratexte et C.D.U.-S.E.D.E.S, 1990) 93–95, draws attention to the fact that the term "word of honor" (*la parole d'honneur*) appears six times in "L'Illustre Gaudissart," an unusually

high repetition in the span of a short story. In the mouth of Jenny or M. Vernier, it seems to mean what it says, though for Gaudissart, it has been emptied of significance to become a mere epithet.

13. See above, in this regard, Chap. 5 on *Le Curé de Tours*.

CHAPTER 8

A Provincial Muse: *La Muse du département*

Adultery and marriage, apostasy and faith, journalism and literature: in other times and in other hands the treatment of such antitheses might have drawn eloquent praise or outrage. But this is Balzac's *La Muse du département* (*The Departmental Muse*—1843), written in a period of great turmoil, when he thought the Church had lost the sense of its high calling, when its priests were willing to serve debased desires for social position and wealth,[1] and when the period's "loathsome literature," according to M. de Clagny, "rests on adultery" (4.680). Oppositions between the debased present and memories of a grander past were the stuff of daily life. Balzac's novel, set in the French Provinces and Paris, provided the writer with another opportunity to dissect the rural, tradition-bound society while considering journalism and literature. The fact that Paris itself takes up an important part of the book, as in *La Rabouilleuse*, throws more light on the relationship existing and growing between the provinces and the capital city. As always, Balzac chose his settings for appropriateness. Nicole Mozet has demonstrated in this regard that each city and town is integrated historically and geographically into Balzac's tales. Among other traits, the author frequently played on the phonic associations and linguistic etymologies of the towns' names. There is, for example, the name, Sancerre, which reminds of the practice of sincere, honest Greek sculptors. Their work was *sans cire* (*without wax*) that inept Greek sculptors used to cover nature's or their own mistakes in their finished work. By setting his story in the phonetically similar

Sancerre, he promises to present reality without subterfuge, giving the whole truth about the provincial middle class and especially about journalism, an industry that had recently expanded prodigiously to employ many writers and influence the whole of society. He raises the issues less to comment on religion and art than to vilipend journalism. One might think newspapers and reviews represent a subject of ephemeral, thus, minor importance. Still, because journalism is merely a semblance of art, in Balzac's recasting of Plato's opposition between imitation and reality,[2] it degrades much that it touches. Balzac announces with heavy disdain that its practitioners belong "to this group of writers called *hacks* or *pen pushers*. In Paris, these days, the journalism trade consists of giving up the pretense of being anything more than a mere job" (4.733).

Bardèche offers a capsule description of one of the novel's main characters, Etienne Lousteau, the journalist picked up from *Illusions perdues* (1837–43) and highlighted in *La Muse*: he is a man "who believes in nothing, a columnist who has trailed about behind the scenes, an easy make from the literary bohemia, who has gotten in the habit of putting his prostitute's soul in everything."[3] Shortly after his arrival in Sancerre, Lousteau makes a telling distinction between journalism and literature. Some proofs have arrived, and Dinah asks, "What? Literature follows you all this way?" No, Lousteau explains, rather than anything so important as literature, it is merely the next installment of a story he has coming out in a review (4.703). Later, the narrator makes the point patent for anyone who has not understood: Lousteau "was working for three or four literary reviews. But, don't worry! he engaged no artistic conscientiousness in what he produced" (4.733). Lousteau is vain (4.786), lazy (4.759), and lacks both courage (4.763) and willpower (4.759). In every way he is a lightweight (4.786). As he says himself, "I am, speaking of literature, a very secondary man" (4.770), and as the narrator explains, he is "an author of the second order, [...] one of the most distinguished serial writers" (4.631). It is then suitable that Lousteau's name suggest a *loustic*, a professional fool or facetious person, and that he would become involved not with *the* Muse at the highest level of art, not even with "*the* French Muse," but merely with "Dinah, the departmental Muse," in short, nothing but a provincial muse. Perhaps even more cruelly, because the name of Dinah's home village of Saint-Satur brings together the images of "holiness" and "saturnalia," this amateur poetess is referred to as the Sappho of Saint-Satur.[4] She is "one of hundreds of tenth muses who ornament the provinces" (4.735), the Sancerre Muse (4.745), a second-rate muse, thus perfectly appropriate for a second-rate writer like Lousteau.

Though Balzac's novel continued to bear the working title *Dinah Piédefer* in the serialized publication in the *Messager*, the author announced a new, definitive title to Achille Brindeau on 12 March 1843. Balzac claimed *La Muse du département* was "more comic and more explicit." Certainly, it draws ironic attention to the arts. I suspect there was as well another reason for the change: because the novelist's onomastics were perfectly obvious to him, so much so in fact that he assumed his audience would read his names as easily as his stories,[5] he may have turned away from *Dinah Piédefer* as a title because it overly emphasizes apostasy to the detriment of the novel's primary focus on journalism and the degradation of art. In a period of constant, front-page archeological discoveries and controversial discussion about the Christian tradition, Balzac could count on his audience's perhaps rudimentary but real knowledge of the Bible. Dinah's biblical eponym was, of course, Jacob's and Leah's daughter who, on going out to "see the daughters of the land" (Gen. 34.1), was violated by Shechem, a Hivite and the son of Hamor. Though Shechem loved and wanted to marry Dinah, she had been "defiled" (Gen. 34.2). The Hebrew word for the King James translation of "defiled" clearly indicates that Shechem forced himself on her.[6] When Hamor came to Jacob with an offer of marriage, Jacob agreed on condition that the men of Shechem's family be circumcised, that is, convert to worship of the God of Abraham. Jacob's sons, however, were bent on revenge. After the males of Hamor's city had been circumcised and "were sore" (Gen. 34.25), Dinah's brothers came and treacherously killed them all. The name then suggests the Genesis story's themes of rape, apostasy, and deceit.

If "Dinah" does not remind readers of the mass circumcision and turning away from the Hivite gods for that of Jacob, which is a clear case of apostasy, her family name, Piédéfer, may be enough to evoke the concept. It is an anagram of *père défi* (father defied). Balzac's Dinah abjures the protestant faith of her grandfather Abraham (4.635). The pseudonym she chooses for her poetry, Jan Diaz, likewise emphasizes the theme, since Juan Diaz was a well-known Spanish apostate of the sixteenth century. In addition, Dinah marries into the La Baudraye family that descends from "a certain departmental magistrate named Milaud, whose ancestors were rabid Calvinists, [but who] were converted to Catholicism at the time of the revocation of the Edict of Nantes." As a reward, Louis XIV gave them the fief, arms, and title of the true La Baudrayes (4.632). Dinah and her husband's family then have apostasy in common.

Finally, the novel reinforces the theme with Dinah's long, adulterous affair. Although Hosea constitutes the most vivid instance of linking adultery and sexual license to apostasy, the themes are commonly linked in other biblical writings. As one biblical exegete puts it, "Sensuality produces religious whoredom and religious whoredom again issues into physical whoredom."[7] To cap off all these indications of apostasy, Dinah converted to Catholicism "for no reason other than ambition" (4.635). Indeed, her conversion paid off richly. The archbishop took an interest in her, and she was able to marry an aristocrat of some wealth. Dinah is then both figuratively and in reality an apostate, and her given, family, and married names suggest apostasy, as does the literary pseudonym she chooses.

The novel's revised title, *La Muse du département*, the numerous references to Dinah as the "Muse of Sancerre" (4.745) or the "dazed Muse" (4.751), comparisons to Mme de Staël (4.753), George Sand (4.668), Camille Maupin (4.662), and her "grotesque nickname of the Sappho of Saint-Satur" (4.665) have the function, however, of insisting on her relationship to literature and suggesting that her most pertinent, if not most important, apostasy is in respect to art. Sappho was of course the great Greek lyric poetess of the sixth century B.C. One legend has it that Sappho, spurned by the handsome Phaon, committed suicide by leaping into the sea from a great cliff. Balzac's Sappho lives at the end of a mountainous path called the *Casse-cou* (*Neck-breaker* 4.648). Sappho was also called the Tenth Muse, as was Dinah (4.736). Some consider the Tenth Muse to be Mnemosyne (memory), the mother of the nine Muses. Dinah is suitably "[g]ifted with a wonderful memory" (4.644), and, for a while, she decides to be a "mother" to Lousteau (4.774, 780). The two children she later has by Lousteau open new complications, since legally they belong to her husband, La Baudraye, though his paternity is not otherwise possible. What makes it all worse is that by the time the local provincials began to call her the "Sapho de Saint-Satur" (4.642), the nickname was dreadfully passé, as one might expect of residents in the hinterlands. As Mary Sherrif points out, "This tradition [tying Sappho to creation] reached its climax only at the beginning of the nineteenth century when Mme de Staël associated her poet Corinne with Sappho and Vigée-Lebrun depicted the novelist as this Sappho–Corinne in an allegorical portrait made in 1806."[8]

The Muses had significant roles both as artists and as inspiration. Dinah writes poetry for a relatively short time. Although few would admire the examples of her verse that Balzac provides for our delectation, as Anthony Pugh points out, the novel has worse poetry,[9] and as Guyon states in reference to the verses of Dinah's *Paquita*, "I for one do not find that so ridiculous!" (4.117). Still, the novel's narrator has a much harsher judgment—"[I]n another time, [the poem] would have been held in contempt" (4.663). A number of critics have taken this judgment to indicate that Balzac confused Dinah's portrayal, perhaps because he changed his mind about her, since they find it unlikely that a superior woman could write contemptible verse,[10] but it seems to me rather a matter of realism. Few knew as well as Balzac that it was not enough to have talent and a reputation for superiority. As the narrator puts it, "[N]o great talent exists without great will power [...] The will can and should be more a matter for pride than talent. If talent is germinated in a cultivated predisposition, the will is a conquest heroically made moment by moment over instincts, over repressed, dominated tastes, over fantasies and hindrances, over all kinds of difficulties" (4.759–60). Dinah eventually stops writing, except when she ghostwrites for her lover, the hack journalist, Etienne Lousteau. This constitutes a turning away from art for journalism, and, as a result, she is an aesthetic apostate.

The text refers to her as "a superior woman," repeating the label with heavy irony, thus calling into question the social standards of Dinah's admirers. The text explains her lofty position so frequently and so unconvincingly that her "superiority" becomes less believable and finally dissolves in mockery.[11] "The superior woman made Sancerre people burst with pride" (4.632). Of course, "France has an exorbitant number of superior women" (4.632). "Sancerre's superior woman lived in the La Baudraye house" (4.632). Indeed, on learning that "she was seventeen when she converted [from Calvinism], uniquely because of ambition, you may judge her superiority" (4.635). When locals saw her dressed in blue velvet, it "confirmed the superiority of this beautiful young lady" (4.640). On being admitted to her fashionably furnished home and seeing her play the piano without being begged, people's conception of her "superiority took on enormous proportions" (4.640). The exaggerated praise of her cultivation, taste, and refinement eventually subjected her to jealous mockery and criticism for her "pedantry, since she spoke correctly [... The narrator adds, w]hen everyone is hunchbacked, a lovely figure becomes a monstrosity" (4.642). Women stopped visiting her. When she asked Monsieur de Clagny about it, he explained, "You are too superior for other women to like you" (4.642). Her male guests "said to Monsieur de La Baudraye: 'How fortunate you are to have a superior woman.... And he finally said, 'I am fortunate to have a superior woman, etc.' Madame

Piédefer [...] allowed herself to say such things as, 'My daughter who is a very superior woman'" (4.642–43). Should readers be tempted to read literally, the narrator says pointedly that she was a "woman whose apparent superiorities were false and her hidden superiorities real" (4.651). And, of course, even Dinah comes to think of herself as "superior" (4.653). How could she not?

One of the more significant impediments to Dinah's rising to the pinnacles of artistic success is her provincialism.

> However great, however beautiful, however strong may be a girl born in any department at all, if, like Dinah Piédefer, she marries in the provinces and if she remains there, she will soon become a provincial woman. Despite her firm plans, the sublime being hidden in this fresh soul is invaded by clichés, mediocre ideas, careless dress, vulgar growths, until it is done, and the plant wastes away [...] From their youth, provincial girls see only provincial people around them, they invent nothing better, they can only choose among the mediocrities. Their provincial fathers marry their daughters only to provincial boys. No one would ever think of mixing the races. The spirit degenerates inescapably [...]. Talented people, artists, superior men, every rooster with magnificent plumage flies to Paris. (4.652)

Married at seventeen years of age, Dinah's older husband is variously described as a "dwarf" (4.648), a "runt" (4.650), and a provincial miser (4.649) with "a sickly constitution" but a "heart of bronze" (4.650). Because we know that prior to his marriage he suffers from "enforced virtue" (4.634), and are told that years after her marriage, Dinah still maintains her "conjugal innocence" (4.647), we may reasonably infer that, though extremely capable at handling money and at agronomy, he is sexually impotent, which makes her designation as "the Sappho of Saint-Satur" even more cruel. Sappho, of course, was thought to be a lesbian.

Unfortunately, surrounded and relentlessly praised by doting nonentities, "Dinah became, alas! a provincial woman" (4.652). Balzac even advances the opinion that she might be saved by a truly outstanding lover. "Still, in the country, if the husbands have no superiority, there is even less in bachelors. Consequently, when a provincial woman commits her little sin, being enamored of a so-called handsome fellow or a local dandy," her failure is exacerbated (4.653). She becomes ridiculous because her choice is necessarily inferior. "This phenomenon is one of the natural results of provincial life" (4.655). Poor Dinah, through no fault of her own, is condemned. Her decision to become a poet does not take into consideration the progressive calcification of her own character that has made that noble profession virtually impossible for her. The fact that she lacks the stimulus of Paris and is circumscribed by mediocrity encourages her to settle into the role of a provincial woman.

Even if Balzac had not discussed the matter of will power, energy, and work so frequently and at such length, his own case serves as an instructive example. Balzac's initial, creative efforts perhaps did not surpass Dinah's in quality. His own judgment is in his refusal to accept the attribution of all those early pot boilers attributed to various pseudonyms. And even in the early 1840s when, except for brief periods of depression, he knew that he was a writer of considerable importance, his continuing travails through successive sets of proofs is chronicled in his letters to Mme Hanska and should be obvious to anyone who has seen the results of his work. In Dinah, Balzac created a young woman of exceptional abilities and talent who, unfortunately, has not been honed by the normal struggles of those artists who succeed. Her first, faltering efforts are published, idolized by her acquaintances, and then, before she can go on and gain real skill, discouraged. The vicount de Chargeboeuf, Monsieur de Clagny, and Monsieur Gravier are all waiting for the beautiful young woman to mature and to fall like a ripe fruit into the arms of one or the other. Unfortunately for the hopeful lovers, several Parisians arrive at just the right time to interfere with their plans.

Dinah's husband Jean-Athanase-Polydore Milaud de La Baudraye's given names may provide insight into his impact on the novel's plot. The etymological "grace of the Lord" or "God gives" of the first of his given names, "Jean,"[12] may imply the help the Restoration Catholic Church provided him in collecting on the loans his father made to various aristocrats during the emigration. The church's blessing, then, provides the base for his fortune and gives him a socially advantageous wife. La Baudraye's financial enterprises are moreover extraordinarily successful. If he had died early on, Dinah's "remarriage" to Lousteau would have provided "much gold" (Polydore) to the couple, though the journalist's hopes and dreams are frustrated by the miser's longevity (Athanase—"undying"). M. de Clagny is devastated to learn that Lousteau's love for Dinah grows from "self-interest" (4.764), but Lousteau's sexual exploitation of Mme de La Baudraye is overshadowed by her husband's masterful manipulation of both her and her inheritance in order to provide himself with heirs, a significant fortune, and an enviable social position. Monsieur de La Baudraye was well aware that according to the Civil Code, he was the father of all of his wife's children. What was a problem for Monsieur de Restaud in "Gobseck," since he worried about his family bloodlines, was an advantage for the impotent La Baudraye, who needed heirs.

Despite Monsieur de La Baudraye's success, he remains a provincial, and it is no accident that Balzac's contemporaries recognized La Baudraye as an inverted rendering of "La" Reybaud (the deputy Chapuys-Montlaville gave a broad hint to the key when he attacked *La Muse du département* in the Chamber of Deputies).[13] Mme Reybaud was the author of a book on Protestantism and wrote many serialized novels about the life of small provincial towns. For readers, who like Chapuys-Montlaville decipher Balzac's onomastic reversal, La Baudraye signifies the provinces. It is but one more indication of the importance of the July Monarchy reality as Balzac grapples with its sociological interactions. When Dinah marries, it is to be expected that she begins a narrow, stultifying provincial life. After all, the text insists on two occasions that Dinah's spouse is an insect (4.769, 779). But if La Baudraye/Reybaud suggests the provinces, the names point to journalism, as well, since it was well known that Mme Reybaud's husband, Charles, was editor in chief of the *Constitutionnel*, and his brother, Louis, ran *Le Corsaire*.

The novel leaves no doubt that Dinah used literature to compensate for her frustrations (4.657, 661), which may not constitute the best of motivations, but it is "what explains certain poets" (4.657). While readers might sympathize and excuse her amateurish work, the consequences of quitting cannot be mitigated, for without constant exercise, the "muse of Sancerre" (4.745) can never hope to improve the quality of her poetry. On realizing that she has offended her husband by allowing her verse to reveal the state of their unconsummated marriage, "she promised to never again write a verse, and kept her word" (4.665).

Writing requires ongoing practice to hone skills. Great writing requires assiduous practice to hone skills. This fact is implicit in the words of Father Duret: "Don't write anything else," he warns Dinah, "you would no longer be a woman, you would be a poet" (4.661). Balzac understood this advice very well, and he never allowed anything to impede his constant struggle to produce outstanding literary works. While Jules Janin tossed off minor pieces to satisfy momentary financial needs, Alexandre Dumas *père* hired "slaves" to increase his production, and Eugène Sue consistently chose quantity over quality, Balzac differed. He made special arrangements and paid extra to have several sets of proofs so he could continue revising until his text satisfied his exacting standards (he exploited successive proofs the way today's writers might use computer printouts). He imprisoned himself at his desk for long periods with the self-imposed tasks of rewriting; in short, he refused to make significant compromises because of financial need, mistresses, or, until close to the end, sickness.[14] As he put it, "Certainly, the mind obeys nothing but its own laws; it recognizes neither the necessities of life, nor the imperatives of honor. You don't produce a beautiful work because a wife dies, or in order to pay demeaning debts, or to feed children. [...] Elite people keep their minds in a usable condition, the way valiant knights once kept their arms in a state of readiness. They subdue laziness, they refuse to indulge in enervating pleasures, or only give in to the small degree allowed by the extent of their faculties" (4.759). Balzac's letters chronicle and his manuscripts and proofs testify to his commitment to Herculean labors and little sleep that distinguish him from the likes of Dinah and Lousteau. More and more scholars and critics recognize, despite the facile condemnations of such writers as Emile Faguet or Martin Turnell, that the end results of Balzac's arduous creative process are masterful.[15] Unlike Lousteau who only seems to create, Balzac demanded an original vision, commitment to art, and a terminal masterpiece. There is an enormous gulf between the original desire, whether attitude or goal, and the final completed creation.

The story Balzac tells in *La Muse du département* presented a significant challenge. How, after all, could one make a female failure interesting? There was, of course, a great novel published a score of years previously that told the tale of such a failure, not of a woman, but of a man. Balzac knew Constant's masterwork well. As Balzac had his character Camille say in his *Béatrix* of 1839, "*Adolphe*, this dreadful book [...] has only told of Adolphe's pain. But those of the woman? eh? He has not observed them sufficiently to paint them for us" (2.773). While Balzac is not being entirely fair, there is no question that Constant focused on the epigone, leaving Ellénore in a barely differentiated background. Perhaps it was Gustave Planche's "gloss" (4.775), giving equal weight to the two characters, that made Balzac realize that such balance was in fact not the case with Constant's novel.[16] As Alison Fairlie understood, in alluding to *Adolphe* (1816), Balzac "has in a sense used [the novel] as the equivalent of the classical author's treatment of ancient and familiar myth: trebly suggestive in underlining the permanence of certain experiences."[17] Balzac's use of *Paul et Virginie* in *Pierrette* was similar. In both cases he tells a more detailed story than the original and thus creates an interlocking structure (see above, Chap. 4). In *La Muse du department*, he needs little to make

Lousteau come alive, for by alluding to *Adolphe* he brings into his novel Constant's feckless, unstable, brilliantly lucid character who is too self-absorbed to be capable of love for Ellénore and too flaccid to break away. Neither Adolphe nor Lousteau loved or indeed were capable of loving the women who committed themselves to them. By referring repeatedly to *Adolphe*, Balzac leaves no question about his desire to attach the earlier novel's psychological analysis firmly to Lousteau and to emphasize it. Of course, there are differences. Lousteau, unlike the wealthy Adolphe, has so little fortune that he can seemingly do nothing but build debt. Indeed, one of his excuses for not breaking with Dinah is his hope that her husband will pass out of the picture so that she might inherit a substantial fortune (4.751). And while Lousteau continues his sexual pleasures in the demi-monde, despite his ongoing concubinage with Dinah, there is no indication that Adolphe was ever unfaithful to his mistress.

Dinah does not follow the normal provincial pattern of choosing to have a brief affair with one of the local men; she settles rather on the disreputable journalist Etienne Lousteau, a sophisticated Parisian. When she discovers she is pregnant, she follows her letters that have been unanswered for two months and corners her lover trying to arrange a very profitable marriage with a girl who has likewise become pregnant, though by another man. While Lousteau tries to make it look as though he is giving up the opportunity of a lifetime for Dinah, in fact the other pregnant girl's mother has learned of Lousteau's provincial philandering and declares him unsuitable. She arranges her daughter's marriage with her notarial husband's clerk. Dinah, then, gains her paramour Lousteau by default. Deceived as to his motive, she is delighted that Lousteau has chosen her, and they begin their life together. By no means as clever as a courtesan, she promises to be his slave (4.750). She is overwhelmed by "a love that is so true, on the one hand, and so well played, on the other" (4.758), though she quickly becomes aware of the poverty stalking this second-rate journalist. It is not long until she decides to economize by providing his meals and serving him as a house maid. Like Adolphe's mistress, her scandalous behavior has brought about her rejection by society. Even her childhood friend, Anna de Fontaine, snubs her (4.754, 779). Neither Constant's Ellénore nor Adolphe needed to worry about money, though the reader is regularly informed about the sources of the funds that meet their expenses. Lousteau, however, combines the ways of both a spendthrift and a shirker, and is less and less capable of supporting the couple. Dinah arranges an allowance. Lousteau's contribution to their relationship sinks to little more than charm and sperm. Perhaps for this reason, when the baby is born he feels the need to announce that he has sired a child with the Baroness de La Baudraye, borrowing from the contemporary reality of Jules Janin's contemptible stunt when the Marquise de La Carte gave birth to their illicit child (4.1426n1).

After failing as a poet, Dinah tries to succeed as Lousteau's muse. "Dinah wanted to be necessary, she wanted to restore energy to this man who was beginning to enjoy his weakness [...], she found subjects for him, she sketched in the basic outline, and if need be she wrote entire chapters. She renewed the veins of this dying talent with fresh blood; she gave him her ideas and her conclusions. More than once, by dictating, correcting, or finishing up the next installments of his columns, she saved Etienne's self-esteem when he was despairing about his lack of ideas" (4.765–66). There is, however, the converse to Balzac's law that excellence is impossible without the will. It is simply put and repeatedly exemplified in *La Comédie humaine*. Here we confront the paired truth: failure awaits the weak willed. However lacking Lousteau was in the drive to succeed, he was by no means stupid. He recognizes Dinah's potential—"This woman is *made to produce copy*" (4.736), and he later tells her that she has "one of those beautiful minds that would make a poet's fortune" (4.780). When her financial situation deteriorates to the point of becoming truly oppressive (largely because Lousteau is squandering their funds in the demi-monde), she stops caring for herself. She even wears nothing but the inexpensive black clothing of poor people. "She stinks black" (4.766, 771). Still, she turns to the one talent she might be able to exploit. She begins once again to write. Not surprisingly, her aesthetic skills improve as she takes up her pen once more. Dinah's role as the nurturing, care-providing mistress morphs into that of an enabling mother figure for Lousteau. Her story of La Palférine in "Un Prince de la Bohème" that she wrote for Lousteau and under his byline demonstrates that she is no longer a neophyte.[18] Written by Dinah, an imaginary character of the novelist's invention, it shows up later as a real creation by Balzac himself. Unlike Balzac's early, unacknowledged work, he not only put his name on this story, but also included it in *La Comédie humaine*. To return to the fictional world of *La Muse du département*, once again material and personal considerations come between Dinah and her art. She senses "that Lousteau turned to her only when he had nothing better to do [...], when the voice of common sense, dignity, family interest, all the things that go under what the Restoration called 'public morality' (thus avoiding the words, 'Catholic religion') were added to hurts that were rather too painful." She sets in motion the machinery for breaking with Lousteau and reconciling with her husband (4.777). She will write no more.

Dinah makes Monsieur de Clagny understand the power of her love (4.773). Indeed, she is incapable of controlling it, and Balzac compares this destructive addiction to magnetism. She sacrifices everything to Lousteau's tastes, even her beauty (4.771). "[S]he was so much a part of him that she lost the consciousness of her own being" (4.771). Even after breaking with Lousteau, she is unable to resist the temptation of his presence. When the journalist comes to beg money from her, she disappears for a dozen days. Balzac thus reminds his readers of Stendhal's analysis. There are loves that are so violent that ordinary measures provide no protection. "In nature, these varieties of violent situations do not end, as they do in books, by death or by cleverly arranged catastrophes. They end much less poetically by revulsion, by the withering of all the flowers of the soul, by the vulgarity of habit, but very often by another passion that strips women of the attractions that traditionally surround them. But when [...] there is a particularly demeaning hurt, one of these cowardly acts that men allow no one to see but women whom they think they still rule, the women are overwhelmed with disgust, with disillusionment" (4.777). Following Stendhal, whom the text proclaims the great analyst of love, Balzac lists stages of affection: "heart love, head love, passion, capricious love, love of common tastes" (4.772). Helped by her mother and her confessor, Dinah recognizes that distance is the only solution to the terrible effects of what Stendhal called "amour-passion." Unable to resist Lousteau, she leaves Paris for the provinces to devote herself to her family and, the text implies, to give birth to a daughter (4.790).

Although Dinah was marked by immense devotion and talent, she was poorly matched to a second-rate hack. She settles on a lesser writer to inspire. Nonetheless, Balzac makes it clear that she is not entirely to blame for her failure. Though a beautiful, talented, intelligent, subtle, in truth, potentially superior woman (e.g., 4.642), by the time she is ready for a lover, provincial life and marriage have so affected her that she is no longer capable of choosing a suitable partner for "her sexual peccadillo [*sa petite faute*]."[19] She illustrates Balzac's understanding of the process that takes place among provincial wives: "[T]he mind necessarily deteriorates" (4.652). During the period when commitment to an exceptional man might have saved Dinah, there are none immediately available. "One of the most agreeable ways a woman can flatter herself is to feel as though she is important in the life of a superior man that she herself has knowingly chosen" (4.653). Dinah was preserved from the local crop of country dandies by "the feeling she had been given about her superiority" (4.653).

When an outstanding man finally does arrive in Sancerre in the person of Bianchon, she passes him by. There are several reasons for her decision. (1) Bianchon has to leave soon, (2) the "straightforward common sense, the perspicacious gaze of a vitally superior man made Dinah uncomfortable" (4.719), and (3) Bianchon perhaps sincerely leads her to believe that she can have an important effect on Lousteau: "Believe me," Bianchon tells her, "he needs to be seriously loved, and if he changes his way of life, his talent will gain" (725). She then chooses Lousteau, and, despite her ministry as muse, "Etienne produced little literature and was considerably indebted" (752). It may be that the characteristics which Balzac gives Dinah would have been enough to make her a great writer, if she had been born in Paris, if she had not been held down by her liaison with a mediocre person, if she had had the will and the courage to continue her efforts. Instead, she becomes enamored of a failure, and while illustrating the mediocrity of journalists and journalism, her love affair follows the path Stendhal describes in *De l'amour*. Balzac's allusion to *Adolphe* allows him to borrow the previous work's intensity to illuminate the interpersonal and social outworking of *La Muse du département*, while completing it with the vivid description of Dinah's self-immolation. Although Lousteau's history is only sketched in here, the emphasis on an allusion to Constant's hero makes it seem as though Adolphe too had everything necessary but willpower and courage. Lousteau "had more than once let things slip that allowed Dinah to understand how much his talent had been diminished by poverty, perverted by bad examples, thwarted by difficulties that were too much for his courage" (4.758). Balzac will return to the sorts of choices Lousteau made in *Illusions perdues* with the brilliant, talented, effeminate, personable but indolent Lucien de Rubempré.

Dinah brings the novel's various themes together in her apostasy, adultery, love, and journalistic writing. All four can be considered lapses or misappropriations. Just as the apostate was traditionally considered to have profaned faith to satisfy greed and elicit personal benefits, the adulterer has misused sex for mere pleasure. Balzac was convinced that, as adulterers prostitute marriage, journalists prostitute art. Journalists merely seek themes or judgments that they can develop in amusing ways. "Since this is the way it is, the profession suits lazy minds, people without the sublime ability to imagine or who, possessing it, do not have the courage to cultivate it."[20] Journalistic reviewing has no consistency, no comprehensive understanding, no "lucid overview of a period's tendencies" (4.761). It is frivolous, ephemeral, shallow, and, indeed, dishonorable, for it lacks standards and impartial integrity. Too often it succumbs to pragmatic pressure, whether commercial, political, or social. With Olympian disdain, Balzac looked down his nose at journalists. They are mere "acrobats who, as long as they have legs, do tricks to make a living" (4.761).

The novel does not develop the understanding of other kinds of journalistic writing and practice in the same way, though the narrator mentions that even writing criticism as practiced by the newspapers of his time could pervert a serious writer, who needs to be committed to a point of view that cannot change according to other influences. He also notes that practitioners of the trade regularly cultivate serialized novels and the short story, both considered minor genres.[21] Lousteau dashes off his articles, columns, reviews, and fiction to pay the tab for what matters most to him: his way of life, his amusements. He does reviews, for they produce the additional income that he gains by selling the books given him for evaluation. Lousteau's days "were filled by dinners, his evenings by the theatre, his mornings by his friends, by visits, by loafing around town. His columns, his articles and the two short stories he wrote each year for the daily papers were the taxes that he paid on this happy life" (4.734). This the narrator tells us directly. The rest we must glean from the examples. Certainly, the novel emphasizes the degree to which journalism, however much Balzac despised it, was changing society. It was one of the most influential social forces of the nineteenth century, and Balzac will return to it in *Illusions perdues*.

According to the *La Muse du department*, society is infused with stories and fragments of stories. "[A]ll clever people have a certain fund of anecdotes" (4.688), which they may have heard (4.682), read in a novel (4.775) or newspaper (4.697), almost witnessed (4.688), experienced (4.661), or even found on printer's sheets of wastage used for wrapping proofs (4.703). The source matters little. Such material may appear in short fragments, as with the story of *Olympia*; it may be little more than a reference, as in Bianchon's briefly sketched tale (Balzac directs readers to *Autre étude de femme* for the complete version). M. de Clagny's account is also abbreviated, though M. de Gravier's memories from Spain are more fully developed. Or it may be known through a full-blown masterpiece like *Adolphe*. Far more interesting than the source is how an author exploits such stories. They may be used appropriately, as when Dinah tries to learn from *Adolphe* ("[S]he did not want to be Ellénore"—4.775) or when Balzac alludes to Constant's masterpiece not merely, as he tells Mme Hanska on 19 March 1843, to treat the subject "realistically," but to insist on the way children and poverty can exacerbate the corrosion of love. They may also be used inappropriately, as when Lousteau and Bianchon build stories as tools to diagnose Dinah's virtue, or blasphemously, as when Lousteau suggests that the biblical Mary and Joseph are adulterers. They may occur in a context, as when Bianchon tells the tale of adultery and revenge in "La Grande Bretèche," or they may be only marginally related as when M. de Clagny gives the account of the man killed and salted by his wife. With the exception of *Adolphe*, any of these stories could have been transferred, much as they stood, to a newspaper. For this purpose, they would require no further depth or polish. Art requires much more, whether insight, or complexity, or depth of relationship, or perfection, or a sense of "trailing clouds of glory." Although the fragments of the anonymous novel *Olympia* found wrapping Lousteau's proofs indicate fiction of the most popular and least aesthetic value, they carry implicit lessons about the structure of fiction and the effects of adultery. The reader is expected to fill in the blanks. In much the same way that Balzac structured *La Comédie humaine* using the plot and the reappearing characters, the person holding the book or hearing the bits and pieces is expected to complete the vision, making a whole.[22]

For Balzac journalistic anecdotes are but passing diversions, written hastily at the last moment (4.761), with no depth of perception (4.761), imagination (4.760), or commitment (4.760). The journalist, a pen-pushing hack (4.760), tosses them off, "*whipping them out [lâchant]*, as painters say of works that lack *craftsmanship*" (emphasis in original 4.761). While the journalist's primary goal and focus are his way of life, everything in the true writer's entire life turns around and is yet subsumed to "the construction of an immense edifice to glory" (4.759). This goal explains the orientation of writers like—Balzac provides a list—"Scribe, Rossini, Walter Scott, Cuvier, Voltaire, Newton, Buffon, Bayle, Bossuet, Leibniz, Lope de Vega, Calderon, Boccaccio, Aretino, Aristotle, in short, all those people who have amused, led, or dictated to their epoch" (4.759–60). Finally, journalists indiscriminately adopt any convenient point of view, while "[t]he Writer exists only through his [personal] positions" (4.760).

La Muse du département weaves one of Balzac's most complicated tapestries. It even includes one of Lousteau's poems, written some ten years before, during the Restoration. If one were to make allowances for the author's youthfulness when he composed it, the poem unquestionably shows potential. Likewise, Dinah's *Paquita la Sévillane* demonstrates talent that needs to be developed. The liberal extracts and summary indicate that it does have value, despite several weak rimes and inconsistent rhythms. The narrator informs us that her next effort, *Le Chêne de la messe*, is "infinitely superior to *Paquita*" (4.661). The two poems' romantic pathos and stunning improbabilities seem mild, however, compared with the fragmented novel *Olympia* found on the spoilage that wrapped Lousteau's proofs. Should a reader wish to consider more extensive, complete works sketched out by one of the storytellers, Bianchon's "La Grande Bretèche" or Dinah's account of La Palférine are available outside of the pages of *La Muse*. Both tales have obvious links with *La Muse du département*, but create additional, independent contexts with works near and far which give them a different significance.[23] Without the Balzacian context, however, provided on the one hand by *Autre étude de femme* and on the other by "Un Prince de la Bohème," neither story has much to recommend it. Both are skillfully recounted, but they lack the depth, overview, and complexity that mark a masterwork like *La Muse du département*, which has these distinctive qualities. Balzac also thought the novel was "better" than *La Rabouilleuse* and "much superior" to *Honorine*,[24] and it seems to me that this is true if one looks at the degree to which all the diverse elements mentioned above are intricately integrated.

The story Dinah wrote provides the framework within *La Muse du département* where Balzac, the sociologist, can compare the hasty, shallow, limited, uncommitted, if not malicious, and certainly ephemeral work of journalists. Like apostasy and adultery the examples fit handily within his novel as betrayals of the higher standard of literary artistry. Almost any of the numerous fragmentary stories could have satisfied the members of Dinah's Literary Society, where their taste is so undeveloped that "[i]n respect to literature, they read newspapers and reviews" (4.646). Of course, neither are what the novelist (or Bianchon—4.714) would call literature. Nor does Balzac neglect the major themes of the *Scènes de la vie de province*. He continues to lay bare the limited life, shallow thought, and greed in the provinces which encourage mediocrity and destroy talent. It is by comparison with the sweep of *La Muse du département* that one begins to understand the disquieting traits of journalism. The trivial motivation for Dinah's religious apostasy (she wanted to be on an equal footing with her schoolgirl friends—4.635) shows no more thoughtfulness or commitment than her decision to have an affair. She gives up poetry to avoid offending her husband. She gives up her children for money. She gives up writing fiction for the comfort of a wealthy lifestyle. If not at the beginning, when she might well have had the potential to become a truly superior woman, as the novel proceeds, she repeatedly compromises and abandons eternal values for ephemera. Because of her choices, she is degraded. In the end she appears to have developed the soul of a lightweight, of a journalist, of a second-rate muse, indeed, of a provincial.

Notes

1. Balzac returns again and again to the theme throughout *La Comédie humaine*. In *La Muse du département*, e.g., "Father Duret [...] spoke of the world when the voice of religion was powerless" (4.664). And, of course, as Dinah owes her wealth and social position to the church, so her husband.
2. "Lousteau lived by his pen [...]. Is that not creating? creating today, always..." the narrator asks facetiously, "or seeming to create, the semblance of which costs as much as the real thing!" (4.733).
3. Maurice Bardèche, ed., "Notice," *La Muse du département*, HH 6.393.
4. Annette Smith has recognized and discussed the irony created "either by the almost comical use of the definite article which always puts the character in pejorative quotes (for example, the spicy oxymoron, 'the Sappho of Saint-Satur,' or 'the departmental superior woman')"—"A boire et à manger dans l'écuelle de Dinah: Lecture de *La Muse du département*," *French Forum* 15 (1990): 304. See, also, in addition to other work cited by Smith, Nicole Mozet, *La Ville de province dans l'œuvre de Balzac: L'Espace romanesque: Fantasmes et idéologie* (Paris: CDU-SEDES, 1982) 261. Bernard Guyon believes Balzac tempered the irony: "She is almost never ridiculous. [...] She is nicknamed '*the Sappho of Saint-Satur*' but he [i.e., Balzac] takes care to add that the nickname was given to her by fools and jealous people"— "Introduction," *L'Illustre Gaudissart; La Muse du département* (Paris: Garnier, 1970) 116.
5. For overviews of Balzac's names, see: Jean Pommier, "Comment Balzac a nommé ses personnages," *Cahiers de l'Association des Etudes Françaises* 3–5 (1953): 223–35 (Pommier specifically addresses Balzac's onomastic anagrams and reversals on 227); Wayne Conner, "Un Aspect de l'onomastique balzacienne: L'Elaboration des noms

de personnage," *Actes du XIIIe congrès international de linguistique et philologie romanes tenu à l'Université Laval* (*Québec, Canada*) *du 29 août au 5 septembre 1971*, ed. Marcel Boudreault & Frankwalt Möhren (Québec: PU de Laval, 1976) 943–51; Anne-Marie Bijaoui-Baron, "La Symbolique des noms chez Balzac," *Vie et langage* 271 (1974): 558–70.
6. R. Laird Harris, ed., *Theological Wordbook of the Old Testament*, 2 vols. (Chicago: Moody Press, 1980) 2.682.
7. Ibid. 2.543. Cf. Hosea 4.11, 14.
8. Mary D. Sheriff, *Moved by Love: Inspired Artists and Deviant Women in Eighteenth-Century France* (Chicago: U of Chicago P, 2004) 70.
9. Anthony R. Pugh, "Balzac's *La Muse du département*: The Status of Fiction," *L'Esprit créateur* 31.3 (1991): 61.
10. For a summary of the various positions taken in respect to Dinah's "contradictory" character, see Smith 302, to which one might add Albert Béguin's "Préface," *La Muse du département, L'Œuvre de Balzac*, vol. 9 (Paris: Formes et Reflets, 1951), 9–14. Béguin believes that "this novel [...] often gives the impression of hasty composition, and almost always of trudging along under a gray sky," because the novelist became disillusioned with Dinah: "The novelist perhaps began by loving this creature which came from his imagination, as he loved almost all of them. But you would say that she let him down and that he became disenchanted with her. He gets even and showers abuse on her, as though he carried a grudge against her for not being able to rise above her fate" (9).
11. Balzac used the same device of ridicule by repetition of "le grand homme de province à Paris" in *Illusions perdues*.
12. Albert Dauzat, *Dictionnaire étymologique des noms de famille et prénoms de France* (Paris: Larousse, 1951) 343.
13. Anne-Marie Meininger quotes from the deputy's speech, first published in *Le Moniteur* of 14 June 1843, in her notes to the Pléiade edition I am using (4.1418–19; see, also, "Introduction" 4.609). After presenting the basic facts of Mme Reybaud's literary career, Meininger points out that Balzac considered Mme Reybaud his enemy and had little affection for either her husband, Charles, or for the latter's brother, Louis, who is today known chiefly as the creator of the satirical character, Jérôme Paturot (4.1419, 1425).
14. As just one of legions of examples, Balzac writes to Mme Hanska on 24 April 1843, "In the midst of furious necessity, I write 3 leaves per

hour. A. Dumas does, as well. But afterwards, you have to correct them, which Dumas does not do, you have to correct them 10 or 12 times."

15. Faguet, "Balzac," *Etudes littéraires sur le dix-neuvième siècle* (Paris: Lecène et Oudin, 1887) 413–53; and his *Les Grands Ecrivains français: Balzac* (Paris: Hachette, 1913); Turnell, "Balzac," *The Novel in France* (London: Hamish Hamilton, 1950), 211–46. For a passionate, expert analysis and defense of Balzac's style, see Pierre Larthomas, "Sur le style de Balzac," *Année Balzacienne* 1987: 311–27. In an earlier study, "Sur une image de Balzac," *L'Année Balzacienne* 1973: 301–26, he expresses the conclusion that may have been responsible for the growing appreciation of Balzac's writing: "If Balzac is a great novelist [...] he necessarily writes well. And if we find that he writes poorly, it is that the criteria we use to judge his style are inadequate. The sole goal of this study was to define other criteria" (326).

16. Planche, "Essai sur Adolphe," *Adolphe: Anecdote trouvé dans les papiers d'un inconnu*, by Benjamin Constant (Paris: Charpentier, 1903) 5–26. The text refers to it several times (4.775, 780).

17. Alison Fairlie, "Constant's *Adolphe* read by Balzac and Nerval," *Balzac and the Nineteenth Century: Studies in French Literature presented to Herbert J. Hunt*, ed. D.G. Charlton, J. Gaudon, and Anthony R. Pugh (Leicester: Leicester UP, 1972) 211. For useful bibliography on Balzac and Constant, see 210n1.

18. For further consideration of this story, see my *Balzacian Montage: Configuring* La Comédie humaine (Toronto: Univ. of Toronto Press, 1991) 108–13.

19. 4.653. The degree to which this upper-class promiscuity was accepted is apparent in the hundreds of conduct manuals written for young woman. See my "Miss Manners and Fooling Around: Conduct Manuals and Sexual Mores in Eighteenth-Century France," *Sex Education in Eighteenth-Century France*, ed. Shane Agin (SVEC; Oxford: Voltaire Foundation, 2011) 29–46.

20. 4.760. To some degree, with more distance, Balzac's view of journalism can be explained by the publishing crisis of the period: increasing numbers of readers and writers, high production costs, multiplication of reading rooms, serial publication by such organs as Girardin's *La Presse*, and the continuing problems of Belgian counterfeits. See L. Casssandra Hamrick, "La Crise d'identité littéraire en 1837 selon la presse périodique," *Autour d'un cabinet de lecture*, éd. Graham

Falconer (Toronto: Centre d'Etudes du XIXe Siècle Joseph Sablé, 2001) 69–90.

21. As James Baltzell puts it, "[T]he short story is a genre which the French have rarely seemed to take seriously"—quoted from Michel Viegnes, *L'Esthétique de la nouvelle française au vingtième siècle* (New York: Peter Lang, 1989) 1. Nor was the novel taken seriously as a potential work of art until Flaubert's demonstration in *Madame Bovary*.

22. Sandrine Aragon has recognized that *Olympia*'s role is to exemplify creation, as the audience creates the interstices: "*Olympia ou les vengeances romaines*, ou le manuscript de l'ère industrielle," *Le Topos du manuscript trouvé*, éd. Jan. Herman, Fernand Hallyn, and Kris Peeters (Louvain, Belgium: Peeters, 1999) 312. For a more complete argument about the structure of *La Comédie humaine*, see my *Balzacian Montage*.

23. See my study of "Un Prince de la Bohème," mentioned above in n. 18. For further consideration of *Autre étude de femme*, see Ross Chambers' "Misogyny and Cultural Denial," *L'Esprit créateur* 31.3 (1991): 5–14; Armine Kotin Mortimer, *La Clôture narrative* (Paris: José Corti, 1985) 142–54; and my *Balzacian Montage* 76–83.

24. See letters of 29 March and 24 April 1843 to Mme Hanska. Not everyone would agree, of course. The matter hangs on whether or not Balzac succeeded in pulling together the various texts which he composed at other times and for other purposes. William Paulson, who considers it "one of his most thrown together novels," argues that Balzac recuperates an order—"De la force vitale au système organisateur: *La Muse du département* et l'esthétique balzacienne," *Romantisme* 55 (1987): 33–40. For Aline Mura-Brunel it is a "disturbing" (576), "disconnected" (578) novel: "Le Livre et le lecteur dans *La Muse du département*," *L'Année Balzacienne* 20.2 (1999): 576, 578. For Lucien Dällenbach, as in a series of studies on other texts, the novel's structure is invented by the reader from the interstices—"Reading as Suture," *Style* 18.2 (1984): 196–206. See, also, the quotation from Guyon above, n. 4, and Smith, who believes that "the novel resists any monolithic interpretation" (301).

CHAPTER 9

Empty Wombs: *La Vieille Fille*

One might question an author's sensitivity to his audience when, commissioned to write a novel for serialization in a newspaper, with no requisite but that it attract a large audience, he decides to write about a pathetic old maid desperate to have a baby. The heroine of this epic was so frustrated that she was reduced to cold footbaths (4.858). With 18,000 pounds of yearly income (4.853), she should have had no difficulty finding a husband, especially since she has enormous good will and a certain charm. Nonetheless, the difficulties multiplied as the novelist thought about his subject. She would be stupid, and her feminine charms would be overwhelmed by fat. She further would have a number of demands. Not only would she want to be loved for her ample self, she would want someone suitable. Though members of her upper bourgeois class have often married into the aristocracy, Revolutionary Tribunals made this dangerous. It was not just aristocratic husbands that went to the guillotine, wives often went as well. Likewise, military men were also a problem, since Napoleon, the great widow maker (4.854), continued his wars until 1815 when Mademoiselle Rose Cormon was 42 (4.859), and the field of potential spouses had become limited. When the novel opens, she is being pursued by three suitors: a young middle-class man, a fifty-year-old noble, and a failed bourgeois speculator. Where is the titillating adventure in that? The possibility that the newspaper was publishing the work as a comic novel seems the only plausible explanation, at least until the story turns tragic, leaving the old maid childless, the young man dead, and the aristocrat hopeless. Of course, by turning the promise of comedy into despair, Balzac emphasized the horror of contemporary society.

Balzac told Madame Hanska that he whipped out *La Vieille Fille* (*The Old Maid* 1837) "in three nights."[1] Emile de Girardin, the brilliant publisher of *La Presse*, had charged him with the task of providing a novel that when broken into appropriate increments would bring readers back day after day for more. Because the serialized novel had, it seems, never before been tried in the French popular press and because Girardin was walking a financial tightrope, Balzac's novel had without fail to succeed in drawing an audience to the newspaper. Indeed, it *was* successful, and the paper's circulation grew at a surprising rate, though Balzac pointed out that it "raised a cloud of print against me" (Hanska 1.483). In fact, as Nicole Mozet concludes, the flurry of interest and criticism cost him his position with *La Presse*. There is no doubt, however, that *La Vieille Fille* brought readers to the newspaper, or that they enjoyed reading the sequential episodes, however scandalous, while screaming their protests about the novel's questionable morality. And in sacrificing the novelist to their prudish complaints, as Mozet concludes, Girardin could prove his sensitivity to his subscribers' demands, thus assuring their faithfulness to his newspaper. When the publisher broke with Balzac because of all the complaints, Girardin was doubly right both in putting Balzac under contract and in later discharging him ("Introduction," 4.795–96).

The reading public found Balzac's *La Vieille Fille* both fascinating and problematic. In the tempest of protests and complaints while it was appearing in *La Presse* from October 23rd to November 4th of 1836, some claimed it was indecent, others that it was downright immoral, others obscene. The continuing attacks castigated the characterization, the style, the descriptions, the very subject. For the ladies' paper *Psyché*, it revealed the decadence of Balzac, for the *Nouvelle Minerve*, it was the production of Balzac's decrepitude. Another writer might have been encouraged when *Le Corsaire* claimed that the "deplorable obscenity" was not written by Balzac, though that paper is alone in disputing the novel's authorship. Only Alphonse Karr took an opposing position. It was, he said, "the capital production of recent days."[2] In short, Balzac had little corroboration when, several months later, on February 10th, he wrote Mme Hanska that *La Vieille Fille* was "one of my best things" (Hanska 1.483). Posterity has not borne him out. Only Léon Pierre-Quint has gushed, "It is one of the greatest, one of the most beautiful of Balzac's novels."[3]

It remains difficult to justify Pierre-Quint's praise, given the bleak conclusion of *La Vieille Fille*. "Death and despair" were overused themes in the first half of the nineteenth century and unquestionably weary when Balzac turned to them. In literature, however, the thematic exploitation of disaster multiplies in effectiveness when it is employed as a device that organizes or increases the significance of other elements. Usage of a theme as a tool, for example, narrows the compass, imposes categories of certain future decisions, and opens a paradigm of choices. The romantics loved the topic of death and worked it mercilessly, leaving the subject lusterless and tattered. Proust's famous scene turning around the death of the Marquis d'Osmond and of their good friend Swann successfully overcomes the wear and tear of death in *A la recherche du temps perdu* (1913–27). In effect, an everyday reality becomes a device that exposes the selfish nature of the Duke and Duchess de Guermantes. The pair is hurrying to leave for an evening on the town, desperate to get away before officially receiving the expected news that their cousin has passed away, since the required mourning would begin immediately and interfere with their projected pleasure. The scene tells the reader something important about the characters of these self-centered socialites. Or one might remember Julien Sorel's death in *Le Rouge et le noir* (1830), and the implication that he is a Messiah ushering a new class into the halls of power. Camus picked up the allusion and exploited it once again in *L'Etranger* (1942) to focus on new changes of attitude in society. Occasionally, death can be a weapon, as when Madame Riccoboni's Mme de Cressy uses her own suicide to take revenge on her errant husband (1758). Most commonly, of course, death serves as a means of closure. The classic bildungsroman begins with the hero's birth; it ends with his or her death. In traditional tragedies, were it not for the *bienséances*, bodies could litter the stage when the playwright is ready to send the audience home. As Lamartine put it near the end of *Jocelyn* (1836), "You would have said that death had closed the book."[4] Nonetheless, it takes skill to make well-worn "despair, disaster, and death" come alive and serve effectively once again.

Real-world suicides were regularly reported in the newspapers, with the official statistics and with all manner of pathetic details. Maigron gives the references to a number of "dramatic" suicides reported in the *Constitutionnel*, and he quotes S. de Sugny's *Le Suicide* to write that from 1833 to 1836 at least, almost every morning, on reading the paper and "'while drinking one's very hot coffee [...] the reader may let himself feel a very slight but delicious shiver.'"[5] In addition, hundreds of novels, stories, plays, and poems had given suicide a key role—I think, of course, of such early works as Chateaubriand's *Atala* (1801) and Senancour's *Obermann* (1804), and later works like Sainte-Beuve's *Joseph Delorme*, Vigny's *Stello*, Stendhal's *Armance*, Philothée O'Neddy's "Nuit Quatrième: Nécropolis," all published in 1829, Musset's "Le Saule" and Hugo's *Hernani* produced in 1830, Petrus Borel's "Champavert" of 1833, Soulié's *Le Conseiller d'Etat* of 1835, as well as legions of others. Maigron goes so far as to suggest that almost all contemporary literature touched on the subject (315n1). By the mid-1830s, literary despair, death, and especially suicide had become a cliché, not quite yet ready for the grave but exhibiting senescence. As a means of arousing readers' sympathy or of shocking, suicide had lost much of its effectiveness. Using it for closure had become a bore. By the early 1840s, suicide had become sufficiently mundane, even trite, for Louis Reybaud to exploit in his burlesque prose epic, *Jérôme Paturot à la recherche d'une position sociale* (1843). Jérôme tries to convince his sensible Malvina to join him for a "[d]ouble crown" when he kills himself. He explains: "Malvina [...] suicide gives a man a position." Malvina responds, "What bull! [...] That's it, kick off like a seamstress with a charcoal heater."[6] It was not long before an anonymous writer declared in the *Chronique de Paris*, "Suicide is no longer fashionable."[7] In *La Vieille Fille*, Balzac needed to revivify the theme and make the death of the young suitor, Athanase, arouse readers' sympathy. To do so, he had to dampen its tedium as a common, literary theme and increase its verisimilitude as a frequent, real tragedy among the young. His strategy was simple. After setting the stage to make the reader expect a comedy, the novel gives depth and complexity to stock characters and a plot typical of *fabliaux* and insists with delight on the ramifications, encourages expectations of a happy ending, before suddenly confronting readers with a heart-wrenching tragedy that leaves the all too human characters in despair.

Although Balzac was sensitive and, indeed, responsive to Girardin's need to attract subscribers for *La Presse*, while writing *La Vieille Fille* the novelist never compromised his own sociological interests or aesthetic demands. The fabled, supposedly unreasonably rewritten Balzacian proofs that elicited such wailing from printers were, in fact, a previously planned and contracted way for Balzac to perfect his work. He paid a substantial portion of his earnings for the privilege. His high standards required that whatever he wrote had to be well done, and it had to present the scope of the push and pull among the interacting groups in society that he was incrementally reflecting in *La Comédie humaine*. In *La*

Vieille Fille he wanted to reveal the entrenched, ineffectual position of the hereditary upper middle class, coupled with brief but significant glimpses at aristocratic leftovers from the *ancien régime*. The small but very significant hereditary bourgeoisie had for generations held major positions in government. By the early nineteenth century, the class had dithered away its power. The remains of this now disappointing slice of society are represented by the withdrawn abbé de Sponde committed to prayer as well as his niece the frantic Rose Cormon desperate to have babies but without the conjugal means to do so. To properly highlight this now unimpressive class, the novelist rolled out his most successful devices, including a cunning emphasis on the mock heroic and the equally effective use of allusion.

In addition, Balzac returned to one of his most pressing social fears. He had for some time been concerned with the way the July Monarchy was bypassing youth and catering, indeed toadying, to the older generations. In his opinion, the nation had fallen under the sway of a "gerontocracy." In "Ferragus" of 1834, he wrote, for example, "The youth of today is unlike the youth of any other period: it is caught between memories of the Empire and memories of the Emigration, between old traditions of the court and the studied consciousness of the bourgeoisie. [...] This youth is uncertain in everything, blind and clairvoyant, and is completely discounted by the old men determined to keep the reins of the state between their feeble hands. The monarchy could be saved if they would retire, and allow access by the youth of France whom the old doctrinaires, having come back to power from the Restoration, continue to mock" (5.801). Balzac repeatedly returned to the theme. In *Un Prince de la Bohème* of 1844, he insisted that "the admirable French youth that Napoleon and Louis XIV sought after [has been] neglected by the gerontocracy under which everything is withering in France" (7.808). This, I suggest, is the central focus of *La Vieille Fille*. Indeed, it colors the entire *Comédie humaine*. Balzac wanted to insist on the suicidal despair of youth wasted by a society ruled by monstrously self-indulgent aristocrats and self-centered, greedy, middle-class leftovers from the Restoration and Directory. Balzac chose to highlight and revivify death with comedic burlesque, much as Ionesco and others would exploit the device more than a hundred years later.[8] Unfortunately, while it was once possible to shock readers and quicken their sympathy by having a young hero kill himself, the contrivance had lost its power. In order to use it again, it was necessary to give renewed impact to a suicide—yet another suicide.

It should not be forgotten that Balzac considered himself a historian of manners and *La Comédie humaine* a history of manners (*histoire des mœurs*, e.g., 1.9–11). Scholars have pronounced him a novelist interested primarily, if not uniquely, in telling stories, and they have virtually ignored his insistence on the historical and sociological unity of his composition, which he thought echoed the design he found in nature, culture, and religion ("Avant-propos" 1.5–20). In fact, he said in 1842 that he believed that "everyone perceives the overriding idea presiding over all the details" of his work (1.1110). The prospectus that he surely inspired, if not wrote, goes on to explain, "The author's plan consisted in tracing in its infinite details the faithful history, the exact representation of the manners of our modern society" (1.1109). To this end, as he insisted repeatedly, all the details speak to the whole. He was a highly observant proto-sociologist.

Take, for example, Suzanne, who, though a minor character in the plot of *La Vieille Fille*, serves in herself as a major allusive complex, that is, as a system of different allusions working together to emphasize one or more traits and helping to produce the final aesthetic experience.[9] It all begins because Suzanne needs money to finance her move to Paris, where she can capitalize on her youthful beauty. Rather like the Suzanne of Beaumarchais's *Marriage de Figaro*, she is both good looking and quick witted (4.842). "[L]a magnificent Suzanne" (4.824) is also sexy and willing to use her attractiveness, to achieve her goals, even before she truly understands the biological realities and consequences she is playing with. It is by no means clear that she knows how a woman becomes pregnant. Where "the chaste Suzanne of the Bible" was in every way innocent of adultery (4.845), Balzac's "chaste Suzanne" (4.842) is likewise innocent of sexual license, at least, though she peddles the story of seduction in order to raise money. Her accurate perception that there is nothing for her in the provinces, forces her to reach for another opportunity. Where else could a beautiful teenager go but to Paris? Sadly, despite the increasing efficiency of public transportation, as mentioned in relation to *Ursule Mirouët*, it was still costly to travel. Without means, Suzanne turns to the old men she has met in the attempt to squeeze them for funds by claiming to be carrying their child. She grasps the means available to her for coercing males but remains vague about the details that would give it credence. The Chevalier de Valois understands that the girl has little choice, and with affection and charm, puts her off: "[Y]ou would more easily put some salt on a sparrow's tale than to make me believe that I had anything to do with your problem" (4.825). He sics her onto du Bousquier, his competition for the hand of the epigonic old maid, Rose Cormon.

What makes the adolescent think that she can get away with the blackmail? As she later admits, she is not pregnant. Sexual ignorance was by no means uncommon among adolescents of the day.[10] Moïse Le Yaouanc, perhaps influenced by Michel Millet's seventeenth-century *L'Ecole des filles*, suggests that she uses the wiles of someone much experienced in encouraging elderly men with faded capacities to initiate some semblance of intercourse, but there is no evidence of this possibility.[11] In fact, du Bousquier says very explicitly, "May the devil take me if I can remember even wrinkling anything other than her collaret!" (4.836). Why then does he pay her off? Suzanne seemingly suffers from a lack of sexual instruction, if not innocence. Nonetheless, like Beaumarchais's Suzanne, she displays her ability to manipulate the old roué, du Bousquier, so as to extort some of the needed funds. Perhaps du Bousquier opens his purse because of his fervent desire to believe in a revival of his former powers, lost from having "pressed the orange of pleasure too much" (4.832). Certainly, his bald pate beneath his toupee, his "flattened nose" (4.828), and the fact that "[he] did not have the voice that should have gone along with his muscles" (4.829), or, perhaps even more obviously, the narrator's comparing him to a "fallen Sardanapalus" (4.831), leave no question that he has become impotent. The narrator tells us that Rose's "little air of deliberate craftiness that distinguishes young women after a marriage of love" (4.925) comes from something other than coitus. Is Rose Cormon as ignorant as Suzanne of what it takes to make a baby? Whatever the case, Suzanne's role in the novel prepares readers to read the signs and recognize Rose Cormon's naiveté.

Du Bousquier is well aware that however innocent he is of Suzanne's proclaimed pregnancy, she can soil his name by spreading word of his guilt, as indeed she maliciously does by complaining of her supposed plight to Madame Granson and the two Societies of Charity and Maternity. Everyone involved thinks that du Bousquier's reputation will be fatally damaged by Suzanne's tale. The girl even thinks that she has successfully convinced him of the truth of her tale, whereas he merely fears that being branded a philanderer will fatally damage his courtship of Mlle Cormon. Valois has similar thoughts, as does Mme Granson. To that end, they happily spread Suzanne's tale. If all goes well, du Bousquier will be out of the running. The field is indeed decreased when Valois successfully derails Athanase's potential suit for Rose with vague accusations hinting at his involvement in the perversions common in Imperial schools. Little do they know that the desperate Rose Cormon cares far less about the reputation than the potency of her chosen mate. Above all else, she wants babies.

The comedy goes on at length. Neither Suzanne nor Rose seem entirely aware of what is required to conceive a child, and Rose mistakes the physical signs of male strength for those of sexual potential.

Suzanne's final role in the novel is defined by the love she suddenly feels for Athanase, the "electric spark [...] the flair [...] the lightning strike [...] a broadside of thoughts to the heart" (4.843). It is love at first sight (4.843), love that inspires her to dream of returning from a successful career in Paris to provide the young man with the funds he needs. With Athanase portrayed as a man filled with potential but like a Christ figure destined for death, Suzanne reminds readers that there was a biblical Suzanne who joined with others to minister to Jesus "of their substance" (Luke 8.3). Balzac's allusive Suzanne would have done similarly (4.920).

The novelist had a clear sense of plot as a malleable device, amenable to innumerable permutations. As he knew, it was an empty structure that could incorporate different types of characters working toward different ends. He understood that just as there are stock characters, there are also stock plots and situations. Molière, for example, used tragic narratives to comic ends. We can study the results as the dramatist walked the line between tragedy and comedy in *Don Juan*, *Le Misanthrope*, and *Tartuffe*. By reversing Molière's sequence, Balzac's comedy almost always turns into calamity, thus serving to enhance his analyses of social behavior and interactions. As a consequence, he illuminates the amusement, only gradually encouraging the reader to see that beneath the farcical humor there are human beings who dramatize the wasted potential of a disintegrating society that is approaching a catastrophic conclusion. When Athanase Granson kills himself, he writes large the hopelessness of the entire younger generation. They are helpless in a society composed of a self-indulgent aristocracy, a rapacious but impotent middle class, and the pathetic incomprehension endemic in provincial France.[12] Perhaps for this reason Balzac ennobled him with the name Athanase, which derives from an etymon meaning *immortal*, for the author hoped that the ideals of the young man and of youth itself would not die and that however much they were currently pushed to the side, threatening the death of the future, they would eventually rise above the slough of the July Monarchy.

Most of the characters in *La Vieille Fille* are nothing, if not comic. The thought of three bachelors of varying ages and classes vying for the hand (and fortune) of an aging spinster who desperately wants a baby has considerable comic potential. Nonetheless, but for reasons having to do less with comedy than with sociological realism, Balzac was especially proud of their portrayal. As he said in his letter of 10 February 1837, "Du Bousquier is quite a nice reflection of people who did business during the Republic and who became liberals during the Restoration, likewise the Chevalier de Valois is a nice image of the leftovers from the century of Louis XV. Mlle Cormon is also a very original creation, I think. These figures are beyond most novelists because there is so little to hold onto" (Hanska 1.483).

First we make the acquaintance of the impoverished, aging, but still elegant beau, the Chevalier de Valois. He is "an old bachelor" (4.819, 906), we are told, "a retired Adonis" (4.814), and one of several supposed offspring of the Valois line—"if the Valois exist," the narrator adds (4.811). This particular Valois had a graceful way of handling his gold snuffbox that gives off the redolence of the fast life at the end of Louis XV's reign and the beginning of the Revolution of 1789. It is decorated with a portrait of the Princess Goritza, over whom he claims to have dueled with the Duke de Lauzun, (4.812). A semblance of verisimilitude is added on remembering that Lauzun, the elegant, historic courtier who became a hero in the American Revolution, may have had a brief affair with Princess Goritza.[13] His memoirs say nothing about any such duel, however. Still, the mere mention reminds readers of Lauzun's and by association Valois's success with the ladies. In a contemporary novel, for example, Paul de Musset has the Marshall of Turenne say to Lauzun, "You do your campaigning in bedrooms, my dear Lauzun."[14]

Born under the *ancien régime*, destined to die with the Bourbon Monarchy in 1830, this Valois is a delightful addition to the generic tribe. One has to admire his ability not only to support his impoverished self with social gambling but also to make his benefactors believe that his quasi-prosperity comes from the repayment of an old debt dating from the emigration. His linen is always dazzlingly white, and the rouge applied tastefully, his manners unimpeachable. "In no country of the world does parasitism present such a graceful form" (4.817). Despite his many effeminate traits, we know that he is well endowed and potent, for he has "a prodigious nose" (4.812). Furthermore, "the chevalier had the voice that goes with the nose; his organ would have surprised you with its ample, redundant tones" (4.814). As Jameson has pointed out, "The symbolism of the Chevalier's nose, which the [...] context makes it impossible to overlook, derives [...] from the oldest sexual folklore of the human race."[15] Unfortunately for Balzac's memorable old maid, Rose Cormon neither knows the significance of long noses, nor is she aware of the chevalier's activities and popularity with the girls who work in the laundry downstairs from his apartment. The narrator describes his rather free manner with them. Some years later Valois would father a child by Césarine (4.815), and, at the moment of what the narrator calls "the current scene," when the chevalier takes aim at Mlle Cormon, Suzanne would like him to believe that because of him she is with child. As Jameson explains in a version subsequent to the one quoted above, the function of the comedy is to direct the reader's attention to the allegory that recounts the tragic decline of the class and power structure of the Monarchy.[16]

Balzac constructed *La Vieille Fille* on a web of images that point toward conflicting implications. Despite du Bousquier's short nose, which for the knowing indicates his impotence, Rose Cormon is impressed by his strong, manly build. Not just anyone could have carried her when she collapses, and she chooses for apparent rather than real masculinity. Likewise, sadly for the all too elegant chevalier, he too bears mixed symbolism. As history states with more or less assurance, when the Valois died out it established the impotence of the Valois line, and left the Bourbons to enjoy power. Far more important, however, are the earrings, which constitute what is probably the chevalier's most serious mistake. While the novelist's chevalier certainly believes his earrings bring his Valois ancestry to people's attention, he forgets that they also remind those who see them of other historical facts, among which is Henri III's supposed homosexuality and his failure to produce an heir. It does not help that he claims they prove him a descendant of the Valois. The fact that Henri III wore earrings would not be a good sign, for they symbolize the opposite of virility. It has long been believed that Henri III, the last Valois king, was a homosexual.[17] Dumas's *Henri III et sa cour* (1829) provides another indication of the opinions of early nineteenth-century France where Henri's sexual preference was patent. Perhaps because of the well-known portraits of Henri III by Etienne Dumonstier, François Quesnel, Léonard Gaultier, and Marcello Bacciarelli, among others, his love of ostentatious earrings was also well known. A set of earrings is mentioned in a passage Ferguson translates from Pierre de L'Estoile's *Registre-Journal du règne de Henri III*: "[H]e had a wondrous friendship for Maugiron and [Caylus], for he kissed them both when they were dead [... H]e removed from Caylus the earrings which he himself had previously given him and put on with his own hands" (150n15).

Times change, however. The prejudice against males wearing earrings had long been common by the early nineteenth century. Even by the turn of the seventeenth and eighteenth centuries, Madame de La Fayette makes that very clear, for when the Abbé de Choisy continued to wear earrings while dressed as a man, she tried to correct him. As he remembered, "It even happened that Madame de La Fayette, whom I saw very often, seeing me decked out in earrings and carefully applied beauty spots told me, as a good friend, that it was no longer fashionable for men, and that I would do better to dress as a woman."[18] In short, both the Chevalier and du Bousquier bear mixed symbolism, and given the choice that Mlle Cormon finally makes, Valois overestimates Rose's intelligence and education. His allusions to the Duke de Lauzun, his impressive nose and deep voice cannot overcome his effeminate mannerisms and svelte figure. Rose Cormon was certainly not interested in marrying a homosexual, since she fervently wanted children. And neither Henri III nor his brother, Charles IX, had heirs, thus bringing the Valois line to an end, forcing France to turn to Henri IV, known for his knightly (i.e., manly) valor, and the Bourbons. Tragically for poor Rose, the chevalier's sexually promising proboscis lost out to his equally suggestive earrings, and the nefarious and impotent du Bousquier has his way with Rose's fortune and the provincial city of Alençon.

Du Bousquier, a former military supplier, is sufficiently husky to allow the delightful but stupid Mlle Cormon to view his physique as corroboration of the rumors of his successful philandering with Suzanne. Certainly, she wants to believe, for she desperately hungers for an heir (a desire that is important for justifying the position of this novel in the *Scènes de la vie de province*). Because his father was an examining magistrate, du Bousquier is something of a country squire, but he has a murky history. Lacking a fortune, he had the initiative to head for Paris, where he had considerable success during the troubled Directory. To his misfortune, however, he made the mistake of squandering his funds in riotous living and then of gambling against Napoleon's victory at Morengo. He was ruined as a result. After paying his enormous debts, he salvaged a small income and returned to Alençon, a reasonably well-preserved quadragenarian. Du Bousquier tried to recoup his fortunes by offering his hand to the two eligible old maids, Mlle Armande, the half-sister of the town's ranking aristocrat, and the other, Mlle Rose Cormon. On being refused by both, he considers the possibilities carefully and returns to courting Mlle Cormon.

The third suitor of the ample old maid is the already mentioned twenty-three-year-old youth, Athanase Granson. Son of a lieutenant-colonel killed at Iéna and an impoverished widow, the intellectually gifted Athanase has a minor position at the local mayor's office. The narrator judges from the character's looks that he is exceptional. "[A]nywhere other than the town of Alençon his appearance would have earned him the assistance of superior men or women who recognize unproclaimed genius" (4.839). Unhappily, we are in the provinces. "Closed-in provincial life, without any way out, without praise, without encouragement, created a circle within which ideas that were not yet quite born died at their sunrise" (4.839). Not a man of action, Athenase is rather contemplative, retiring, easily discouraged, waiting to be recognized for his potential. His love for Mlle Cormon was at first inspired by her fortune, but as time went on he falls truly in love with her. "His passion was true," insists the narrator (4.840). It was "a real passion" (4.841).

In the midst of the suitors who remain in the lists, rumors proliferate. Rose is hindered in her desire to sort out the unsuitable suitors by a maze of bizarre tests that only she understands. Equally disastrous is the influence of rumor, which is rife.[19] Finally, she comes to the point where her only wish is for a husband who can provide her with a baby. Too limited to make a reasonable judgment between her lovers, she listens to the rumors and responds passively to circumstances. She whips poor old Pénélope to a gallop in order to return to the house and prepare things for M. de Troisville's visit, only to learn that this guest, at least, is already married. Then M. de Valois dallies, forcing her to faint into the only available arms of the physically strong du Bousquier.

The cast is appropriate: an elderly aristocrat, an aging bourgeois speculator, and a charming young poet with black eyes "sparkling with thought" (4.838). If d'Aubignac was correct in 1657 to suggest that the genres of tragedy and comedy correspond respectively to noble and middle-class life, the fact that *La Vieille Fille* is set in a bourgeois world prepares readers for a comedy.[20] With three engaging characters in pursuit of a skittish but wealthy old maid, readers are encouraged to settle back and enjoy. The stage is set. Beaumarchais's Chérubin is mentioned in a reference to his embracing Marceline, an event which as Castex points out does not actually happen in *Le Mariage de Figaro*,[21] but which emphasizes the possibility of a happy ending. Perhaps the young, pale, thin intellectual, Athanase, will move into the sunset with his buxom heiress. Comic tradition would lead us to expect that the worthy young man will win the prize, and that we will come to the end of the adventure with a glow in our hearts. As a possible reminder of Molière, the long introduction takes readers on a tour of the imposing house built during the reign of Henri IV to meet the people who gather there nightly and to learn the history of Mlle Cormon's problematic courtship. Only the phrase "The poor man," which repetitively marks *Tartuffe*, is lacking when, over one-third of the way through the book, Rose finally comes "on stage," like Tartuffe, and we meet the object of all this maneuvering.

The tone changes somewhat when Rose actually appears. She is indeed ridiculous, but she is also quite engaging, and it becomes increasingly difficult to deny her humanity. "Not only did she receive everyone in town, she was charitable, pious, and incapable of saying anything spiteful or malicious" (4.864). Too "foolish" to recognize the sincere love of Athanase Granson, she attempts to calm her tormented yearnings with foot baths and the confessional. "Pure as an angel, healthy as a child, and full of good will" (4.856), she is made for motherhood. Furthermore, "what, in her celestial ignorance, she wanted more than anything else were children" (4.859). When 1815 arrives, Rose Cormon is 42 years old. It will not be long before she is too old to have a baby. "Her desire then took on an intensity neighboring monomania" (4.859). As the narrator points out, her story is rather special, "why not consider the distresses of stupidity, as one considers the distresses of genius? One is a social reality that is infinitely more abundant than the other" (4.863). Nonetheless, in *La Vieille Fille*, Balzac complicates the laughter cued by devices from farce on making the audience aware of the individual tragedy taking place. As Philippe Berthier points out, it is surely not one of the novelist's accidents that reversing the syllables of Cormon creates "mon cor[ps] [my body]."[22]

As the text encourages readers to continue to expect a happy ending, the mention of Rose's horse, Penelope, may raise another possibility. We remember what befalls Penelope's suitors in the *Odyssey* who persist even though Ulysses's wife has long sought to discourage them. They have become decidedly unruly during Ulysses's absence, making free with his property and hoping to make free with his wife. The Greek hero, however, is more than a match for them, and all the suitors die. In Balzac's *La Vieille Fille* only the husbands are safe from similar punishment. Because the Vicount de Troisville is, to Rose's consternation, already married, he lives on, and du Bousquier's successful marriage apparently protects him to pursue his nefarious plans. But, as already mentioned, the young Athanase drowns and the Chevalier de Valmont "died while living" (4.921).

Rose would probably have been happy with the chevalier de Valois. He subsequently proves that he can sire a child, and he is kind, a kindness mingled with intelligence and the savoir-faire that can cover up Rose's worst faux pas. Athanase Granson would also have made her happy. In addition, the young man could have continued to care for his mother and gone on to do significant work that would have brought glory and honor to Alençon. Only his mother and Suzanne, the nascent courtesan, believed in him enough to encourage him. Since this is the story of a lack of insight, of an inability to judge, in short, of stupidity, Rose Cormon picks the brutal, selfish, destructive du Bousquier, and readers slug through the ten long pages of Athanase's suicide and his mother's grief-filled efforts to bury him in sacred ground. "Athanase was promptly forgotten by society, which wants and, indeed, must forget its mistakes" (4.921). Likewise, the community is spared nothing of the discouraging details of the spurned Valois's slow, painful disintegration and death. His linen is no longer spotless, his hair remains uncombed, he appears with missing teeth and disheveled apparel, and he is physically unclean. "Alençon," the narrator confides, "was a witness to a particularly pitiable suicide that continued [...] The pathetic Chevalier de Valois died while [he continued to] live. He committed suicide every morning for fourteen years" (4.921). "Finally, right in the middle of the Restoration, the impotent Republic won out over the valiant aristocracy" (4.922). The further warning is unmistakable: because both Suzanne and the epigonic old maid have empty wombs, unless France changes its ways, it too will be condemned to sterility.

Married to Rose Cormon, du Bousquier explodes into a thoroughly unpleasant but imposing supplier from the days of the Directory (4.924). He "restores" the once imposing house, painting nude women on the walls, cutting down the beloved linden trees, and replacing the comfortable yard with an English garden (4.923). Supported by middle-class liberals and the reoriented church, he works successfully to ruin local aristocrats, while speculating with his wife's money to bring in industry. The Revolution of 1830 is for him the triumph of the republican tricolor flag. He makes a fortune and gains widespread respect, though "[he] is despotic in his home and completely devoid of conjugal love" (4.929). Compelled to drink the lees of her choice, Rose is blamed by the community for her failure to have children. In 1830, the pitiable Rose confided to a friend "that she couldn't stand the idea of dying a virgin" (4.836). Her bad choice in husbands causes Rose's despair, but also the destruction of traditional provincial culture, and the death of Athanase. Given that du Bousquier's name recalls *brusquer* or *bousculer*, either one of which suggests treating another person roughly and without regard, the reader has been prepared. Rose might have been saved "from the terrible misery of conjugal life" had she read Ariosto's *Orlando furioso*, that Balzac cites, "where Angélique prefers Médor, a blond Chevalier de Valois, rather than Roland" (4.935). As one perceives with increasing clarity, Rose Cormon resembles provincial France. "[S]he conformed with the general spirit and behavior of the local people, who loved her as the best example of their own lives, because she was encrusted in the provincial way of life [...]. Despite her eighteen thousand pounds of income from her land [...], she got along well with families that were not as rich as she" (4.864). Like Rose, provincial France lacks the wisdom to choose wisely between alternate prospects, and, like Rose, it consequently condemns itself to a barren future. The middle class lacks refinement; the aristocracy lacks energy. France's only hope is in the young.

Balzac's marvelous exploitation of comedy in conjunction with the worn-out device of Athanase's suicide works very effectively, and *La Vieille Fille* may be one of Balzac's masterworks. The many allusions encourage reflective readers to follow the signs and seek to uncover the novel's major thrust: a warning that the people of France are blind to the shifting social patterns and thoughtlessly driving to their death, a formulation analyzed by Jameson, Georges Laffly, and others that neatly opposes the virtuous potential of youth to the charming but ineffective aristocracy and the brutal greed of the middle class.[23] Treating the banal tale of an ignorant virgin past her prime who is wild to have a baby as though it were an incredibly significant episode makes the reader expect an entertaining resolution, as would be the case of most mock heroic (*burlesque*) accounts. Surely, one might hope that, if not the bright-eyed Athanase, then the sympathetic Valois will be chosen. It does seem that Balzac was correct in his favorable assessment of the characterization of Rose Cormon.[24] She and the Chevalier de Valois are two of the novelist's most successful characters. As Henri Queffélec said, Rose Cormon "is, for the reader, better than sublime... she exists" ("Préface" 4.896). I would say something similar for the Chevalier de Valois. Rose and Valois are better than superb characterizations; they give the effect of real life. More important, *La Vieille Fille* provides an excellent example of a way of reviving the impact of a theme like suicide by disrupting expectations, much as Ionesco would a century later. Even more important, it proves Balzac's innovative brilliance in the techniques of fiction, skill that has been too often ignored, if not denigrated. Most important, his sociological dissection effectively portrays the final defeat of both the aristocracy and the hereditary upper middle class, which in a bloody revolution emphasized their feckless lack of the power and character needed to maintain their position at the top of society. They are sterile.

NOTES

1. Letter of 6 October 1836, Hanska 1.445. Nicole Mozet, the Pléiade editor of *La Vieille Fille*, believes he was in fact talking about the two first chapters *La Vieille Fille* (4.1435).
2. For this summary, I have used Patricia Kinder's "Un Directeur de journal, ses auteurs et ses lecteurs en 1836: Autour de *La Vieille Fille*," *L'Année Balzacienne* 1972: 173–200. See, also, René Guise, "Balzac et le roman feuilleton," *L'Année Balzacienne* 1964, esp. 283–97. Dominique Massonnaud mentions a number of earlier serializations: *Faire vrai: Balzac et l'invention de l'œuvre monde* (Geneva: Droz, 2014) 330.
3. Quoted from Bardèche, ed., "Préface," *La Vieille Fille*, HH 6.558.
4. Alphonse-Marie-Louis de Lamartine, *Jocelyn*, ed. Jean des Cognets (Paris: Garnier, 1960) 253.
5. Louis Maigron, *Le Romantisme et les mœurs* (1910; rpt. Geneva: Slatkine Reprints, 1977) 333.
6. Reybaud, *Jérôme Paturot à la recherche d'une position sociale*, 2 vols. (Paris: Paulin, 1847) 1.162.
7. I quote this from, Charles Simond, ed., *Paris de 1800 à 1900 d'après les estampes et les mémoires du temps*, t. 2. 1830–1870, *La Monarchie de juillet, La Seconde République—Le Second Empire* (Paris: Plon, 1900) 383.
8. Armine Mortimer's insight shows how Balzac turned a comic detail into the image of the whole—"The Corset of *La Vieille Fille*," *For Love or for Money: Balzac's Rhetorical Realism* (Columbus: Ohio State UP, 2011) 218–38. For Michel Riffaterre, when the novel is considered as literature, rather than history, it is "a story of disillusionment [...], but above all, a comical story"—"Fear of Theory," *Romanic Review* 93.1–2 (2002): 190. See, also, Michael Tilby's fine "Balzac and the Poetics of Ignorance: *La Vieille Fille*," *Modern Language Review* 100.4 (2005): 957–58.
9. See Pasco, *Allusion* 77–97.

10. The ignorance about sex that was common throughout the eighteenth century—see, e.g., Shane Agin, ed., *Sex Education in Eighteenth-Century France* (Oxford: Voltaire Foundation, 2011)—continued well into the nineteenth. Writers may refer to it with amusement (see, e.g., Barbey d'Aurevilly, "Le Plus Bel Amour de don Juan") or outrage (Emile Zola considered the typical adolescent girl an ignorant "Sleeping Beauty" awaiting the first passing knight to kiss her awake—see *La Faute de l'abbé Mouret, Les Rougon-Macquart*, 15 vols., Bibliothèque de la Pléiade (Paris: Gallimard 1966–69) 1.1251). In numerous newspaper articles, he expressed his concern about the dangers for teenage girls caused by a lack of parental guidance, see, e.g., Zola, *Œuvres complètes* (Paris: Cercle du Livre Précieux, 1969) 9.353, 355, 359, 385–86; 13.187.
11. Le Yaouanc, "Le Plaisir dans les récits balzaciens," *L'Année Balzacienne* 1973, 209. Albert Béguin, as well, terms her a "professional of love"—quoted from Philippe Berthier, ed. *La Vieille Fille, Le Cabinet des antiques* (Paris: Garnier-Flammarion, 1987) 382. While she eventually becomes a sex worker, there is reason to doubt that her professionalism was very advanced before leaving Alençon. Even today, Balzacians have not been able to agree on the sexual knowledge of either Suzanne, at the beginning of her career, or Rose, through much of hers.
12. Cf., "Why did Balzac add the story [of Athanase Granson]? You could remove this protuberance without affecting the core of the plot!"—Henri Queffélec, "Préface," *La Vieille Fille, L'Œuvre de Balzac*, ed. Albert Béguin and Jean A. Ducourneau, vol. 1 (Paris: Formes et Reflets, 1949) 897; Maurice Bardèche, who cites Paul Souday's similar position, puts the position in his own words: "What is the idea behind the destiny of Athanase Granson? [...] Why give him an important development, even though it is unnecessary? We do not understand what he [Balzac] wanted to do in introducing a character and event that he does not succeed in integrating into the plot [and] that remains foreign to the character and to the novel's thrust without successfully establishing a contrast. It leaves the impression of a sin against the laws of composition and of the conception of a subject as Balzac conceived them"—"Notice," *La Vieille Fille*, HH 6.557. While I would agree that Balzac was not completely successful in an attractive characterization of Athanase, the young man remains an important part of *La Vieille Fille*, for he represents the promise of the

beleaguered youth of France. For a sympathetic and, I think, appropriate view of the character, see Pierre Barbéris, *Mythes balzaciens* (Paris: Armand Colin, 1972) 81–82; and Anne-Marie Baron, *Balzac ou les hiéroglyphes de l'imaginaire* (Paris: Champion, 2002) 168.
13. Valois's memory may have slipped a bit here. According to Armand Louis de Gontaut, duc de Biron, *Mémoires du duc de Lauzun (1747–1783)*, tran. E. Jules Méras (NY: Stirgis & Walton, 1912), first published in 1822, Isabelle Czartoryska, princess Goritza, was Polish, rather than Hungarian, and although Lauzun quarreled with M. Braniski over the princess, as mentioned before, there was no duel, either with him or anyone else (95, 136, 171).
14. Paul de Musset, *Lauzun*, 2 vols. (Paris: Dumont, 1835) 1.96.
15. Fredric Jameson, "The Ideology of Form: Partial Systems in *La Vieille Fille*," *Sub-stance* 15 (1976): 34.
16. Jameson, "Realism and Desire: Balzac and the Problem of the Subject," *The Political Unconscious: Narrative as a Socially Symbolic Act* (London: Routledge, 1989) 162–63.
17. Of late, the matter has been reconsidered, and it seems likely that if Henri III was not homosexual, he was bisexual, although his sexuality remains elusive. See the summary of this work in, Gary Ferguson, *Queer (Re)Readings in the French Renaissance: Homosexuality, Gender, Culture* (Aldershot, Hampshire: Ashgate, 2008) 147 and n2, 172, 179–90; and Keith Cameron, *Henri III, A Maligned or Malignant King? (Aspects of the Satirical Iconography of Henri de Valois)*, (Exeter: U of Exeter P, 1978) 84. In fact, for Balzac's purposes, the reality was less important than *ce qu'on dit* (what people said). As Georges Bordonove reminds us in his consideration of King Henri III (though with no documentation), "the king shut himself up with his darlings [*mignons*—the word can also mean "familiars"] to indulge in unnatural vice"—*Les Rois qui ont fait la France: Henri III, roi de France et de Pologne* (Paris: Pygmalion/Gérard Watelet, 1988) 216. Although for most scholars, the dinner served by nude women of the court on Henri's return from Poland had no particular import in the normal libertine surroundings, for Balzac it was Catherine de Médici's attempt to turn Henri from "his bad habits"—Balzac, *Sur Catherine de Médicis, La Comédie humaine*, Bibliothèque de la Pléiade, Vol. 11 (Paris: Gallimard, 1980) 169.

18. L'abbé de Choisy, *Mémoires de l'abbé de Choisy habillé en femme* (Paris: Mercure de France, 1983) 324.
19. See Jean-François Richer, "Bruits et rumeurs dans *La Vieille Fille* d'Honoré de Balzac," *Dix-neuf* 17.3 (November 2013): 265–75.
20. See Edouard Morot-Sir, "La dynamique du théâtre et Molière," *Romance Notes* 15, supplement no. 1 (1973–74): 39. Morot-Sir argues that "*comic form* is revealed in a clear idea of the obstacle standing in the way of destiny, as a *setback* or a *hiccup*, and how it is put into a complicitous relationship with love and subterfuge; there are then good and bad *deceits*—justifiable and dishonorable *impostures*. Besides, the imposture controls both the enemy and the friend; and the way it is revealed as it relates to complicity of love and subterfuge: the comic function, which becomes the essence of comedy, is the play of ignorance and deceit, the behavior of 'the one who does not know' causes the laughter." *La Vieille Fille* would illustrate Morot-Sir's view nicely, at least up to the point where Rose makes her decision.
21. Pierre-Georges Castex, ed., *La Vieille Fille*, by Honoré de Balzac (Paris: Garnier, 1957) 62n1.
22. Berthier, "Introduction," *La Vieille Fille / Le Cabinet des antiquités* (Paris: Garnier-Flammarion, 1987) 10.
23. Jameson, "Ideology" 29–49; Laffly, "La Politique dans *La Vieille Fille*," *Ecrits de Paris*, novembre 1970: 66–75; Robert Kopp, "Préface," *La Vieille Fille*, by Balzac, Folio (Paris: Gallimard, 1978).
24. Hanska 12 February 1837, 1.483; and 4 May 1843, 2. 210.

CHAPTER 10

Restoration Boneyard: *Le Cabinet des Antiques*

Le Cabinet des antiques was begun rather early in 1833. The Restoration had failed in France, and the glow of the new July Monarchy was already beginning to fade. Balzac wrote to Mme Hanska on several occasions that he had composed the introductory pages. He took them to Geneva to read to her, and mentioned them again subsequently. Although Bardèche assures us that we can be quite certain the 1833 draft existed, neither Louvenjoul nor anyone else has been able to locate it; therefore we cannot be sure that the "seventeen pages" that Balzac announced were that lengthy. The text that he published in *La Chronique de Paris* in 1836 may in fact be this very early manuscript of 1833. Whatever the case, it is interesting that the draft was written near the beginning of his composition of the *Scènes de la vie de province*, while he was working on *Eugénie Grandet* ("Notice," HH 11–21). The major themes of *Le Cabinet des antiques* reappear throughout these scenes focused on the provinces, and most of them in other works as well.

Balzac's intentions for *Le Cabinet des antiques* were clear, at least to him, for he was able to tell Mme Hanska that "*Le Cabinet des antiques* will serve as closure for *La Vieille Fille*."[1] Nonetheless, despite his assurance, the novel has long been controversial, for it seems to lack focus. The d'Esgrigneux family obviously portrays the faded, impoverished, virtually forgotten remnants of a once important house. Though they are aware of their long, distinguished history, they resemble antiques in a museum (*cabinet*). They lack almost everything except historical, hereditary value.

The most troublesome issue concerns their names, which repeatedly arise in critics' discussions. Although easily identifiable from their earlier life in *La Vieille Fille*, major characters who appear in *La Vieille Fille* have acquired new names when they reappear in *Le Cabinet des antiques*. Why would Balzac make such changes, especially since he meant for the two novels to have an intimate relationship and to appear together under the collective title of *Les Rivalités*? Nicole Mozet refused to take a position on the renaming, "It is impossible to determine with certitude why Balzac [...] struggled to mask the relationship that unites these two novels."[2] Castex suggested that the novelist might have wanted to make the publisher Souverain believe he was getting a brand-new conception, rather than the continuation of a previous effort.[3] We have to note, however, that if Balzac had wanted to deceive Souverain in 1839, he made no effort to undo the alterations in the Furne edition of 1844, when Souverain was no longer involved. Whether because of the onomastic puzzle or for some other reason, major critics have moreover failed to provide their normal depth of analysis toward unwrapping the novel's hidden components and thus to permit more adequate readings.

Balzac's decision to use the same characters in *La Vieille Fille* and *Le Cabinet des antiques*, though with new names in the latter novel, is a variation on his oft-used device of reappearing characters. This particular arrangement has several possible justifications. His personages are types, if not archetypes. Though he often exploits names in an allusive manner, using them to emphasize qualities of both the character and the underlying thrust of the novel's meaning, they are in effect mere labels, one among many related details. By changing them, Balzac was able to purge the previous characters of some of their old connotations and to shift the emphasis of the new novel to a different social class, moving from the upper middle class with a long, distinguished history, to the old, provincial aristocracy. In a way, he thus assures the anonymity of his fictional "sources," whether bourgeois families like that of Rose Cormon of *La Vieille Fille* or the provincial nobility, the subject of *Le Cabinet des antiques*.

The Chevalier de Valois of *La Vieille Fille* has lost his family name and becomes simply the Chevalier, though he is still remembering his flirtations with Princesse Goritza (4.1093). Rose Cormon's entire name disappears. Her husband's new name of du Croisier replaces her previous married name of du Bousquier. And the setting, which several scholars have identified as Alençon, is never explicitly designated. Nonetheless, despite the revisions and apparent contradictions between the two novels, the final text of *Le Cabinet des antiques* "is admirably integrated [; ...] the unity of tone and the unity of emotion are perfect," as Bardèche judges.[4] The problem comes when these two panels of *La Vieille Fille* and *Le Cabinet des antiques* are viewed together as a diptych.

The incongruous names that have long bedeviled critics in their introductions to the different editions is resolved on taking particular notice of the overture to *Le Cabinet des antiques*. Balzac has the narrator make his reasons for the name changes clear. As he says: "[T]he names of this street and of this city must remain hidden here. Everyone will appreciate the motives for this wise restraint required by conventional propriety [... T]he names of the main personages will also be changed [...] to hide the truth" (4.965–66). The reader is asked to understand that had the real situation been exposed, it would have harmed important people. Thomas Conrad recognizes that Balzac is exploiting the roman à clef.[5] By the very pseudonyms, the text suggests that there exists another "true" reality behind the surface, just as the roman à clef implies true personages behind the fictional names and characters or a capital letter followed by ellipses. In short, this particular application of aliases or onomastic drift allowed Balzac to play on the device of realism, as though by shielding the imaginary characters of *La Vieille Fille*, he was protecting the identity and reputation of living sources. In fact, Balzac is merely borrowing an old device to enhance realism that is found in many eighteenth-century novels: pseudonyms declared to be such or a capital letter followed by ellipses suggests real people whose identity must be kept secret if the true story be told. Such devices are of course a variation on the imaginary sources of a "diary found in an old trunk" or "letters tucked away," all for the later narrator to discover. Marivaux's *La Voiture embourbée* (1714) or Constant's *Adolphe* (1816) provide examples. Without pretending to have found an aged, hidden manuscript, Balzac simply changed the names when he wrote *Le Cabinet des antiques*.

The very pretense to truth, of course, indicates fiction, as Boris Tomashevsky points out.[6] Still, there is a hidden reality in *Le Cabinet des antiques*. If readers have been reading in the sequential order that Balzac chose for *La Comédie humaine*, they have already come to know several of the main characters of *La Vieille Fille*, though with different names.[7] Like the shells which decorate Judge Blondet's house, these characters are shells, similar to those washed up on a beach.[8] The inner being is either gone or in the process of dying and rotting away. Likewise, almost all the major characters in *Le Cabinet des antiques* are a variety of a shell character. To a large degree, it is for the reader to remember the physical traits, attitudes, behavior, and background that have already been detailed in *La Vieille Fille* under different names and to recall so as to fill in their carapace in *Le Cabinet des antiques*. Readers should draw on the earlier descriptive characterization labeled with the name of du Bousquier to judge the substance of this aggressive but impotent man. The later novel assumes the continuation of many details and even hints at du Croisier's sexual deficiencies (4.1071), with which readers of the previous creation are acquainted.

Balzac deployed the device not to confuse readers and not just to emphasize the current subject but to serve to increase verisimilitude of both *La Vieille Fille* and *Le Cabinet des antiques* and to encourage readers to find the "hidden" truth. After all, the latter tale is a shocking story about the only child of an ancient, noble family, who fraudulently draws a substantial sum on a major bank. Balzac claimed that the real-life story inspiring him told of a conviction, prison, and branding.[9] Though his fictional rapscallion, Victurnien d'Esgrignon, is not so brutally treated, what he did and what happened to him is implicitly so terrible that it would, if revealed, provide the whole of France with a scandal that could mortally wound what remained of the aristocracy and, in addition, would have cast a damaging light on the period's system of justice. By masking the names of the characters in *Le Cabinet des antiques*, Balzac suggests not only that the novel is true, but that *La Vieille Fille* is, as well.

The king provokes further thought about Balzac's characterization. The monarch is mentioned several times in *Le Cabinet des antiques*, while the Duchesse Diane de Maufrigneuse and others act in the background to save the young Count d'Esgrignon from condemnation and branding, if not worse (Diane brings a mortal poison for his use, in case he should be convicted). As a *deus ex machina*, the monarch is somewhat better prepared in Balzac's text than is Molière's in *Tartuffe*, though both kings function in the same way. In neither *Tartuffe* nor *Le Cabinet des antiques* is the king himself ever incarnated; his influence is, however, manifested at the last moment by his agent who brings regal justice and promises. The king, in short, is a shell character, lacking the pretense of flesh and blood or even a visual image. After having said that Chesnel "would have had the eternal Father intervene if he had had the power" (4.1052), Balzac's narrator calls attention to the king's absence when he has Chesnel cry out, "Open in the name of the King!" and then points out that the faithful notary "was getting mixed up, he was delirious" (4.1053). The king certainly does not accompany Chesnel—only his title. Actually, Molière's depiction of his seventeenth-century monarch has a much easier time than his regal offspring represented in Balzac's nineteenth-century fiction. Louis XIV has the power to have the despicable Tartuffe hauled off to jail, while Balzac's Louis XVIII has to await Diane's successful manipulations before showering appointments on his obedient servants.

The absent king is an indication of the importance of missing substance. Just as *Le Cabinet des antiques* is designed to shine a brilliant light on the value of the French aristocracy, now deficient in true nobility, and on the corrupt French legal system that undergirds the monarchy, so it also illuminates the Restoration itself which had only an inadequate grasp on power. In this novel the fragile system resembles Emile Blondet's childhood vision of the d'Esgrignon circle seen through the windows, "some with wobbling heads, others dried up and black like mummies; these stiff, those bent over, all wrapped in fantastic clothes that were out of style" (4.976). The poorly articulated parts of mechanical people seemed to lurch and jolt, all with terrifying rapidity that makes the boy, Emile Blondet, think of the sinister, imaginary creations of Maturin and Hoffmann (4.796). Like ossified museum pieces, they have no real life, though they are theatrical, pompous, even seemingly supernatural. The mature Blondet says he imagined them occupying the furniture of museums in major European cities.

However active these noble figures may appear to the watching boy, they lack the most important thing. Implicitly, though continuing to move, they are effectively defunct, empty of true life, and lacking in value. Rather than exploiting their hereditary talents and virtues to establish new positions that would benefit the whole of France, nobles have chosen the easy path of self-centered enjoyment. It is precisely the life Vautrin recommends in *Illusions perdues*: "a life of pleasure, of honors, of continuing parties" (5.703). While hoping for reinstatement to former glories, the aristocracy is unwilling to devote the effort and authentic nobility of character required to rise to its previous position at the apex of a society that would lead to better lives for everyone. Their power is gone, as, in the case of the d'Esgrignons, are the accouterments of former glories. Despite moments after the defeats of Napoleon, when these leftovers of bygone days muster hope of regaining their former positions, the marquis's declarations of a better future seem utterly ludicrous. Mlle Armande suddenly sees the truth. "There are terrible deaths for the noble races that are falling," she says (4.1030).

Similar to the "noble" characters, justice has nothing but the shell-like outer appearance of the virtue it represents. As the empty nature of the old aristocracy is revealed to Emile through the windows of the d'Esgrignon house, so the evisceration of Restoration justice is illuminated behind the panes of Judge Blondet's greenhouse, where the most powerful of the local judges happily spends his time puttering with his peregoniums, a rarified variety of geraniums. Perhaps it was a simple matter for his learning and authority to be suborned in his greenhouse, since he "had enormous disdain for his legal knowledge" (4.1064). The way desired outcomes are effected has become unimportant for both the aristocratic class and the judicial institution; only the goal matters. Aristocrats and legal authorities sink to vile acts in order to accomplish desired ends that are possible only when the motivations and means are kept secret (5.701). Likewise, because Victurnien's judicial condemnation might embarrass the king, the judge closes his eyes to the truth. Vautrin uses a biblical reference to explain the new world: "Your society no longer loves the true God, but rather the Golden Calf!" (5:701). As Vautrin, in the guise of the abbé Carlos Herrera in *Illusions perdues*, puts it to Lucien de Rubenprès, "Work to be rich!" (5.701). Forget true virtue. In short, adopt the morality of the bourgeoisie, which by definition lacks nobility. Buy a title, much as du Croisier purchases the aristocratic Victurnien for marriage to his niece. Subvert justice, as does the king. Balzac reveals the middle class in all its corrupt baseness. Likewise the aristocracy of the Restoration, however beautiful its external appearance, is rotten within its shell, and willing to use any means whatsoever to succeed. "Take up a brilliant goal and hide your way of reaching it" (5.701), advises Vautrin in *Illusions perdues*. The means are unimportant, only appearances matter (5.700).

The other reality beneath *Le Cabinet des antiques* and *La Vieille Fille* is neither people nor events. It is rather the attitudes, influences, movements, in short, the very relationships within society. Balzac, as "a historian of the manners" of the Restoration ("Préface," 4.962), wanted to paint as accurate a picture as humanly and artistically possible. In *Le Cabinet des antiques* he uses consideration of an old provincial family to reopen questions of class, parenting, celibacy,[10] the gerontocracy, and justice, all with the social relationships and interactions between Paris and the provinces clearly in mind. With each of his novels, the sociologist in Balzac attempted to grip the reader's attention while providing a fuller perspective on the reality of post-Revolutionary France. It is neither an accident nor a unique event that du Croisier (aka du Bousquier) and Victurnien went to Paris, only to return ingloriously, nor that Emile Blondet left the provinces, where he could not succeed because of his illegitimacy, for Paris and a noteworthy career. As Balzac told Madame Hanska, "I believe I will have well painted the triple movement that leads poets, nobles, and bourgeois from the provinces to Paris. *Le Cabinet des antiques, Le Député d'Arcis* and *Illusions perdues,* which will themselves form two of the volumes of *La Comédie humain* [and] do a good job at representing our period" (Hanska, 21 December 1842). The novelist had been struck by the importance of this movement of people, money, and ideas between the provinces and Paris. Because it marked a significant stage in the modernization of France, he returned to it repeatedly in *Les Scènes de la vie de province.*

The novel's title came to Balzac as early as 1833, for he discusses it in the already mentioned letter to Madame Hanska (1.108). As usual with the titles of his fictions, it has considerable depth of significance, multiple meanings, and plural implications for Balzac to exploit and his audience to enjoy. While the *cabinet* of the title does not in this novel have the sense of an office where work or study takes place, as the French word still does, since the d'Esgrignons do no worthwhile work, it reminds us that under the Valois kings, the marquises d'Esgrignon were quasi-princes with enormous power. In the sixteenth-century court of Henri IV they were a part of the close friends and high-ranking officials that surrounded and counseled the monarch, thus a part of the king's cabinet (4.993, 1008). Now, their day has passed, and their fortunes have declined. As said before, they remain rather like antiques in a museum (a *cabinet des antiques*). They are able to gain the anonymous, secret help of the king and his trusted associates only through the influence of intermediaries and that effort is made only to preserve the monarchy from embarrassment. After all, it would not look good for an old-line, aristocratic family to be accused of thievery, much less be convicted. Still, I suspect that the most important reason for the title is its suggestion of one of the popular spectacles during the eighteenth and nineteenth centuries: a waxworks (a *cabinet de cire*) like those of Curtius and Tussaud, where images of famous or notorious people and important events were portrayed, often caricatured, in wax, then put on display and preserved.

The family's isolation is highlighted by Emile Blondet telling how he used to admire Mlle Armande d'Esgrignon through the windows of their salon, which he likens to a "glass cage" (4.975, 977). As a boy, he watched corseted and powdered "mummies" with wax-colored skin ("teint de cire" 4.976), dressed in outmoded styles, as though preserving a past reality (4.976). These are but the ruins of history that have little resemblance to life. The beauty of Mlle Armande, her emerald eyes, fair skin, and slim figure projected the spirit of the feudal age for Emile (4.972–73) and made him believe in the superiority of the family heir, Victurnien (4.977). Still, despite the d'Esgrignon family's previous importance, everything has changed. "[N]o one thought at court or in the government of the house of Esgrignon's grandeur. [B]eyond the gates of the city, [it] was completely unknown" (4.982). This has become increasingly clear, since the marquis has remained isolated "in the depths of his province, where poverty had kept him" (4.997). The family's power passed away definitively with the money and lands they lost during the Revolution, a period that the marquis denigrates by referring to it merely as "the troubles" (4.967).

The truth about the real world of nineteenth-century France is quite different from the elegance the Esgrignon family projects for the young Emile gazing through their windows and serving as the reader's surrogate. The d'Esgrignons are lost in a past that no longer exists. "[T]here were more than sixty leagues between the *cabinet des antiques* and the Tuilleries; there was a distance of several centuries" (4.1007). Whatever vanity that the old marquis feels about his distinguished family and history, his heredity is almost devoid of value in the Restoration world. Money has become "the only power of the period,"[11] and the marquis, unfortunately, has no insight into "the great changes produced by industry and modern attitudes" (4.983). Importance is measured not in titles, not in land, not in aristocratic lineage, but in the amount of taxes paid (4.994). The old marquis's incomprehension of present reality is remarkable.

Chesnel, who handles the financial affairs of most of the department's families, has a better understanding. "For him the Revolution had formed the spirit of the new generation" (4.984). Rastignac's summary is accurate: "[W]e have passed from the Fact to the Idea, from brutal force to intellectual force" (4.1013). He means that Parisians are capable of generalization and abstraction and are thus able to transform the meager items that come to them from the provinces into productive ideas. A hundred francs unearthed in the provinces and taken to the bankers in Paris, for instance, can be lent out over and over again, thus multiplying its "value" accordingly. Provincial exceptions like Monsieur Grandet, who are able to work on a high, intellectual plane similar to Parisians, can often act resourcefully at the right moment to vanquish those in the capital city. Such individuals are capable of independent action and thought and do not need to be a part of a group, unlike most provincials. They can perceive the complex, multiple systems operating in the modern, industrial world and are themselves capable of systematic manipulation. As the narrator says, "In Paris, men are systems, in the Provinces systems become men, and some of these are men with unceasing passions, always present, spying on home lives, discussing what has been said, observing each other like duelists ready to thrust six inches of a blade in the [opponent's] side" (4.979–80). Provincials' analytical ability is always oriented toward the particular, the individual, the material event. "When they move from Thought to Fact" (4.1033), they have succeeded, although their success is far short of what their Parisian cousins attain by utilizing a more comprehensive mental activity that proceeds from fact or event to meaning, implication, and potential, that is, to thought.

With the destruction of the Esgrignon chateau during the Revolution (4.967) and the demolition of the imposing mansion the family formerly owned in town (4.968), they have been forced to occupy a much less regal residence that the local dignitaries who have been socially excluded mockingly term the *hôtel d'Esgrignon* (the d'Esgrignon mansion 4.966). Two factories now occupy the location of the earlier much grander residence (4.968). The august character of the old marquis and the beauty of his sister have been enough to invest the pathetic, present reality and the house's name with a certain dignity. Still, even on a reduced scale, the 9000-franc income from the remaining, modest, family estate would not be able to support the marquis and his wastrel son, were it not for the generosity of the family retainer, Chesnel, who has made a fortune as a local notary, while continuing to serve the d'Esgrignon family faithfully. His name suggests *chenil*, or kennel (Berthier 44), and highlights the retainer's canine devotion to the family. In the end it is no surprise that he dies "like an old, faithful dog in his triumph" (4.1094). The novel's progression of episodes shows that the old order carapace of the aristocratic shell is pierced and opened, allowing the reader to perceive another, less impressive reality.

On remembering that a *cabinet* is also a piece of furniture used to store jewels and other precious objects, often in secret drawers, it is worth wondering whether the author might have had the family's heir in mind. Victurnien d'Esgrignon would give reason to believe that he was special (4.982), that, as the Chevalier puts it, "he will go far; I see in him the excesses of men who later accomplish great things..." (4.995). The Chevalier is not disturbed that the boy has run up debts of 100,000 pounds, caused some property damage while hunting, and impregnated several local girls, for he was, after all, educated in eighteenth-century France and considers such infractions of little importance (4.987). The boy is unquestionably the hope of his father and aunt (4.982), who are unaware of the extent of Victurnien's dissipation. Chesnel has simply paid the boy's gambling debts and bought off angry parents and proprietors, a service that the boy took as his due. After all, the Esgrignon heir knew that his family had once held near-absolute power. His father, the aged marquis, had moreover indoctrinated him in the belief that the unpleasant realities of 1822 would eventually be put aright. "[T]his foolishness will pass like all the others. [...] 'God swept aside Buonaparte, his armies, and his great vassals, his thrones and his vast conceptions! God will deliver us from the rest!'" (4.984). The old man expressed his disdain for the Emperor Bonaparte by adding the "u," as was not uncommon among the monarchists of the day. Born in Corsica, Napoleon Buonaparte was a foreigner, they thus implied, not really French.

Another task the sociologist in Balzac confronted was the education of the noble heir, Victurnien. The governing pedagogy was out of date. It did not attempt to raise the boy to be honest, financially responsible, and respectful toward others. Indeed, the Chevalier and the Vidame de Palmiers join together to make it perfectly clear that the young Count d'Esgrignon was raised to be a part of an incredibly privileged class that no longer exists (Péraud 69–72). As Diane de Maufrigneuse explains to Mlle Armande and Chesnel, "So you want to remain in the fifteenth century when we are in the nineteenth? My dear children, nobility no longer exists; there is no longer anything but the aristocracy" (4.1092). She means that nobility retains nothing of its previous rights, privileges, and virtues. All that remains is aristocratic heredity, which no longer has any importance. The courts are as ready to judge aristocrats as they judge bourgeois. It is consequently time for Victurnien to learn to obey the laws and attitudes governing the whole of bourgeois France, for unlike his ancestors he is accountable. For this reason Péraud argues that *Le Cabinet des antiques* is "a degraded epic poem that tells of the fall of the nobility" (66). Of course, in times of transition, like those of the Restoration, there are occasional miscarriages of justice that prolong the very life of the hereditary aristocracy, as the story of the young Victurnien illustrates. In the end, however, France was being transformed into a new world, where the middle class reigns. Balzac did not view this as a happy result, but it was indeed the sociological reality of competing classes, motives, and outcomes that he recorded. Beneath the enfeebled aristocratic government invented during the Restoration and

July Monarchy, there existed the brash, ill-mannered, uncultured, corrupt bourgeoisie bearing France into the Industrial Revolution and, indeed, into modernity.

Victurnien is an exceptional young man. Handsome to a fault, he is also blond, with fair skin and grace of movement. In addition, he is athletic and both a superb shot and horseman. Finally, if good looks are not enough, he has an excellent memory, and he is intelligent, quick, perceptive, and, at least for a provincial nobleman, well educated. How could his family not believe that these gifts "should one day suffice to bring the marquis d'Esgrignon's ambitions to fruition" (4.987)? How could such a child not be indulged? Naturally, as the family's hope for the future, he was pampered and became a vain egotist (4.987, 1007). The narrator makes it clear that the boy was very poorly parented. His father, the marquis, was so distant as to be almost absent, ignored his responsibilities, and depended on others to discipline his son (e.g., 4.1006). As was demonstrated in *La Rabouilleuse*, Balzac concurred with twenty-first-century psychologists that children lacking fathers commonly fail to have respect for the law. It is perfectly in character, then, that while ready to defend his honor against any challenge, Victurnien is not above lying to local girls about the possibility of marriage in order to facilitate his little affairs (4.988). The fact that Chesnel is always available to get him out of trouble, even when he is guilty of corrupting a minor, encourages his lack of respect for the law. "He regarded the courts as though they were scarecrows that had no impact on him" (4.989). He was wrong.

Victurnien is further deprived of a real mother, for his had died in childbed. While his aunt idolizes him to the point of relinquishing the possibility of marriage in order to take on the duties of a mother, like all unmarried women she lacks a fundamental maternal gift: she is simply unable to treat him rigorously, as a mother would and should. Consequently, lacking this maternal closeness and sensitivity, she cannot foresee and forestall catastrophe. An aunt like Mlle Armande "will not have these sudden warnings, these uneasy hallucinations of mothers [...]. [A] mother is irreplaceable. A mother foresees evil long before an old maid like Mlle Armande recognizes [a problem], even after it has [already] occurred. One foresees disaster, the other remedies it" (4.985). Chesnel has a better sense of what is taking place with the boy than does the aunt, but he is of so little account in the family that he fails to make an impression, much less a difference, at least not until they are faced with disaster. As Chesnel tells Mlle Armande, "[H]e needed a severe guide, and that could be neither you, who are unmarried, nor me to whom he didn't listen" (4.1030).

We soon learn that the young man is not merely spoiled and vain; he is weak (e.g., 4.1093). Thanks to complacent tutors and his unrestrained companions, his moral fiber has become highly elastic. As Chesnel discovers, Victurnien is able to confess and repent one day, only to indulge in the same error the next. "Victurnien [...] had suddenly developed the weakness of sensualists, at the point when, to exercise and strengthen his character, he needed a diet of frustrations and distress" (4.991). Because of his wretched upbringing and his isolation from the real demands of nineteenth-century France, which keeps him from forming an accurate view of this new society, he judges everything according to his own egotistical needs and desires. He is, then, "struck with a frightening weakness at his center" (4.1006). He is destroying himself through his pleasures (4.1000). Beneath his handsome shell, he is empty of substance and lacks character.

Du Croisier manifests the provincial talent of analysis that allows him to delve into the Esgrignon heart and mind and recognize that the family's weakness lies in the heir (4.1033). As an ambitious bourgeois parvenu, he was infuriated when Mlle Armande turned down his request for marriage, which would have opened the whole of local society to him. Furthermore, as additional reason for his hatred, despite his marriage to a bourgeois woman of considerable wealth and prestige, the d'Esgrignons never welcomed him into their home. Likewise, du Ronceret, another closet liberal around du Croisier, "had aspired to the honors of the *cabinet des antiques* without having been able to obtain them" (4.981–82). As a result, as Chesnel explains to Mlle Armande, the official "radiates nothing but revenge against you and the whole of nobility" (4.1000). While their anger and bitterness simmer beneath the surface, du Croisier and his allies are reduced to forming a salon composed of commoners like the local prefect, various judges, and a gathering of administrators and government employees, all of whom have felt the ridicule and insulting witticisms directed at them by the Chevalier and other members of the aristocratic salon. They are also aware of their own inferior status, which whets their desire for revenge. Du Croisier becomes the point man, *un croisé* or crusader, in a crusade of vulgar, heartless, bourgeois modernity against the very nobility that once led crusades against the infidels. It constitutes a war between the nobility and the bourgeoisie (4.1057).

Despite having ostensibly adopted conservative ideas, du Croisier leads the local liberals. In fact, he is purely a man of the left. He would be happy to sweep all nobles aside, but particularly pleased if he can expose them to public shame and humiliation in the process. He surrounds himself with liberals like Monsieur du Ronceret, presiding judge of the district tribunal (whose name derives from a word meaning "filled with brambles"[12]), and M. Sauvager, the deputy public prosecutor, whose name is self-explanatory. Du Croisier decides to exploit his insight into Victurnien's flaws, so as to wreak his vengeance on the entire Esgrignon family (4.985). He and his friends, whom the narrator repeatedly compares to "savage[s]" (4.980, 981, 986), will not be content until Mlle Armande, the marquis, and Chesnel are ruined and disgraced (4.999). Victurnien has been encouraged in his errant ways by Fabien du Ronceret, President du Ronceret's son and an "agent provocateur" (4.990), whom du Croisier uses to further tempt and weaken the young count's character. The members of du Croisier's salon "[a]ll hope to ruin [the d'Esgrignons] through [Mlle Armand's] nephew, to see him fall into the sludge of the streets [*boue*]" (4.1000). As Chesnel explains: "Their vengeance was based on this scamp's vices" (4.1005). The notary recognizes that Victurnien's depredations in the region have put him in serious trouble, which affects the family, and he has him sent to Paris, though the young man is unprepared for any useful position in the world of the Restoration, whether at the court or elsewhere. He is, however, all too prepared for Parisian "dissipations which he was unable to resist" (4.1006).

In fact, Victurnien's spendthrift, philandering behavior is not entirely his fault. Balzac described in horrifying detail in such novels as *Pierrette* how the old men of the modern gerontocracy had not only taken authority during the Napoleonic wars, they have refused to give it up.[13] As Victurnien guessed, and as Athanase Granson proved in *La Vieille Fille*, the youthful possessors of talent, intelligence, and energy have been condemned to stand aside. It is nothing but another version of oligarchy, where the young are serfs. As a consequence, they fill their lives with foolish, often harmful activity. On arriving at the court, an event from which Victurnien and his father hoped to gain a position of some sort, the Esgrignon heir "suddenly guessed the serfdom to which the Restoration, enveloped by its eligible old men and its old courtiers, had condemned the noble youth. He understood that there was no suitable place for him either at court or in the government or in the army, in short, anywhere" (4.1009).

Du Croisier and his friends are dismayed to see Victurnien move out of reach. Their avid desire for revenge is merely delayed, however, for du Croisier's earlier analysis was accurate, and it will not be long before the young man destroys himself. Du Croisier nonetheless finds a way to help the process along. In Paris, Victurnien acutely feels the need to follow Henri de Marsay's model and "rise to the height of his period" (4.1008), which of course means imitating high-living dandys like Ronquerolles, Montriveau, Félix de Vandenesse, or Henri de Marsay. In some cases these men are wealthy; in others they are either living on the funds provided by their mistresses or securing loans in the speculation of a future, wealthy marriage. Such men-about-town cannot do without horses, servants, fine runabouts and carriages, suitably equipped lodging, and all the other accouterments of modern luxury. The Count d'Esgrignon happily follows their example. He gambles, repays invitations with luxurious dinners, and, perhaps worst of all, chooses the prodigal Duchess de Maufrigneuse as a mistress. The 100,000 francs provided by the family melts, and Victurnien is forced to return repeatedly to Chesnel, whose purse he erroneously considers inexhaustible.

The young Victurnien d'Esgrignon makes three major mistakes. First of all, he falls in love, an irrational error no true dandy would make. Secondly, like Lucien de Rubempré he does not choose a mistress according to her financial or social potential. No sensible dandy would be so foolish; witness Maxime de Trailles, Rastignac, Ajuda-Pinto, and others. They understand that money is the single most important item in any plans for a future in Restoration society. Furthermore, Victurnien takes on debt that he cannot possibly either pay himself or delay until he has the requisite fortune or deflect to someone else for payment. Balzac's world is full of dandys who easily find solutions to any of these strictures. Victurnien would certainly have done so, had he not been paralyzed by his vain incapacity to let his need be known early in his Parisian stay. In fact, he did very well in beginning at the top of Parisian society as a modish aristocrat. With deeper pockets, he might have been successful. Victurnien does not understand that "you succeed at everything through women" (4.1020). Phrased crassly, he does not know how to exploit his mistress, the highborn duchess de Maufrigneuse. As a final, crucial error, he breaks the law in a way that is almost impossible to deny or hide. The sum total of his foolishness is inexcusable, as Henri de Marsay and his friends agree. Victurnien simply does not have the qualities needed to succeed in Paris. Jealous of the dazzling success the young man enjoyed while emptying the very limited family coffers, his malicious friends watch his failure with some pleasure (4.1014, 1023).

Had the count's mistress, Diane de Maufrigneuse, known of his need, she might have been able to help him, for she is extremely well connected.

Marriage to Victurnien is of course impossible, since she has a husband living separately, and as economically as possible, though major debts were paid off with Diane's dowry (6.990). After her marriage, Diane was left overwhelmed by her own outstanding loans. She still enjoys an income of 60,000 pounds per year, but she spends 200,000 (4.1023–24). As a result of her social position and borrowed money, she has been able to remake herself into an angel of innocence, at least for the naïve Victurnien (and later for d'Arthez). While one of the queens of society, her financial distress makes her unable to extricate Victurnien from his financial trouble and unwilling to run away with him. Only after he has committed a fraud does she become actively involved in attempting to rescue the hapless young man.[14]

Victurnien's abysmal failure is self-induced. After almost immediately running through the cash that he brought from home and that he begged from Chensnel, he returns again and again to the family for more. Finally, a 6000-franc gambling debt pushes him over the edge. The notary Cardot, who has already advanced 30,000 francs, refuses to provide more. Promising to repay the loan quickly, Victurnien secures permission to draw 10,000 francs on du Croisier's account at the Keller bank, which reduces some of the pressure. The gambling debt is personal, yet imperative. As for the loan he accumulated to maintain a luxurious lifestyle, it remains, grows, and eventually comes due. In a show of insouciant generosity, Henri de Marsay gives him 20,000 francs, which allows Victurnien to ignore his debt and continue his pleasures, while writing Chesnel to ask for more money (4.1022). Balzac's readers have met Marsay numerous times in other novels and short stories. The narrator says in this fiction that he "enjoys evil" (4.1023). Elsewhere we learn that he paid for the privilege of raping the kidnapped Lydie Peyrade (6.661). Marsay watches with pleasure as Victurnien, who already owes a significant amount, adds to his loans. During the winter of 1823–24, his debt with Keller and, more important, with du Croisier increases to 227,000 francs. Du Croisier apparently concludes that it is enough for his purposes. He presents the notes to Chesnel with the demand for forty-eight-hour repayment, a demand that the family notary meets only by mortgaging the rest of his personal property. Du Croisier then writes to Keller, closing off that source of funds for Victurnien, and another letter informing the latter of the action he has taken (4.1033).

An additional gambling loss and the understanding that he has already "devoured" Chesnel and that his friends will provide no more money leaves the wastrel count desperate (4.1035–38). He considers suicide, but chooses instead to fraudulently draw another 300,000 francs on du Croisier's account, money that he offers his mistress with the proposal that they flee together (4.1038–39). Diane refuses to leave. At first dismayed by his petulant reaction, then distressed, she puts the money away and dismisses him with "a deluge of epigrams [... S]he humiliated, she jabbed, all by herself she wounded the way ten Savages could wound when they wanted to make their enemy suffer while tied to a post" (4.1041). Learning that his aunt has come from the provinces to protect him, Victurnien accompanies her home and hides with Chesnel. He is soon discovered, arrested, and imprisoned, of course, for there are no secrets in the provinces.

Victurnien believes mistakenly that his legal problems come from his fraudulent withdrawal of 300,000 francs from du Croisier's account. Actually, there has not yet been time for this to be discovered; it is his enormous debt that has come due. When Diane de Maufrigneuse bursts upon the provincial scene, dressed as a man, she knows the entire story and comes with the blessing of the invisible king. Balzac then opens the panel representing the second major thrust of the novel. He exposes the hollow reality of a justice that does not rest on eternal, fundamental juridical principles like rectitude and truth; it depends rather on influence and secrecy. Like the pelargoniums that Judge Blondet cultivates, France's system of justice is fragile and needs protection.[15] It is furthermore for sale. The duchess brings 100,000 francs "that the King gave me out of his private funds to buy Victurnien's innocence, if his adversary is corruptible" (4.1077). She has also brought the 300,000 francs Victurnien stole and that she had tucked away. Were there any doubt of the king's willingness to corrupt justice, the narrator goes on to inform us that Chesnel did not hesitate to "suborn" the examining magistrat Camusot in the middle of the street (4.1072).

Balzac, who seldom represses his love of onomastics, tells us that Camusot "has the [snub] nose of his name" (4.1078). He is also married to a woman who desperately wants her husband appointed to a position in Paris and who knows that such an appointment will surely follow from helping the noble family of d'Esgrignons, crown, and church. Mme du Croisier joins the representatives of the monarchy when assured by her confessor that she may lie without displeasing God about the predated receipt for the repayment of the 300,000 francs. The socially illustrious but morally corrupt group standing for God and King is complete. These warriors recognize that neither God's appointed King, nor the court, nor in fact the government would be "pleased to see a name like that of the d'Esgrignons dragged through criminal court" (4.1080). They believe it is important to the whole of France that there exist "a highly regarded aristocracy consecrated by time." While equality has become the ineffective watch cry of the liberal opposition (4.1080), aristocrats feel the demand for equality and justice is patently absurd, though they and their minions feel perfectly justified in postulating the rightness of their cause, while perjuring themselves and corrupting the law, the church, and, indeed, the court. The beautiful aristocratic "shell" is open to reveal the decay within what is left of the formerly ruling class.

The infidel "crusaders" (as mentioned before, in French the word is *croisés*), spearheaded by du Croisier, have been equally busy implementing their plans to discredit the aristocracy. Du Ronceret, the presiding magistrate, intends to replace the absent public prosecutor, who, because he is politically sophisticated, would not abide the liberal attempt to condemn Victurnien. He also attempts to replace the examining magistrate Camusot with Sauvager, for Sauvager has been bought with the promise of marriage to du Croisier's wealthy niece. (Whoever serves as examining magistrate will have authority over the investigation.)

Despite the maneuvering on both sides and however ethically questionable their actions, the defense has been cárefully arranged. The camp of the nobles stands ready to spin the facts as necessary: Victurnien may have been "foolish," he may even have been "imprudent" (4.1080), but at worst he is guilty of an "irregularity" (4.1086). Selectively emphasizing a few facts, they concoct the protective shield. Du Croisier has long made the young count believe that he could borrow whatever he might need. The minute Chesnel learned about the young man's "mistake," as he and his cohorts invent the defense, he returned the 300,000 francs to Madame du Croisier, receiving in return the (predated) receipt. Because Mme du Croisier's husband is traveling, the story goes, he does not learn of the repayment before charging the Esgrignon heir with fraud. The monarchists maintain that the ignoble bourgeois liberals have done nothing but lay a trap. As long as the only son of the noble Esgrignon house is not pressured into damaging admissions, as long as Madame du Croisier is not forced to recant her priest-sanctioned story about the falsely dated receipt, and as long as the sympathetic judicial authorities are firmly in place and retain their prejudice in favor of the nobility, the law can decide that the young man has been tricked. True, he may have been in error, but he is innocent of any criminal behavior. As a reward, Judge Blondet is also promised that his much loved but dullard son, Joseph, will end with an appointment to the magistracy. The judge can vote his conscience, but only if he does not question the elaborate fiction proving Victurnien's innocence, fiction that would not pass the smell test. Aristocratic suborners are not above their bourgeois enemies; they are simply more skilled, better equipped, and in point of fact more audacious.

Le Cabinet des antiques allows us to see into the reality of a provincial nobility that has not lived up to either its responsibilities or its potential. As the young Emile Blondet could look through the windows of the d'Esgrignon salon, so readers are able to peek in the various, handsome shells of aristocratic personages and understand what has happened to the "noble" realm. We learn that the prostitute Suzanne takes the working name of du Val-Noble, the street where the Hôtel d'Esgrignon is located. Her decision gives some indication not only of what has happened to the impotent family but also to the provincial aristocracy they represent. As Philippe Berthier concludes, France's fabled nobility is for sale (43). Nonetheless, while du Croisier fails to bring Victurnien to justice as a criminal, he succeeds in marrying him to his niece, Mlle Duval, and in thus purchasing a title for her. Really, the Count Victurnien d'Esgrignon has little choice but to accept the misalliance. He has bankrupted the house of Esgrignon. Like others of his sort, he allows himself to be bought.

Balzac's initial selection for the Esgrignon family name was Gordes (4.829b, 869a). The obvious suggestion of *gourde* and its emptiness makes a certain sense, given the way these aristocrats have continued to justify the void of their hollow existence by nothing other than a long-gone past, however distinguished. Balzac's final choice of a play on *grignoter*—to nibble or to slowly destroy—makes even more sense, since it illustrates what has happened to this potentially valuable family of great age and current incapacity. Like many provincial families of noble descent, the useless d'Esgrignons are content to live on the margin, deliberately eating into their capital, slowly fading away. Victurnien "was much better educated than are other young provincial nobles, who become hunters, smokers, and very distinguished property owners, but who rather cavalierly treat the sciences and letters, the arts and poetry, all the talents whose superiority offends them" (4.986–87). He may be intelligent, he may be educated, he may be a good shot, but he accepts the role of a frivolous, empty aristocrat. Indeed, he is an immoral wastrel who lacks the purpose of action and resources that are necessary in the modern world. He is certainly not alone. "Today names as illustrious as those of sovereign houses like the Foix-Grailly [and] the d'Hérouville, [who] lacking money, the unique power today, are relegated to an obscurity that is equivalent to extinction" (4.1008).

The narrator gives a more detailed view of the demise of the aristocracy in another passage:

> The d'Esgrignons lacked the foundation of [...] modern aristocracy. They also failed to continue [...] real activity of substance, the renown that catches attention at court as on the battlefield, in diplomatic salons as in the law courts, all of which is like a *Sainte-Ampoule* poured on the heads of each new generation. A noble family that is inactive and forgotten is [like] a girl who is silly, ugly, poor, and chaste, the four cardinal points of misfortune. (4.983)

The "Sainte-Ampoule" was a miraculous glass vial containing the always ample anointing oil used for the coronation of all the kings of France from Louis VII in 1131 to Louis XVI in 1774. Balzac could not be clearer. If the aristocracy were truly noble, they surely would have inherent virtues and talents that could actively continue to serve France.

Restoration justice is also an empty shell having nothing to do with the ideal it represents. Because, in effect, the Count d'Esgrignon is declared innocent by the efforts of several corrupt officials, including the highly regarded and decorated Judge Blondet, we perceive the putrid reality of modern "justice." However sympathetic we may be to the young man, in fact, he should not have been released for lack of evidence. Balzac has painted an egregious miscarriage of justice prefigured by the deceptive reality that Emile Blondet saw early in the novel as he peered through the marquis's salon windows. The narrator is likewise present while a compliant priest condones and, indeed, encourages Mme du Croisier in her essential lie. The reader subsequently has a privileged position to consider the judge's corruption behind the windows of his greenhouse. At best, "[t]he integrity of the judge was equal to his passion for flowers" (4.1068). His commitment has shifted, however, from upholding the principles of the law to growing rare flowers and to promoting his unintelligent son Joseph. We soon learn that he is willing to go further and sell out justice in order to give his lackluster offspring an advantage. Judge Blondet accepts the elaborate stage setting allowing Victurnien to slip away. Although money does not directly pay for the final legal judgment, influence serves as coin of the realm. As a result, justice miscarries. Balzac emphasizes the vacuity of Restoration justice by placing the image of a shell above the judge's front door. Further, the courtyard door is likewise topped by an enormous shell (4.1062). A shell is as hollow as the skeletal nobles moving spasmodically in the *hôtel d'Esgrignon*. Slowly, methodically, Balzac evacuates nobility and justice of their traditional virtues.

The fact that the du Croisier clan is as vile as their aristocratic neighbors changes nothing. It merely emphasizes the universal disintegration of the July Monarchy culture. Du Croisier and his allies simply understand the current legal realities, and like the aristocrats are both willing and able to manipulate the Restoration legal system. They bought off the influential presiding judge, du Ronceret, and the deputy public prosecutor, Sauvager, just as Chesnel buys Judge Blondet. Despite less than convincing justifications, France's justice is rotten to its eviscerated core. The narrator explains:

> Justice was then fanaticized by faith in the monarchy that was repairing the errors of the old *Parlements*, and worked in tandem with Religion, perhaps even too ostensibly. Religion was at this point more zealous than clever. It sinned less through Machiavellianism than through the sincerity of her views, although they seemed hostile to the general interests of the country that she tried to protect from the possibility of revolutions. But taken as a whole, justice still included too many bourgeois elements; it was too accessible to the petty passions of liberalism. Sooner or later, it must become constitutional and join with the Bourgeoisie when the day of struggle came [...] There was hypocrisy, or to be more precise, a spirit of imitation that causes France to model itself on the Court, and, thus, to make a very innocent mistake. (4.1060)

The narrator rises above the contemporary reality to recognize that, although the legal system had been radically revised during the Revolution and again under Napoleon, it remains inadequate for dealing with modern problems, and was thus unfair. It is therefore necessary to counter self-serving injustice by any means whatsoever. Balzac exposes the weaknesses of Restoration justice behind the glass of the judge's greenhouse, much as he has exposed the fragility of the provincial aristocracy through the windows of the d'Esgrignon house (4.1006). Indeed, as the d'Esgrignon salon is a "cemetery" (4.977), so Judge Blondet is "one of these curious figures buried in the provinces like old medallions in a crypt" (4.1063). Approaching death casts its shadow on both the aristocracy and the ossified political gerontocracy.

The story of a minor family in a little country town allows Balzac to shatter the glass shield of major cultural and conceptual social structures undergirding the Restoration and July Monarchy. The mirage behind the windows of the d'Esgrignon family may have appeared glorious to Emile Blondet as a child, if nonetheless somewhat sinister because of the prophetic and funereal associations, but it is little more than imagination and pretense. Considering his nobility, even Victurien "had felt its hollowness" (4.1006). As with an opened shell, readers can look under the onomastic covers of *Le Cabinet des antiques* and reveal the names used in *La Vieille Fille*. The shocking existence of these same people further unveils the disappointing truth of the pretentiousness of the Restoration and the monarchy. We look at M. du Croisier, Mme du Croisier, and the Chevalier, to find very similar shells corresponding to Rose Cormon, du Bousquier, and the Chevalier de Valois. Beneath the hollow characters, Balzac has rendered evident the sociology of the time, a general observation of the state of provincial nobility and the post-Revolutionary system of justice. We discover that the comic reality of *La Vieille Fille* develops into a vicious struggle for power in *Le Cabinet des antiques*. The behaviors, the systems, and the movements that instruct us in the causes that have culminated in the disheveled reality of modern France are brilliantly illuminated.

Notes

1. Letter of 10 February 1837, Hanska 1.483. Philippe Berthier comments on the unity of the two novels: "Introduction," *La Vieille Fille, Le Cabinet des antiques*, by Balzac (Paris: Garnier-Flammarion, 1987) 8.
2. "Introduction" to the Pléiade *Cabinet des antiques* 4.939.
3. Pierre-Georges Castex, "Introduction," *Le Cabinet des antiques* (Paris: Garnier, 1958) vi, a position discussed by Alexandre Péraud, *Le Cabinet des antiques, Honoré de Balzac* (Paris: Bordas, 2004) 33. Diana Knight terms the changed names a "curious oversight"— "Celibacy on Display in Two Texts by Balzac: *Le Cabinet des antiques* and the Preface to *Pierrette*," *Dix-Neuf* 2 (2004): 14.
4. HH 7.21. Nicole Mozet has however noticed a number of anomalies (4.941).
5. Conrad, "*Le Cabinet des antiques* dans *La Comédie humaine*, ou comment 'être un système'," *Nexilis* 1 (14 décembre 2008): 1–12. <http://www.revuenexilis.org/issue1/>

6. Tomashevsky, "Thematics," *Russian Formalist Criticism: Four Essays*, ed. Lee T. Lemon and Marion J. Reis (Lincoln, NE: U of Nebraska P, 1963) 85.
7. I argued previously that Balzac very carefully organized the order in which the fictions of *La Comédie humaine* appear: *Balzacian Montage: Configuring* La Comédie humaine (Toronto: U of Toronto P, 1991) 8–21, 99–148.
8. Péraud provides a conservative discussion of the sources for Victurnien's crime (41–45). There is no definitive relationship with a particular person or event, though Balzac always seeks to give the sense of reality.
9. Ezra Pound developed the concept of a shell character in *Canto VII*.
10. See Knight, "Celibacy on Display" 1–6, 11.
11. 4.1008. As Richard D.E. Burton says, money has replaced titles in importance—*The* Flaneur *and His City: Patterns of Daily Life in Paris 1815–51* (Durham: U of Durham P, 1994) 61.
12. Albert Dauzat, *Dictionnaire étymologique des noms de famille et prénoms de France* (Paris: Larousse, 1951) 526.
13. For a description of pre-revolutionary and revolutionary families, see Suzanne Desan, *The Family on Trial in Revolutionary France* (Berkeley: U of California P, 2004) 141–77.
14. For a more detailed consideration of this brilliant socialite, see my "*Anti-Nous* and Balzac's Princess de Cadignan," *Romance Quarterly* 34 (1987): 425–33.
15. Although the fragile *pelagonium* will not live through the European winters, it does well in protected greenhouses. Brought to Europe before 1600, it became particularly popular in the nineteenth century, when wealthy owners of greenhouses appreciated it for its novelty and susceptibility to hybridization. The tender, rare plants are valued especially for the beauty of their flowers, though it is used primarily for perfume and herbal medicines—Maria Lis-Balchin, "History of Nomenclature, Usage and Cultivation of Geranium and Pelagonium Species," *Geranium and Pelargonium: The Genera Geranium and Pelargonium*, ed. Maria Lis-Balchin (London: Taylor & Francis, 2002) 5.

CHAPTER 11

Aeries and Muck: *Illusions perdues*

In *Illusions perdues*, Balzac turned insightfully to issues of class conflict, social mobility, and the concurrent mention of hierarchical stagnation. He particularly delighted in illustrating the interstices of social forces as a means of explaining the unquestioned turmoil of nineteenth-century France. And he returned as well to antithesis, one of his favorite literary devices. Balzac (and his spokesman Davin) said opposition was "the first law of literature" (1.1162). It is particularly prevalent in the *Scènes de la vie de province*. Balzac loved to set a hero up against villains, only slowly allowing his principal protagonist to win out, as was in most cases the *terminus ad quem*. In few novels is the device so obvious and ubiquitous as in the *Illusions perdues* (1839–43), where the forces of Goodness, Light, and Heaven are engaged in a vicious war against those of Evil, Darkness, and Hell. Eventually the powers of good prevail, though the oppositions touch every level from top to bottom and every element from beginning to end. As is often the case, the final resolution is so unexpected that it smacks of something arranged by the gods. Having been hopelessly defrauded by his father and by the Cointets, which reduces David to prison and his family to the depths of poverty, how but by divine intervention could the Séchard offspring have acceded to a comfortable position of wealth and respect?

In considering the novel's main characters, Per Nykrog makes the point that neither David nor Lucien is independently capable of making his way in society.[1] David Séchard, a strong but gentle bull of a man, works persistently to develop a revolutionary new formula for the manufacture of paper. Nonetheless, he cannot exploit his idea. He lacks the money and the knowledge required to take the few, individually produced samples of his successful product and ratchet up to large-scale production runs necessary to feed the requirements of French newspapers. He needs an investment banker who can manage the financial capital for development and act as an agent in marketing the paper, though perhaps not one like the Cointet combine that intends to swallow the whole invention. Still, because David is a "poet," a dreamer able to come up with revolutionary ideas but lacking the skills and discipline to succeed in this nineteenth-century society that runs on power and money, he must have Petit-Claud serve as the intermediary *deus ex machina*, who arranges everything so that the young man and his family end with a modest return for his invention to add to the fortune he will inherit from his father.

Likewise, his friend Lucien Chardon de Rubempré is also a poet. Slender and not just handsome but beautiful and intelligent, he is, however, weak and lacks persistence. He is thus unable to transform his initial flashes of brilliance into great works of art. Herrera, the evil genius who rescues him from suicide, willingly performs the same role for Lucien that Old Séchard and Petit-Claud do for David. Herrera agrees to "administer his social and financial affairs that the poet is incapable of directing for himself" (Nykrog 45). As Piketty has pointed out at some length, because of the stagnant nineteenth-century economy, it was virtually impossible for young people to rise to positions of ease and power without the backing of a fortune, from whatever source.[2] Hererra provides the essential money for Lucien, as old Séchard does at his death for David. The link between the two poets is further emphasized by Lucien's legitimate family name of Chardon (French for "thistle") on remembering that thistles are an essential ingredient of David's paper. David and Lucien form a sort of oxymoron. Though very different, they are linked by their friendship, talent, and love of Chénier's poetry. They bring many of Balzac's antitheses together, thus giving a more complete vision of the intense individual impulsions and social forces creating modern France.

To the interpersonal oppositions on the micro level, there is an additional macro level that organizes the whole. The author exploits the most common plot structure of all literature: the rise to success and the fall to failure. David's story is singular. He successfully invents a new kind of paper, only to have the idea stolen from him. Lucien, however, has three cycles of rise and fall that extend beyond David's story to add a further link with the next novel, *Splendeurs et misères des courtisanes*. *Illusions perdues* concludes with a terminal chiasmus: David inherits considerable wealth in the midst of losing his invention, allowing him to become a middle-class man of substance, while Lucien comes to the end of his second failure and accepts an agreement that will result in his death, but only after enjoying high-flying life in society that will be told in the initial novel of the following *Scènes de la vie parisienne*.

In his home town of Angoulême, Lucien's native genius permits him to rise above his birth as the son of a pharmacist and a disgraced aristocratic mother, to become the companion in a chaste relationship with the noble Madame de Bargeton. Very shortly after arriving in Paris, however, he begins his first descent. His earlier, provincial rise to success is followed by a traumatic introduction to the capital city, when he experiences his initial failure: he becomes the unsuccessful, cast-off lover of Madame de Bargeton. Any male tossed away by a mistress immediately turns into a figure of ridicule, as Lucien understands, for he plays the traditional role of a dependent mistress at the beck and call of the lover in this affair, and his ridiculousness is only exacerbated by his inability to dress appropriately for fashionable Paris. Determined to succeed, he descends further: first as an impoverished failure of a poet, then as a journalist, then, because of his lack of the most rudimentary standards of honor, as a venal journalist, who fails for the second time. Balzac drags him further into the dregs of society. He tumbles in the conclusion of *Illusions perdues* to an adumbrative ninth circle and becomes Herrera's catamite, if not his adopted son (5.703), or, as he says, his "creature."[3] In the following *Splendeurs et misères des courtisanes*, he will enjoy a great love, social success, and the accouterments of wealth, before experiencing his third failure by being thrown into prison, where he commits suicide.

The antitheses only begin with the now expected opposition between Paris and the provinces: Old Séchard proclaims what has become a truism after having been repeatedly highlighted through the entire length of the *Scènes de la vie de province*: "The provinces are the provinces, and Paris is Paris" (5.133). However clumsily phrased, Séchard points to one of the major lessons of this section of *La Comédie humaine*. Paris and the provinces are seemingly irredeemably separate, a disjunction that must be overcome for France to move into the modern age. Only at the end do we watch the powerful Cointets and their aides leave the provinces, to be safely and happily ensconced in Paris, as little by little the emphasis on the capital city increases through the ten novels of the *Scènes de la vie de province*.

At first, Balzac's narrator remains in the provinces and stresses the great differences between two adjacent areas: on the one hand, Houmeau, a section of the greater city, serves as the commercial and financial center, and, on the other, the upper reaches of Angoulême proper houses nobility and authority. In the mind of David Séchard, the printer and friend of Lucien, Angoulême and Houmeau are separated by distance and by jealousy and remain as far apart as Peking and Greenland (5.149, 151). People holding positions in government, the courts, church, as well as those who have traditional authority, reside in the upper-class, "elevated city" of Angoulême, while the "low city" of the suburban Houmeau is the realm of money and power (5.150). Since the sixteenth century the city had been a manufacturing center of paper. And as is explicitly emphasized, "Commerce is rich; nobility is generally poor" (5.152). Balzac never fails to recognize the potential of the real, material world to bear symbolic value. While the ancient ramparts that surround the upper part of Angoulême significantly limit its ability to grow, Houmeau down below has sprouted "like a bed of mushrooms at the foot of a boulder on the edge of the river" (5.150). Almost anyone would understand that the old world has ground to a stop, while the new expands and, indeed, conquers, as exemplified by the Cointet brothers, who become enormously wealthy by stealing David's invention.

Though the aristocrats' doors are closed to most commoners, however powerful their positions might be, it is certainly not true that the two classes never mix. For all the indications of a closed society, significant breaches exist in the fortifications enclosing the upper city. Lucien and his sister Eve result from the marriage of the daughter of an old-line aristocratic family to a pharmacist, and Lucien is welcomed, if not exactly pursued, by the wife of a family dating back to Louis XIII, whom the irrepressible Balzac christens Madame de Bargeton. A *barge* is a small, not particularly attractive boat used for salvage and rescue. Lucien, naturally, sees her as his ticket to the good life, as he prepares to go off to Paris. His poetic genius (perhaps also his extraordinarily good, if effeminate, looks) fascinates Mme de Bargeton, one of the artsy women whose type the novelist mocks in *La Muse du département*. She decides to be his patroness. She exerts her power on one of her influential admirers, the director of the local tax office. Condescendingly, she calls the latter Monsieur Châtelet, thus putting him on notice that she is quite aware of the illegitimacy of the nobiliary particle he has affected in calling himself Monsieur "du" Châtelet. On leaving off the "de," she effectively coerces him into supporting the poet. The blatant blackmail "petrified" the functionary, since he has been accepted as an appropriate member of Angoulême's high society (5.171). Monsieur Sixte du Châtelet grimly decides to "exterminate" Lucien and take the "queen" who has belittled him to bed (5.172). The text gives little reason to admire Madame de Bargeton.

The great gulf separating the classes becomes even more pronounced in Paris. On first arrival, Lucien reveals with every piece of his attire that he has just arrived from the provinces, and, on studying the passersby with care, he learns how far he remains from the elegant young men of Saint-Germain, the aristocratic quarter of Paris (5.269–70). To reduce this distance requires awareness of Parisian fashion, but, even more, it requires the money he does not have. "You had to be enormously rich to play the role of a handsome fellow [*joli garçon*]" (5.270). Madame d'Espard and his rival M. du Châtelet quickly initiate Madame de Bargeton into the requirements of noble Parisian society, and Lucien's erstwhile patron moves with little disruption into the world of the aristocratic Saint Germain. Conversely, Lucien "understood that an abyss separated him from society" (5.270). Madame de Bargeton, his *dulcinea*, dumps him into "the sludge [*boue*] of Paris" (5.291). It is "a very distinctive kind of muck," that gives the city a notably loathsome stench. This unimaginable horror flowing more or less unimpeded to the Seine was composed of offal, rotting human and animal cadavers, overflowing latrines, horse manure, the effluent of chemists and metalworking shops, household garbage, in short, the sewage of a large, active, nineteenth-century city.[4] In literally hundreds of works from the mid-eighteenth through the mid-nineteenth centuries, the "boue" of the streets symbolizes shame and failure, whatever is vile. Balzac exploited this symbolism by liberally applying it to all aspects of journalism and thus indicating the noisome abyss into which Lucien will shortly fall (e.g., 5.349).

The beautiful, the talented, and the rich had long gravitated to Paris, which promised to win and enhance their "glory, power, and money" (5.297). As Madame de Bargeton told Lucien, that is where "superior people" live (5.249). The daily reality was, however, indescribably horrid. Ymbert Galloix, a Swiss of some twenty years of age, gives a brief description of this Paris, where in October of 1827 he had come to make his fortune and where, in 1828, he died. As he wrote to a friend in Florence, "[Paris], an enormous Babylon saturates you with disgust, with sludge [*boue*], with fatigue, and with sadness. I do not know how you feel in Florence, but it would certainly be worse in Paris, without even considering the extreme difficulty of day to day life. To this point, I have earned nothing, and yet I have true friends who are trying to find something for me."[5] Although Balzac's hero, Lucien, will eventually rise above the *boue* of the streets, he does so by immersing himself in the *boue* of journalism.

Because Lucien is handsome and a talented poet of considerable potential, he has risen in his hometown of Angoulême from a common middle-class existence to local renown as a reasonably successful country poet and the courtier of a provincial but authentic aristocrat. Now that Madame de Bargeton has discarded him in the *boue de Paris*, he has little choice but to revert to his role as an impoverished poet, determined to find recognition. While this phase of Lucien's life would hardly be termed a success, in fact he has reached the apex of his career. No reader of Balzac can fail to recognize that turning from poetry to journalism represents a descent. Success in the dismal trade of journalism, like falling in love with a prostitute, betraying his friends and family, and becoming a forger, illustrates his sliding, moral failure until he is left with nothing, forced to try again in Angoulême. His failure at home sets him up to become the protégé of the homosexual predator, the abbé Carlos Herrera, better known as Jacques Collin or Vautrin.

There exists an extreme difference between the life of an aspiring member of the middle class, like David, and someone like Lucien, who dreams of himself comfortably ensconced in the soft life of aristocratic society. Although David's wife Eve recognizes that her father-in-law has a sizeable fortune in Marsac and other properties, David knows only the reality of the poverty to which his father has reduced him—"[M]y father took pleasure in ruining me" (5.216)—which left him with much diminished assets, a nearly worthless press, out-of-date equipment, but nonetheless an acute desire to succeed. His dicotyledonous opposite, Lucien, also wants to make his mark and will shortly experience firsthand the squalor of Parisian poverty. As Séchard impoverishes David, so Madame de Bargeton when she abandons Lucien. David's father is a self-centered drunk, jealous of his son. Madame de Bargeton is equally egocentric. She can measure herself only against the stupidity of her husband and the pretentious simpletons who people her salon, but the oppositions are repeatedly brought to the reader's attention. None of the mediocrities that surround her can understand poetry—only Madame de Bargeton. She, at least, recognizes Lucien's talent as a poet (5.170), though the dazzling luminaries of Parisian society soon give her a better understanding of her own and of his value.

As is so often the case in *La Comédie humaine*, certain characters become symbols. For David, the name of Eve becomes "a symbol of my love" (5.217). She, "a big brunette" (5.179), who even impresses the family's enemies with her intelligence and beauty, will hopefully produce exceptional children, a new race made for the modern world. Daniel's wife Eve gains her full meaning when highlighted by her difference from Madame de Bargeton and, later, from Coralie. The latter, the "Eve of the wings [of the theatre]" (5.418), becomes Lucien's first great love, raised in his eyes, though in no one else's, above her courtesan state.[6]

Elsewhere, a group of hardworking, ethically outstanding intellectuals called the *Cénacle* opposes the newspapers. Consequently, art is set against journalism, creation against imitation. Lucien "did not realize that he stood between two distinct paths, between two systems represented by the *Cénacle* and by journalism, the first of which was honorable and sure, while long, the other sown with reefs and perils, full of the miry gutters where his conscience would be covered with muck" (5.348–49). The genius of Daniel d'Arthez, one of the members featured here and in "Les Secrets de la princesse de Cadignan," confronts the debased scribbler Lousteau. Unlike the latter and his journalistic brethren, d'Arthez has both exceptional ideas, "the beautiful thought of a poet," "a beautiful talent and [...] a beautiful character" (5.311). Through persistence and hard work, d'Arthez will eventually rise above the *boue* that will engulf both Lucien and Lousteau. Newspapers and their denizens value nothing but what pays off in food, women, or cold cash, and in the present, so much so that such rewards easily induce practitioners to praise or vilify the same object or person on succeeding days. While d'Arthez values truth and beauty above everything else, and will one day attract the Princess de Cadignan (also known as Diane de Maufrigneuse), Lousteau frequents prostitutes. Lucien, moreover, prostitutes himself both in respect to his art and when he swings to Herrera. From the smallest detail—"The dazzling flesh of shoulders and breasts sparkling amidst the almost always somber gentlemen's clothing produced the most magnificent oppositions" (5.360)—to the larger realities of Lousteau's "kennel" dwelling, where "poverty was sinister" (5.350), to the indescribable luxury of the theatre and the wasteful excess of the fast lane, the reader is taken on a partial tour of Paris in the 1820s.

Illusions perdues emphasizes both the potential and the abysmal failure of journalism by using the drunk, Séchard, David's elderly father. Despite Old Séchard's inability to read and write (5.124), he claims that people will not believe they are really married if the announcement of their wedding is not printed with his old type font characters (5.133). While this pronouncement seems merely an amusing foible, it is later followed up in a more blanket claim insisting on the importance of the printed word to verify the reality of happenings in readers' minds. Lousteau maintains that by publishing in the newspapers, Lucien will impose his thought on society (5.383). Unfortunately, Lousteau's unscrupulous colleagues seem uniquely motivated by self-centered desires for debauchery. It is an understatement to suggest that they are unethical; in fact, as the text makes abundantly clear, they are profoundly corrupt.

Balzac uses an allusion to prefigure Lucien's fate. In 1819, shortly before the period when *Illusions perdues* was set, the critic and writer Henri de Latouche had rediscovered the work of André Chénier for the French public. Balzac refers to the revolutionary poet a number of times and, as his Pléiade editor Roland Chollet notes, associated him with "an entire mental atmosphere of youth, exaltation, frenzied idealism" (5.147n2). Certainly, for Balzac, Chénier was "the poet of lovers" (5.229), and was unquestionably one of the great poets of France. The novelist tried early on to pastiche him, he cited his poems in his letters, and he took various passages to serve as epigraphs in his pre-*Comédie humaine* novels by the pseudonymous Lord R'hoone. What Chollet terms his delicate appreciation of Latouche's preface to the 1820 edition of Chénier leaves no doubt of the novelist's appreciation: "A poet found by a poet," Lucien says (5.147 and n2). As Balzac wrote in *La Comédie humaine*, and as he put it in one of his letters to Madame Hanska, Chénier was for him "the poet of love, the greatest of French poets" (Hanska 1.71).

The text of *Illusions perdues* refers to Chénier repeatedly in connection with the two enthusiastic young men, Lucien and David, and casts long shadows of meaning forward, particularly as related to Lucien. Such reiterations always indicate importance in *La Comédie humaine*. Most obviously, Lucien resembles Chénier in that he has great, but never fulfilled promise, however different the reasons for this lack of success. As Latouche put it, "In dying, André Chénier [...] had only a name that promised fame."[7] Lucien, as well, fell short of the mark. The text makes it clear that Lucien could have established himself as an outstanding poet had he been stronger and capable of refusing deceptively easy paths to success, first as a journalist, then as a would-be socialite. In opposition to his hardworking friends, David and d'Arthez, he continues to prefer "the easy life" (5.428) through this novel and that of the subsequent *Splendeurs et misères des courtisanes*, as well.

Those who are familiar with Chénier's verse might be struck by curious parallels between the poet's and Balzac's characters. Perhaps the most notable is the revolutionary poet's mention on a number of occasions of the abandonment of a mother, especially on recalling that Lucien failed to care for his mother in her time of need.

> This Neaera, alas! that he named his Neaera, [*Cette Néère, hélas! qu'il nommait sa Néère,*]
> Who for him criminally abandoned her mother [.] [*Qui pour lui criminelle abandonna sa mère*]. ("Néère 68)

Néère (Neaera), Chénier's persona, is feminine, and Balzac insists on the femininity of Lucien's personal beauty. He had, for example, a woman's hands (5.349), delicate feet, and, moreover, "His hips were shaped like those of a woman" (5.145). Even more important, he has one of "these half-feminine natures" (551). Perhaps only on recalling such descriptions will the reader sense the foreshadowing and see the parallel. Like Chénier's Néère, Lucien abandons his mother. The theme of maternal abandonment is emphasized when Chénier picks it up again in "Malade [Sick]" (called the "Jeune malade [The Young Sick Person]" in most editions), this time with a masculine hero.

> [Apollo] have pity on his mother condemned to tears, [*Prends pitié de sa mère aux larmes condamnée,*]
> Who lives only for him, who dies abandoned, [*Qui ne vit que pour lui, qui meurt abandonnée,*]
> Who did not have to remain to see her son die. [*Qui n'a pas dû rester pour voir mourir son fils*]." ("Le malade" 38).
> Child [said the mother] you wish to die? You wish, in her aged years, [*Enfant tu veux mourir? Tu veux, dans ses vieux ans,*]
> To leave your mother alone with her white hair? [*Laisser ta mère seul avec ses cheveux blancs?*]. ("Le malade" 39)

As is clear, the reason for this abandonment is that he fell in love, the kind of extreme, obsessive passion that leaves the lover helpless, oblivious to any other attachment, and without volitional choice before his mistress. However much he feels and anticipates the pain that comes to himself and others from uncontrollable love, he must pursue the young woman of his dreams, leaving behind the maternal encumbrance.

> Oh carry, carry me to the banks of the Erymanthus, [*O portez, portez-moi sur les bords d'Erymanthe,*]
> That I may again see this virgin dancing! [*Que je la voie encor, cette vierge dansante*]!
> Oh! that I may see the long waves of smoke in the distance [*O! que je voie au loin la fumée à longs flots*]
> Rise from the roof at the edge of this enclosure [*S'élever de ce toit au bord de cet enclos...*] . ("Le malade" 41)
> —Ah! my son, it is love, insane love [*Ah! mon fils, c'est l'amour! c'est l'amour insensé*]
> That has so cruelly wounded you? [*Qui t'a jusqu'à ce point cruellement blessé?*]. (Ibid. 41)

As the poet tells his mother, he recognizes that such a love will inevitably lead to his death.

> Throw everything to her feet. Teach her who I am [*Jette tout à ses pieds. Apprends-lui qui je suis*].
> Tell her that I am dying, that you no longer have a son. [*Dis-lui que je me meurs, que tu n'a plus de fils.*].
> . . . .
> Leave; and if you return without having swayed them [these forces], [*Pars; et si tu reviens sans les avoir fléchis,*]
> Good-by, my mother, good-by, you will no longer have a son. [*Adieu, ma mère, adieu, tu n'auras plus de fils.*]. ("Le Malade" 42-43)

It is certainly no accident that in Balzac's text the poem alludes not only to Lucien's mother and to the love that leads him away from home, but also to his repeated threats to commit suicide, as well as to his eventual death by his own hand in the later work, *Splendeurs et misères des courtisanes*.

The means of Lucien's death is indicated by the next poem he and David read, "Elégie XVIII," which Latouche labeled an elegy "in the traditional mode" (*Poésies* 128-29; other editions title it "La Jeune Tarentine"). Although Chénier did not commit suicide, as did Lucien, his repeated desire for death rings forth in a number of his poems and looms over the revolutionary poet's entire oeuvre. For those who have read *Illusions perdues*' sequel, *Splendeurs et misères des courtisanes*, the laments recall the subsequent vision of Lucien's lonely, miserable death in prison. As Chénier puts it, for example, though of course before the fact:

> Today when I am ready to go down to the tomb, [*Aujourd'hui qu'au tombeau je suis prête à descendre,*]
> My friends, into your hands I place my ashes. [*Mes amis, dans vos mains je dépose ma cendre.*]
> Covered with a funereal shroud, I do not wish [*Je ne veux point, couvert d'un funèbre linceul*]
> For the saintly pontiffs around my coffin, [*Que les pontifes saints autour de mon cercueil,*]
> Tolled with slow and somber bronze accents, [*Appelés aux accens de l'airain lent et sombre,*]
> To accompany my shade with their lamentable song. [*De leur chant lamentable accompagnent mon ombre*].
> I am dying. Before evening I have finished my day. [*Je meurs. Avant le soir j'ai fini ma journée.*]. (Elégie VI 92–93)

As another example, in one of the iambes that David and Lucien read aloud, the poet cries: "Come, may death come! let death deliver me!" [*Vienne, vienne la mort! que la mort me délivre!*] "(Iambe III 267), and in the last iambe of the poet's volume, Chénier recognizes that his end approaches: "The sleep of the tomb will press my eyelids. [*Le sommeil du tombeau pressera mes paupières*]" (Iambe IV 270).

Some of Chénier's verses seem to describe a place very much like Lucien's final jail cell where he killed himself in *Splendeurs et misères des courtisanes*.

> Let us become accustomed to oblivion. [*Accoutumons-nous à l'oubli.*]
> Forgotten like me in this awful den, [*Oubliés comme moi dans cet affreux repaire,*]
> . . . .
> What could my friends do? Yes, a word through the bars from their dear hands? [*Que pouvaient mes amis? Oui, de leur main chérie / un mot à travers ces barreaux?*]. (Iambe IV 247–48)

As one would expect, during Lucien's reading at Madame de Bargeton's gathering of her feckless Angoulême acquaintances, Chénier's masterful poem, "L'Aveugle [The Blind Person]" elicited widespread boredom (5.199). Earlier, David and Lucien could scarcely contain their enthusiasm. The latter "kissed the book, and both friends wept, because both of them idolized another person. [...] David's adored Eve had become André Chénier's Camille for him, as the high born lady (i.e., Mme de Bargeton) Lucien was courting had for him " (5.147). In reading and rereading Chénier's "L'Aveugle," a poem about Homer, Lucien emphasizes his aspiration for the Greek poet's greatness.

With the repeated references to the poems celebrating "Camille," where Chénier expresses his passionate love for his mistress, the identification of Balzac's allusion becomes very certain. Chénier's Camille is generally considered to be the lovely bourgeois creole, Mme Bonneuil (1748–1829). Despite differences from the latter's class and appearance, for Lucien she parallels the unattractive Mme de Bargeton, whom Paris views as "a large, dried out woman with broken veins, more faded than brown, angular, stilted, precious, pretentious, provincial in her speech, especially badly put together!" (5.273). Nonetheless, both women are considerably older than their lovers, both are unfaithful, and both eventually break with their impoverished poets. In 1791, Charles-François Le Brun called Mme de Bonneuil "an outdated coquette," a "clever cheat," who "tricks Love, believing she has tricked Time." Perhaps even more to the point, for Le Brun, Chénier's Camille is a "deceptive dowager" with aristocratic pretentions, whose "antiquated youth/Still pleases duped love."[8] Lucien's friend Vernon calls Mme de Bargeton "the cuttlefish bone" (5.447). Nonetheless, their pretentious mistresses continue to beguile (*berce*) both revolutionary and Balzacian poets by false hopes and illusions.

At first, Mme de Bargeton was intensely interested in the young poet Lucien, whose talent she wanted to feature in her social evenings. On at least one occasion before leaving Angoulême for Paris, where she was attempting to highlight his talent, the text portrays her in a turban (5.191), perhaps modeling Madame de Staël, who affected turbans (cf., 5.412), sponsored the writer Benjamin Constant (cf., 5.405), and avidly sought prominence and attention. Like Madame de Staël, Madame de Bargeton was accustomed to "dominate this world from the height of her intelligence" (5.203). When Lucien returns and attempts to regain his position as her favorite, the narrator will term her "the Corinne of Angoulême" (5.455), thus recalling Mme de Staël's novel *Corinne*. Although many years older than Lucien, she saw herself as someone who, similar to the famous revolutionary feminist, essayist, and novelist, could guide and form an artist. Especially if Lucien were the genius she thought him to be, as his mentor/muse her position in society would be reinforced. Although Madame de Bargeton's relations with the young man were chaste, it does not seem that she planned to keep her distance always. When she decides to discard Lucien, she thinks, "What luck for me that I kept this little rascal at a distance and allowed him no liberties!" (5.283). In his poetry, at least, Chénier pretends to be a similarly unhappy aspirant to the beautiful Creole's attentions, rather than the successful lover he was thought to be (Buisson 405–06).

As mentioned before, Balzac's Lucien was the son of a deceased pharmacist and a high-born woman (née Rubempré) who was *déclassée* by her marriage to a commoner and then by her occupation as a nurse/midwife who cared for pregnant women. Lucien's family name of Chardon, or "thistle," is likewise ridiculous, and he will expend an enormous amount of energy attempting to adopt his mother's name officially. In the social circles the young poet would like to penetrate, substituting the name of Lucien de Rubempré for Lucien Chardon would be a distinct advantage, at least he would be spared the most obvious belittling pleasantries. Madame d'Espard makes that very clear, "[I]t would be very hard to call myself Madame Chardon" (5.480). It was an unrefined, coarse country name, after all. As Chevalier and Gheerbrant explain, "The thistle is generally considered difficult to approach, disagreeable, and, also, like donkey food."[9]

Balzac repeatedly insists on the references of many of his evocative names (cf. above, Chap. 8, n.5). Lucien's continued efforts to join with those men "bearing sonorous names encased in titles" draws even more attention to the importance of the novelist's onomastics. As another foreshadowing of Lucien's eventual fate, the novelist turned to a Biblical allusion. Although the young man has no legal right to the name of his mother's Rubempré family, he nonetheless illegitimately assumes it, hoping futilely that the authorities will regularize it. He then parallels the biblical Ruben who, by sleeping with his father's concubine, asserted a privilege that was not lawfully his, and thus lost his birthright (Genesis 35.22, 49.3–4). In *Illusions perdues*, Lucien will be disappointed in his attempt to legitimize the name and become M. de Rubempré. Certainly, when the faubourg's aristocrats deny him the use of the maternal name, they accompany this refusal with rejection and mockery, leaving him in a world of prostitutes, criminals, and journalists.

Lousteau adds emphasis to values in both the literary and political worlds, when he suggests that without exception people can be divided into the corruptor and the corrupted. For him there is no other category (5.344). Many other antitheses occur on the pages of *Illusions perdues*. Parisian *boue* against the glitter of success, sloth against work, liberals against royalists, Madame de Bargeton and Coralie against Eve Séchard, mind against heart, actresses against "the most distinguished women of society" (5.345). Although the text most often insists on the elements that make two poles antithetical, it is not always so. The satanic Herrera, for example, rises above such oppositions, as though there were no difference between good and evil, and Lucien contrasts with David, without impugning their similarity, since the former is weak and lazy rather than evil.

Balzac uses this concluding novel of the *Scenes de la vie de province* to insist once again on provincial inadequacies and the wastage of youth. Lucien is neither the first nor the last of old-line aristocratic families who were destroyed by Paris. His onomastic struggles highlight his death as an aristocrat, similar to those of Savinien de Portenduère and Victurnien d'Esgrignon, depicted in other novels. Dissolution of character also took place in such middle-class immigrants as Charles Grandet and Etienne Lousteau. Lucien serves as a summary character in that he is between bourgeois and noble, and his translation from the provinces to Paris was disastrous. The aristocratic Rastignac, as a contrary example in other of Balzac's works, becomes a financial success, though completely corrupt.

The novelist's zoological analogies have been noted. Not only does the 1842 preface point to "differences between a soldier, a working man, an administrator, a lawyer, a loafer [...] as considerable as those that distinguish a wolf, a lion, a donkey, a crow," but Balzac sprinkles all his works with comparisons that call biology, fables, fairytales, and everyday experiences to mind. Anastasie de Restaud is a "thoroughbred horse," her sister "a swallow," "a nightingale," and "a partridge," Madame de Beauséant "a nanny-goat," Poiret a "donkey," "a turkey," and "a cat," though "an eagle" when compared to Goriot," Mme Vauquer "a rat," "a parrot," "partridge," and "a cat," Christophe "a mastiff," which suffices to give the flavor of much of the author's usage, though these are just a few examples from one novel.

Occasionally, Balzac refers to more esoteric knowledge that was, however, common at the end of the eighteenth and early nineteenth centuries. His knowledge of alchemy, the Kaballah, Swedenborg, somnambulism, mesmerism, and other mystical practices, while not profound, is most obvious in *La Recherche de l'absolu* (1834), *Le Livre mystique* (1835), and *Ursule Mirouët* (1842), though they occur elsewhere, for example, in *Illusions perdues*.[10] While it is perfectly true that typesetters were once familiarly termed "bears [*ours*]," and their compositors, "monkeys [*singes*]," the fact that the text refers to Old Séchard on numerous occasions as a bear (e.g., 5.124, 125, 129, 606), if not "the old bear" (e.g., 5.128, 133), should be understood on several levels. It is likely that Balzac wished to imply other connotations. In alchemy and the Greek religions, both bear and monkey are commonly related to the baser forces, darkness, and the unconscious, that is, to lower forms of life; the bear in particular is regularly presented as a monster.[11] Monkeys were viewed as corrupted, degraded men and cruel tricksters, dominated by their vices (Cirlot 202). These descriptions fit Cérizet, the compositor that David brings from Paris. Not only does Cérizet spy on the Séchards,[12] he wreaks damage by slowing his work and allowing the Cointets to produce a competitive almanac, thus assuring the press's failure. Like his simian designation, Cérizet is "rough, greedy, and lascivious" (Chevalier 708). The bear is usually no better. In alchemy, the animal "corresponds to the *nigredo* of the *prima materia*" (Jung, *Psychology and Alchemy* 178). Related to the lunar myths and Artemis, the bear represents the monstrous and the dangerous side of the unconscious. "Powerful, violent, dangerous, uncontrolled like primitive forces" (Chevalier 574), the beast is crude and cruel, even savage (Cirlot 22).

David's father, the old pressman, likewise fits his evocative designations: "Séchard, faithful to the destiny that his name had given him, was gifted with an inextinguishable thirst" (5.127), and he remains true to his ursine sobriquet. He knows neither how to read nor write. Avaricious and a drunk, his bearlike visage reveals his brutal cupidity for all to see (5.127). Not content to cheat his son on selling the press to him for an exorbitant amount of money, he later takes the press's one viable asset, a local newspaper, sells it to the Cointets, and pockets the money. Had he been able to see David's method when the latter prepares samples of his revolutionary new kind of paper, in the attempt to persuade his father to invest and to some degree solve the young family's financial exigencies, he would have sold the information to the Cointets, as well. Certainly, Old Séchard does not hesitate to serve the Cointet brothers to the detriment of his son. "David experienced the most horrible of humiliations, that caused by the debasement of a father" (5.135). The avaricious old man has betrayed the most basic values of human culture, as György Lukàcs points out. He has turned away from his own son. For Lukàcs, it reveals that capitalism destroys culture, though I would say that the brutish father has simply allowed his greed to erode the very structure of family.[13]

Balzac makes it very clear in the early part of the novel that Lucien is a young eagle (5.147, 173), and that he has reason to hope the king will do more than pun on the possibility of ennobling a Chardon, or *chardonneret* [goldfinch] into an eagle (5.535). Eagles are characterized by their daring flight, speed, and close association with thunder, fire, intelligence, and action.[14] Unfortunately for the young poet, his repeated failures reveal him as at most an "eaglet" [*aiglon*]" (e.g., 5.577), and he gives up his dreams of soaring with poetry to toady to the lions of society: Marsay, Vandenesse, Manerville (5.454–55). Given his desire for "glory" and his love of flashy attire, Lucien's given name appropriately derives from the etymon *lux* or "light."[15] With insistent irony the text calls him "the great man from the provinces" (e.g., 5.314, 365, 390, 484), and one should not forget Satan as a referent. He is, of course, the most widely known "angel of light" (Isaiah 14.12). David, on the other hand, is "this ox" (*ce bœuf*)." He wonderfully characterizes the ox's symbolic qualities of patience, submission, humility, and self-sacrifice.[16] In *Symbols of Transformation*, Jung explains that "the son" may rise above "the father," thus "overcoming animal instinct, and at the same time, [exhibiting] a secret and furtive overcoming of the power of the law" (261–62). Balzac shows at length how David succeeds in his clandestine attempt to invent paper that will benefit the whole of France's printing industry, despite his father's adamant and destructive opposition.

As the novelist did in other novels, he frequently alluded to mythological figures and etymological meanings. On noting that Lucien's mother, Madame Chardon, used the pseudonym Madame Charlotte in her work as a midwife, it is important to recognize that "Charlotte," like Charlemagne, derives from an etymon meaning "man [human being]."[17] The text rapidly offers three of the four most common components of tetramorphs or quaternities: eagle (Lucien), ox (David), and man (Mme Charlotte). One should perhaps wonder about the tetramorph's fourth related, but missing, component of lions. Does Lucien have a duel role? Does he give up one identification to assume the other? Without a lion, the archetype remains unstable. As Jolande Jacobi said, "Four is an age-old symbol, probably going back as early as the Old Stone Age. It occurs in the image of the 'four rivers' of Paradise. [...] The four cardinal points of the horizon, the four phases of the moon, the four seasons, the four primary colors, etc., are fundamental elements in our experience of the world. [... I]t forms a natural pattern of order within all created matter. [...] Examples might be multiplied indefinitely."[18] Doubtless the most common tetramorph of early modern Europe is that of the four Gospels, which may be seen in one form or another on many churches and cathedrals: Matthew is portrayed as a man, often winged like an angel, Luke as an ox, John as an eagle, and Mark as a lion. In the center generally resides Christ (Cirlot 321). All tetramorphs, perhaps especially the one best known in Christian Europe, represent wholeness.[19]

The lion occurs in a rather strange way in *Illusions perdues*. At first, the regal animal is related to the "lions" of society (5.454–55). Then, when Lucien gives up his poetic vocation, "[i]mperceptibly, he renounced literary glory, believing that political success was easier to obtain" (5.491). He becomes a lion, at least of a sort. In Angoulême, "Lucien had been promoted to the rank of *Lion*" (5.675). He is committed to provincial high style, though he lacks the personal qualities and resources that could assure his social success, and sadly, Lucien has already shown that he does not have what it takes to join the Parisian social lions and move from the provinces to power in Paris. He is only a lion in the much restrained and restricted world of Angoulême (5.675). Furthermore, Lucien cannot be counted on. He suffers from "the fatal mobility of his character" (5.254); he "is weak" (5.582); he is "inconsistent" (5.698). In short, he is a shirker, with predictable results. He cannot carry the role of lion, and he abandons his role as eagle, consequently leaving the tetramorph incomplete and infirm.

Finally, good and evil coalesce into one character, the Abbé Carlos Herrera, Balzac's Satan in a priest's cassock. He finds Lucien along the "precipice full of water" between Angoulême and Poitiers, where Lucien intends to end his life. Herrera, standing in the path leading to Paris, an image that reflects Minoret-Levrault, the "brute" compared to Caliban (3.770), who awaits his son Désiré on the bridge leading into Nemours at the beginning of *Ursule Mirouët* and the *Scènes de la vie de province*. Herrera, the priest, is neither Cain nor Abel; rather, he is "of mixed blood: Cain for my enemies, Abel for my friends" (5.704). He occasionally serves the principle of Good, at least in the instance when he sends money to David. For different reasons, the future is bleak for both Désiré Minoret-Levrault and for Lucien, as it has been for most of the other provincials who move to Paris. As Daniel d'Arthez recognized, Lucien "would willingly sign [...] a pact with a demon" (5.578). "If he meets a bad angel, he will go to the depths of hell" (5.580). Lacking the competitive, ruthless intelligence of the Cointets, most provincials are better off living the small, quiet lives of the provinces. Like David

Séchard, who, though ruined by his father and Lucien's depredations before being bested by the Cointet brothers, those who stay at home most often seem to end comfortably well off. The novel illustrates that good can triumph in the provinces. Indeed, the money Lucien and Herrera send to the Séchards might be seen as tribute from the kingdom of darkness. Certainly, the priest's name suggests the French word *errer* (to wander or to err), another indication of Lucien's destiny in this return to Paris, while Eve and David's progeny give hope of a better future. Lucien has modeled the impossible situation of France's youth. Not only did he find it impossible to rise, he exemplifies the inevitable disaster of young people. *Illusions perdues* leaves the reader with few illusions. Neither family, nor friends, nor art, nor indeed love seem able to offer more than haphazard success in a society on its knees in the *boue* worshipping Mammon.

Notes

1. Nykrog, "Illusions perdues dans ses grandes lignes: strategies et tactiques romanesques," *Balzac*: Illusions perdues: *"l'œuvre capitale dans l'œuvre,"* éd. Françoise van Rossum-Guyon, CRIN 18 (Groningue: U de Groningue: Département de français, 1988) 34–46.
2. Piketty, *Capital in the Twenty-First Century* (Cambridge MA: Harvard UP, 2014) 238–43.
3. As Owen Heathcote understands, the relationship of the abbé Herrera and Lucien at the end of *Illusions perdues* prepares Lucien's role in *Splendeurs et misères des courtisanes—Balzac and Violence: Representing History, Space, Sexuality and Death in* La Comédie humaine (Oxford: Peter Lang, 2009) 49.
4. The quotation is from Louis Sébastien Mercier, *Le Nouveau Paris*, éd. Jean-Claude Bonnet (Year VII—1798; Paris: Mercure de France, 1994) 17. Brief, contemporary descriptions are found in Restif de la Bretonnne, *Les Nuits de Paris, ou le spectateur nocturne*, 8 vols. (London, Paris n.p. 1788–94) part xi, night 185 (1788), 2519–20, and Stendhal, *Journal* (10 septembre 1811), *Œuvres intimes*, éd. Henri Martineau, 2 vols., Bibliothèque de la Pléiade, (Paris: Gallimard, 1955, 1982) 1.1088, and throughout *La Comédie humaine*. As the groom tells Balzac's Louise de Chaulieu, "[T]he sludge of Paris [...] does not look like mud of the country" (1.387). For more complete discussion and documentation, see my *Sick Heroes: French Society and*

Literature in the Romantic Age, 1750–1850 (Exeter: U. of Exeter P, 1997) 22–29; and Alex Lascar, "De la boue balzacienne," *L'Année Balzacienne* 2009: 105–25.

5. Quoted from Victor Hugo, "Ymbert Galloix," *Littérature et philosophy mêlées*, *Œuvres complètes*, ed. Jean Massin, vol. 5 (Paris: Club Français du Livre, 1967) 182.
6. For a development of the trinity prostitute/literary writer/journalist, see Victoria E. Thompson, *The Virtuous Marketplace: Women and Men, Money and Politics in Paris, 1830–1870* (Baltimore: Johns Hopkins UP, 2000) 27–51.
7. For André Chénier, I shall quote from the edition that Balzac used (he identifies it by mentioning the in-18 size): *Poésies d'André Chénier* (1819; Paris: Baudouin Frères, 1820), "Néère" 64. All further references to this édition will be cited parenthetically. Néère or Neaera is the woman that the Roman poet Tibullus sings about.
8. George Buisson and Edouard Guitton, eds., "Notes et variantes" to the *Elégies*, *Œuvres poétiques*, by André Chénier, tome 1 (Paris: Paradigme, 2005) 401–07. Le Brun is cited 404–05.
9. Jean Chevalier et Alain Gheerbrant, *Dictionnaire des symbols, mythes, rêves, coutumes, gestes, formes, figures, couleurs, nombres* (Paris: Robert Laffont, 1969) 174, and J.E. Cirlot, *A Dictionary of Symbols*, trans. Jack Sage (New York: Philosophical Library, 1962). I refer to Jung (nn11, 14, 18, 19 below) and such editors as Chevalier and Cirlot as well-documented elucidations of widely recognized associations, but only when Balzac's context is congruent.
10. See Anne-Marie Baron, *Balzac occulte : alchimie, magnétisme, sociétés secrètes* (Lausanne: L'Âge d'or, 2012).
11. C. G. Jung, *Psychology and Alchemy*, trans. R. F. C. Hull (London: Routledge & Kegan Paul, 1953) 178; *The Archetypes and the Collective Unconscious*, trans. R. F. C. Hull (New York: Pantheon, 1959) 195; *Symbols of Transformation*, trans. R. F. C. Hull (New York: Pantheon, 1956) 316. The other side of the bear archétype is the mother, which like Balzac's Ursule, though kindly intentioned as in *Ursule Mirouët*, is ferocious—see above, ch. 2. For another example of Balzac's mystical propensities, and for relevant bibliography, see my, "*Les Proscrits* et l'unité du *Livre mystique*," *L'Année Balzacienne* 1999: 75–92.
12. On the destructive, reprehensible work of spies, see Sarah Horowitz, *Friendship and Politics in Post-Revolutionary France* (University Park: Pennsylvania State UP, 2013) 37–38, 50–54.

13. György Lukàcs, "Balzac: *Lost Illusions*," *Studies in European Realism: A Sociological Survey of the Writings of Balzac, Stendhal, Zola, Tolstoy, Gorki, and others* (London: Merlin P, 1972) 51. Horowitz believes that traditional family values are replaced in *Illusions perdues* by friendship. If so, Lucien's abandonment of his friends is not encouraging (*Friendship* 59–64).
14. Jung, *Psychology and Alchemy* 193, 398; *Alchemical Studies* (Princeton: Princeton UP, 1967) 345; Cirlot 87, 321; Chevalier 750.
15. Patrick Hanks and Flavia Hodges, *A Dictionary of First Names* (Oxford: Oxford UP, 1990) 212–13. As is often the case, Balzac exploits several possibilities of the name, Lucien. He is explicitly termed an eagle, which is closely related to the sun and light, but is also a coordinate of the gold of the goldfinch, mentioned in the royal pun (Jung *Psychology and Alchemy* 417).
16. 5.147, 559, cf. 685–89; Cirlot 236, 321, 750.
17. For Mme Charlotte, see 5.141, 171; for the etymology, see Charlotte M. Yonge, *History of Christian Names* (London: Macmillan, 1884) xl, 384–87.
18. Jacobi, *Complex / Archetype / Symbol in the Psychology of C.G. Jung*, trans. Ralph Manheim (New York Bollingen, 1959) 167. Cf., *Psychology and Alchemy* 35.
19. Jung, *Psychology and Alchemy* 112, 210; *Alchemical Studies* 280, 281, 282.

CHAPTER 12

Conclusion

As Balzac observed the social machinations of the Restoration and July Monarchy, his understanding was infused with a firm grasp of the facts of the arts and sciences of his day, especially of literature, history, and psychology. He apprehended both the interplay of relationships between reappearing characters and situations within the social scene and the political, aesthetic, and spiritual movements that were radically changing his society. He was sensitive to those ideas that were dysfunctional on the large and small scale and to the more positive conceptions, dreams, and insights that held potential for the future. While he was aware of the catastrophes lying in wait at every turn as history was being made, and was determined to illustrate examples that impelled them, he was by no means hopeless as he considered the possible avenues that might be redirected or reformed to avoid chaos. Unfortunately, he has often been viewed as a mere storyteller, and in fact he did tell stories brilliantly, but readers need to read intelligently and carefully, ready to perceive both his expert deployment of literary devices working throughout the evocative imagery of his depictions and his purposeful implications. He expected readers to be knowing participants in the experiences he creates and to distill their overriding meaning. Balzac is a good read, but an adequate reading is neither fast nor easy. Unlike most popular writers he worked on several levels, and carelessness opens his work to misinterpretation and incomplete comprehension. Reading Balzac's stories at face value alone leads to an appreciation for his portrayal of his society. Nonetheless, a shift in perception must also take place which reveals the scope of his lucid sociological comparisons, much like the "double vision" of M. C. Escher's tesselations awaken new concepts and understandings.

Since the panoply of Balzac's favorite devices and themes are on display in the *Scènes de la vie de province*, the first step toward an adequate interpretation of his artistry is to recognize that his "fiction" is rather shallow, consisting of little more than characters and actions occupying the foreground, but that he has with considerable accuracy recreated an entire "background" society. Rich relationships bind each of his various levels, characters, themes, and details to each other and to external reality. Though I am not sure that I would agree when W. S. Lilly suggests that Balzac is the French Shakespeare, given the English master's integration into the whole of Western civilization, I have no trouble at all when he claims that Balzac was a competent historian. He says simply that it "would hardly seem open to doubt [... that Balzac's] marvelous faculty of observation is indeed conceded on all hands [...] He brought, too, imagination to idealize and will to realize what he saw."[1] Even Sainte-Beuve agreed that "M. de Balzac was indeed a painter of the manners of this time, and he is perhaps the most original, the most appropriate, and the most penetrating."[2] He was indeed a historian, but the aspect of his world that drew him was what we today would call sociology. His insight was particularly acute in his explanations of the motives for the behavior he saw in people and social units.

Balzac was particularly proud of his use of detail (e.g., 1.1164, 1175), the items that other writers might have left out as inconsequential but that in *La Comédie humaine* set the scene for the vision to follow. It is not true as some Balzacians claim that one can divine the subsequent story in the initial details without actually reading beyond the overture, but the opening developments of his novels set the subsequent story on a solid foundation, becoming a part of everything that happens afterward. No one can doubt the importance of family after reading *Le Père Goriot*, for example, but like this famous novel, the creations of the *Scènes de la vie de province* point to the glorification of healthy families by their absence. They were a large-scale "minus device," raised in the reader's mind because they should be, but are not, where they are expected. Who would praise the Grandet family? or the Minoret-Levraults? Even admirable couples, like David and his wonderful wife Eve, are rare. Artificial families are at least as numerous, whether good like Denis Minoret's group of friends, or questionable, like the group captained by Maxence Gilet. Most common, however, are fatherless families and children, from Ursule, to Pierrette, to Philippe and Joseph, and including both Lucien and, in essence, David, whose unnatural father made every possible attempt to destroy his son. Detail reveals real or absent thematic constructs of importance.

It has been common for critics to denigrate Balzac's details. Emile Faguet, among others, insistently mocked the novelist's comparisons and descriptions. In "Gobseck," for example, the text describes the miser as having a "lunar" face, which stimulated the critic: "Wrong note [...] 'lunar face' will suggest in everyone's mind the idea of a round blossoming countenance, and a miser's countenance is always [...] the exact converse." Faguet did not accept Balzac's connotations and wanted the miser to have an emaciated visage, but Balzac would have justified his image by explaining that the moon suggests reflective power and frigidity, of undoubted importance in illuminating Gobseck. Traditionally the moon moreover symbolizes psychic power and, as well, submission to matter. Balzac's exploitation of the image was extensive and tied directly to this particular miser.[3] I could easily fill all of these pages with such examples, for Balzac's details are enormously significant. As he said, "[T]he author firmly believes that details alone will henceforth constitute the merit of works that are improperly called *romances*" (1.1175). Balzac's details are generally anchored in material reality, but they bring with them related complexes of other traits and traditions from a cultural context playing on literature, history, legend, myth, and the religious tradition. Immediately, they should begin to construct in the reader's mind the web that both circumscribes and lifts the novel's meanings above the banal and mundane (1.1164). Because the details come from the real world and are true (1.15), they also suggest the truth of the characters, stories, and descriptions they accompany, thus adding to verisimilitude.

Balzac frequently mentioned his use of types. Especially exploited by the *Commedia dell' arte*, they can, on the one hand, be the stock characters that are found throughout literature: the pretty young ward, the handsome lover, the crotchety guardian, the sly servant, the pretentious doctor, the deceitful wife, the dullard of a husband, and so on. Generally, they are what E. M. Forster would term "flat" characters, included to fulfill a limited function, like serving a meal, or holding open a door, or driving a carriage. In Balzac's hands, however, such limited figures quickly acquire qualities and complexity that give them the characteristics of human beings, thus distinguishing them from the configurations of other writers. Gobseck turns into a greedy personage who is sufficiently complex to go beyond his miserliness and show a glint of human compassion when he refuses to take advantage of a young man with no other hope. The miser as a type seldom shares such humanity. Father Chaperon provides a different example of a character developed well beyond his type. His avariciousness is explained by his desire to give as much as possible to the poor. Often Balzac's types are even more "round," that is, more realistic. When a handsome young man sings outside Pierrette's window, for instance, we expect the most vapid of tales, where love conquers all. In this case, however, Balzac is setting up an opposition, hoping to encourage his reader to expect a joyous conclusion, so as to the contrary to afflict him with the discouragement and disgust that comes when the guardian in fact abuses the guileless young woman. Pierrette is all the more thoroughly a victim when the abuse kills her.

Balzac's types are seldom dull. "The Idea, having become a Character," the novelist once wrote, "has a more comely intelligence" (*La Revue Parisienne*, HH 24.217). Fredric Jameson goes so far as to suggest that any of Balzac's characters could potentially serve as the focus of any of his narrative texts. As he understands, all are susceptible of being filled out, so as to function in a more complex literary environment, where the novelist works to unveil a significant aspect of his world.[4] With this quotation about ideas, the proto-sociologist and reformer, Balzac, explains why he was not content to stop with essays, with "non-fiction" describing his society. Instead, he thought that his analysis and insight would have a better chance at making sense, and thus have a beneficent influence, if they were clothed in narration with the attitudes and actions of real characters struggling for success at their various enterprises and goals in an enormous, multifaceted representation of Restoration and July Monarchy society.

The novelist's models gain profundity and interest when he moves away from character types to situational and plot types. Such plot patterns were also exemplified in the *Commedia dell'arte*. As Balzac pointed out, these latter kinds of figures or types are essential if an author wishes to represent a realistically complex world. In short, they are "indispensable in modern literature" (HH 24.217). "Not just men, but in addition the principal events of life may be formulated by types. There are situations, typical phases, which take place in all stories about human beings, and that is what I have sought to represent the most precisely" (1.18). His approach infused his narrations with a sense of universality leading to an appreciation of his creation as it expanded beyond its constituent parts. I usually term similar constructions "plot armatures." Often, they are too tenuous to function as allusions. Such constructions provide vectors and cantilevered frameworks anchoring characters and stories. An armature would be devoid of interest if it were not fleshed out with the idiosyncratic and detailed characteristics that provide literary dimensionality with color and action. I think, for example, of the two women who, accompanied by soldiers, are moving through an embattled zone. One of their apparent guardians turns out to be a vicious traitor, bent on revenge, who escapes before being discovered. The group eventually stops to rest, having been assured that they will be safe. Unfortunately, the authority who offered his nominal enemies safety is betrayed by his own minions, and many are treacherously killed as they set their weapons down and relax. At the end of the novel, the comely male and female characters lie holding hands in death. This abstract description briefly describes both James Fenimore Cooper's *The Last of the Mohicans: A Narrative of 1757* and Balzac's *Les Chouans, ou La Bretagne en 1799*.[5]

This summary is far too imprecise to be identified as one creation or the other; it is nonetheless accurate and further analytical reflection leaves little doubt of the kinship. Within the similar, schematic framework, close consideration reveals many differences between the two texts. In the Balzacian novel, two women are being transported through Brittany when the accompanying troupes are joined by the brutish Marche-à-Terre, who slips away when his treachery is about to be revealed, much as does Cooper's Magua. Balzac's villain is a local peasant, and Cooper's an American Indian. Both groups are accompanied by the man who will eventually commit himself to one of the women. Balzac's numerous characters are on their way to Fougères. Those of Cooper are less numerous and hope to bring the girls to their father. Motivated by his commitment to church and king, Marche-à-Terre is capable of the worst sorts of brutality. He and his Chouans, like Magua and his Herons, do not hesitate to betray their leaders by killing the opponents who believed the leaders promising safety. These and other parallels cannot be denied, for they are sufficiently clear when put side by side to highlight their family resemblance in the midst of striking distinctions. Although Balzac was enamored of the very popular novel *The Last of the Mohicans*, and surely would not have objected to being compared to the American novelist, he added so many dissimilar details to *Les Chouans* that a comparison of the stories highlights their differences.

It was not a matter of plagiarism, if the word had any meaning in this period. On Balzac's part it was simply a convenient plot armature that the French novelist could exploit. Nor does it seem an adaptation, since it makes no attempt to deal with Cooper's major themes. Most significant in the effort to distinguish types from allusions, unlike the allusions I have studied in *Allusion: A Literary Graft*, the discovery that this text has some similarity with *Les Chouans* adds very little to Balzac's novel, for the latter author does not bring Cooper into his text and engage some aspect of the predecessor. Like the form of a sonnet, it is possible to fill Cooper's plot armature in many different ways. Perhaps the most obvious example of types that Balzac exploits occurs in *Même histoire*. He solved the fragmentary nature of this work by turning the heroines who were unquestionably of the same type into the same character and *Même histoire*, the work where they first appeared, into *La Femme de trente ans*, where they converged.[6] Conversely, when he felt, for what I argued are very good reasons, that *La Vieille Fille* was too tightly linked to *Le Cabinet des antiques*, he changed several of the main characters' names.

One of Balzac's more potent tools was allusion, whether on the grand scale, as with the metaphoric construct bringing Sappho to bear on *La Muse du department*, or with the more restrained allusion to the revolutionary poet Chénier or the Biblical Reuben in *Illusions perdues*. The novelist was also very conscious of names, calling attention to them with frequent references to Laurence Sterne and with the sheer appropriateness of his choices, whether historical, etymological, or analogical. In a related device, he chose titles that key the major image or "seminal idea" of his novels. Elsewhere, I have called attention to the importance of the etymological meaning of the name Goriot, since it bore the sense of Rabelais's *Grande Guorre* or syphilis, and, as well, points to the sordid sickness that afflicts the July Monarchy's institution of family. Similarly, it is worth remembering that Dinah de La Baudraye is not THE muse, and certainly not the muses' mother, Mnemosyre, or any of the nine Greek muses, or even the French muse. She is nothing but a minor departmental muse, writing in the provinces for a gathering of lackluster mediocrities.

Balzac's most common device depended on his ability to combine contrasts and analogies, antiphrasis and parallels or even doubles. Contrast is "the first law of literature" (1.1162), he says through Félix Davin, and he uses the device centrally in all of his work. As Madeleine Fargeaud summarizes from Balzac's prefatory remarks, contrasts and analogies are the very stuff of life, and of Balzac's work (1.1133). Often, pairs provide him with the opportunity to insist upon related oppositions and more fully explain the concept that he wishes to project. I think, for example, of Joseph and Philippe Bridau, one ugly and the other handsome, one honest to a fault and the other a thief who steals from his very family, one a painter who works to support his family and the other a murderer, who panders uniquely to his own needs. Or Lucien and David, one an eagle and the other an ox, one a gifted writer and the other an inventive genius, one weak and the other strong, but both of whom share a deep friendship. Of course, the oppositions may be on a larger scale over the span of several of his works, as with *Splendeurs et misères* or *Grandeur et decadence*, where on the one hand the rise and fall of vice is highlighted and on the other the honesty of César Birotteau is contrasted with the profound dishonesty of Baron Nucingen, as Balzac pointed out (HH 24.535).

Balzac's revolutionary structuring is accompanied by the production of texts designed to stimulate far-reaching complexes or images rather than long sequences. More attention should be paid, for example, to oppositions that make encompassing frames. I think of the colossus Minoret-Levrault, on the introductory bridge of *Ursule Mirouët*, who should be coupled in the reader's mind with an image of the monstrous Abbé Herrera in the last pages of *Illusions perdues*. Or, the way the occult group committed to good works at the end of the *Scènes de la vie parisienne* in *L'Envers de l'histoire contemporaine* configures a masterful opposition to the nefarious group of baleful characters described in the *Histoire des treize* that opened this portion or "scenes" of Balzac's cycle.

Descriptive images can easily confuse readers who, well trained in the Aristotelian tradition of the tragedy, elevate plot to dominate their mental screen. The Greek theorist has been interpreted as calling for a sort of single-strand pearl necklace in which the main character moves from episode to episode like a *picaro* in a picaresque novel. For many a reader, tragedy is held together by a sequence of incidents, in which the main character acts out the main thought. Such simplistic plots are seldom Balzac's most salient strategy. For the nineteenth-century novelist, plots are but one sequence held together by numerous metaphoric chains of images that form the crosshatching of a web-like text. While they may correspond to the beginning and end of a particular novel's plot, in fact they may not. Usually keyed by some central thought, Balzac's novels project various aspects of his vision of society. Like a three-dimensional version of a *dot-to-dot* picture, his readers are left to draw "lines" from one number to its sequel and, thus, to fill in the empty spaces—be it with color, event, depth, thought, implication, episode, or time—turning the "fragments" into a four-dimensional image. The reader is expected to draw conclusions from the web of the description.

Perhaps the most interesting aspect of the criticism of Balzac's *La Comédie humaine* is the fact that, even while regularly quoting the novelist's claims, scholars have seldom gone on to discuss the unity of the Balzacian cycle.[7] Given Félix Davin's reticence, Pierre Citron suspects that the young critic himself had some doubt about the unity of *La Comédie humaine*.[8] That may also be true of other distinguished Balzacians that have long dominated the criticism dealing with Balzac's cycle. Davin establishes a much repeated pattern. He quotes Balzac's claims, but leaves them with a paucity of explanation or defense. Whether on the part of Davin or other scholars, this implicit position is puzzling, considering the frequency of the novelist's insistence on the unity of his masterpiece and in the light of the outstanding quality of the Balzacian secondary literature over the last fifty years or so. In the novelist's letters, in his various prefaces, and in his very public pronouncements, he insists on the organization that wrestled the multiplicity of his work into a unity. We know that Balzac had much to do with both of the prefaces signed by Félix Davin, who served as his spokesman.

Edouard Monnais tells that in late 1835 or early 1836 he listened to Davin complain about the difficulty of writing a preface that would satisfy Balzac and "tie all of his productions together, to demonstrate the claimed unity, and to erect a philosophic system! What I do on one side, is undone on the other: I am never considered sufficiently positive, sufficiently laudatory" (quoted by Citron, "Article" 184). As Anne-Marie Meininger established, not only did Balzac inspire, correct, and augment the material published in the introductions to the *Etudes philosophiques* and the *Etudes des mœurs*, he actually cribbed from them (or his previous notes) when he was forced to give in finally to his publisher's demands that he not republish Davin's introductions but that he actually write his own "Avant-propos" to the 1842 Furne edition of *La Comédie humaine*. Balzac had even tried to enlist "le bonhomme Sand [good fellow Sand]" to no avail, or at least not until some years after his death, when she published the very intelligent, insightful article "Honoré de Balzac."[9]

We do not know when Balzac conceived a way to bring unity to his work. Whether it was very early on, perhaps even as early as *Les Chouans* (1829), as the Furne prospectus published in 1842 seems to suggest (1.1119), or in 1831, when he was working with Chasles Philarète on the

"Introduction" to his *Romans et contes philosophiques*, or in 1834, when he was struggling with Félix Davin about the "Introduction" to the *Etudes philosophiques*, or at some point beyond our ken. We can, however, be certain that it was by no means as late as the 1840s. By 1834, Balzac certainly knew his cohesive aims for his enormous work, and he had a sense of how that goal could be achieved. The novelist said as much in his letters to Madame Hanska of 26 October 1834 and 8 July 1837, in the "Introduction" he and Davin wrote in 1834 to the *Etudes philosophiques*, in the 1835 Davin/Balzac "Introduction" to the *Etudes de mœurs*, and in the novelist's "Avant-propos" of 1842. His various prefaces often make considerably briefer but parallel comments. There can be no question that he believed and had long believed his work to be unified, a unification that was illustrated by the novels and stories themselves, for he used similar structural methods overall and in individual novels. *La Comédie humaine* was unified by the idea, the organizational, generative idea, or "idée mère," that he saw bringing the whole of this society into unity.

The crucial role of money was both the overarching and the permeating influence on the stories that he envisioned within the social context that he described in detail, and Balzac was perfectly correct to insist on its importance throughout *La Comédie humaine* and his July Monarchy society. Certainly, no thoughtful person could consider his tumultuous, industrial/commercial age without grappling with the effects of the media of exchange. At the root of every action, every decision, and most thoughts, was "the omnipotence, the omniscience, the omniexpediency of money" (6.331). Ownership of land that had been at the base of the social, religious, and economic spheres of France before the Revolution continued to have significance in many of the functions that it served previously. Land still justified positions of authority and importance (7.763), for example, but it was rapidly becoming little more than one among many other components of capital, like gold, or precious stones, or art, or other physical property, or currency. Indeed, even a person like Maxime de Trailles saw himself as a factor of exchange or value, as he bragged to Gobseck. And there were of course the slaves that Charles Grandet bought and sold as human capital in the accumulation of his fortune. Capital, in short, whether termed gold or money or whatever constituted exchange value and became a key factor in this period when the French Industrial Revolution was gaining strength. It was the "idée mère" that was more than just a "master key." It was the seminal idea that served as the nucleus of forces driving this rapidly changing society. Although the details of some of the more sophisticated financial strategies, such as purchasing debt, forward selling, leveraging, and various kinds of speculation, will be worked out in other creations of *La Comédie humaine*, like "La Maison Nucingen," *La Cousine Bette*, and *César Birotteau*, the dominant sway of capital is obvious throughout the entire cycle. It was to this new god that people did obeisance, that infiltrated every decision, for which they would sell spouses, children, or, indeed, themselves. Although the economy of society was overall stagnant, few were the individuals that were not attempting to claw their way to wealth and power. The abbé Herrera put it simply in the *Illusions perdues*: "Your society no longer adores the true God, but rather the golden calf" (5.701; cf. Exodus 32.4–8).

In attempting to explain the various features of his description of society, Balzac illustrated his organizational method with a literary type attached to an armature and both filled out and animated the extended framework with descriptive details, so that it became a web including many metaphoric chains. This "type" resembles the disembodied consciences in Nathalie Sarraute's *Tropismes* (1938). She described them nonetheless as living creatures or consciences that matured as their understanding increased, on the one hand, or, on the other, that existed simultaneously with various other similar creatures at different points in their development. Balzac's character types could echo the growth of real people from infancy to maturity. Of course, while the novelist did not need to project a chronological connection between individual or collective types, since the forms of the various ages could co-exist, he paused in his introductions to regret that he could not place each work including these types precisely where it should go to make chronological or causal or, simply, thematic sense at the moment of its publication. Merchandizing his creations unfortunately required shuffling particular works from one part of *La Comédie humaine* to another, as he explains, although the temporary displacement might well lose the additional meaning that particular works would have in the final carefully arranged version. Still, he insisted that these temporary changes of position were in effect no different than an architect changing the position of the stones stored for later use in his planned monument (1.1202). Nonetheless, when one of his works is extracted from the whole, stand-alone versions lose the rich texture of what would eventually be their context in the author's final version, the larger structure of his magnum opus.

Long before the 1842 Furne edition, Balzac planned on six *scènes*, that he also called galleries (1.18), for the most voluminous section of his oeuvre, the *Etudes des mœurs*. These major sections follow the maturation of an imagined human being. (On several occasions, Saint-Simon also configured the development of human history as the growth of a human being, from infancy to maturity.[10]) Balzac's first section of *La Comédie humaine* and of the major section he called the *Etudes des mœurs* open the sub-section which he titled the *Scènes de la vie privée* (*Scenes from Private Life*). It includes works that he felt portrayed the brilliant freshness of new life in individuals and their families. Davin, and by implication the novelist who was looking over his shoulder, claim that we see human life in its matinal glory at this stage, the nascent traits of which will eventually mark a person's character profoundly, preparing to blossom into the first sensations of youth (1.1204). Later in the century, a number of authors attempted to reinvent in the same vein the Garden of Eden of Genesis that could be developed to show civilized mankind forming societies and moving out into the world with the intent to control their own and others' lives and, in addition, to improve on what happened the first time, after Adam and Eve were expelled from Eden.[11] For Balzac, the "*Scènes de la vie privée* represent childhood, adolescence, and their lapses" (1.18). Later in Balzac's work, when he could organize his creation as he wished in the Furne *Comédie humaine*, he expected this stage of human development to mature and lead into the next configuration of scenes.

In the second grouping of fictions, the *Scènes de la vie de province*, Balzac's incarnated "consciousness" or "creature" has grown older, and the author announces that the novels and stories he will insert in this section will illustrate "this phase of human life when the passions, the calculations, and the ideas take the place of sensations, impulsive movements, images taken as reality" (1.1146). They live in the present without second thoughts and seem more aware of themselves as individuals. With multifaceted plans and manoeuvers destined to implement and give them what they wish, they pass from the previous state. "Life becomes serious" (1.1146). As the more or less naïve desires and plans are set in motion, egotism brings people into conflict with each other both within the family and in local society. Violence and crime may result from the daily conflict of spiritual or financial aggression, since extraordinarily important, individual passions may oppose the similar emotions of others. "Passion is what makes humanity," Balzac explained (1.16). In this more mature stage, "passions, calculations, interests, and ambition" (1.18) replace sensations, ill-considered impulses, and thoughts imagined as though they are real (10.1205). Success in this "gallery" space (10.1204) of stories requires being or becoming part of a cohesive group. Family is best, for there are generally strong ties holding the group together ("Family and not the Individual [is] the true social element"—1.13), but, since real families had become somewhat rare, given that Napoleon's militant politics left multitudes of widows, other kinds of groups can be almost as successful. The situation turns on whether the desires of the individual can be sufficiently hidden, disguised, submerged, or integrated into a group to succeed. A tightly knit gathering of people can turn against an individual, however, which is of course devastating for the person either duped or harmed. When the groups remain united in contrast to the larger "society without ties, without principles, without homogeneity," however, they have enormous power to change the cultural environment or to better the group's situation within the larger social complex (1.1169).

The third gathering of novels, the *Scènes de la vie parisienne* (*Scenes from Parisian Life*), offer a distillation of unbridled tastes and vices that especially occur in the capital city where the extremes of good and evil are found (1.18, 10.1206). The traits that were exhibited in the "creature" of the two preceding sections of "private life" and in the provinces move onto a larger stage and gradually afflict men's minds, hearts, and bodies until they suffer decrepitude in the end (10.1205). The results are those pathetic, gray individuals that people the first part of "La Fille aux yeux d'or." Masks, disguises, and counterfeit gestures are common, and demeanor seldom reveals true sentiments. Sincerity is the exception. Moral excellence can rarely resist the play of self-interest in Paris and is generally crushed in the cogs of society's mechanism, where uprightness is disdained and innocence sold. Individual passions that were the prevailing traits of youth in the first two ages have gained power over their victims and become ruinous tastes and vices (10.1205).

Everything has become so analyzed, sold, and bought that people habitually put a price on every virtue, relationship, and position. There are only two kinds of people: the deceiver and the deceived, the workers of iniquity and those harmed. Success is for those who can dominate others. People sit around waiting for grandparents' and other relatives' deaths, so that they may inherit. Honest people are taken for fools. Generous ideas are not *caritas*, or sacrificial giving, but rather a means to a self-centered end, and religion is viewed simply as an instrument of governance. Honesty becomes a tactical position. Everything is exploited, everything is for sale, and abject poverty and luxury appear side by side. Corruption makes young men age quickly and resemble jaded, centenarians. They insult the elderly and respect nothing. It is a La Rochefoucauldian society in which all of the virtues can be reduced to self-interest. In short, Paris is a place of incredible sophistication that has become rotten through its very civilizing elements. Balzac wanted to expose and illustrate society at its most violent, as it extends beyond itself for defense and conquest (1.1206). Such are the *Scènes de la vie parisienne*.

Continuing beyond the episodes set here and there across the great city of Paris to complete his vision of *La Comédie humaine*, Balzac envisaged the fourth section of the *Etudes des mœurs* (Studies of Manners), the *Scènes de la vie politique* (*Scenes from Political Life*), where he planned to describe those truly powerful men charged with foreseeing the future needs of society. The *Scènes de la vie militaire* (*Scenes from Military Life*), which would consider those men and interests that put masses of people in movement in order to do battle, come next. Only then should the reader move into the fifth "gallery" and the *Scènes de la vie de campagne* (*Scenes from Country Life*), which he termed the evening of the long progression starting with the matinal *Scènes de la vie privée* and ending with the principles of order, politics, and morality in a country thoroughly infiltrated or modernized by Parisian ideas (1.19). Given the pressure of time in his short life, the author was unable to do more than sketch them into his work, but he wrote that the six scenes or galleries lay out the general ideas that he understood to be governing society and the types of people and events or situations that reveal social impetus and interactions. Each "section" has a meaning and formulates an epoch, and each constitutes both an important part of the *Etudes des mœurs* and an essential element in Balzac's study of society (Hanska, 26 October 1834, 1.269).

There remain the *Etudes philosophiques* that allow us to see the ravages of thought and sentiment as they come to grips with desire, which Balzac terms the principle of all passion. In this major section, he maintains that he will show thought becoming an organizing force, completely abolishing sentiment, rather than merely subjecting it to ideas (1.1148). This was to demonstrate the victory of the intellect and the will over the fleeting impulsions of passion. Finally, in the last section, the *Etudes analytiques* look back and offer a general view of the results of his sociological analyses detailed in the realities that he has painted. While perhaps the most important part of his monumental *Comédie humaine*, the *Etudes analytiques* are the least developed, though there is little doubt that Balzac was not particularly worried by the incompletion. He felt that the whole meaning was fully established, at least if he had competent readers of good will who would accompany him as he examined the personal motivations and social constructs, exposing the problems and pointing to solutions. His vision of his society was conceived, represented, and completed, and he felt that the lessons and remedies would rise with perhaps varying force but inexorably from across his work. Readers would be able to grasp the problems and the solutions that maximized human possibility as social relations were actualized in his creation and in life. Had Balzac lived longer, he would have been even more comprehensive and filled in more of the gaps. Nonetheless, as George Sand said, "[N]othing more complete has ever come from the mind of a writer" ("Honoré de Balzac" 203). And, as should be obvious to any careful reader of the whole, the "idée mère" or generative idea is capital (HH 24.253), whether money, gold, property, or other media of value. It translates into power.

In the above chapters, I have focused on the second gallery of novels, novellas, and short stories, the *Scènes de la vie de province*, for they provide an excellent understanding of what the author does in major sections of his work and in the whole. Having experienced the first section, the *Scènes de la vie privée*, and on entering the second *Scènes de la vie de province*, we immediately confront the provincial giant, Levrault-Minoret, occupying the bridge over the Loing. He seems a Cerberus that marks the separation of Paris and the provinces. We might well remember an outdated truth declaimed by David Séchard's illiterate, brutish father: "[T]he provinces are the provinces, and Paris is Paris" (5.133). But those days are past, for France is unifying. Through the course of the novels in this section of *La Comédie humaine*, we will be made aware of numerous characters who go to the capital and either succeed or fail on the larger, Parisian stage. The capital city is the center of power and finance. Money, talent, beauty, and power are being siphoned out of the provinces for the sake of Paris. Because it was not often possible to earn the sizable income or a fortune by one's own means, all but one of these novels focus on the scramble to corner inheritances. As France would emerge from the financial doldrums toward the end of the nineteenth century, the dissipation of the stagnation would open society to more exciting possibilities.

The particular reality depicted in the *Scènes de la vie de province* describes the pulsating Parisian society of the early nineteenth century as it slowly imposed its inhuman mercantile values on the whole of France. Perhaps most salient among the interlocking tableaux hung in this gallery of *scènes*, the novelist stresses his opposition to the gerontocracy and the rigid old men who have moved into positions of power, not because of their talent or wisdom, but because they are simply the "last ones standing." They are solidly entrenched, lacking competition, because their own sons and those of their neighbors have died of disease and in the numerous wars that have continued almost without stop since 1789. The country suffers as a consequence. The institutions of government, church, and family foster the reflexive resistance to modernity and general mediocrity of the elderly that have taken over with the aim of maintaining the status quo. More shocking is the depth of the corruption that spreads across France, infecting even French justice. The legal system is fully capable of ignoring Ursule's stolen inheritance and of allowing Pierrette's murderer to slip out from under justifiable punishment. We are allowed to see the king himself buy and whitewash Victurnien's lawless thievery, explicitly aware that he is suborning justice. Those young men who survived the revolutionary wars and who could have been a source of new ideas are blocked, pushed to the side, and given little or nothing to occupy their time and energies. Revolutionary and Napoleonic wars had also deprived many children of their fathers, who could have given them support, advice, contacts, and other help, and thus aided youth in moving into positions of consequence. Mothers are depicted as being incapable of effectively parenting fatherless children, and lacking encouragement from the missing generation of fathers, indeed confronting stern opposition to their success, young men find other activities. They make trouble for their families and their communities, and they deprive France of their potentially beneficent influence by emigrating or, with increasing frequency, committing suicide.

    Balzac marshaled reappearing characters, recurring themes, and continuing plots to link novels and major sections—such as Lucien's story as he falls further and further into depravity and victimization from *Illusions perdues* into *Splendeurs et misères des courtisanes*. More commonly than such uninterrupted plots, the joints between novels are cemented by repeated themes brought to more completion. Paris takes a gradually enlarging role as we move through the *Scènes de la vie de province*. Even the case of reappearing characters, where we left Lucien in *Illusions perdues* selling himself for 15,000 francs—and other considerations—he fully invests his role as a prostitute. We are further introduced to Esther, a famous courtesan, and to the principle theme of *Splendeurs et misères*. Esther and Lucien are but "exemplars of an entire society of sycophants, ready to pander to any vice whatsoever" (*Balzacian Montage* 49). Elsewhere, one might think of the importance of religion and the "finger of God" tying *Ursule Mirouët* to *Eugénie Grandet*, which prepares the reader for His absence in later creations like *Pierrette*. In successive novels, God is replaced by corrupt priests like Troubert or, in *Le Cabinet des antiques*, by the abbé Couturier, who finds Madame du Croisier's lie permissible. Similarly, the celibates and related themes of egotism and jealousy that dominate *Pierrette*, *Le Curé de Tours*, and *La Rabouilleuse* offer significant linkage in the metaphoric chain tying provincials to their attitudes and lives. Given the dearth of natural families, substitute family-like groups are established to help members strip position and wealth from the outsider, the foreigner, or simply the "other." These unnatural families were not for the most part organized around mutual love, but rather around individual self-interest.

It is not simply that as a social category fathers had been decimated in thirty or forty years of disease, revolutions, and wars. For other reasons due to changes brought about by political revolution and industrialization, the very concept of the patriarchy was dying and its vestiges had been replaced by a gerontocracy. The result of children and families without fathers has been widely studied in recent sociology and psychology. Their conclusions are summarized by David Blankenhorn, who sees such individuals as infected with a narcissism that is outwardly hostile and violent, especially toward women and authority.[12] One hundred and fifty years ago, Balzac recorded the horrendous results of fatherless France, to an important degree a society limited to grandfathers, women, and children. For many reasons he believed that fathers were essential in order to resist the crumbling society surrounding him in the 1830s and 1840s and to restore social functionality and cohesiveness.

Ancien régime education was the provenance of fathers, though Madame de Maintenon was an exception who worked wonders in her school for orphaned, aristocratic girls. If fathers were no longer functioning appropriately, substitutes were needed. Saint-Just is widely cited as having pronounced in the revolutionary National Convention that "[c]hildren belong to the Republic before they belong to their parents."[13] Unfortunately, the French state was far from having developed an adequate educational system to replace earlier methods. Convents and tutors filled in to some degree, though not always with admirable results. Balzac was aware of this lacuna and considered the possibilities of home schooling in *Ursule Mirouët*.

In Balzac's work, a theme may disappear the way it does in a tapestry and then reappear appropriately elsewhere, as the theme of journalism and the character Lousteau are introduced in *La Muse du department* and recur in *Illusions perdues*. Nicole Moset has pointed out that the arrival of a stranger constitutes the precipitating event of most of the novels.[14] Equally important is the theme of inheritance. Balzac clearly understood the reality described by Thomas Piketty: success without significant capital in this society is impossible. As Piketty puts it, "The structure of the income and wealth hierarchies in nineteenth-century France was such that the standard of living the wealthiest French people could attain greatly exceeded that to which one could aspire on the basis of income from labor alone."[15] And, with few exceptions, success was measured in respect to capital without regard to how it was accumulated.

The traditional values of church, family, king, and country no longer seemed important. Money had usurped both spiritual and secular thrones. But as gold was deified, it moved ineluctably to the capital city. Bardèche concludes appropriately, "[S]erious men [...] accumulate fortunes that their sons will dissipate, and silently prepare this enormous movement that drains the provinces of its life blood in favor of Paris."[16] This activity, of course, brought with it not only the fortunes necessary to fuel the Industrial Revolution but also the talent required to bring France into the modern world. Granted, it was a society dominated by the selfish, vain, often corrupt individuals who continually generated the flow of money. Balzac's work touches on the social forces that were giving birth to a transformed economy necessary for this new world based on capital and commerce. Napoleon had established the central Bank of France, and the financial system had gained sufficient liquidity to make slow but continuing development possible. Transportation and communication were modernizing rapidly, allowing people and information to travel faster than before on improved roads. The profound changes marking France's development from an agricultural to a capitalistic society were illustrated and to a large degree explained by Balzac. He dedicated all his literary skills to elucidating the disintegrating class structure and the overarching social forces that constituted the tangible and intangible workings of post-revolutionary France. More than a simple storyteller, he was a sociologist *avant l'heure*, who had carefully studied his society. He even proposed a cure for the nation's troubles. He was, after all, a self-described "doctor of the social sciences."[17] It was time to set the gerontocracy aside and give their creaky old bones and indolent minds a rest. It was time to open society to the energy and talents of youth, thus to a better future for France. And it was time for the provinces and provincials to leave behind their obstructive attitudes and move into the modern age. As he elucidated what had happened to family, to sincere affection, to children in fatherless families, to justice, to religion, to an entire society gone astray, readers are brought to regret the terrible effects of the changes that were being wrought and to yearn for the imagined perfection, if not of the *ancient régime*, then of a benign monarchy.

NOTES

1. Lilly, "The Age of Balzac," *The Contemporary Review* June 1880: 1004, 1031. I would be more sympathetic to Dominique Massonnaud's suggestion that Balzac is the French Gœthe—*Faire Vrai: Balzac et l'invention de l'œuvre-monde* (Geneva: Droz, 2014) 142.
2. Charles-Augustin Sainte-Beuve, "M. de Balzac" (2 September 1850), *Causeries du lundi*, 3e ed., Vol. 2 (Paris: Garnier, 1852) 443.
3. See, for references and extended consideration, Pasco, "Balzac's 'Gobseck' and Image Structure," *Novel Configurations*, 2nd ed. (Birmingham, AL: Summa Publications, 1994) 51–71.
4. Fredric R. Jameson, "Introduction," *Eugénie Grandet*, Everyman's Library (New York: Knopf, 1992) xv.
5. See my "Personalizing Violence in Balzac's *Les Chouans*," *Nineteenth-Century French Studies* 41.3–4 (2013): 191–203. For a more adequate consideration of Balzac's treatment of war, see Max Andrioli, "La Guerre vue par Balzac dans *La Comédie humaine*," *Le Courrier balzacien* 31 (2015): 41–51.
6. See my *Balzacian Montage* 18–19, 21, 59–64.
7. For exceptions, see above, chapter 1n45.
8. Citron, "Un Article sur la mort de Balzac," *L'Année Balzacienne* 1977, 179–92.
9. George Sand, "Honoré de Balzac," *Autour de la table* (Paris: Michel Lévy, 1876) 197–213.
10. E.g., Henri de Saint-Simon, *Science de l'homme: Physiologie religieuse* (Paris: Victor Masson, 1858) 342–46. I put this statement between parentheses, since I do not have sufficient evidence to suggest that Saint-Simon influenced Balzac directly. There are, however, many similarities, and the subject might reward further study. For the moment, however, I wish only to suggest that sociology was in the air.
11. Cf., Robert Couffignal, "*Aux premiers jours du monde…*": *La Paraphrase poétique de Hugo à Supervielle* (Paris: Minard, 1970).

12. Blankenhorn, *Fatherless America: Confronting Our Most Urgent Social Problem* (New York: Basic Books, 1994) 4. See my discussion in *Sick Heroes* 54–82, 159–65.
13. Quoted from J. Mulliez: "La Volonté d'un homme," *Histoire des pères et de la paternité*, ed. Jean Delumeau and Daniel Roche (Paris: Larousse, 1990) 291.
14. Mozet, "Introduction" to *Eugénie Grandet* 3.1010.
15. Piketty, *Capital in the Twenty-First Century*, trans. Arthur Goldhammer (Cambridge, MA: Harvard UP, 2014) 240. For an expanded discussion, see, e.g., pp. 239–41, 401–29.
16. Maurice Bardèche, "Notice," *Scènes de la vie de province, Etudes de mœurs, Œuvres complètes* HH 5.13.
17. Hippolyte Taine, "Balzac" *Nouveaux Essais de critique et d'histoire* (Paris: Hachette, 1886) 66.

WORKS CITED

Abraham, Pierre. *Créatures chez Balzac*. Paris: Gallimard, 1931.
Adamson, Donald. *Balzac: Illusions perdues*. Critical Guides to French Texts, no. 7. London: Grant & Cutler, 1981.
Agin, Shane, ed. *Sex Education in Eighteenth-Century France*. Oxford: Voltaire Foundation, 2011.
Ambrière-Fargeaud, Madeleine. "Madame Balzac, son mysticisme et ses enfants." *L'Année Balzacienne*, 1965 : 3–34.
___. "Prospectus de *La Comédie humaine*," "Avant-propos." *La Comédie humaine*. By Honoré de Balzac. Ed. Pléiade, 1.1109–10, 1110–72.
Amossy, Ruth, and Elisheva Rosen. *Les Discours du cliché*. Paris: C.D.U.-S.E.D.E.S., 1982. 50–56. (Also in, "Les 'Clichés' dans *Eugénie Grandet*, ou les 'négatifs' du réalisme balzacien." *Littérature* 25, 1977 : 114–28.
Andréoli, Max. "A propos d'une lecture d'*Eugénie Grandet*: Science et intuition." *L'Année Balzacienne*, 1995 : 9–38.
___. "La Guerre vue par Balzac dans *La Comédie humaine*." *Le Courrier balzacien* 31, 2015: 41–51.
___. *Le Système balzacien: Essai de description synchronique*. 2 vols. Lille: Atelier National Reproduction des Thèses, Université de Lille III, 1984.
Anonymous. *Les Confessions d'une courtisane devenue philosophe*. Londres et Bruxelles: B. Le Francq, 1784.
Antoine, Gérald. "En relisant *La Muse du département*." *Travaux de Linguistique et de Littérature* 8.1, 1970: 35–44.
Aragon, Sandrine. "*Olympia ou les vengeances romaines*, ou le manuscrit de l'ère industrielle." *Le Topos du manuscrit trouvé*. Ed. Jan Herman, Fernand Hallyn, and Kris Peeters. Louvain, Belgium: Peeters, 1999: 307–18.

Aston, Nigel. *Religion and Revolution in France, 1780–1804*. Washington, D.C.: Catholic UP, 2000.

Balzac, Honoré de. *La Comédie humaine*. Ed. P.-G. Castex. 12 vols. Bibliothèque de la Pléiade. Paris: Gallimard, 1976–81.

___. *Correspondance d'Honoré de Balzac*. Ed. Roger Pierrot. 6 vols. Paris: Garnier, 1960–69.

___. *Lettres à Madame Hanska*. Ed. Roget Pierrot. 4 vols. Paris: Robert Laffont, 1990.

___. "Etudes sur M. Beyle (Frédéric Stendalh [sic])." *La Revue Parisienne*. 25 septembre 1840, *Œuvres diverses*. *Œuvres complètes*. Ed. Maurice Bardèche. 24 volumes. Paris: Club de l'Honnête Homme, 1968–71: 24.213–68.

Baran, James J. "Statues, Statutes and Status in Balzac's *Le Curé de Tours*." *Journal of Evolutionary Psychology* 14.3–4, 1993: 250–59.

Barbéris, Pierre. *Balzac et le mal du siècle, 1799–1833*. 2 vols. Paris: Gallimard, 1970.

___. "La Province comme langage romanesque: La Dramatisation provinciale dans la constitution du héros balzacien." *Stendhal et Balzac II: La Province dans le roman. Actes du VIIIe Congrès International Stendhalien, Nantes 27–29 mai 1971*. Éd. Alain Chantreau. Nantes: Société Nantaise d'Etudes Littéraires, 1978: 130–41.

___. *Mythes balzaciens*. Paris: Armand Colin, 1972.

Bardèche, Maurice, ed. *Œuvres complètes*. 24 v. Paris: Club de l'Honnête homme, 1968–71.

___. *Balzac, romancier*. Paris: Plon, 1940.

Baron, Anne-Marie. *Balzac, ou les hiéroglyphes de l'imaginaire*. Paris: Champion, 2002.

___. *Balzac occulte: alchimie, magnétisme, sociétés secrètes*. Lausanne: L'Âge d'or, 2012.

___. "La Symbolique des noms chez Balzac." *Vie et Langage* 271, 1974: 558–70.

Bazard, Amand. *Exposition de la doctrine de St. Simon*. 2 vols. 1828–1830. Paris: Rivière, 1924.

Béguin, Albert. "Préface." *La Muse du département*. *L'Œuvre de Balzac*. Vol. 9. Paris: Formes et Reflets, 1951: 9–14.

Bell, David F. "Balzac S.A.R.L." *French Forum* 14, 1989: 43–53.

___. *Real Time: Accelerating Narrative from Balzac to Zola*. Urbana: U of Illinois P, 2004.

Bérard, Suzanne J. *La genèse d'un roman de Balzac: Illusions perdues, 1837*. 2 vols. Paris: A. Colin, 1961.

___. *Honoré de Balzac: Illusions perdues, le manuscrit de la Collection Spoelberch de Lovenjoul*. Paris: A. Colin, 1959.

___, ed. "Préface." *Le Curé de Tours; La Grenadière; L'Illustre Gaudissart*. Paris: Garnier-Flammarion, 1971: 17–35.

Bernard, Claudie. "La Dynamique familiale dans *Ursule Mirouët* de Balzac." *French Forum* 24.2, 1999: 179–201.
Berthier, Patrick. "La Critique littéraire dans *Illusions perdues*." *L'Année Balzacienne*, 2008: 63–80.
___. "La Dot de Dinah." *Romantisme* 13.40, 1983: 119–28, 1983.
Berthier, Philippe, ed. "Introduction." *La Vieille Fille et Le Cabinet des antiques*. By Balzac. Paris: Garnier-Flammarion, 1987: 7–43.
___, ed. "Préface" (to *Pierrette*). *L'Œuvre de Balzac*. Vol. 6. Paris: Formes et Reflets, 1950: 621–31.
___. "La Province comme langage romanesque: La Dramatisation provinciale dans la constitution du héros balzacien." *Stendhal et Balzac II: La Province dans le roman. Actes du VIIIe Congrès International Stendhalien, Nantes 27–29 mai 1971*. Ed. Alain Chantreau. Nantes: Société Nantaise d'Etudes Littéraires, 1978: 130–41.
___. "Structure et signification d'un espace provincial chez Stendhal et Balzac: la ville." *Stendhal et Balzac II*. Ed. A. Chantreau. Nantes: Société Nantaise d'Etudes Littéraires, 1978: 187–201.
Biron, Armand Louis de Gontaut, duc de. *Mémoires du duc de Lauzun (1747–1783)*. Trans. E. Jules Méras. NY: Stirgis & Walton, 1912.
Blankenhorn, David. *Fatherless America: Confronting Our Most Urgent Social Problem*. New York: Basic Books, 1951.
Blix, Göran. "The Occult Roots of Realism: Balzac, Mesmer, and Second Sight." *Studies in Eighteenth-Century Culture* 36, 2007: 261–80.
Bloom, Harold. *The Anxiety of Influence: A Theory of Poetry*. London: Oxford UP, 1973.
Bluche, F., S. Rials, and J. Tulard. *La Révolution française*. *Que sais-je?*. Paris: PU de France, 1989.
Bonnet, J.-C. "De la famille à la patrie." *Histoire des pères*. Ed. Jean Delumeau and Daniel Roche: 235–58.
___. "La Malédiction Paternelle." *Dix-Huitième Siècle* 12, 1980: 195–208.
Booker, John T. "Starting at the End in *Eugénie Grandet*." *L'Esprit Créateur* 31.3, 1991: 38–59.
Bordonove, Georges. *Les Rois qui ont fait la France: Henri III, roi de France et de Pologne*. Paris: Pygmalion/Gérard Watelet, 1988.
Bowman, Frank Paul. *Le Christ des barricades 1789–1848*. Paris: Cerf, 1987.
___. *Le Christ romantique*. Geneva: Droz, 1973.
___. *French Romanticism: Intertextual and Interdisciplinary Readings*. Baltimore: Johns Hopkins UP, 1990.
Burton, Richard D.E. *The Flaneur and His City: Patterns of Daily Life in Paris 1815-51*. Durham: U of Durham P, 1994.
Butler, Ronnie. "Les Émigrés dans *La Comédie humaine*." *L'Année Balzacienne*, 1978: 189–224.

Butor, Michel. "Balzac et la réalité." *Répertoire [1]*. Paris: Minuit, 1960: 79–93.
___. "Les Parisiens en province." *Répertoire III*. Paris: Minuit, 1968: 169–83.
Byatt, A.S. "The Death of Lucien de Rubempré." *The Novel*. Ed. Franco Moretti. Vol. 2. Princeton: Princeton UP, 2006: 389–408.
Cabanis, Pierre Jean George. *Rapports du physique et du moral de l'homme*. 2nd ed. Paris: Chez Crapart, Caille et Ravier, An XIII, 1805.
___. *Œuvres philosophiques*. Ed. Claude Lehec et Jean Cazeneuve. 2 vols. Paris: P.U.F, 1956.
Cabantous, A. "La Fin des patriarches." *Histoire des pères*. Ed. Jean Delumeau and Daniel Roche: 323–48.
Cameron, Keith. *Henri III, A Maligned or Malignant King? (Aspects of the Satirical Iconography of Henri de Valois)*. Exeter: U of Exeter P, 1978.
Carlisle, Robert B. *The Proffered Crown: Saint-Simonianism and the Doctrine of Hope*. Baltimore: Johns Hopkins UP, 1987.
Castex, Pierre-Georges. "L'Ascension de Monsieur Grandet." *Europe* 43, 1965: 247–63.
___. "Aux sources d'*Eugénie Grandet*. Légende et réalité." *Revue d'Histoire Littéraire de la France* 64.1, 1964: 73–94.
___, ed. "Introduction." *Le Cabinet des Antiques*. By H. de Balzac. Paris: Garnier, 1958: i–xxxv.
___, ed. "Introduction." *Eugénie Grandet*. By H. de Balzac. Paris: Garnier, 1965: xv–lxvi.
___, ed. "Introduction." *La Vieille Fille*. By H. de Balzac. Paris: Classiques Garnier, 1957: iii–xli.
Chambard, Lucette, and Marguerite Rochette. *Pierrette de Honoré de Balzac*. Folio Guides 2. Paris: Armand Colin/Gallimard, 1976.
Chambers, Ross. "Misogny and Cultural Denial (Balzac's *Autre étude de femme*)." *L'Esprit créateur* 31.3, 1991: 5–14.
Chasles, Philarète. "Introduction" to the *Romans et contes philosophques*. By H. de Balzac. *La Comédie humaine*. Pléiade. 10.1185–97.
Chénier, André. *Elégies, Œuvres poétiques*. Ed. George Buisson and Edouard Guitton. Paris: Paradigme, 2005.
___. *Poésies d'André Chénier*. 1819. Paris: Baudouin Frères, 1820.
Cherpillod, André. *Dictionnaire étymologique des noms géographiques*. Paris: Masson, 1986.
Chevalier, Jean, and Alain Gheerbrant. *Dictionnaire des symboles: Mythes, rêves, coutumes, gestes, formes, figures, couleurs, nombres*. Paris: Laffont, 1969.
Choisy, François-Timoléon, abbé de. *Mémoires de l'abbé de Choisy habillé en femme*. Paris: Mercure de France, 1983.
Cholvy, Gérard. *La Religion en France de la fin du XVIIIe siècle à nos jours*. Paris: Hachette, 1998.
Christiansen, Hope. "Exchanging Glances: Learning Visual Communication in Balzac's *Eugénie Grandet*." *European Romantic Review* 6.2, 1996: 153–61.

Cirlot, J.E. *A Dictionary of Symbols*. New York: Philosophical Library, 1962.
Citron, Pierre. "Un Article sur la mort de Balzac." *L'Année Balzacienne*, 1977: 179–92.
___. "Le Cabinet des antiques." *L'Année Balzacienne*, 1966: 370–73.
___. "Coralie et Faublas." *L'Année Balzacienne*, 1969: 311–14.
___, ed. "Introduction." *La Rabouilleuse*. By H. de Balzac. Paris: Garnier Frères, 1966: ii–c.
___. "Préface." *Eugénie Grandet*. By H. de Balzac. Paris: GF-Flammarion, 1964: 5–21.
___. "Préface." *Pierrette*. By H. de Balzac. Paris: Garnier-Flammarion, 1967: 21–47.
___, ed. *La Rabouilleuse*. By H. de Balzac. Coll. Intégrale. Paris: Seuil, 1966: 86–87.
Clark, Roger J. B. "Un Modèle possible de 'L'Illustre Gaudissart'." *L'Année Balzacienne*, 1969: 183–86.
Cocteau, Jean. *Journal d'un inconnu*. Paris: Grasset, 1953.
Collomp, Alain. "L'Impossible mariage : violence et parenté en Gelvaudan, XVIIe, XVIIIe et XIXe siècles. Ed. Elisabeth Claverie and Pierre Lamaison. Paris: Hachette, 1982: 157–77.
Comte, August. *Cours de Philosophie Positive*. Vols. 4, 5, 6. Paris: Bachelier, 1830–42.
Condorcet, Marie Jean Antoine Nicolas de Caritat, marquis de. *Esquisse d'un tableau historique des progrès de l'esprit humain*. Ed. Olivier H. Prior. Paris: Bovin, 1933.
Conner, J. Wayne. "Un Aspect de l'onomastique balzacienne: L'Elaboration des noms de personnage." *Actes du XIIIe congrès international de linguistique et philologie romanes tenu à l'Université Laval (Québec, Canada) du 29 août au 5 septembre 1971*. Ed. Marcel Boudreault and Frankwalt Möhren. Québec: PU de Laval, 1976: 943–51.
___. "On Balzac's Goriot." *Symposium* 8, 1954: 68–75.
Conrad, Thomas. "*Le Cabinet des antiques* dans *La Comédie humaine*, ou comment 'être un système.'" *Nexilis* 1, 14 décembre 2008: 1–12. http://www.revuenexilis.org/issue1/.
Conroy, William T., Jr. "Imagistic Metamorphosis in Balzac's *Eugénie Grandet*." *Nineteenth-Century French Studies* 7, 1979: 192–201.
Constant, Benjamin. *Adolphe: Anecdote trouvé dans les papiers d'un inconnu*. 1816. Paris: Charpentier, 1903.
Couffignal, Robert. "*Aux premiers jours du monde...*": *La Paraphrase poétique de Hugo à Supervielle*. Paris: Minard, 1970.
Dällenbach, Lucien. "Du fragment au cosmos (*La Comédie humaine* et l'opération de lecture, 1)." *Poétique* 40, 1976: 420–31.
___, and Susan H. Léger (trans.). "Reading as Suture: Problems of Reception of the Fragmentary Text: Balzac and Claude Simon." *Style* 18.2, 1984: 196–206.

___. "Le Tout en morceaux (*La Comédie humaine* et l'opération de lecture II)." *Poétique* 42, 1980: 156–69.
Danino, Emile. "Contrats et castration dans *Le Curé de Tours* (Balzac)." *(Pré)publications* 61, 1980: 3–13.
Dargan, Joan. *Balzac and the Drama of Perspective: The Narrator in Selected Works of* La Comédie humaine. Lexington, KY: French Forum, 1985.
Darnton, Robert. *Mesmerism and the End of the Enlightenment in France*. Cambridge: Harvard UP, 1968.
Daumas, Maurice. *L'Affaire d'Esclans: Les Conflits familiaux au XVIIIe siècle*. Paris: Seuil, 1988.
Dauzat, Albert. *Dictionnaire étymologique des noms de famille et prénoms de France*. Paris: Larousse, 1951.
___. *Les Noms de lieux: Origine et évolution: villes et villages, pays, cours d'eau, montagnes, lieuxdits*. Paris: Delagrave, 1963.
David, Marcel. *Fraternité et Révolution française*. Paris: Aubier, 1987.
Davin, Félix. "Introduction," *Etudes de mœurs au XIXe siècle*. By H. de Balzac. *La Comédie humaine*. Pléiade, 1.1143–72.
___. "Introduction," *Etudes philosophiques*, by H. de Balzac. *La Comédie humaine*. Pléiade, 10.1185–1218.
Debray-Genette, Raymonde. "Le Jardin-Miroir d'Eugénie." *Territoires de l'imaginaire. Pour Jean-Pierre Richard*. Ed. Jean-Claude Mathieu. Paris: Seuil, 1986: 95–103.
Delumeau, Jean, and Daniel Roche, ed. *Histoire des pères et de la paternité*. Paris: Larousse, 1990.
Desan, Suzanne. *The Family on Trial in Revolutionary France*. Berkeley: U of California P, 2004.
___. *Reclaiming the Sacred: Lay Religion and Popular Politics in Revolutionary France*. Ithaca: Cornell UP, 1990.
Donnard, J.-H. *Les Réalités économiques et sociales dans* La Comédie humaine. Paris: A. Colin, 1961.
Dubois, Charles Pinot. *Mémoires secrets sur le règne de Louis XIV, la Régence et le règne de Louis XV*. Paris: Formin Didot, 1854.
Du Camp, Maxime. *Souvenirs littéraires*. 2 vols. Paris: Hachette, 1906.
Dufour, Philippe. "Les Avatars du langage dans *Eugénie Grandet*." *L'Année Balzacienne*, 1995: 39–61.
Dunn, Susan. *The Deaths of Louis XVI: Regicide and the French Political Imagination*. Princeton: Princeton UP, 1994.
Dupâquier, Jacques. "La Population française de 1789 à 1806." *Histoire de la population française*. Ed. J. Dupâquier. 4 vols. Paris: P.U.F., 1988: 3.64–83.
Durkheim, Emile. *Le Socialisme. Sa Définition, ses débuts. La Doctrine saint-simonienne*. Paris: P.U.F, 1971.
Evans, Henri. "A propos de *Louis Lambert*: Un Illuminé lu par Balzac: Guillaume Oegger." *Revue des Sciences Humaines* 57–58, 1950: 37–48.

Fabre, Lucien. "Préface." *Eugénie Grandet. L'Œuvre de Balzac.* Vol. 5. Paris: Formes et Reflets, 1950: 715–29.
Faguet, Emile. "Balzac." *Etudes littéraires sur le dix-neuvième siècle.* Paris: Lecène et Oudin, 1887: 413–53.
___. *Les Grands Ecrivains français: Balzac.* Paris: Hachette, 1913.
Fairlie, Alison. "Constant's *Adolphe* Read by Balzac and Nerval." *Balzac and the Nineteenth Century: Studies in French Literature Presented to Herbert J. Hunt.* Ed. Donald G. Charlton, J. Gaudon, and Anthony R. Pugh. Leicester: Leicester UP, 1972: 209–24.
Fargeaud, Madeleine, ed. "Prospectus de *La Comédie humaine*," "Avant-propos." Ed. Pléiade 1.1109–10, 1110–72.
Farrant, Tim. *Balzac's Shorter Fictions: Genesis and Genre.* Oxford: Oxford UP, 2002.
Felman, Shoshana. "Folie et discours chez Balzac: *L'Illustre Gaudissart.*" *Littérature* 5, 1972: 34–44.
Ferguson, Gary. *Queer (Re)Readings in the French Renaissance: Homosexuality, Gender, Culture.* Aldershot, Hampshire: Ashgate, 2008.
Fischler, Alexander. "Eugénie Grandet's Career as Heavenly Exile." *Essays in Literature* 16.2, 1989: 271–80.
___. "Show and Rumor. The Worldly Scales in Balzac's *Eugénie Grandet.*" *French Review* 8.2, 1981: 98–105.
___. "The Temporal Scale and the Natural Background in Balzac's *Eugénie Grandet.*" *L'Hénaurme siècle: A Miscellany of Essays on Nineteenth-Century French Literature.* Ed. Will McLendon. Heidelberg: Carl Winter Universitätsverlag, 1984: 35–45.
Fouchet, Max-Pol. "Préface." "L'Illustre Gaudissart." *L'Œuvre de Balzac.* Vol. 8. Paris: Formes et Reflets, 1951: 9–14.
Fox-Genovese, Elizabeth. *The Origins of Physiocracy: Economic Revolution and Social Order in Eighteenth-Century France.* Ithaca: Cornell UP, 1976.
Frappier-Mazur, Lucienne. "Lecture d'un texte illisible: *Autre étude de femme* et le modèle de la conversation." *MLN* 98, 1983: 712–27.
___. "Max et les chevaliers, famille, filiation et confrérie dans *La Rabouilleuse.*" *Balzac, pater familias.* Ed. Claudie Bernard and Franc Schuerewegen, Cahiers de Recherche des Institutes Néerlandais de Langue et de Literature Française 38. Amsterdam: Département de Langues romanes, U de Groningue, 2001: 51–71.
Gemie, Sharif. "Balzac and the Moral Crisis of the July Monarchy." *European History Quarterly* 19, 1989: 469–94.
Genette, Gérard. *Palimpsestes: La Littérature au second degré.* Paris: Seuil, 1982.
___. *Figures II.* Paris: Seuil, 1969.
Grange, Julienne. *Saint-Simon.* Paris: Ellipses, 2005.
Guichardet, Jeannine. *Balzac-Mosaïque.* Clermont-Ferrand: PU Blaise Pascal, 2007.
Guise, René. "Balzac et le *Bulletin de Censure.*" *L'Année Balzacienne*, 1983: 269–301.

___. "Balzac et le roman feuilleton." *L'Année Balzacienne*, 1964: 283–97.
Gurkin, Janet. "Romance Elements in *Eugénie Grandet*." *Esprit Créateur* 7, 1967: 17–24.
Guyon, Bernard. "*Adolphe, Béatrix* et *La Muse du département.*" *L'Année Balzacienne*, 1963: 149–76.
___. "Balzac, héraut du capitalisme naissant." *Europe* 429, 1965: 126–45.
___. "Balzac 'invente' les *Scènes de la vie de province.*" *Mercure de France* 333, 1958: 465–95.
___, ed. "Introduction." *L'Illustre Gaudissart; La Muse du département*. Paris: Garnier, 1970: ix–xlix, 49–148.
___. "Pages retrouveés de 'L'Illustre Gaudissart'." *L'Année Balzacienne*, 1960: 65–72.
___. *La Pensée politique et sociale de Balzac*. 2nd ed. Paris: A. Colin, 1967.
___. "La Province dans l'œuvre romanesque de Balzac." *Stendhal et Balzac, II*. Ed. A. Chantreau. 117–27.
Hamrick, L. Casssandra. "La Crise d'identité littéraire en 1837 selon la presse périodique." *Autour d'un cabinet de lecture*. Ed. Graham Falconer. Toronto: Centre d'Etudes du XIXe Siècle Joseph Sablé, 2001: 69–90.
Hanks, Patrick, and Flavia Hodges. *A Dictionary of First Names*. Oxford: Oxford UP, 1990.
___. *A Dictionary of Surnames*. Oxford: Oxford UP, 1988.
Harris, R. Laird, ed. *Theological Wordbook of the Old Testament*. 2 vols. Chicago: Moody Press, 1980.
Hayward, Margaret. "Superchérie et hallucination: *La Peau de chagrin*: Balzac orientaliste et mesmérien." *Revue de Littérature Comparée* 56.4, 1982: 437–56.
Heathcote, Owen. *Balzac and Violence: Representing History, Space, Sexuality and Death in* La Comédie humaine. Oxford: Peter Lang, 2009.
F. W. J. Hemmings, F. W. J. *Culture and Society in France 1789–1848*. Leicester: Leicester UP, 1987.
Heyndels, Ralph. "Théorie du roman/Roman de la théorie: Une Réflexion critique à partir de *Jacques le fataliste* (Diderot), *Ursule Mirouët* (Balzac) et *La Mise à mort* Aragon)." *French Literature Series* 11, 1984: 23–32.
Hoffmann, Léon-François. "Eros en filigrane: *Le Curé de Tours.*" *L'Année Balzacienne*, 1967: 89–105.
Hoffmann, Léon-François & the Princeton Balzac seminar, 1974. "Thèmes religieux dans *Eugénie Grandet.*" *L'Année Balzaciennne*, 1976: 201–29.
Holoch, George. "A Reading of *Illusions perdues.*" *Romanic Review* 69, 1978: 307–21.
Horowitz, Sarah. *Friendship and Politics in Post-Revolutionary France*. University Park: Pennsylvania State UP, 2013.

Hubert, J. D. *Molière & The Comedy of Intellect*. Berkeley: Univ. of California Press, 1962.
Hugo, Victor. "Ymbert Galloix." *Littérature et philosophy mêlées*. *Œuvres complètes*. Ed. Jean Massin. Vol. 5. Paris: Club Français du Livre, 1967: 173–91.
Hunt, Herbert J., ed. *Eugénie Grandet*. By Honoré de Balzac. Oxford: Clarendon, 1967.
Hunt, Lynn. *The Family Romance of the French Revolution*. Berkeley: U of California P, 1992.
Jacobi, Jolande. *Complex/Archetype/Symbol in the Psychology of C.G. Jung*. Trans. Ralph Manheim. New York: Bollingen, 1959.
Jacobus de Voragine. *The Golden Legend*. Trans. Granger Ryan and Helmut Ripperger. 2 vols. London: Longmans, 1941.
Jakobson, Roman. "Linguistique et poétique." *Essais de linguistique générale*. Trans. Nicolas Ruwet. Paris: Minuit, 1963: 209–48.
Jameson, Fredric. "The Ideology of Form: Partial Systems in *La Vieille Fille*." *Substance* 15, 1976: 29–49.
___. "Imaginary and Symbolic in *La Rabouilleuse*." *Social Science Information* 16.1, 1977: 59–81.
___. "Introduction." *Eugénie Grandet*. Everyman's Library. New York: Knopf, 1992: v–xxiii
___. *The Political Unconscious: Narrative as a Socially Symbolic Act*. Ithaca: Cornell UP, 1981.
___. "Realism and Desire: Balzac and the Problem of the Subject." *The Political Unconscious: Narrative as a Socially Symbolic Act*. London: Routledge, 1989: 151–84.
Jones, Colin. *The Great Nation: France from Louis XV to Napoleon 1715–99*. New York: Columbia UP, 2002.
Jung, C. G. *Alchemical Studies*. Princeton: Princeton UP, 1967.
___. *The Archetypes and the Collective Unconscious*. Trans. R. F. C. Hull. New York: Pantheon, 1959.
___. *Psychology and Alchemy*. Trans. R. F. C. Hull. London: Routledge & Kegan Paul, 1953.
___. *Symbols of Transformation*. Trans. R. F. C. Hull. New York: Pantheon, 1956.
Karr, Alphonse. *Sous les tilleuls*. Paris: Calmann Lévy, 1881.
Kinder, Patricia. "Un Directeur de journal, ses auteurs et ses lecteurs en 1836: Autour de *La Vieille Fille*." *L'Année Balzacienne*, 1972: 173–200.
Knight, Diana. "Celibacy on Display in Two Texts by Balzac: *Le Cabinet des antiques* and the Preface to *Pierrette*." *Dix-Neuf* 2, 2004: 1–15.
Kopp, Robert. "Préface." *La Vieille Fille*. By H. de Balzac. Folio. Paris: Gallimard, 1978.
Laffly, Georges. "La Politique dans *La Vieille Fille*." *Ecrits de Paris*. November 1970: 66–75.

Laguérenne, Lise de. "D'un portrait de Mademoiselle de Maupin à la duchesse de Maufrigneuse dans *Le Cabinet des Antiques:* Une Lecture créatrice de Balzac." *L'Année Balzacienne,* 1997: 413-27.
Laisney, Vincent. "Du Cénacle à l'élite." *Le Miroir et le chemin: l'univers romanesque de Pierre-Louis Rey.* Ed. V. Laisney. Paris: Sorbonne Nouvelle, 2006: 271-80.
Lamartine, Alphonse-Marie-Louis de. *Jocelyn.* Ed. Jean des Cognets. Paris: Garnier, 1960.
Landes, Joan B. "Representing the Body Politic: The Paradox of Gender in the Graphic Politics of the French Revolution." *Rebel Daughters: Women and the French Revolution.* Ed. Sara E. Melzer and Leslie W. Rabine. New York: Oxford, 1992.
Larthomas, Pierre. "Sur le style de Balzac." *L'Année Balzacienne,* 1987: 311-27.
___. "Sur une image de Balzac." *L'Année Balzacienne,* 1973: 301-26.
Lascar, Alex. "De la boue balzacienne." *L'Année balzacienne,* 2009: 105-25.
Le Breton, André. *Balzac: l'homme et l'œuvre.* Paris: Armand Colin, 1905.
Le Calvez, Eric. "Gobseck and Grandet: Semes, Themes, Intertext." *Romance Studies* 23, Spring 1994: 43-60.
Le Huenen, Roland, and Paul Perron. "Balzac et la représentation," *Poétique* 61, 1985: 75-90.
___. *Balzac: Sémiotique du personnage romanesque: L'Exemple d'*Eugénie Grandet. Paris: Didier; Montréal: P de l'U de Montréal, 1980.
___. "Balzac et la representation," *Poétique* 61, 1985: 75-90.
Levin, Harry. *The Gates of Horn: A Study of Five French Realists.* New York: Oxford UP, 1963.
Le Yaouanc, Moïse. "Le Plaisir dans les récits balzaciens." *L'Année Balzacienne,* 1972: 275-308; 1973: 201-33.
Lilly, W. S. "The Age of Balzac." *The Contemporary Review* 37, June 1880: 1004-44.
Lis-Balchin, Maria. "History of Nomenclature, Usage and Cultivation of Geranium and Pelagonium Species." *Geranium and Pelargonium: The Genera Geranium and Pelargonium.* Ed. Maria Lis-Balchin. London: Taylor & Francis, 2002: 5-10.
Lubbock, Percy. *The Craft of Fiction.* 1921. New York: Viking, 1966: 203-35.
Lubin, Georges. "Sur la piste du poète Jan Diaz." *L'Année Balzacienne,* 1987: 297-307.
Lukács, Georg. *Balzac et le réalisme français.* Trans. Paul Laveau. Paris: Maspero, 1967.
Lukács, György. "Balzac: *Lost Illusions.*" *Studies in European Realism: A Sociological Survey of the Writings of Balzac, Stendhal, Zola, Tolstoy, Gorki, and others.* London: Merlin P, 1972: 46-64.
___. *The Historical Novel.* London: Merlin, 1962.
Magette, Dorothy. "Trapping Crayfish: The Artist, Nature, and *Le Calcul* in Balzac's *La Rabouilleuse.*" *Nineteenth-Century French Studies* 12.1-2, Fall-Winter 1983-84: 54-67.

Maigron, Louis. *Le Romantisme et les mœurs*. 1910; rpt. Geneva: Slatkine Reprints, 1977.
Mainardi, Patricia. *Husbands, Wives, and Lovers: Marriage and Its Discontents in Nineteenth-Century France*. New Haven: Yale UP, 2003.
Manuel, Frank Edward. *The New World of Saint-Simon*. Cambridge: Harvard UP, 1956.
___. *The Prophets of Paris*. Cambridge: Harvard UP, 1962.
Marincic, Katarina. "*Eugénie Grandet* d'Honoré de Balzac: L'Histoire secrète d'une écriture romanesque." *Acta Neophilologica* 33.1–2, 2000: 49–60.
May, Georges. *Le Dilemme du roman au XVIIIe siècle. Etude sur les rapports du roman et de la critique (1715–1761)*. New Haven: Yale UP, 1963.
Mazahéri, Jean Homayoun. "La Conversion du Dr. Minoret dans *Ursule Mirouët* de Balzac." *Lettres Romanes* 55.1–2, Feb–May 2001: 53–66.
McCall-Saint-Saëns, Anne E. "Une Certaine Idée de la copie: Jeux de genèses pour une Société de gens de lettres." *Genèses du roman: Balzac et Sand*. Ed. Lucienne Frappier-Mazur (ed.). and Eric Bordas (preface). Amsterdam, Netherlands: Rodopi, 2004: 79–95.
McManners, John. *Church and Society in Eighteenth-Century France*. 2 vols. Oxford: Clarenden P, 1998.
___. *The French Revolution and the Church*. New York: Harper & Row, 1970.
Meininger, Anne-Marie. "*Illusions perdues* et faits retrouvés." *L'Année balzacienne*, 1979: 47–78.
___. "Sur *Le Cabinet des antiques*." *L'Année Balzacienne*, 1973: 384–85.
Mercier, Louis Sébastien. *Le Nouveau Paris*. Ed. Jean-Claude Bonnet. Year VII—1798; Paris: Mercure de France, 1994.
Merrick, Jeffrey W. *The Desacralization of the French Monarchy in the Eighteenth Century*. Baton Rouge: Louisiana State UP, 1990.
Mileham, James. *The Conspiracy Novel: Structure and Metaphor in Balzac's Comédie humaine*. Lexington: French Forum, 1982.
Mirabeau, Honoré-Gabriel Riqueti. *Lettres à Sophie* (1792). *Œuvres de Mirabeau*. 8 vols. Paris: Brissot-Thivars, Dupont, 1825–26. Vol. 1.
Morot-Sir, Edouard. "La Dynamique du théâtre et Molière." *Romance Notes* 15, supplement no. 1, 1973–74: 15–49.
Mortimer, Armine. *La Clôture narrative*. Paris: José Corti, 1985.
___. *For Love or for Money: Balzac's Rhetorical Realism*. Columbus: Ohio State UP, 2011.
___. "Myth and Mendacity: Balzac's *Pierrette* and Beatrice Cenci." *Dalhousie French Studies* 51, 2000: 12–25.
___. *Writing Realism: Representations in French Fiction*. Baltimore: Johns Hopkins UP, 2000.
Mozet, Nicole. "De sel et d'or: *Eugénie Grandet*, une histoire sans histoire." *Corps/décors: Femmes, orgie, parodie*. Ed. Catherine Nesci, Gretchen Van Slyke, et Gerald Prince. Amsterdam: Rodopi, 203–20.

___. "*Le Curé de Tours*, un espace œdipien?" *L'Œuvre d'identité: Essais sur le romantisme de Nodier à Baudelaire*. Ed. Didier Maleuvre and Catherine Nesci. Montreal: Département d'Etudes Françaises, University de Montréal, 1966: 21–27.

___. "*Ursule Mirouët* ou le test du bâtard." *Balzac, Œuvres complètes: Le Moment de* La Comédie humaine. Ed. Claude Duchet, et Isabelle Tournier. Saint-Denis: PU de Vincennes, 1993: 217–28.

___. *La Ville de province dans l'œuvre de Balzac: L'Espace romanesque: Fantasmes et idéologie*. Paris: C.D.U.-S.E.D.E.S., 1982.

Mulliez, J. "La Volonté d'un homme." *Histoire des pères*. Ed. Jean Delumeau and Daniel Roche. 279–312.

Mura-Brunel, Aline. "Le Livre et le lecteur dans *La Muse du department*." *L'Année Balzacienne*, 1999: 575–92.

Musset, Paul de. *Lauzun*. 2 vols. Paris: Dumont, 1835.

Neefs, Jacques. "*Illusions perdues*: Représentations de l'acte romanesque." *Le Roman de Balzac: recherches critiques, méthodes, lectures*. Ed. Roland Le Huenen et Paul Perron. Montréal: Didier, 1980: 119–30.

Nykrog, Per. "*Illusions perdues* dans ses grandes lignes: strategies et tactiques romanesques." *Balzac:* Illusions perdues*: "l'œuvre capitale dans l'œuvre."* Ed. Françoise van Rossum-Guyon. CRIN 18. Groningue: U de Groningue: Département de français, 1988: 34–46.

Pannier, Sophie. *L'Athée*, 2 vols. 1835. Paris: Fournier, 1836.

Pasco, Allan H. *Allusion, A Literary Graft*. First published by U of Toronto P, 1994; rpt. Charlottesville: Rookwood P, 2002.

___. "*Anti-Nous* and Balzac's Princess de Cadignan." *Romance Quarterly* 34, 1987: 425–33.

___. *Balzacian Montage: Configuring* La Comédie humaine. Toronto: U of Toronto P, 1991.

___. "Balzac's 'Gobseck' and Image Structure." *Novel Configurations*. 2nd ed. Birmingham, AL: Summa Publications, 1994: 51–71.

___. "Image Structure in *Le Père Goriot*." *French Forum* 7, 1982: 224–34. Print.

___. "Miss Manners and Fooling Around: Conduct Manuals and Sexual Mores in Eighteenth-Century France." *Sex Education in Eighteenth-Century France*. Ed. Shane Agin. SVEC; Oxford: Voltaire Foundation, 2011: 29–46.

___. "Personalizing Violence in Balzac's *Les Chouans*." *Nineteenth-Century French Studies* 41.3–4, 2013: 191–203.

___. "*Les Proscrits* et l'unité du *Livre mystique*." *L'Année balzacienne*, 1999: 75–92.

___. *Revolutionary Love in Eighteenth- and Early Nineteenth-Century France*. Burlington, VT: Ashgate, 2009.

___. *Sick Heroes: French Society and Literature in the Romantic Age, 1750–1850*. Exeter: U. of Exeter P, 1997.

Paulson, William. "De la force vitale au système organisateur: *La Muse du département* et l'esthétique balzacienne." *Romantisme* 55, 1987: 33–40.
Péraud, Alexandre. Le Cabinet des antiques: *Honoré de Balzac*. Paris: Bordas, 2004.
___. *Le Crédit dans la poétique balzacienne*. Paris: Garnier, 2012.
Perri, Carmela, et al. "Allusion Studies: An International Annotated Bibliography, 1921–1977." *Style* 13, 1979: 178–225.
Persson, Karl Gunnar. *An Economic History of Europe: Knowledge, Institutions and Growth, 600 to the Present*. New York: Cambridge UP, 2010.
Pichois, Claude. *Littérature et progress: Vitesse et vision du monde, essai*. Neuchatel: La Baconnière, 1973.
Picon, Gaëtan. "Suite balzacienne." *L'Usage de la lecture*. Vol. 2. Paris: Mercure de France, 1961: 9–97.
Piketty, Thomas. *Capital in the Twenty-First Century*. Trans. Arthur Goldhammer. Cambridge, MA: Harvard UP, 2014.
Planche, Gustave. "Essai sur *Adolphe*." *Adolphe: Anecdote trouvé dans les papiers d'un inconnu*. By Benjamin Constant. Paris: Charpentier, 1903: 5–26.
Pommier, Jean. "Comment Balzac a nommé ses personnages." *Cahiers de l'Association des Etudes Françaises* 3–5, 1953: 223–35.
Popkin, Jeremy D. *A Short History of the French Revolution*. 3d ed. Upper Saddle River, NJ: Prentice Hall, 2002.
Pound, Ezra. *The Cantos*. London: Faber, 1975.
Prendergast, Christopher. *The Order of Mimesis: Balzac, Stendhal, Nerval, Flaubert*. New York: Cambridge UP, 1986.
Prioult, Albert. "Du Mémorial catholique à 'L'Illustre Gaudissart'." *L'Année Balzacienne*, 1975: 263–78.
Proust, Marcel. *A la recherché du temps perdu*. Ed. Jean-Yves Tadié. 4 vols. Bibliothèque de la Pléiade. Paris: Gallimard, 1987–89.
___. *Contre Sainte-Beuve*. Bibliothèque de la Pléiade. Paris: Gallimard, 1971.
Pugh, Anthony R. "Balzac's *La Muse du départment*: The Status of Fiction." *L'Esprit créateur* 31.3, 1991: 60–66.
___. *Balzac's Recurring Characters*. Toronto: U of Toronto P, 1974.
___. "Du *Cabinet des antiques* à *Autre étude de femme*." *L'Année Balzacienne*, 1965: 239–52.
___. *Unité et création dans* Illusions perdues. *Le Roman de Balzac: recherches critiques, méthodes, lectures*. Ed. Roland Le Huenen et Paul Perron. Montréal: Didier, 1980: 99–107.
Queffélec, Henri, ed. "Préface." *La Vieille Fille. L'Œuvre de Balzac*. Vol. 1. Paris: Formes et reflets, 1949: 893–901.
Queffélec, Lise. "*La Vieille Fille* ou la science des mythes." *L'Année Balzacienne*, 1988: 163–77.
Réau, Louis. *Iconographie des saints*. Tome 3 of *Iconographie de l'art chrétien*. 3 vols. Paris: P.U.F., 1958.

Reboussin, Marcel. "Balzac et la presse dans *Illusions perdues*." *French Review* 32, 1958: 130–37.
Reid, Martine. "Introduction." *Eugénie Grandet*. Paris: Classiques de Poche, 1996: 7–52.
Restif de La Bretonnne, Nicolas-Edme. *Les Nuits de Paris, ou le spectateur nocturne*. 8 vols. London, Paris: n.p. 1788–94.
Reybaud, Louis. *Jérôme Paturot à la recherche d'une position sociale*. 2 vols. Paris: Paulin, 1847.
Ricardou, Jean. "Le Nouveau Roman existe-t-il?" *Nouveau Roman: hier, aujourd'hui*. Communications et interventions du colloque tenu du 20 au 30 juillet 1971 au Centre Culturel de Cerisy-la-Salle. 2 vols. Paris : 10/18, 1972. 1.9–34.
Richer, Jean François. "Bruits et rumeurs dans *La Vieille Fille* d'Honoré de Balzac." *Dix-huit* 17.3, November 2013: 265–75.
Riffaterre, Michael. "Fear of Theory." *Romanic Review* 93.1–2, 2002: 185–99.
Robb, Graham. *Balzac: A Biography*. London: Picador, 1994.
Robbe-Grillet, Alain. *Pour un nouveau roman*. Coll. Idées. Paris: NRF, 1963.
Roche, Daniel. *Le Peuple de Paris: Essai sur la culture populaire au XVIIIe siècle*. 1981. Rpt. Paris: Fayard, 1998.
Sacy, S. de. "Préface." *Ursule Mirouët*. *L'Œuvre de Balzac*. Ed. Albert Béguin and Jean A. Ducourneau. Vol. 8. Paris: Formes et Reflets, 1951.
Sainte-Beuve, Charles-Augustin. "Frochot, Préfet de la Seine." *Nouveaux lundis*. t. 11. Paris: Lévi frères, 1869: 21–37.
___. "M. de Balzac" (2 September 1850). *Causeries du lundi*. 3e ed. Vol. 2. Paris: Garnier, 1852: 443–63.
___. "Poètes et romanciers modernes de la France: Balzac," *Revue des Deux Mondes* 333.4, 1834: 440–58.
Saint-Pierre, Jacques-Henri Bernardin de. *Paul et Virginie* (1788). Ed. Pierre Trahard. Paris: Garnier, 1964.
Saint-Simon, Henri de. *Mémoire de la science de l'homme* (1813). 2e partie. Ed. Prosper Enfantin. *Science de l'homme*. Paris: Victor Masson, 1858.
___. *Science de l'homme: Physiologie religieuse*. Paris: Victor Masson, 1858.
Sand, George. "Honoré de Balzac." *Autour de la table*. Paris: Michel Lévy, 1876: 197–213.
Sarraute, Nathalie. *L'Ère du soupçon: Essais sur le roman*. Paris: Gallimard, 1956.
Schilling, Bernard N. *The Hero as a Failure: Balzac and the Rubempré cycle*. Chicago: U of Chicago P, 1968.
Schor, Naomi. "*Eugénie Grandet*: Miroirs et Melancholia." *Breaking the Chain: Women, Theory, and French Realist Fiction*. New York: Columbia UP, 1985: 90–107.

___. *Reading in Detail: Aesthetics and the Feminine.* New York and London: Methuen, 1987.
Schuerewegen, Franc. "'L'Illustre Gaudissart': Le Mal des mots." *Balzac contre Balzac: Les Cartes du lecteur.* Toronto: Paratexte, 1990: 89–104.
Scott, Edouard-Léon. *Les Noms de baptême et les prénoms: Nomenclature, signification, tradition, légend, histoire: Art de nommer.* Paris: Alexandre Houssiaux, 1858.
Sheriff, Mary D. *Moved by Love: Inspired Artists and Deviant Women in Eighteenth-Century France.* Chicago: U of Chicago P, 2004.
Simond, Charles, *Paris de 1800 à 1900 d'après les estampes et les mémoires du temps.* 2 vols. Paris: Plon, 1900.
Sjödén, K.-E. "Remarques sur le swedenborgisme balzacien." *L'Année Balzacienne,* 1966: 33–45.
___. "Balzac et Swedenborg." *Cahiers de l'Association Internationale des Etudes Françaises* 15, 1963: 295–307.
Smith, Annette. "A boire et à manger dans l'écuelle de Dinah: Lecture de *La Muse du department.*" *French Forum* 15, 1990: 301–14.
Smith-Di Biasio, Anne-Marie. "'Le Texte de la vie des femmes': Female Melancholia in *Eugénie Grandet.*" *Nottingham French Studies* 35.2, 1996: 52–59.
Sonnet, M. "Les Leçons paternelles." *Histoire des pères.* Ed. Jean Delumeau and Daniel Roche: 259–78.
Stendhal, *Correspondance.* 3 vols. Bibliothèque de la Pléiade. Paris: Gallimard, 1962–68.
___. "Les Cenci" (1837). *Chroniques italiennes, Romans et nouvelles.* Vol. 2. Bibliothèque de la Pléiade. Paris: Gallimard, 1952: 678–709.
___. *Journal* (10 septembre 1811). *Œuvres intimes.* Ed. Henri Martineau. 2 vols. Bibliothèque de la Pléiade. Paris: Gallimard, 1955, 1982.
___. *Lucien Leuwen. Romans et nouvelles.* Vol. 1. 765–1384.
Stern, Daniel (pseud. Marie de Flavigny Agoult). *Esquisses morales et politiques.* Paris: Pagnerre, 1849.
Taine, Hippolyte. "Balzac." *Nouveaux Essais de critique et d'histoire.* 4th ed. Paris: Hachette, 1886: 51–140.
Thompson, Victoria E. *The Virtuous Marketplace: Women and Men, Money and Politics in Paris, 1830–1870.* Baltimore: Johns Hopkins UP, 2000.
Tilby, Michael. "*Ursule Mirouët,* or Balzac and the Coach to Paris." *Moving Forward, Holding Fast: The Dynamics of Nineteenth-Century French Culture.* Ed. Barbara T. Cooper, Mary Donaldson-Evans. Amsterdam, Netherlands: Rodopi, 1997: 53–66.
___. "Balzac and the Poetics of Ignorance: *La Vieille Fille.*" *Modern Language Review* 100.4, 2005: 957–58.

___. "Playing with Risk: Balzac, the Insurance Industry and the Creation of Fiction." *Journal of European Studies* 4.2, 2011: 107–22.
Tomashevsky, Boris. "Thematics." *Russian Formalist Criticism: Four Essays*. Tran. Lee T. Lemon and Marion J. Reis. Lincoln, NE: U of Nebraska P, 1963: 61–95.
Traer, James F. *Marriage and the Family in Eighteenth-Century France*. Ithaca: Cornell UP, 1980.
Trillat, A. "Les Savants et la théorie unitaire dans *La Comédie humaine*." *Revue d'Histoire de la Philosophie* 3, avril 1935: 137–55.
Tritter, Jean Louis. "A propos des épreuves de *Pierrette*." *L'Année Balzacienne*, 1973: 19–29.
Turnell, Martin. "Balzac." *The Novel in France*. London: Hamish Hamilton, 1950: 211–46.
Urquhart, Steven. "Le Savoir moralisateur d'*Eugénie Grandet*." *South Carolina Modern Language Review* 3.1, Spring 2004: no pagination.
Van der Elst, Jo. "Autour du *Livre mystique*: Balzac and Swedenborg." *Revue de Littérature Comparée* 10, 1930: 88–123.
Vanoncini André. "*Pierrette* et la rénovation du code mélodramatique." *Balzac: Œuvres complètes: Le Moment de* La Comédie humaine." Éd. Claude Duchet et Isabelle Tournier. Saint-Denis: PU de Vincennes, 1993: 257–67.
Viatte, August. "Les Swedenborgiens en France." *Revue de Littérature Comparée* 11, 1931: 416–50.
Viaud, J. "Egyptian Mythology." *New Larousse Encyclopedia of Mythology*. London: Prometheus Press, 1968: 9–48.
Viegnes, Michel. *L'Esthétique de la nouvelle française au vingtième siècle*. New York: Peter Lang, 1989.
Watts, Andrew. *Preserving the Provinces: Small Town and Countryside in the Work of Honoré de Balzac*. Oxford: Peter Lang, 2007.
___. "An Exercise in International Relations, or the Travelling Salesman in Touraine: Balzac's 'L'Illustre Gaudissart'." *Currencies: Fiscal Fortunes and Cultural Capital in Nineteenth-Century France*. Ed. Sarah Capitanio, et al. Oxford: Peter Lang, 2005: 161–73.
Wetherill, P.M. "A Reading of *Eugénie Grandet*." *Modern Languages* (London) 52, 1971: 166–72.
White, Andrew Dickson. *Fiat Money Inflation in France*. New York: Appleton-Century, 1933.
White, Matthew. "Selected Death Tolls for Wars, Massacres and Atrocities Before the 20th Century." *Historical Atlas of the 20th Century*. n.d. http://necrometrics.com.
Wille, Georges. *Mémoires et journal*. Ed. Georges Duplessis, 2 vols. Paris: Jules Renouard, 1857.
Williams, Timothy J. "Dessein hagiographique balzacien: A propos de *Pierrette*." *Dalhousie French Studies* 28, 1994: 87–97.

———. "Martyrdom in *Pierrette*: Balzac's Unmasking of Scapegoat Violence." *Renascence: Essays on Values in Literature* 61.2, Winter 2009: 91–102.
Winkler-Boulenger, Jacqueline. "La Durée romanesque dans *Eugénie Grandet*." *L'Année Balzacienne*, 1973: 75–87.
Wirtz, Dorothy. "Animalism in Balzac's *Curé de Tours* and *Pierrette*." *Romance Notes* 11.1, 1969: 61–67.
Wollen, Geoff. *Le Curé de Tours*. Glasgow: University of Glasgow French and German Publications, 1988.
———. "*Le Curé de Tours* and the Ten Year Itch." *French Studies Bulletin: A Quarterly Supplement* 29, 1988–89: 7–9.
Yonge, Charlotte. *History of Christian Names*. 1884; rpt. Detroit: Gale, 1966.
Zola, Emile. *La Faute de l'abbé Mouret. Les Rougon-Macquart*. Ed. Henri Mitterand. Vol 1. Bibliothèque de la Pléiade. Paris: Gallimard, 1966–69: 1213–527.
———. *Œuvres complètes*. Ed. Henri Mitterand. Vols. 9, 13. Paris: Cercle du Livre Précieux, 1969.

Index

A
Abbott, Edwin A, 60, 107
Abel, 229
Abraham, Pierre, 102, 153
Adolphe (Constant), 159, 160, 163, 164, 165, 169n16, 169n17, 193
adultery, 4, 14, 58, 121, 151, 154, 163, 165, 166, 176
Affaire d'Esclans, L' (Daumas), 63
Agin, Shane, 169n19, 187n10
A la recherche du temps perdu (Proust), 23, 32n46, 173
Alençon (city), 181, 182, 184, 187n11, 192
allusion, 5, 59, 60, 66, 73, 78n18, 83, 84, 88, 89, 90, 91, 92, 93, 95, 96, 97, 98n11, 99n13, 126, 134n12, 163, 173, 175, 176, 181, 185, 220, 224, 225, 237, 238
   antiphrastic, 73
   Eugenie Grandet and allusive opposition, 57–79, 83, 92
   Illusions perdues and, 163, 213–230
   La Muse du département and, 151–167, 238
   La Vieille Fille and, 83, 96, 98n5, 171–186, 238
   Pierrette and, 81–97, 99n13
   types *vs.*, 238
   zoological, 121, 226
Allusion (Pasco), 83, 97n4, 132–133n2, 238
allusive complex, 83, 92, 95, 176
ambition, 36, 37, 44, 45, 82, 92, 102, 108, 110, 145, 154, 155, 201, 243
Ambrière-Fargeaud, Madeleine, 37, 48, 55n18
amour-passion, 63, 162
analogies, 226, 238
   zoological, 226
ancient régime, 12, 42, 51, 58, 77n1, 108, 128, 175, 179, 248, 250
Andrioli, Max, 31–32n45

Note: Page numbers with "n" denote notes.

Angers, David d', 107
Angoulême, 215, 216, 217, 218, 223, 224, 229
Annales, 4
antithesis, 74, 213. See also opposition
apostasy, 151, 153, 154, 163, 166
Aragon, Sandrine, 170n22
Aretino, 165
Ariosto, 185
aristocracy, 2, 5, 6, 7, 61, 65, 138, 171, 178, 184, 185, 186, 192, 194, 195, 196, 200, 207–210
Aristotle, 120, 165
Armance (Stendhal), 174
armature, 40, 41, 113, 120, 237, 238, 242
arrivals, 40, 47
art, 4, 11, 19, 20, 21, 38, 70, 121, 122, 129, 133n9, 152–155, 159, 161, 163, 165, 170n21, 214, 219, 230, 241
  failure in, 4, 159, 161, 163, 214, 219
Ashton, Kevin, 25
Arthez, Daniel d', 26, 123, 205, 219, 220, 229
Atala (Chateaubriand), 174
atomization(ed), 42, 123
Aubignac, d', 182
Augustine, St., 7
Auray, Anne d', Ste., 99n18
Austria, 85
Autre étude de femme (Balzac), 35, 36, 164, 166
Avare, L' (Molière), 40
"Aventures administratives d'une idée heureuse" (Balzac), 113
"Aveugle, L'" (Chénier), 224

B

Bacciarelli, Marcello, 180
Bainville, Jacques, 12, 30n32

Balanche, Pierre-Simon, 147
Baltzell, James, 170n21
Balzac and the Drama of Perspective (Dargan), 78n16
Balzac and Violence (Heathcote), 230n3
Balzac contre Balzac (Schuerewegen), 149n12
Balzacian Montage (Pasco), 23, 31n42, 32n47, 117, 212n7, 247
Balzac occult (Baron), 55n20
"Balzac's *Gobseck* and Image Structure" (Pasco), 114n11
Balzac's Recurring Characters (Pugh), 53n4
Bank of France, 10, 65, 249
Barbéris, Pierre, 97n3, 114n7, 187–188n12
Bardèche, Maurice, 60, 77n8, 92, 97n1, 113n1, 118, 152, 187n12, 191, 193, 249
Bargeton, Marie-Louise, 215–219, 223–226
Baron, Anne-Marie, 55n20, 231n10
Baudelaire, 3, 76
Bayle, 165
bear, 37, 48, 71, 103, 121, 122, 153, 180, 181, 216, 227, 231n11, 238
Béatrix (Balzac), 159
Beaumarchais, 6, 176, 177, 182
Béguin, Albert, 168n10, 187n11, 187n12
Bell, David F., 55n16
Bérard, Suzane, 136
Bernanos, 73
Bernard, Claudie, 40, 132n1
Bertault, Philippe, 102
Berthier, Philippe, 22, 114n7, 183, 187n11, 208, 211n1
Bible, 38, 59, 70, 72, 73, 74, 153, 176. *see also specific* biblical figures

Eugenie and, 73
Exodus, 242
Genesis, 122, 132, 153, 225, 243
Gospels, 229
John, 38, 69, 229
Luke, 71, 178, 229
Mark, 229
Matthew, 229
1 Corinthians, 38
Bichat, 2, 16
Birotteau, Abbé François, 101–108, 110–114
Bildungsroman, 173
Biron, duc de, 188n13
Blanchard, Pierre, 13
Blankenhorn, David, 123, 133n9, 248
Bluche, F., 55n14, 98n8
Blondet, Emile, 98n11, 195, 197, 208, 209, 211
Blondet, Judge, 193, 196, 206, 208–210
Boccace, 165
"A boire et à manger dans l'écuelle de Dinah" (Smith), 167n4
Bonald, Louis de, 75
Bonneuil, Mme "Camille," 224
Bordonove, Georges, 188n17
Borel, Petrus, 174
Bossuet, 165
Bougainville, 3
Bourbon monarchy, 10, 11, 12, 179
bourgeoisie, 10, 11, 12, 61, 68, 122, 128, 131, 175, 196, 201, 202, 210
Bourget, August, 136
Bourlin, Antoine-Jean, 9
Bowman, Frank Paul, 27n1, 59, 77n3
Braniski, M., 188n13
bridges, 39
Brazier, Flore, 118, 119, 121, 128
Brillat-Savarin, 17
Brindeau, Achille, 153

Bridau, Agathe Rouget, 121–123, 129
Bridau, Joseph, 41, 121–124, 129, 132, 139, 239
Bridau, Philippe, 120–124, 129, 239
Brigaut, Jacques, 83–85, 90, 95, 123, 145
Buffon, 23, 165
Burton, Richard D.E., 212n11
Butor, Michael, 133n3

C
Cabanis, 2, 16
Cabinet des antiques, Le (Balzac), 31n44, 47, 126, 138, 187n11, 191–211, 238, 248
 critical evaluation of, 60
 hidden reality in, 193
 La Vieille Fille and, 192, 193, 194
 names, 192, 193, 194, 209, 211, 238
 title, 192, 195, 196, 197, 198, 208, 238
Cain (biblical figure), 229
Cadignan, Princess de, *see* Maufrigneuse, Diane de
Calderon, 165
Calvinism, 155
Camus, Albert, 173
Canada, 15, 167–168n5
capital, 5, 9, 11, 26, 36, 47, 65, 66, 67, 76, 104, 108, 128, 136, 139, 147, 151, 172, 193, 198, 208, 214, 215, 241, 242, 244, 246, 249. *See also* money
Capital in the Twenty-First Century (Piketty), 29n27, 134n16, 149n1, 230n2, 251n15
capitalism, 25, 135–148, 227
Carpaccio, St. Ursula, 37
Carraud, Zulma, 136
Carroll, Lewis, 38

274 INDEX

Castex, Pierre-Georges, 22, 27n5, 33n52, 61, 77n10, 78n19, 182, 192
catallaxy, 2
Catholic Church, 57, 59, 65, 75, 157
  celibacy and, 102
  Concordat and, 58
  conversion to, 58
  corruption of, 76
  decline of, 123
  education and, 57
  Eugenie Grandet and, 23, 92
  intangible *vs.* tangible values and, 101–113, 114n11, 140, 148, 249
  Napoleon and, 10, 12, 58, 65, 93
  occult and, 52
  property confiscated, 13, 57
celibacy, 21, 102, 108, 196
Célibataires, Les (trilogy of *Pierrette, Curé*, and *Rabouilleuse*), 103
Cénacle group, 219
"Cenci, Les" (Stendhal), 99n13
César Birotteau (Balzac), 24, 239, 242
"Champavert" (Borel), 174
Chants modernes, 1
characters
  shell, 193, 194, 196, 199, 202, 207–211
  as symbols, 120, 219
  as types, 82, 236, 242
Charles IX, 181
Charles X, 113
Charte of, 109
Chartier, Roger, 28n11, n12
Chasles, Philarète, 22, 240
Chateaubriand, 59, 75, 119, 174
Châtelet, Sixte du, 217
Chénier, André, 214, 220–225, 231n7, 238
Cherpillod, André, 134n12
Chevalier, the, 192, 199, 200, 202, 211. *See also* Valois, Chevalier de

Chevalier, Jean, 37, 38, 53n5, 99n17, 115n13, 180, 181, 199, 200, 202, 211, 225, 227, 231n9
Chevaliers de la Désoeuvrance, 123, 125, 131, 145
childcare methods, 44
children, 13, 18, 21, 43, 44, 45, 48, 49, 58, 59, 62, 63, 76, 84, 85, 86, 89, 96, 121–125, 128, 141, 142, 143, 148, 154, 158, 159, 165, 167, 181, 183, 184, 200, 210, 219, 235, 242, 247, 248, 249. *See also* fathers, absence of; illegitimacy; mothers, inadequate; young
  desire for, 43, 128, 148, 159, 181, 183
Choisy, Abbé de, 181
Chollet, Roland, 220
Cholvy, Gérard, 59, 75
Chouans, Les (Balzac), 29n23, 237, 238, 240, 250n5
Christ des barricades, Le (Bowman), 27n1, 77n3
Christianity, 57, 59, 67, 68. *See also* Church
Christ romantique, Le (Bowman), 99n16
Chronique de Paris, La, 191
Chronus, 96
Church and Society in Eighteenth Century France (McManners), 76–77n1
Cirlot, 53n5, 227, 229, 231n9
Citron, Pierre, 60, 98n6, 126, 240
Civil Code, 10, 15, 124, 131, 146, 157
class conflict, 213
class structure, 21, 47, 249
Cobban, Alfred, 29n26
Cobb, Richard, 7, 28n10

Coralie, 212, 219, 226
Cormon, Rose, 83, 171, 175–177, 179–815, 192, 211. *See also* du Bousquier, Madame du Croisier
colonies, 26, 65, 69
Collin, Jacques, *see* Herrera, Abbé Carlos
Comédie humaine, La (Balzac), 4, 5, 20, 21, 23, 25, 26, 27n5, 29n23, 31–32n45, 35, 36, 40, 43, 44, 46, 48, 53, 65, 81, 117, 121, 123, 135, 138, 143, 145, 161, 165, 167n1, 170n22, 174, 176, 188n17, 193, 212n7, 215, 219, 220, 230n4, 234, 240, 241, 242, 243, 245, 246. *See also* and stories; sections; *specific* novels
  ages represented in, 36, 242
  arrangement of works in, 5
  "Avant-propos," 20, 23, 121, 176, 240, 241
  concept of unified society in, 20
  critical evaluation of, 60
  detail in, 26, 234, 241
  "Foreword," 36
  Furne edition, 240, 242
  historical and sociological unity of, 176
  history of manners, 176
  image structure and, 114n11, 118, 132–133n2
  "L'Illustre Gaudissart" included in, 138, 145
  links within, 35
  order of, 35
  overtures of novels in, 48, 234
  reappearing characters and themes, 165, 247
  Scènes de la vie de province as major section of, 5, 20, 23, 24, 26, 35, 36, 40, 53, 138, 215, 234, 246
  sociological insight in, 25
  Sterne's influence on, 121
  structure, 21, 26, 40, 165, 170n22, 242
  titles of novels, 103, 197, 225, 238
  unity of cycle, 5, 23, 176, 193, 240
  comedy, 57–76, 83, 84, 114n4, 137, 138, 145, 147, 172, 174, 178, 180, 182, 185, 189n20
    turned to despair, 172
Commedia dell'arte, 40, 236
"Comment Balzac a nommé ses personnages" (Pommier), 167n5
commerce, 18, 19, 25, 86, 216, 249
communication, 15, 16, 25, 26, 46, 71, 138, 147, 148, 249
Comte, Auguste, 16, 17, 19, 20, 31n40
Concordat (1801), 58, 108
Condorcet, Marquis de, 2, 16
Confessions d'une courtisane devenue philosophe (anonymous), 43
Conner, J. Wayne, 133n8
Conrad, Thomas, 193
Conseiller d'Etat, Le (Soulié), 174
Constant, Benjamin, 4, 169n16, 224
Constitutionnel, 158, 173
contrasts, 226, 238. *See also* opposition
conversation, without communication, 138
Cooper, James Fenimore, 237
Corbeill, Anthony, 32n47
Corinne (de Staël), 224
Corneille, 11
corruption, 11, 37, 76, 88, 209, 244, 247
Corsaire, Le, 158, 172
"Corset of *la Vieille Fille*, The" (Mortimer), 186n8

courts, 14, 15, 51, 55n19, 200, 201, 209, 216. See also justice; law and legal system
Cousine Bette, La (Balzac), 59, 118, 133n8, 140, 242
Cousin Pons, Le (Balzac), 20
Cultural Origins (Chartier), 28n11, 28n12
Curé de Tours, Le (Balzac), 96, 101–113, 148, 248
   conclusion added to, 102
   critical evaluation of, 60
   narratological repetitions, 101
   overture, 48, 104
   title of, 109, 112
Custine, Marquis de, 99n13
Cuvier, 23, 165

D

Dällenbach, Lucien, 31n42, 170n24
Dante, 72, 114n4
Dargan, Joan, 78n16
Darnton, Robert, 7
Daumas, Maurice, 63
Dauzat, Albert, 37, 38, 134n12
David, Marcel, 42
Davin, Félix, 5, 22, 36, 213, 238, 240, 241, 243
Davis, Natalie Z., 15, 30n34
death, 4, 21, 38, 42, 48, 50, 71, 75, 82, 85, 87, 88, 91–5, 104, 111, 120, 121, 123, 127–9, 132, 145, 147, 162, 173, 174, 175, 178, 184, 185, 195, 210, 214, 215, 222, 223, 226, 237, 240, 244
Deaths of Louis XVI, The (Dunn), 54n10
debt, 7, 32n46, 137, 148, 159, 160, 179, 181, 199, 200, 204–6, 242
"De la force vitale au système organisateur" (Paulson), 170n24

De la gérontocratie (Fazy), 109
De l'amour (Stendhal), 163
Delmas, General, 30n32
Delphic oracle, 133n6
Delphine (Madame de Staël), 14
Denis, St., 38
Denon, Vivant, 11
Député d'Arcis, Le (Balzac), 197
Desan, Suzanne, 55n19, 59, 76n1, 134n17
description, web of, 240, 242
detail, 1, 19, 22, 23, 25, 26, 41, 55n19, 64, 86, 88, 96, 106, 128, 136, 173, 176, 184, 192, 194, 203, 219, 234, 235, 237, 241, 242
Diary of a Country Priest, The (Bernanos), 73
Diaz, Juan (Spanish apostate), 153
Dictionnaire ètymologique des noms géographiques (Cherpillod), 134n12
Diderot, 1, 3, 6, 17, 27n2
Dinah (Biblical figure), 155–7, 162
Dionysos, 86
"Directeur de journal, Un" (Kinder), 186n2
Directory, 9, 10, 12, 98n8, 175, 181, 184
Divine Comedy (Dante), 114n4
divorce, 4, 13, 14
Don Juan (Molière), 178, 187n10
Doyle, William, 28n12
dreams and visions, 122, 127
Droits de l'homme, 16
Du Camp, Maxime, 1, 27n1
du Bousquier, Madame, 184, 192. See also Cormon, Rose; du Croisier, Madame
du Bousquier, Monsieur, 25, 104, 130, 139, 176–177, 179–184,

192, 194, 196, 211. *See also* du Croisier, Monsieur
du Châtelet, Sixte, 216–217.
du Croisier, 192, 206, 207, 209, 211, 248. *See also* Cormon, Rose; du Bousquier, Madame
du Croisier, Monsieur, 192, 194, 196, 202–203, 205–211. *See also* du Bousquier, Monsieur
Ducray-Duminil, 82
Dumas, Alexandre, *père*, 126, 158, 169n14, 180
Dumonstier, Etienne, 180
Dunn, Susan, 50n10
Durkheim, Emile, 19, 25, 31n40
du Ronceret, Fabien, 202, 203, 207, 210

E
eagle, 226, 228, 229, 232n15, 239
earrings, 180, 181
Ecole des femmes, L' (Molière), 83, 95
Ecole des Filles, L' (Millet), 177
Economic History of Europe, An (Persson), 29n27, 55n14
economics, 2, 4, 10, 15, 21, 26, 29n27, 113, 131, 138, 141, 241
education, 10, 21, 26, 38, 45, 75, 77n1, 88, 181, 200, 248
egotism, 70, 82, 87, 88, 102, 109, 111, 123, 243, 248
Egyptians, 17, 125, 126
emigration, 14, 157, 175, 179
Empire period, 10, 11
Encyclopédie (Diderot), 6
Enfant du carnaval, L' (Pigaut-Lebrun), 82
Enlightenment, 15, 16
Envers de l'histoire contemporaine, L' (Balzac), 35, 239
equality, 9, 207

"Eros en filigrane" (Hoffmann), 114n10
Escher, M.C., 234
Esgrignon, Armande d', 195, 197, 198, 200–203
Estournelles, Louise d', 43
Esgrignon, Count Victurnien d', 25, 139, 194, 196–204, 206–209, 211, 226
Etranger, L' (Camus), 173
Etudes analytiques (Balzac), 245
Etudes des mœurs (Balzac), 20, 240, 243, 245
Etudes philosophiques (Balzac), 22, 240, 241, 245
Eugenia of Alexandria, Saint, 70
Eugenia of Alsace, Saint, 70
Eugénie Grandet (Balzac), 20, 23, 41, 57–79, 83, 86, 92, 103, 114n11, 118, 148, 191, 247
  allusive opposition of God *vs.* Mammon in, 83
  analogical resonances, 89
  artistic economy and, 64
  critical evaluation of, 60
  image structure, 118
"Exercise in International Relations, An" (Watts), 149n7

F
Faguet, Emile, 159, 235
failures, 4, 5, 6, 26, 32n46, 48, 89, 104, 123, 127, 135, 145, 146, 156, 159, 161, 162, 180, 184, 204, 205, 214, 215, 217, 218, 219, 227, 228
Faire Vrai (Massonnaud), 250n1
Fairlie, Alison, 159
family, 4, 13–16, 21, 25, 26, 38, 39, 41–7, 51, 54n13, 55n17, 63, 67, 69–71, 73, 85, 90, 91, 101, 103,

108, 112, 119, 121–8, 130, 131, 136, 140, 145, 148, 153, 154, 158, 161, 162, 191, 192, 194, 196–206, 208, 209, 211, 213, 214, 216, 218, 219, 225, 227, 230, 234, 237, 238, 239, 243, 244, 247, 248, 249
   friends, as artificial, 26, 42, 47, 234
   individualism *vs.*, 43
   marriage and, 63
   weakened, 13, 42, 124
Family on Trial in Revolutionary France, The (Desan), 28n17, 55n19, 134n17
Farge, Arlette, 27n7
Fargeaud, Madeleine, 33n52, 238
Farrant, Tim, 105
fathers and fatherhood, 13, 21, 42–45, 48–49, 54n10, 60–73, 84–85, 91, 117–134, 147–148, 218, 219, 227, 228, 235, 246–249. *See also* patriarchy
Fazy, James, 109
"Fear of Theory" (Riffaterre), 186n8
Felicitas, 72
Felman, Shoshana, 137, 138, 146
Femme de trente ans, La (Balzac), 63, 238
Ferguson, Gary, 180, 188n17
"Ferragus" (Balzac), 82, 109, 140, 175
Feydeau, Ernest, 1
fiat currency *(assignat)*, 8, 61
Fiat Money Inflation in France (White), 76n1
Figures II (Genette), 74
"Fille aux yeux d'or, La" (Balzac), 22, 130, 244
financial system, 137, 249
Fischler, Alexander, 67, 78n18
Flatland (Abbott), 60, 107
Flaubert, Gustave, 1, 43, 89, 170n21
Fleming, William, 11

For Love or for Money (Mortimer), 5n17
Forrest, Alan, 9
Forster, E.M., 235
Fouché, Joseph, 12
"Fragments," 23, 53n4, 164, 165, 240
Frappier-Mazur, Lucienne, 117, 133n4
fraternity, 42, 43
freedoms, 9, 13, 58, 62
French Academy of 1635, 11
French National Assembly, 75
French parliament, 109
French Revolution and the Church (McManners), 77n2
French Revolutionary Assembly, 8, 9, 85
French Revolutionary National Convention, 248
French Romanticism (Bowman), 99n16
Frères de la consolation (Balzac), 35
friendship, 25, 42–5, 108, 180, 214, 239

G
Gamard, Sophie, 101, 104, 105, 107–110, 113
Gaudissart, Félix, 20, 25, 27n1, 135–150
"Galloix, Ymbert" (Hugo), 217, 231n5
Garden of Eden, 243
Gatien, Saint, 105, 111
Gaultie, Léonard, 180
Gautier, Théophile, 76
Gemie, Sharif, 141
generosity, 40, 67, 199, 205
gerontocracy, 45, 81–99, 109, 175, 196, 203, 210, 246, 248, 249
Gheerbrant, Alain, 53n5, 225

"Ghosts, Kin, and Progeny" (Davis), 30n34
Gide, André, 74
Gilet, Maxence, 118–119, 123–126, 128–129, 131, 234
Girardin, Emile de, 172, 174
"Gobseck" (Balzac), 3, 40, 41, 110, 118, 158, 235, 241
God, 14, 35, 42, 51, 52, 59, 60, 63–5, 67–9, 72, 90, 92–5, 103, 111, 122, 132, 147, 153, 157, 196, 200, 206, 242, 247, 248
  false god of money *vs.*, 59, 64, 69
  France abandoned by, 94
  as protector, 51
Goethe, 250n1
gold, 3, 8, 22, 46, 62, 64, 66–8, 70, 72, 74, 76, 106, 114n111, 137, 144, 148, 157, 179, 196, 228, 241, 246, 249. *See also* money
goldfinch, 228, 232n15
Goritza, Princess, 179, 188n13, 192
government, 8, 10–16, 104, 128, 141, 142, 175, 198, 200, 202, 203, 207, 216, 247
Grande Guorre (syphillis), 238
Grandeur et décadence (Balzac), 239
Grandet, Charles, 41, 62–63, 57, 69–74, 226, 241
Grandet, Eugénie, 41, 60–79, 86
Grandet, Félix, 41, 60–76, 78n16, 148
Granson, Athanase, 83, 123, 145, 177, 178, 181–184, 187n12, 203
Great Nation, The (Jones), 30n31
Greece, 86, 121, 122
  three wise men of, 122
greed, 41, 45, 50, 60, 62, 65, 66, 73, 82, 88, 92, 93, 163, 166, 185, 227
group, local, 41, 89
  individual *vs.*, 243

Guichardet, Jeannine, 32n45
Guignard, R., 133n5
Guise, René, 24, 186n2
Gutman, David, 123
Guyon, Bernard, 31n41, 33n52, 72, 137, 154, 167n4, 170n24

H
Halévy, Léon, 19
Hanska, Madame, 22, 27n3, 81, 117, 157, 165, 168n14, 170n24, 172, 179, 191, 197, 220, 241, 245
hare, 37, 38, 87
Hayek, Friedrich, 2
Heathcote, Owen, 230n3
Helenus, 70
Henri III, 180, 181, 188n17
Henri III et sa cour (Dumas), 180
Henri IV, 58, 181, 182, 197
Herrera, Abbé Carlos, 25, 35, 196, 214, 215, 218, 219, 226, 229, 230, 239, 242. *See also* Vautrin
Héritiers Boirouge (Balzac), 37
Hernani (Hugo), 174
Histoire des treize (Balzac), 35, 239
Hobbes, Thomas, 3
Hoffmann, Léon-François, 38, 114n10, 195
Holy Spirit, 38, 65, 66, 68, 69
Homer, 224
homosexuality, 180
"Honoré de Balzac" (Sand), 240, 246
Honorine (Balzac), 166
Horowitz, Sarah, 12, 42, 44
Hugo, Victor, 76, 174, 231n5
humanity, ages of, 36, 122, 183, 236, 243
human nature, 22
Hunt, Lynn, 42

Hyacinthe, Bishop, 102, 108, 112, 139. See also Troubert, Abbé

I
ideas
  character and, 236
  values and, 140
idée mère (generative idea), 2, 24, 27n3, 241, 246
Iéna, battle of, 181
illegitimacy, 49, 131, 197, 216
  inheritance and, 40–2
Illusions perdues (Balzac), 23, 26, 35, 152, 163, 164, 195, 196, 197, 213–32, 238, 239, 242, 247, 248
  names, 214, 220, 225, 227, 230
  opposition and, 152, 213, 215, 218–20, 226
  Ursule Mirouët and, 35
"Illustre Gaudissart, L'" (Balzac), 135–49
  critical evaluation of, 137
images, 2, 3, 20, 23, 24, 35–40, 45, 52, 53, 60, 62, 64, 67, 70, 78n16, 83, 90, 91, 113, 117, 118, 147, 152, 179, 180, 186n8, 194, 197, 210, 228, 229, 233, 235, 238–40, 243
image structure, 31n42, 114n11, 118, 133n2, 250n3
"Image Structure in *Le Père Goriot*" (Pasco), 31n42
impotence, 13, 124, 180
individualism, 43
Industrial Revolution, 5, 15, 17, 25, 59, 65, 137, 144, 145, 148, 201, 241, 249
inheritance, 4, 13, 37, 40, 41, 42, 48, 50–3, 55n19, 61, 66–8, 71, 77, 78n16, 93, 94, 102, 112, 119–21, 126, 127, 129, 131, 135, 136, 141, 148, 157, 246, 247, 249

illegitimate children and, 48, 58
insurance companies, 140
intangible *vs.* tangible values, 101–15, 249
intertextuality, 83
Ionesco, 175, 185
Isis, 125, 126, 132, 134n12
Issoudun, 118, 124–30, 132, 134n12, 143

J
Jacob (biblical figure), 122, 127, 153
Jacobi, Jolande, 228
Jakobson, Roman, 91, 99n14
Jameson, Fredric, 97n3, 117, 132n1, 179, 180, 185, 236
Janin, Jules, 158, 161
Jérôme Paturot (Reybaud), 168n13, 174
Jesus Christ, 64, 66, 69, 70, 71, 78n18, 89, 90, 95, 178
Jews, 58
Jocelyn (Lamartine), 173, 186n4
John, St., 38
Jones, Colin, 30n31
Joseph and Mary, 64
Joseph (Old Testament),
Joseph (biblical figure), 122, 132. (*See also* allusion)
Joseph Delorme (Sainte-Beuve), 174
journalism, 21, 26, 104, 151–3, 155, 158, 163, 164, 166, 169n20, 217–19, 248
July Monarchy, 3, 5, 12, 14, 15, 22, 23, 26, 31n44, 37, 42, 43, 47, 53, 57, 59, 64, 82, 85, 89, 92, 97, 113, 118, 122, 132, 135, 149n10, 158, 175, 191, 201, 210, 211, 233, 236, 238, 241
Jung, C.G, 37, 53n5, 227, 228
justice, 10, 22, 42, 51, 52, 53, 90, 108, 124, 194, 196, 200, 206–11, 247, 250.
law and legal system

INDEX 281

K
Kaballah, 226
Karr, Alphonse, 43, 54n12, 172
Kinder, Patricia, 186n2
Knight, Diana, 211n3
Kristeva, Julia, 98n4

L
La Bretonne, Restif de, 27n2
La Bruyière, 11
La Baudraye, Dinah Piédefer de, 153–158, 161–162, 238
La Carte, Marquise de, 161
Lacordaire, 75
La Fayette, Madame de, 181
Laffly, Georges, 185, 189
La Maisonfort, 6, 9, 28n14
Lamartine, Alphonse de, 173, 186n4
Lamennais, 75
land ownership, 241
La Rochefoucauld, 245
Larthomas, Pierre, 169n15
Last of the Mohicans, The (Cooper), 237
Latouche, Henri de, 220, 222
Lauzun, Duc de, 179, 181, 188n13
  inheritance and, 13, 48, 55n19, 61
  marriage and family and, 14, 48
law and legal system, 2, 8, 9, 12–14, 16, 19, 21, 48–50, 52, 55n19, 68, 111, 126, 159, 161, 187n12, 201, 204, 207, 209, 213, 218, 228, 238. *See also* courts; justice
Le Breton, André, 117, 132n1
Le Brun, Charles-François, 224, 231n8
Leibniz, 165
Lépinard, Commissioner, 16
L'Estoile, Pierre de, 180

Le Yaouanc, Moïse, 177, 187n11
liberals, 42, 86, 89, 91, 92, 94, 95, 148, 166, 179, 184, 202, 207, 226
Lilly, W.S., 234, 250n1
linguistic construction, 137
lion, 226, 228, 229
literary devices, 5, 82, 213, 233
Literary Eclecticism, 24
Littérature et progress (Pichois), 55n16
Listomère, Madame de, 108, 110, 112, 113
"Livre et le lecteur dans La Muse de departement, Le" (Mura-Brunel), 170n24
Livre mystique, Le (Balzac), 226, 231n11
Lousteau, Etienne, 104, 152, 154, 155, 157, 159–167, 219, 220, 225–226, 248
Locke, John, 3
Lope de Vega, 165
Lorraine, 90
Louis-Philippe, King of France, 1
Lorrain, Pierrette, 41, 42, 81–99, 235, 236, 247
Louis VII, 209
Louis XIV, 5, 30n31, 153, 175, 195
Louis XV, 7, 12, 30n31, 58, 179
Louis XVI, 7, 11, 12, 42, 54n10, 209
Louis XVIII, 195
Louvenjoul, 191
Louvre Museum, 11
love, 13, 21, 25, 39, 43, 44, 48, 49, 52, 59, 60, 62–4, 69–72, 75, 76, 84–7, 90, 91, 93, 95, 96, 98n11, 119, 123, 125, 126, 128, 129, 131, 157, 160, 162, 163, 165, 177, 178, 180, 182–4, 187n11, 189n20, 196, 204, 214, 215, 218–22, 224, 228, 230, 236, 248

lower classes, 10, 14, 68
Lubbock, Percy, 60, 77n9
Lucien Leuwen (Stendhal), 10
Lukàcs, György, 227
Lutherans of Montbéliard, 75
Lyon, 75

M
macrosociology, 25
Madame Bovary (Flaubert), 170n21
madness, 137, 144
Magette, Dorothy, 117, 132, 133n7
Maigron, 173, 174
Maintenon, Madame de, 248
"Maison Nucingen, La" (Balzac), 65, 242
Maistre, 75
Manuel, Frank E., 18, 19, 31n39
Marie Antoinette, 7
Marivaux, 193
marriage, 14, 25, 35, 40, 41, 45, 47, 48, 60, 62, 63, 65, 71, 73, 84, 94, 121, 125, 127, 129, 133n3, 142, 151, 153, 156, 158, 160, 162, 176, 183, 196, 201, 202, 204, 205, 207, 216, 225
Marriage de Figaro (Beaumarchais), 176
martyrdom, 37, 38, 89, 90, 98n10
"Martyrdom in Pierrette" (Williams), 98n10
Mary, Virgin, 70, 78n18, 154
Massonnaud, Dominique, 32n45, 186n2, 250n1
Maturin, 195
Maupin, Camille, 154
Maufrigneuse, Diane de (*later* Princess de Cadignan), 194, 200, 204, 206, 219

Maxence, Emperor of Rome, 124, 128, 129, 234
McManners, John, 76n1
Médici, Catherine de, 188n17
Meininger, Ann-Marie, 168n13, 240
Même histoire (Balzac), 238
Mémoire sur las science de l'homme (Saint-Simon), 19
Mercadet, le faiseur (Balzac), 66
Mercier, Louis Sébastien, 230n4
Merrick, Jeffrey W., 6, 58
Mesmer, Anton, 37, 39, 47, 52, 226
metaphoric chains of images, 239, 242, 248
metaphoric speech, 138
metonoymy, 137
Michelet, 42
Millet, Michel, 177
Minoret, Dr. Denis, 25, 37–52, 139, 229, 246
Minoret-Levrault, François, 37–39, 45–48, 229, 234, 239, 246
mirrors and mirroring, 38
Mirouët, Ursule, 37–55, 62, 65, 96, 103, 231n11, 235, 247
Misanthrope, Le (Molière), 178
misers, 40, 66, 68, 76, 78n16, 156, 157, 235, 236
Mises, Ludwig von, 2
"Miss Manners and Fooling Around" (Pasco), 169n19
Mnemosyne, 154
mock heroic, 5, 101, 113, 175, 185
modernity, 53, 143, 147, 201, 202, 247
Molière, 40, 51, 83, 84, 95, 178, 182, 189n20, 194, 195
monarchy, 2, 6, 7, 10, 11, 82, 85, 109, 180, 195, 197, 206, 210, 211, 250
money, 2, 3, 8, 10, 21, 22, 47, 51, 59, 61, 62, 64–8, 70, 72, 73, 76, 90, 94, 119, 120, 124, 125, 127, 130, 131, 136, 137, 141, 144,

145, 148, 156, 160, 162, 167, 176, 184, 186, 197, 198, 204, 205, 206, 209, 214, 216, 219, 227, 229, 230, 241, 246, 249. *See also* gold; inheritance; silver
Moniteur, Le, 168n13
monkey, 227
Monnais, Edouard, 240
Montalambert, Charles Forbes, comte de, 75
moon, 228, 235
morality, 124, 161, 172, 196, 245
Morot-Sir, Edouard, 189n20
Mortimer, Armine Kotin, 55n17, 97n1, 99n12, 124
mother
  abandonment of, 44, 221
  ineffective, 21
  lack of, 44, 47, 71, 126, 201, 215
Mozet, Nicole, 22, 31n41, 40, 48, 54n7, 60, 77n8, 97n1, 113n2, 114n5, 129, 151, 167n4, 172, 186n1, 192
Mura-Brunel, Aline, 170n24
Muse du département, La (Balzac), 41, 151–70, 216
  names, 151–4, 158, 161, 167n4
  plot type, 41
  title, 153, 154
muses, 152, 154, 238
Musset, Paul de, 174, 179
Mythes balzaciens (Barbéris), 188n12

N
names, 7, 37, 38, 40, 43, 46, 53, 67, 70, 72, 83, 85, 86, 89, 92, 93, 95, 96, 102, 110, 120, 121, 122, 131, 142, 151–4, 157, 158, 161, 177, 178, 184, 192–4, 199, 203, 206–9, 211, 214, 219, 220, 225, 227, 228, 230, 232n15, 238
  ability to choose, 43, 54n13
  Cabinet and, 192, 193
  Cabinet vs. Vieille Fille and, 187n11, 192, 193, 194, 196, 203, 211, 238
  Eugénie Grandet and, 67, 92
  Illusions perdues and, 214, 219–21, 238
  La Rabouilleuse and, 120, 121, 123, 128, 131
  Muse and, 151–4
  Pierrette and, 83, 85, 86, 89, 92, 93, 95, 96, 123
  Ursule and, 37, 38, 40, 46, 53
  Vieille Fille and, 83, 177, 178, 192–4, 211
Nantes, Edict of, 114n7, 153
Napoleon, 10–12, 15, 45, 51, 58, 65, 69, 75, 85, 93, 98n8, 124, 130, 131, 171, 175, 181, 195, 200, 210, 244, 249
Napoleonic wars, 55n14, 98n8, 124, 203, 247
narcissism, 123, 248
narration, 21, 47, 64, 82, 88, 112, 117–20, 127, 236
Néère or Neaera, 221, 231n7
neo-classicism, 11
Nephthys, 125, 126
Newton, 165
noble savage, 17
Nodier, 76, 126
Noms de lieux, Les (Dauzat), 134n12
Nougaret, Pierre-Jean-Baptiste, 27n2
Nouveaux Romanciers, 118
Nouvelle Minerve, 172
"Nuit Quatrième" (O'Neddy), 174
Nuits de Paris, Les (Restif de la Bretonne), 230n4
Nykrog, Per, 213, 214

O

Obermann (Senancour), 174
occult, 37, 39, 40, 52, 53, 55n20, 65, 107, 131, 239
Odyssey (Homer), 183
Olympia (anonymous novel in *Muse*), 164–6, 170n22
"On Balzac's Goriot" (Conner), 133n8
O'Neddy, Philothée, 174
oppositional allusion, 60, 66, 84, 92, 95
oppositions, 3, 14, 21, 36, 45, 59, 60, 63, 65, 68, 69, 72, 74, 82, 83, 94, 121, 122, 126, 136, 149n7, 151, 152, 207, 213, 214, 215, 218–20, 226, 228, 236, 239, 246, 247
Origins of the French Revolution (Doyle), 28n12
Orlando furioso (Ariosto), 185
orphans, 44, 82, 84, 85, 130
Osiris, 125, 126, 132
Ourliac, Edouard, 82
ox, 228, 229, 239

P

paradigm change, 18, 41
parenting, 126, 196, 247. *See also* fathers; mothers
Paris
  ability to succeed in, 144
  back and forth migration and, 26
  beautification of, 10, 22
  "boue" of, 217, 218, 226
  bridge to provinces from, 38–9
  class conflict in, 213
  enlarging role of, 247
  finances in provinces and, 140, 145
  individualism and, 43
  infernal vision of, 130
  influence of, 36
  movement to, 1, 197
  population of, 13, 142
  provinces *vs.*, 5, 13, 21, 25, 26, 36, 40, 66, 104, 121, 125, 130, 138, 142, 162, 196, 197, 215, 217, 226, 229, 246
  society of, 5, 25, 36
  St. Denis as patron saint of, 38
  success or failure and, 26, 48, 163, 227
  vice *vs.* honesty and, 244
Pasco, Allan H., 14, 27n6, 63, 83
passion, 14, 20, 36, 63, 66, 83, 89, 91, 93, 109, 111, 121, 162, 169, 182, 199, 209, 210, 221, 224, 236, 243–5. *See also* love
Passion of Christ, 83, 89
paternalism, 124
patriarchy, 63, 85, 117–34, 141, 248
Paul et Virginie (Bernardin de St. Pierre), 83, 87, 88, 90–2, 98n11, 99, 159
Paulson, William, 170n24
peasants, 9, 13, 15, 25, 86, 129, 237
Peau de chagrin, La (Balzac), 22
pelagonium, 212n15
Péraud, Alexandre, 135, 200, 211n3, 212n8
Père Goriot, Le (Balzac), 20, 21, 31n42, 118, 234
  image structure, 31n42, 118
  names, 118
periodicals, 141, 143
"Personalizing Violence in Balzac's *Les Chouans*" (Pasco), 250n5
Persson, Karl Gunnar, 10, 29n27, 55n14, 135, 149n1
Petit Carrillonneur, Le (Ducray-Duminil), 82
Petrarch, 72
Peytel, 92
Phaon, 154

Philarète, Charles, 22, 240
Physiocrats, 82
Physiologie du goût (Brillat-Savarin), 17
Physiologie du mariage (Balzac), 17
physiologies, 138
Pichois, Claude, 55n16
Piédefer, Dinah, *see* La Baudraye, Dinah Piédefer de
Pierre de Vérone, St., 89–92, 95, 97
Pierre-Quint, Léon, 172, 173
Pierrette (Balzac), 41, 42, 81–99, 123, 159, 203, 235, 236, 247, 248
  Béatrice Cenci and, 83, 91, 92
  critical evaluation of, 60
  names, 67, 70, 72
  Virginie and, 83, 87–93, 95, 96, 98n11
Pigaut-Lebrun, 82
Piketty, Thomas, 16, 29n27, 131, 135, 214, 249
Pius VII, Pope, 58
Planche, Gustave, 147, 159, 169n16
Plato, 152
"Playing with Risk" (Tilby), 149n9
plot, 5, 13, 15, 35, 37, 41, 48, 51, 52, 53, 62, 64, 84, 94, 112, 113, 117, 120, 121, 127, 157, 165, 174, 176, 178, 187n12, 214, 236–9, 247
  armatures, 41, 113, 120, 237, 238
  continuing, 247
  malleable, 178
  rise and fall, 214, 239
  stock, 178
  types, 236
  variations on, 53
  vector, 121
poetry, 153, 154, 158, 166, 208, 214, 218, 225, 228
political affiliations, 42
political conflicts, 92

Pommier, Jean, 167n5
pope, 58, 75, 91, 92, 102, 111
Popkin, Jeremy D., 98n7, 98n9
population decline, 13
Pound, Ezra, 212n9
Portenduère, Savinien de, 25, 36, 38, 43, 44, 47, 48, 52, 104, 139, 226
poverty, 9, 58, 127, 129, 160, 163, 165, 169, 213, 218, 219, 244
power or authority, 7, 112, 131, 196, 216
Presse, La, 169n20, 172, 174
priests, 2, 6, 41, 44, 57, 59, 68, 73, 76, 86, 96, 101–8, 127, 151, 207, 209, 229, 230, 248
"Prince de la Bohème, Un" (Balzac), 161, 166, 170n23, 175
property requirments, 109
property rights, 18
Propp, Vladimir, 41
Proscrits et l'unité du Livre mystique, Les (Pasco), 231n11
prostitution, 21, 58, 127, 129
Protestants, 58, 75, 153
Proust, Marcel, 23, 32n46, 132, 173
Provins, 87, 88, 93, 94, 96
pseudonyms, 70, 153, 154, 157, 193, 220, 228
Psyché, 172
Pugh, Anthony R., 53n4, 154, 168n9, 169n17
puns, 123
Pyramus de Candolle, Augustin, 20, 41n31

Q
Queffélec, Henri, 185, 187n12
Quesnel, François, 180

R
Rabelais, 133n5, 238
rabouilleuse, definition of, 133n5

Rabouilleuse, La (Balzac), 45, 103, 117–134, 143, 144, 151, 166, 201, 248
   critical evaluation of, 137
   image structure, 117, 118
   names, 120–3, 131, 151
   plot armature, 120
Raphaël d'Urbin, *Transfiguration*, 91
Rastignac, Eugene de, 21, 26, 130, 139, 198, 204, 226
Reactions (Cobb), 7
"Reading as Suture" (Dällenbach), 170n24
Real Time (Bell), 55n16
reappearing characters, 5, 165, 192, 233, 247
reappearing themes, 5
Recherche de l'absolu, La (Balzac), 20, 132n1, 226
Reclaiming the Sacred (Desan), 76n1
Registre-Journal du règne de Henri III (L'Estoile), 180
Reni, Guido, 91
Renouveau (Renewal of faith), 75
Republican periodicals, 141
Réstif de la Bretonne, Nicolas-Edme, 230n4
Restoration, 3, 5, 11, 12, 23, 42, 44, 57, 58, 64, 108, 109, 113, 132, 157, 161, 165, 175, 179, 184, 191–212, 233, 236
Return of the Prodigal Son, The (Gide), 74
Reuben (biblical figure), 238
Revolutionary Love (Pasco), 4, 14, 63
revolutionary wars, 247
Révolution française, La (Bluche, et al.), 55n14, 98n8
Revolution of 1789, 61, 179
Revolution of 1830, 92, 96, 184
Reybaud, Charles, 158

Reybaud, Louis, 174
Reybaud, Mme, 158, 168n13
Rials, S., 55n14, 98n8
Riccoboni, Madame, 173
Richard III, 126
ridicule by repetition, 168n11
Riffaterre, Michael, 98n4, 186n8
Robbe-Grillet, Alain, 118, 133n3
Robespierre, 9, 13
Rodrigues, Olinde, 19
Rogron, Jérôme-Denis, 41–42, 83–87, 93–94, 139
Rogron, Sylvie, 41–42, 83–87, 93–94
roman à clef, 193
Romans et contes philosophiques, (Balzac), 241
Romantic God, 93, 99n16
Romantics, 13, 43, 44, 54n10, 76, 93, 99n16, 166, 173
Rome, 6, 91
Rossini, 165
Rouge et le noir, Le (Stendhal), 173
Rouget, Jean-Jacques, 119, 121, 122, 126–129
Rougon, Jean-Jacques, 119, 133n7
Rousseau, Jean-Jacques, 3, 13, 122, 133n7
royalists, 85, 89, 94, 226
Rubempré, Lucien Chardon de, 22, 35, 104, 139, 163, 196, 204, 213–226, 228–230, 232n13, 235, 239, 247

S

Sacy, S. de, 37
Sainte-Ampoule, 209
Sainte-Beuve, Charles-Augustin, 9, 60, 62, 77n8, 174, 234, 250n2
Saint-Estève, 43
Saint Gatien Cathedral, 105
Saint Hilaire, Geoffroy, 23

Saint-Just, 9, 248
Saint-Paterne Church, 128
Saint-Pierre, Bernardin de, 87
saints, 37, 38, 40, 59, 65, 66, 70, 76, 89, 91, 95, 99n13, 102
Saint-Satur, 152, 154, 156, 157n4
Saintsbury, George, 134n11
Saint-Simon, Henri de, 1, 2, 6, 16–20, 22, 27n1, 31n39, 36, 141, 142, 147, 148, 243, 250n10
Sancerre, 151, 152, 154, 155, 158, 163
Sand, George, 25, 154, 240, 246, 250n9
Sappho, 152, 154, 156, 167n4, 238
Sappho of Saint-Satur, 152, 156, 167n4
Saracens, 17
Sarraute, Nathalie, 118, 133, 242
Satan, 228, 229
"Saule, Le" (Musset), 174
Saumur, 61, 62, 66, 67, 71
Sauvage de l'Aveyron, 17
Savinien, St., 38
Scènes de la vie de campagne (Balzac), 245
Scènes de la vie de province (Balzac). See also specific characters; novels; stories; and themes
  background society in, 234
  Comedie humaine as whole and, 242, 245, 246
  critics on, 22
  Etudes des mœurs and, 20
  ideas and images in, 24
  importance of, 35
  link with *Scènes de la vie privee*, 35, 39
  literary devices and, 5, 82
  opening of, 36
  organization of, 19, 32, 104, 240, 242
  quest for unified society in, 20
  stages in life represented by, 36, 243–5
Scènes de la vie militaire (Balzac), 245
Scènes de la vie parisienne (Balzac), 35, 215, 239, 244, 245
Scènes de la vie politiques (Balzac), 243
Scènes de la vie privée (Balzac), 35, 36, 39, 243, 245, 246
Schor, Naomi, 102, 114n5
Schuerewegen, Franc, 132n1, 149n12
science, 2, 17, 18, 19, 31n39, 53n3, 111, 208, 233, 249
Scott, Walter, 165
Scribe, 99n13, 165
Second Coming, 64, 66, 74, 78n18
Séchard, David, 213–220, 222–224, 226–230, 234, 235, 239, 246
secrecy, 30n31, 44, 206
Séchard, Eve, 218, 219, 224, 226, 230, 234
Séchard, Old, 214, 215, 218–220, 227, 230
"Secrets de la princess de Cadignan, Les," 219
"Selected Death Tolls for Wars, Massacrews and Atrocities" (White), 98n8
Senancour, 174
serialization, 171, 186n2
sex, 4, 58, 70, 109, 136, 163, 187n11
Sex Education in Eighteenth Century France (Agin), 169n19, 187n10
Shakespeare, William, 22, 234
Shechem, 153
Sherrif, Mary D., 154
Short History of the French Revolution (Popkin), 98n7, 98n9

Sick Heroes (Pasco), 44, 54n10, 98n12, 133n9, 230n4
signifying, 92, 120, 141
Silvanus, 86
silver, 8, 76, 104, 106, 107
Sixtus V, Pope, 102, 111
slavery, 18, 69
Smith, Annette, 167n4, 168n10, 170n24
Social Interpretation of the French Revolution, The (Cobban), 29n26
society
   Balzac's stories as insight into, 21, 65, 137, 141, 233
   Church and need to stabilize, 74
   creation of new, 21
   discontent in, 5, 15
   Saint-Simon and idea of, 18
   search for peoples uncorrupted by, 3
   turmoil in, 1, 4, 10, 14
sociology
   Balzac and, 16, 20, 21, 26, 138, 211, 234, 248
   Comedie humaine as work of, 176
   quest for, by French thinkers, 17
   term created by Comte, 19
somnambulism, 226
Souday, Paul, 187n12
Soulié, 174
Sous les tilleuls (Karr), 43
South Sea islands, 3
Souverain publisher, 192
speculation, 137–9, 140, 144, 146, 204, 242
Splendeurs et misères des courtisanes (Balzac), 24, 215, 221, 222, 223, 230n3, 247
   critical
Staël, Madame de, 14, 59, 154, 224
stagnation, 15, 85, 128, 130, 132, 148, 213, 246
Stello (Vigny), 174

Stendhal, 10, 27, 30n32, 43, 59, 63, 91, 99n13, 162, 163, 174, 230n4
Stern, Daniel, 59, 121
Sterne, Laurence?, 37, 121
stranger, 40, 41, 45, 249
St. Pierre, Bernarndin de, 87
Sue, Eugène, 126, 158
Sugny, S. de, 173
suicide, 4, 7, 13, 26, 28, 58, 83, 85, 123, 145, 154, 173–5, 184, 185, 206, 214, 215, 222, 247
Suicide, Le (Sugny), 173
Sur Catherine de Médicis (Balzac), 82, 188n17
"Sur le style de Balzac" (Larthomas), 169n15
"Sur une image de Balzac" (Larthomas), 169n15
Suzanne, 176–178, 180, 181, 184, 187n11
Suzanne (biblical figure), 178
Suzanne (Ourliac), 82
Swedenborg, 20, 52, 226
Symbols of Transformation (Jung), 228, 231n11
synecdoche, 146
Système de politique positive (Comte), 19

T
Taine, Hippolyte, 22, 27n1
Tartuffe (Molière), 51, 178, 183, 194, 195
taxation, 5, 14, 57
tetramorphs or quaternities, 228, 229
Thermidor, 8, 9, 44
Thierry, Augustin, 19
Thompson, Victoria E., 65, 231n6
thought, sentiment *vs.*, 245
Through a Looking-Glass (Carroll), 38

INDEX 289

Tibullus, 231n7
Tilby, Michael, 149n9, 186n8
time, compression of, 55n16
Tocqueville, 6, 7, 10
Tomashevsky, Boris, 193
Toulouse, 75
Touraine, 96, 110, 111, 149n7
Tours, 101, 102, 108, 110–13
tragedy, 84, 88, 89, 95, 174, 178, 182, 183, 239
transportation, 16, 46, 47, 148, 176, 249
Trillat, A., 24, 32n48
Trinity, 68, 69, 71
Tritter, Jean-Louis, 81, 92, 99n12
Tropismes (Sarraute), 242
Trotsky, Leon, 11
Troubert, Abbé, 101–104, 107–108, 110–113, 139, 248. *See also* Hyacinthe, Bishop
Tulard, J., 55n14, 98n8
Turnell, Martin, 159
types, 5, 17, 40, 41, 82, 86, 138, 139, 178, 192, 216, 220, 235, 236, 238, 242, 245

U
universality, 236
Ursula, St., 37, 38
Ursule Mirouët (Balzac), 35–55, 62, 64, 65, 103, 176, 226, 229, 231n11, 239, 247, 249
  names, 37, 38, 40, 43, 46, 53
  overture, 39, 48, 53

V
Valois monarchy, 197
Valois, Chevalier de, 176, 179–181, 183–185, 192, 211. *See also* Chevalier, the

Vendean uprisings, 58
venereal disease, 13, 63
vengeance, 41, 102, 103, 170n22, 203
Viaud, J., 125
Vautrin, 102, 195, 196, 218. *See also* Herrera, Abbé Carlos
Vicq-d'Azyr, 2, 16
Viegnes, Michel, 170n21
Vieille Fille, La (Balzac), 82, 96, 122, 123, 124, 130, 171–89, 191–4, 196, 203, 211, 238
  Cabinet and, 187n11, 189n22, 191–4, 196, 203, 211
  critical evaluation of,
  names, 192–4, 199, 203
  serialization of, 171
  web of images, 180
Vigée-Lebrun, 154
Vigny, 174
Virtuous Marketplace (Thompson), 65
Voiture embourbée, La (Marivaux), 193
Voltaire, 122, 165, 169n19, 187n10
voting rights, 109
Vouvray, 144–8
Vulgate Bible, 72

W
wars, 4, 8–11, 13, 22, 25, 29n26, 43, 44, 45, 48, 55n14, 58, 82, 85, 95, 98n8, 103, 124, 171, 202, 203, 213, 247, 248. *See also* Napoleonic wars; revolutionary wars
Waterloo, 10–12, 45, 85
Watts, Andrew, 22, 31n44, 96, 149n7
waxworks, 197
Weimar republic, 8
White, Andrew Dickson, 76n1

White, Matthew, 55n14, 98n8
Willes, Jean-Georges, 4
Williams, Timothy J., 89, 95, 98n10
womb, 105, 171–89

Y
Yonge, Charlotte, 72
young
   absence of fathers and, 85
   gerontocracy and, 81–99
   hopelessness and waste of, 123, 175, 178
   as hope of France, 85, 97, 185
   mistreatment of, 131
   ungoverned, 124

Z
"Z. Marcas" (Balzac), 82, 132
Zola, Emile, 89, 187n10

The manufacturer's authorised representative in the EU is Springer Nature Customer Service Centre GmbH, Europaplatz 3, 69115 Heidelberg, Germany. If you have any concerns regarding our products, please contact ProductSafety@springernature.com

Printed and bound by CPI Group (UK) Ltd, Croydon, CR0 4YY
23/03/2026
02076736-0012